# Reason and Its Other

# BERG EUROPEAN STUDIES SERIES

GENERAL EDITOR: **Brian Nelson** (Monash University, Melbourne)

ADVISORY BOARD: Michael Biddiss (University of Reading), John Flower (University of Exeter), Paul Michael Lützeler (Washington University, St. Louis), David Roberts (Monash University, Melbourne), Tony Judt (New York University), Walter Veit (Monash University, Melbourne)

Marko Pavlyshyn (ed.), *Glasnost in Context*

David Roberts and Philip Thomson (eds.), *The Modern German Historical Novel*

Brian Nelson (ed.), *Naturalism in the European Novel*

Brian Nelson, David Roberts and Walter Veit (eds.), *The Idea of Europe*

Alun Kenwood (ed.), *The Spanish Civil War*

*Forthcoming*

Mirna Cicioni and Nicole Prunster (eds.), *Visions and Revisions: Women in Italian Culture*

# Reason and Its Other

## Rationality in Modern German Philosophy and Culture

Edited by

## DIETER FREUNDLIEB

and

## WAYNE HUDSON

## BERG

*Providence / Oxford*

Published in 1993 by
**Berg Publishers, Inc.**
Editorial offices:
221 Waterman Street, Providence, RI 02906, U.S.A.
150 Cowley Road, Oxford OX4 1JJ, UK

**Library of Congress Cataloging-in-Publication Data**
Reason and its other : rationality in modern German philosophy and culture /
    edited by Dieter Freundlieb and Wayne Hudson.
        p.   cm. —(Berg European studies series)
    Incudes bibliographical references and index.
    ISBN 0–85496–372–3
    1. Reason.  2. Philosophy. German.  3. Philosophy, Modern—18th century.
4. Philosophy, Modern—19th century.  5. Philosophy, Modern—20th century
6. Germany—Civilization.  I. Freundlieb, Dieter. II. Hudson, Wayne,  III.
Series.
B2748.R37R37    1993
128'.3—dc20                                                    93–18012
                                                                      CIP

**A CIP catalogue record for this book is available from the British Library.**

Printed in the United States by E.B. Edwards Brothers, Ann Arbor, MI.

# Contents

# –1–

# Reason and Its Other: Some Major Themes

## DIETER FREUNDLIEB AND WAYNE HUDSON

### I

The title *Reason and Its Other* echoes the provocative title of Gernot and Hartmut Böhme's book *Das Andere der Vernunft* published in 1983. In conjunction with the impact of French poststructuralist thought on German philosophy, this book sparked important debates among a number of German philosophers and critics: debates that may, in the longer term, lead to significant realignments in contemporary German philosophy and culture.

Following the publication of *Das Andere der Vernunft,* much of the immediate debate centered on the question of how far it was justified to use psychoanalysis in order to imply structural connections between the rigidly puritanical and psychopathological nature of Kant's personal lifestyle, and technical features of his philosophical system. At least one critic, Jürgen Habermas, was sufficiently challenged by the book to clarify and reassert his own view that it was now necessary to move from a subject-centered concept of reason to a concept of reason grounded in the communicatively structured life-world. Thus Habermas wrote,

> During the last decade, the radical critique of reason has become fashionable. A study by Hartmut and Gernot Böhme, who take up Foucault's idea of the rise of the modern form of knowledge in connection with the work and biography of Kant, is exemplary in theme and execution. In the style of a historiography of science expanded by cultural and social history, the authors take a look, so to speak, at what goes on behind the back of the critique of pure and practical reason.... The authors marshal before our eyes the "costs of reason" in terms of psychohistory. They undertake this cost/benefit accounting ingenuously with psychoanalytic arguments and document it with historical data, though with-

out being able to specify the place at which such arguments could claim any weight – if indeed the thesis they are concerned with is supposed to make sense.

Kant had carried out his critique of reason from reason's own perspective, that is to say, in the form of a rigorously argued self-limitation of reason. If, now, the production costs of this self-confining reason (which places anything metaphysical off limits) are to be made clear, we require a horizon of reason reaching beyond this drawing of boundaries in which the transcending discourse that adds up the bill can operate.[1]

Another and more enduring issue was the question of how far it was possible to recognize and take account of an "Other" of reason. As Gernot Böhme subsequently pointed out,[2] the Böhmes' critics, including Jürgen Habermas, failed, for the most part, to realize that the Böhmes intended to advance a critique of reason *by reason*. In insisting on the importance of the "Other" of reason, they sought to draw attention to the inability of the Western metaphysical tradition to think this "Other," without either excluding it from reason, or assimilating it to reason.

Another important issue was the status and contemporary tasks of philosophy. According to Gernot Böhme, philosophy had to change its self-conception if it was to overcome the false alternatives between excluding the "Other" of reason from reason or assimilating it to reason. Reason and nature, or the mental and the corporeal, were not, Böhme insisted, completely separate, as modern philosophy often seemed to imply, but intimately linked. Philosophy also needed to take references to experiences more seriously, including the experience of an "Other" of reason. Here Böhme saw his project as continuous with, and not outside of, the discursive tradition of a "dialectic of enlightenment" theorized by Horkheimer and Adorno. The fact that the Böhmes stirred up so much controversy by reasserting the need for philosophy to think the nonconceptual – a theme familiar enough – after all, from the work of Adorno, points to an underlying fear of irrationalism in postwar German philosophy and culture. The debates about reason and its "Other" touched a political as well as a philosophical nerve. Following the debates about reason and its "Other," there has been a significant change of temper in German thought, including a willingness to problematize the heroic position previously attributed to "reason." Today the implication that the relations between reason and its Other need to be radically rethought reverberates across large strands of contemporary German culture, and opens these strands up for reevaluation and redefinition.

The need, however, to distinguish between "reason" and "non-reason"

---

1. J. Habermas, *The Philosophical Discourse of Modernity*, Cambridge, 1987, pp. 301/302. For Habermas's response to the Böhmes more generally, see chapter XI.
2. G. Böhme, "Vorwort" to *Philosophieren mit Kant*, Frankfurt, 1986.

is an old theme in a German context. German thought since at least Christian Wolff has witnessed endless arguments about how *Vernunft* should be understood, as well as many different assertions of antirationalist points of view, of which existentialism, the philosophy of life (*Lebensphilosophie*), and philosophical anthropology are among the most important. In the first part of this century, Ludwig Klages, whose distinction between "logocentric" and "biocentric" thought foreshadowed some of the issues raised by, or arising out of, contemporary French philosophical thought, drew a famous distinction between intellect (*Geist*) and soul (*Seele*), and his doctrine that *Geist* and *Seele* were intrinsically in tension with one another left its mark both on the rampant anti-intellectualism of the Nazis, and on the more philosophically sophisticated reserve toward instrumental reason apparent in the work of Heidegger and Adorno. Indeed, it is significant that despite their many and deep disagreements, both Heidegger's notion of Being and Adorno's conception of the nonidentical seek to delimit the range and universal validity of discursive thought.

The idea of a contrast term that can be opposed to *Vernunft* has been an important theme of modern German culture since at least the Romantics. The tension between *Vernunft* and *Verstand* (understanding) was basic to several forms of German idealism, just as the contrast between *Vernunft* and *Glaube* (faith), the ecstasis of faith, was central to pietism, and also played a certain role in Lutheran thought. What is new in the more recent literature is the idea that neither *Verstand* nor *Glaube* are the relevant "Others" of reason. The foreshortened alternative of faith in reason or irrationalism has been transcended in favor of a quest for a less hegemonic and more pluralist notion of reason. There is a new willingness to allow for the extent to which reason may be hegemonic and repressive of whatever falls outside its ambit.

The recent German debates about "the Other" of reason can also be seen as part of a longer-term process of modernization going on in German philosophical thought. Since the end of World War II, German philosophy has struggled to find the right relationship to the achievements of ancient Greek philosophy, eighteenth and nineteenth-century classical German philosophy, contemporary Anglo-American philosophy, and the postphilosophical trends associated with the philosophy of life (*Lebensphilosophie*), philosophical anthropology, and Martin Heidegger's history of Being (*Seinsgeschichte*). Immediately after the war there was a vogue for the philosophy of Jaspers and Heidegger read as existentialists, as well as major attempts to clarify problems raised by Husserl's phenomenology (Ludwig Landgrebe, Eugen Fink). In the philosophy of science a renewed engagement with the logical empiricism of the Vienna Circle led to a reception of Karl Popper's ideas in the critical rationalism of Hans Albert.

When in the early sixties the advocates of critical rationalism clashed with Adorno and the defenders of "dialectics," the scene was set for a wide range of methodological controversies, particularly in the philosophy of the social sciences. For example, Peter Winch's Wittgensteinian conception of the social sciences and Anglo-American debates about the logic of action explanation, i.e., the reasons versus causes debate, were taken up by Karl-Otto Apel and Rüdiger Bubner. In social philosophy the revival of the work of the Frankfurt School by Adorno and Horkheimer was crucial. The pattern of postwar development in social philosophy was decisively influenced by the existence of the German Democratic Republic, and the divisions in German intellectual and cultural life consequent upon it. Philosophy in the *Bundesrepublik* strove to find a critical voice, while in the East an official Marxism-Leninism flourished alongside a cult of German classical philosophy designed to lay claim to the legacy of the "good" Germany.

Another important postwar development was the reception of Anglo-American analytical philosophy, and the belated reception by many German philosophers of the so-called "linguistic turn." Here the work of Ernst Tugendhat on the philosophy of language is of outstanding importance. Other German philosophers, however, continued doing philosophy in a more traditional mode by commenting upon, and reinterpreting the "great texts" in an established canon. The methodological differences between those philosophers who attempted to adopt new methodological programs – for example, the constructivist program of Paul Lorenzen, Oswald Schwemmer, and Friedrich Kambartel (the Erlangen School) – and those philosophers who reworked the texts by Kant, Fichte, Hegel, Schelling, Schopenhauer, Nietzsche, Husserl, Heidegger or Jaspers, were striking, but the points of substantive contact were relatively few.

There were also obvious tensions among those philosophers who concentrated on problems in the theory and philosophy of science, such as Wolfgang Stegmüller and Wilhelm K. Essler; hermeneutic scholars in philosophy and literature influenced by Gadamer's *Truth and Method*; those who worked on the problems pertinent to the philosophy of history, such as Reinhardt Koselleck, Hans Blumenberg, Hans Michael Baumgartner, and Odo Marquard; and those primarily interested in political philosophy, such as Joachim Ritter, Hans Lübbe and Robert Spaemann. In some cases the revival of classical authors and movements substituted for methodological refinements, and this was true both of radicalizations of Heideggerian historicism in the philosophy of history and of revivals of practical philosophy by Joachim Ritter and Manfred Riedel, although there were also major insights into the limits of ahistorical and purely theoretical approaches to philosophy respectively. Subsequently, Jürgen Habermas's and Karl-Otto Apel's transformations of Critical Theory, Gadamer's philosophical hermeneutics, and Luhmann's systems theory emerged as the outstanding achievements of contemporary German thought. Tensions among these three schools of thought, however, were again inevitable, as witnessed in the Gadamer-Habermas debate (which also involved Apel, who is still continuing this debate) over the question of the primacy of language and tradition (Gadamer), over the power of critical reflection (Apel, Habermas), and the debate between Habermas and Luhmann concerning their different conceptions of the individual and society.[3] While retaining his generally critical stance toward Luhmann, Habermas later attempted to integrate aspects of Luhmann's systems theory into his theory of communicative action.

Tensions also arose in the field of ethics between the proponents of a procedural and universal concept of practical reason (Apel, Habermas, Böhler, Kuhlmann) and those who argue that reason is irreducibly context-bound (Bubner, Schnädelbach and others). These debates are centered on the question to what extent the historical and the contingent needs to be excluded, as an Other of reason, or whether a universalist conception of ethical principles is ultimately without practical relevance. In many ways this debate is a conscious renewal of Hegel's critique of Kant in terms of the distinction between *Moralität* (morality) and *Sittlichkeit* (ethical life).[4]

To understand recent developments in German philosophy it is important to recognize how unreconstructedly *German* much contemporary German philosophy still is, in spite of the broadly based reception of the so-called "linguistic turn" within Anglo-American analytical philosophy, including, particularly in the case of Apel and Habermas, Peircean pragmatism. Individual German philosophers can be found who reject the philosophy of the subject, the neo-Kantian critique of knowledge, quasi-Hegelian philosophy of history, Romantic hermeneutics, critical theory, Heideggerian postontology – and so forth. Nonetheless, the spirit of those traditions, and aspects of the methodologies associated with them, have not entirely disappeared. On the contrary, residues of the terminology and the mind-sets of both Kantian transcendentalism and Hegelian idealism are strikingly evident in the work of thinkers who may be seen as struggling against them.

When during the eighties French structuralism and its aftermath broke on the German scene, it initially seemed to many Germans as though the French had abandoned the Enlightenment and its emancipatory politics

---

3. For the debate between Habermas and Luhmann, see J. Habermas and N. Luhmann, *Theorie der Gesellschaft oder Sozialtechnologie*, Frankfurt, 1971. Material on Habermas's integration of systems theory into his own theory is contained in his *Theory of Communicative Action*, vol. 2, Boston and Cambridge, 1984.

4. See for example Wolfgang Kuhlmann (ed.), *Moralität und Sittlichkeit. Das Problem Hegels und die Diskursethik*, Frankfurt, 1986.

for philosophical surrealism and irrationalism. To some it seemed as if the French were reimporting some of the worst aspects of the work of Nietzsche and Heidegger, from which contemporary Germans were trying finally to escape. To others, such as Gernot Böhme and his brother Hartmut, the French pointed to genuine *lacunae* and *aporiae* in modern philosophy, and the task was to rethink the "great texts" of German philosophy in the light of the French challenges.

From an Anglo-Saxon standpoint it sometimes seems as though many of the German receptions of the French thought of the 1960s, 1970s and 1980s take the form of very un-French constructions of French thought, as if there was some coherent movement emanating from Paris called "neostructuralism" or "poststructuralism," addressing issues which German rather than French thinkers associate with the Enlightenment. This pattern of reception has had two major consequences. One consequence has been to persuade some Germans that texts that they know well are again at the front of world fashion. Specifically: texts by Friedrich Schlegel, Nietzsche, Heidegger and Adorno, all of whom are said to anticipate later French debates. The second consequence has been to suggest that recent French thought is really a reincarnation of radicalisms already implicit in German idealism. For example: in Fichte, Schelling or Schopenhauer. Both readings are no doubt to some extent correct, but they can also be misleading, in the sense that they prevent German philosophers from exploring the specific French contexts and backgrounds to French debates, including both the intense, but very local, French internal quarrels underlying texts by Barthes, Lacan, Derrida and Foucault, and also the relevant relations back to nineteenth-century French philosophers, such as Ravaisson.

The issues raised by the German receptions of the new French thought are complex, and the controversies continue. In far-ranging discussions, the status of reason, science, the Enlightenment, modernity and progress have all been called into question. There have also been various attempts to rehabilitate the significance of the body, desire, nature, art, and religion as "Others" of reason. Similarly, reevaluations of premodern culture and experience have appeared. Here there are fascinating parallels with the so-called "crisis of reason" debates in Italy. As in France and Italy, delayed impacts of Nietzsche and Heidegger as critics of Western civilization, reason and modernity have reopened debates explored earlier in the century about the historicity of philosophy and rationality. These debates involve a problematization of the fundamental idea usually attributed to the European Enlightenment: the idea that the major problems of human life can be managed by the application of "reason" to human affairs. Contemporary discussions now tend to problematize this idea along with the heroic moralism that it implies. Critiques of the philosophy of reflection, and of the claim that reason can turn back upon itself and examine itself, are becoming more prominent.

More recently, apart from a renewed attention to, and a critical assessment of, Heidegger's philosophy, particularly with regard to its alleged political implications, there has been a renewed involvement with the German idealist version of transcendental philosophy. Philosophers such as Herbert Schnädelbach have worked across these traditions in methodologically fruitful ways. There has also been a major revival of philosophical hermeneutics, indebted either to Heidegger, as in the case of Hans-Georg Gadamer, or to Schleiermacher, as in the prolific work of Manfred Frank. In Frank's work the project of retrieving hermeneutics is combined with an attempt to rethink the philosophy of consciousness and subjectivity, taking into acount both Dieter Henrich's important defense and reformulation of Fichte's notion of self-consciousness, as well as recent Anglo-Saxon work on the idea of the self. Like his teacher Henrich, Frank insists that all reflexive theories of the self are untenable, and emphasizes the crucial role of a nonconceptual knowledge, or "acquaintance" of the self with itself, as the basis for all reflexive self-knowledge. From the point of view of Habermas, Henrich's attempt to continue the German tradition of metaphysical thought through a theory of subjectivity must, of course, appear as a source of irritation. Recently, therefore, Habermas has foregrounded the "postmetaphysical" character of his own philosophy, and reasserted that subjectivity must be explained in terms of an interactionist, linguistically mediated constitution of the self along the lines of G. H. Mead.[5] Although Habermas by no means accepts Mead's theory uncritically, the tenability of his theory of the constitution of subjectivity based on Mead remains open to question. This raises the possibility that the advance beyond the problematic of German idealism, which Habermas's work assumes, has yet to be successfully argued.[6]

The reassertion of the irreducible importance of subjectivity in the work of Henrich and Frank gives the work of German idealists such as Fichte and Schelling new contemporary significance, and opens up the vista of a rationally argued end to rationalism. It may also, in the longer term, have serious implications for the purely procedural definitions of communicative reason proposed by Karl-Otto Apel and Jürgen Habermas. It clearly challenges Habermas's idea that the philosophy of consciousness has defin-

5. See his *Nachmetaphysisches Denken. Philosophische Aufsätze*, Frankfurt, 1988.
6. Henrich has expressed serious doubts that Habermas's reliance on G. H. Mead (and on Tugendhat's critique of Henrich in Tugendhat's *Self-Consciousness and Self-Determination*, translated by Paul Stern, Cambridge, Mass., 1986) is justified in his essay "The Origins of the Theory of the Subject" in *Philosophical Interventions in the Unfinished Project of Enlightenment*, edited by Axel Honneth et al., and translated by William Rehg, pp. 29–87. See in particular p. 87, footnote 28.

itively been superseded by the linguistic-pragmatic turn. In fact, it suggests that there may be nonconceptual forms of knowledge which, far from being in any way "irrational", are indispensable for the development of an acceptable notion of reason. Frank combines this reassertion of the subject with a major rereading of early German romanticism. In effect, he shows that the challenges of recent French thought involve many revivals of problems raised by the early German romantics and German idealism, that "neostructuralism" or "poststructuralism" is not the break with old European philosophy it is often alleged to be, and that French thinkers may be guilty of dubious originality when they attempt to break with the subject while advancing philosophical programs that require it for their coherence.[7]

The challenge posed by the particular kind of poststructuralist thought that came to be known as deconstruction was taken up, among others, by Hans-Georg Gadamer, the most eminent contemporary proponent of philosophical hermeneutics and hermeneutic reason.[8] Yet the encounters between Derrida and Gadamer, in spite of Gadamer's attempts to engage in a dialogue based on "good will," remained largely inconclusive, and failed to lead to a real confrontation between the two thinkers. One of the differences that emerged in the contributions to this "improbable debate," as it was called, was the different interpretations of Nietzsche and Heidegger by Gadamer and Derrida, but even here the dispute did not reach any final results. What this debate, which never really took place, demonstrates, however, is not that contemporary German thought is necessarily impervious to "French Theory." Rather, it is an example of a difficulty encountered on similar occasions when German and French philosophers of public renown were brought together in order to stage a debate for a large academic audience.[9]

7. A similar point is made forcefully by Frank's British disciple Andrew Bowie in his book *Aesthetics and Subjectivity: From Kant to Nietzsche*, Manchester and New York, 1990.

8. The confrontation between philosophical hermeneutics and deconstruction began at a meeting between Gadamer and Derrida arranged by the Goethe-Institut in Paris in April 1981. The most important documents arising from this meeting and from subsequent work are collected in *Dialogue and Deconstruction. The Gadamer-Derrida Encounter*, edited by Diane P. Michelfelder and Richard E. Palmer, Albany, 1989. Some of this material was previously published in Germany under the title *Text und Interpretation*, edited by Philippe Forget, Munich, 1984.

9. As D. P. Michelfelder and R. E. Palmer point out in a footnote to their "Introduction" to *Dialogue and Deconstruction*, a second encounter between Derrida and Gadamer in 1988 at the University of Heidelberg "involved no appreciable further dialogue on hermeneutics and deconstruction" (p. 295). It should be mentioned in this context that Manfred Frank has devoted a small monograph to an imaginary debate between Lyotard and Habermas. See his *Die Grenzen der Verständigung: Ein Geistergespräch zwischen Lyotard und Habermas*, Frankfurt, 1988. Frank suggests that one of the problems encountered in the debates between French and German philosophy is a lack of familiarity with the work of German writers among at least some of the French participants in the debate, but this observation can also be argued conversely, at least at the level of hermeneutically sensitive interpretations of French texts.

Finally, the reception of contemporary French thought in Germany has revitalized the field of philosophical aesthetics and its relevance to debates about reason. Whereas Habermas accused Nietzsche of subordinating questions about reason and the argumentative justification of truth claims under a comprehensive aestheticism, others take aesthetic experience seriously as an Other of reason, without relegating it to the realm of the non-rational. Thus Albrecht Wellmer, who in many ways is supportive of Habermas's program of developing a universal notion of communicative reason, and who shares his belief in the "linguistic turn," has been trying to reconceptualize Adorno's aesthetic theory in order to bring out the emancipatory and rational potential of aesthetic experience, without the aporias in which it is embedded within Adorno's conceptual framework. Wellmer emphasizes that the experience of art is only in part a cognitive process open to discursive analysis and representation, but that this does not make it any less important or less "rational." This rediscovery of the relevance of nonconceptual mental experiences, of the nonrepresentable, suggests that the overly enthusiastic reception of the "linguistic turn" by some of the major figures in contemporary German philosophy as heralding the end of the philosophy of the subject, and also perhaps of the philosophy of consciousness, was premature. Wellmer, who has spoken of a discovery of an Other of reason *within* reason by Freud as well as by the philosophy of language (Wittgenstein),[10] would not wish to go that far. But his insistence on the importance of noncognitive aesthetic experiences is an indication that he is prepared to defend a more encompassing concept of reason than initially envisaged by Habermas.

While the widespread German skepticism toward the more extreme claims of contemporary French thought is understandable, it is also now evident that German philosophy can benefit from the French challenges in so far as they lead to a renewed investigation of significant nonlinguistic and nonconceptual experiences. The renewed interest in aesthetics and the sublime, witnessed in the work of younger scholars such as Wolfgang Welsch, Martin Seel and Christoph Menke-Eggers, points precisely in this direction. In fact, it is becoming increasingly obvious to Habermas himself that aesthetic experience cannot be easily subsumed under, or correlated with, any or all of the three validity claims raised in discursive speech acts, i.e., the claims to objective truth, normative correctness and subjective truthfulness or authenticity. The holistic and integrative nature of such experience is now admitted by Habermas.[11] To this extent the philosopher

10. See *Zur Dialektik von Moderne und Postmoderne. Vernunftkritik nach Adorno*, Frankfurt, 1985, p. 80.

11. A detailed analysis of this change and its consequences for Habermas's philosophical project can be found in David Ingram's paper "Habermas on Aesthetics and Rationality: Completing the Project of Enlightenment," *New German Critique* 53, 1991, pp. 67–103.

who urgently needs to be re-read and made more accessible is Schelling. For it was Schelling rather than Nietzsche who understood the radical role that aesthetics could play in a future philosophy, just as it was Schelling who saw that rationality had to be combined with awareness of the workings of nature and the unconscious.

## II

The contributors to this volume differ in nationality, in disciplinary orientation, and in areas of primary specialization. All the contributors, however, relate to the same central problem of how to construct notions of rationality that neither obstruct human cultural, political and economic development, nor encourage excessively homological approaches to a plural and heterogeneous world. All the contributors have a sense that the legacy of the European Enlightenment must be problematized in essential respects, and all recognize that there is a need to get past the dichotomies and dualisms in terms of which reason and unreason, modernity and antimodernity, science and nonscience have too long been discussed. All the contributors want to allow for the plurality and heterogeneity of human life, without abandoning some basis for human solidarity, and all accept that some of the organizing doctrines of post-Enlightenment Western thought now have to be given up. The crucial differences are about which doctrines to give up, and what to put in their place.

Karl-Otto Apel's essay is a response to what he sees as the totalizing critique of reason mounted by postmodern French thinkers such as Foucault, Derrida and Lyotard and their German precursors Nietzsche and Heidegger. Adorno and Horkheimer, as well as Gadamer and Rorty, are seen as possible sources of such a radical critique of reason. A totalizing critique of reason must be distinguished clearly from a Kantian critique of reason from within reason itself. Apel notes that Heidegger postulated a form of thinking beyond and more rigorous than occidental "logos," a thinking that claimed to take into account the ontic-ontological difference between Being and mere beings, and which took the whole of traditional metaphysics as only a contingent moment in the history of Being. Apel, however, tries to show that the idea of an argumentative justification of scientific and philosophical claims to truth is not dependent on a prior ontology of the kind developed by Heidegger. While we must accept Heidegger's insistence on the disclosure of meaning in language, it is also possible, Apel argues, to postulate cognitive progress spelled out in terms of the learning processes human cultures go through. A Heideggerian or a Derridean critique of Western "logocentrism," on the other hand, is obliged to provide an answer to the question of how its own truth claims can be redeemed.

Apel argues that Heidegger fails to provide a satisfactory answer to this question. The truth claims made by Heidegger (and Derrida) seem to appeal to a notion of justification whose validity is simultaneously denied. Their attempts to provide totalizing critiques of reason involve them in a pragmatic self-contradiction. Apel concludes that an internally consistent critique of reason cannot be a totalizing one.

Apel conceives of his own theory of types of rationality as an alternative to the postmodern critique of reason. This theory is based on the idea that everyone who participates in an argumentative discourse must presuppose the validity of a number of basic cognitive and ethical norms, norms that we cannot criticize argumentatively without, in the process, appealing to precisely those norms. In this way, Apel's theory of a discursive theoretical and practical rationality claims to be foundationalist without being circular. Apel concedes that Heidegger's critique of "logos" is justified insofar as it is aimed at the instrumental reason underlying the natural sciences, but modern societies have developed different types of rationality associated with different spheres of social life. Apart from the instrumental reason of science, there is a complementary hermeneutical *logos*, Apel claims, underlying the interpretive sciences. The process of occidental rationalization and disenchantment would be misunderstood if it were defined as the development of a purely instrumental rationality. The presuppositions of hermeneutical reason, guided by an interest in mutual agreement, on the other hand, allow us to provide a noncircular justification for the idea of natural and human rights: for the justification of an ethics of discourse (*Diskursethik*) that builds on, but goes beyond, a Kantian ethics.

The contemporary status of "reason" is also a central issue for Herbert Schnädelbach. Schnädelbach accepts that today the philosophy of reason must become the theory of rationality focussed on language. Given a transcendental-pragmatic transformation of philosophy, the critique of pure reason becomes the critique of linguistic reason, and following Karl-Otto Apel, the analysis of communicative competence must replace attempts to analyze the faculties of consciousness. However, such a transformation has still to be worked out in detail. According to Schnädelbach: (1) a critique of linguistic reason must encompass all of what Kant divided into reason, understanding and judgment; (2) it is impossible to represent rationality completely in principles, rules or norms, so that there is always an unbridgeable gap between what we are capable of in the area of rationality and what we can explicate discursively as rationality that we currently possess; and (3) a way must be found to reconcile reason and historicity.

Manfred Frank's essay is a different response to the challenge of the "postmodern" critique of reason. Whereas Apel tries to counter this critique by pointing out what he sees as its internal inconsistency, and by setting against it a comprehensive notion of rationality grounded in the cognitive and ethical presuppositions of argumentation aimed at a universal consensus, Frank is not convinced that a consensus theory of discursive rationality is what we need to prevent the relativism and the decentering of the subject advocated by some poststructuralist thinkers. For Frank there is an "Other" of reason that needs to be protected from the idea of a universal reason, including the discursive reason advocated by Apel and Habermas. This "Other" of reason is the individual in its absolute uniqueness and nonidentity in relation to any other individual.

Frank discusses the issue of the critique of reason in an historical context as well as in a systematic one. Like Apel, he points to Nietzsche and Heidegger as precursors of the contemporary critique of reason, and shows how Heidegger put Nietzsche's critique on a more profound epistemological basis. He also discusses Weber's thesis about the rationalization and disenchantment of the world of Western capitalism in the context of Heidegger's theory of the history of Being. Frank traces back the critique of a total rationalization of the life world to early German romanticism and idealism. This allows him to establish a link between problems of rationality and the beginnings of romantic hermeneutics in Herder, Friedrich Schlegel, and Schleiermacher, and to argue that any grounding of rationality is dependent on a prior process of interpretation. Knowledge claims cannot be founded on an axiomatics because even axioms, as linguistic signs, would have to be interpreted, and their meaning exists only in the consciousness of individuals. Analysis is grounded in synthesis. The legitimation of rationality is dependent on something beyond the limits of rationality.

According to Frank neither Sartre's existentialism nor Adorno and Horkheimer's neo-Marxism have been able to provide a satisfactory answer to the question of how we should deal with the dialectic of enlightenment. Instead, they repeat the dilemma that was already obvious to the romantics: the dilemma between an idea of an order requiring an ahistorical *telos* for its legitimation and the historicization implied by hermeneutics. Frank argues against Habermas that a consensus theory of rationality based on the idea of an ideal speech situation and the unavoidable normative presuppositions built into language, fails to take into account the irreducibly individual character of our interpretations. Such a theory threatens to impose universalistic norms and meanings on individuals without giving them the right to interpret these in their own specific ways. Frank therefore accepts, to some extent, the radical critique of reason that Germans find in contemporary French thought, but he rejects its concomitant attack on the subject.

Gernot Böhme, on the whole, is far more sympathetic toward the challenges discussed in the context of the idea of a radical critique of reason. In a brief historical overview from Kant's critique of reason to Horkheimer and Adorno's *Dialectic of Enlightenment*, he discusses the ways in which the subversive potentialities implicit in the Enlightenment's ambivalent attitude toward reason were drawn out and increasingly radicalized. Like Frank, he believes that Habermas's conception of a communicative rationality is not an acceptable solution to the problems arising out of a radical critique of reason. He argues that true communication must allow for the irrational behavior of our dialogue partners, that rational behavior has roots in nature, and that Habermas's conception of communicative rationality suppresses the human being's relationship with nature, which in part at least is one of necessity, and thus calls into question the entire program that Habermas associates with modernity.

Böhme does not himself promote a radical critique of reason. On the contrary, he believes that it is necessary to go beyond any such critique and to develop a new philosophical anthropology.[12] Böhme asserts that we need to stop thinking of ourselves as autonomous rational beings and to orient ourselves instead toward our bodily existence. We also need to take account of all those more intangible matters related to moods and the "atmospherics" of emotionally charged situations. In addition, we need to foreground nature in a new way: to understand human beings as part of nature, and to stop viewing nature as nonhuman. The independence of nature as an agency has to be recognized, just as the opposition between nature and society has to be overcome.

Albrecht Wellmer compares the views of the Paris-based Greek social philosopher Castoriadis with those of an imagined pragmatic philosopher of language (PPL), a composite figure, modelled largely on Jürgen Habermas and Wellmer himself. Wellmer's aim is to show that the objections that seem to follow from Castoriadis's work to the strong conceptions of truth and reason advocated by the pragmatic philosopher of language are not, in fact, very damaging. The three basic arguments he considers are: that the institution of a new social imaginary is creative; that the signifying relationship is irreducible and the condition of all other relations, and so has a holistic character; and that the institution of a common world has a practical character. All three arguments might seem to suggest that the idea of truth and reason have only limited applicability to an instituted world, and do not apply at all to the event of its institution. Wellmer, however, attempts to show that a revised version of Habermas's ideas can avoid most of these difficulties.

Wellmer argues that given a dialogue paradigm of rationality, both the

12. See, for example, his book *Anthropologie in pragmatischer Hinsicht*, 3rd ed., Frankfurt, 1991.

creative character of the institution of a social imaginary can be admitted, and the holistic character of the instituting dimension of language can be accepted without abandoning the framework of rational argument, especially since breaks are never total and continuities are also prominent. He concedes, however, that there is a problem about the practical character of the institution of a common world, and that fundamental changes in a form of life can never be understood as a manifestation of a rational choice. Nonetheless, Wellmer believes that Castoriadis's project of an autonomous society can be integrated with an attempt to rethink modern democratic and liberal universalism on the basis of a critique of traditional European rationalism and scientism, and with an attempted self-transcendence of modern reason.

Wayne Hudson reads Habermas's *The Philosophical Discourse of Modernity* in the context of the debates about "reason and its Other." In a spirit of critical sympathy with Habermas's work he raises scruples about aspects of Habermas's discursive practice in *The Philosophical Discourse of Modernity*, which he suggests do not help to advance Habermas's project. Specifically, Hudson examines Habermas's use of "high" terminology which tends to homologize or conflate issues that need to be distinguished if their connections are not to be oversimplified, and his regimentive readings of the work of other thinkers, such as Nietzsche, Heidegger, Derrida and Foucault. Hudson concludes that it may be a mistake simply to contrast Habermas's work with the advocates of "the Other of reason" since the problem of an extrarational dimension arises in Habermas's work itself.

Richard Campbell's paper assays the problem of reconceiving truth and reason after Habermas. Campbell traces the different conceptions of truth developed by Hegel, Kierkegaard and Heidegger in response to the collapse of the medieval Christian-Aristotelian synthesis and to the dichotomy between thought and reality that it opened up. Campbell sees Hegel as having an objectual conception of truth as opposed to modern attempts to set language, thought and judgment over against "reality." Kierkegaard, on the other hand, breaks up the link between truth and reason assumed by the Enlightenment, and shifts truth into the Other of reason. Truth is subjectivity and consists in the self-activity of personal appropriation – a reading that unexpectedly links Kierkegaard's position with later views of Foucault. Heidegger relocates truth as a revelatory event that makes possible the disclosure underlying assertions. Campbell argues that Habermas's view of truth as warranted assertibility leads him to exclude the disclosure of Being from the sphere of reason. Such disclosure then becomes the *mysticum* of an "Other of reason." Instead, Campbell recommends a turn to Kierkegaard and to truth as faithfulness, located primarily in action. A conception of reason that encompassed both insight and discursive rationality might, Campbell believes, be able to overcome the modern narrowing of reason to the instrumental calculation of the cost-benefits of various possible means for attaining preferred ends. It might also avoid constructing an "Other of reason" out of the many aspects of reality to which such a narrowed conception of rationality is inadequate.

Dieter Freundlieb examines K.-O. Apel's conception of the explanation of human action as an example of the ontological and epistemological dualism characteristic of large parts of German post-Kantian philosophy. Freundlieb addresses the question of whether a dualism of reason and nature in Apel's work does not result in a tendency to make nature an Other of reason that needs to be assimilated to, and ruled over by, reason. He argues that Apel's conception of human beings as "denizens of two worlds," who belong to the natural order as well as to the order of the rational and the normative, even though it differs in important respects from Kant's distinction between the phenomenal and the noumenal, makes it impossible for Apel to provide a satisfactory account of human action. While not pretending to be able to offer a solution to the difficult question of the relation between the factual and the normative in human action, Freundlieb suggests that a more naturalist and less dualist conception that recognizes the importance of the natural in the human world would be a more promising philosophical project.

Tuan Nuyen relates the German critique of scientistic reason to analytical philosophy as its apparent "Other." He examines arguments from Husserl and Gadamer which he believes deserve better recognition within the analytical tradition. Nuyen denies that such views can be characterized as irrationalism, or that they lead to relativism. He also suggests that the standard dualism between "continental philosophy" and "analytical philosophy" has been overstated. Indeed, insofar as modern German *Vernunftkritik* includes an attempt to draw limits around the reason of science, Nuyen shows that similar arguments can be found in analytical philosophy, most obviously in the work of David Hume, Peter Winch and Elizabeth Anscombe.

Michelle Walker poses the problem of the relationship between the German *Vernunftkritik* and French feminist theory. She reads Adorno with and against French feminist philosopher Luce Irigaray. She rereads Adorno's exploration of the limits of reason and the concept in the light of Irigaray's work on the body. Walker reads Adorno as prefiguring deconstruction and interprets both negative dialectic and deconstruction as attempts to demolish hierarchical oppositions within rational thought. Like Irigaray, Walker implies that a psychoanalytical reading of philosopy is possible, and that the refusal of philosophers to acknowledge the gaps in reason can be interpreted along Freudian lines. She calls into question "the construction of reason" in the Western tradition, insofar as it is characterized by a desire to unify, to find a single ultimate meaning. Walker also takes seriously Adorno's negative dialectics, interpreted as an attempt to change the direction of conceptuality toward nonidentity. The implication is that an alternative to the Western construction of reason can be envisaged, that conceptuality can be emancipated from the logic of identity, and opened to what escapes or lies beyond reason.

Niklas Luhmann, in his interview with Wayne Hudson, takes a characteristically individual approach to the debates about "reason and its Other." Luhmann rejects the terms of these debates as belonging to "old European thought." He criticizes traditional discussions of the distinction between reason and nonreason on the grounds that they fail to discuss what is the same on both sides of the distinction. Nonetheless, although Luhmann rejects talk of "reason" in favor of "rationality," and proposes to reinterpret the subject and consciousness in terms of systems theory, his interview makes it clear that he is not an antirationalist or an enemy of the Enlightenment. Rather, Luhmann advances a series of technical distinctions in place of familiar everyday ones, and attempts to show that a systems-theoretical approach can produce the theory which, while it is antihumanist, claims to be able to take better account of the individual, and also to be more useful in the context of both historical research and practical administration than approaches, such as Critical Theory, that continue to deploy the distinctions of "old European thought."

Such highly theoretical issues relate directly to more specific critical and historical studies of modern German culture. For a contrast between reason and nonreason, rationalism and non-rationalism, has played an organizing role in constructing modern German political, literary and cultural history. Hence, philosophical debates that question standard dualisms and one-sided correlations of reactionary politics with rationalism and irrationalism respectively, lead to major reevaluations of specific authors and trajectories. Such reevaluations are operative in the contributions by Hohendahl, Bonnell, and Alter that follow.

The problems associated with over-schematic and dualistic constructions of "the Other of reason" are taken up *in concreto* by Peter Uwe Hohendahl. Hohendahl raises these themes by means of a critical analysis of Adorno's attempt to reevaluate the status of Heine in German culture. The question of Heine's status in a German context was recently reopened by Jürgen Habermas in an essay on "Heinrich Heine and the Role of the Intellectual in Germany".[13] In this essay Habermas emphasizes that Heine, the representative of radical enlightenment and of materialist and rational

13. J. Habermas, *The New Conservatism: Cultural Criticism and the Historians' Debate*, trans. S.W. Nicholsen, Cambridge, Mass., 1989, chapter 3.

utopian thought, was not well received in Germany, even by Weimar intellectuals. His independent involvement with both the Enlightenment and Romanticism upset both left and right, and there was no room for an intellectual of Heine's type in Germany, even at the start of the First World War. Heine the patriotic Jewish emigré living in Paris at a distance from his homeland, and critical of the German restoration, represented a type of intellectual that only really flourished in France with the Dreyfus affair, and which Germany tragically lacked even much later.

Hohendahl takes up the implication that Heine needs to be rehabilitated precisely because of the complexity of his modernity. Whereas in Germany "intellectuals" were constructed as "an Other," with disastrous consequences, an enlightened cultural politics needs to be open to the "Other" within reason, in a way that avoids such misleading polarizations. Adorno's reading of Heine, Hohendahl argues, is distorted by dualistic distinctions and contrasts. Thus Adorno condemns Heine's poetry by reference to "modernity" because he fails to break with "tradition," which Adorno dubs a "premodern" category. In this way, Adorno makes Heine into a second-generation Romantic. Adorno also criticizes Heine for his alleged reified language, and for his alleged lack of "resistance" in working with the linguistic materials of the Romantics. Judged by the standard of Baudelaire, Adorno's paradigm for modernism, Heine fails to achieve modernist status. Hohendahl shows how hegemonic all this is. He shows that Adorno fails to grasp Heine's particular version of modernity because he ignores how Heine refunctions the Romantic elements in his poetry. Adorno resists Heine's modernity and finds a lack of authentic language in his poetry. But this follows from the schematic oppositions he brings to Heine's work. Hohendahl stresses that Heine's poetry at once both imitates and mocks Romantic poetry. It makes the reader feel uncanny because it points to a troublesome fact about modernity: namely, that the processes of modernization cannot preserve authentic language. Whereas Adorno requires Heine to conform to his own historicist aesthetics and to produce the demanded "rupture" with Romantic language, in fact Heine was conscious of the problem of language, and used irony and parody to subvert institutionalized aesthetic materials. In this way Hohendahl's essay subverts, through an example, some of the more global theses associated with dualistic approaches to "reason and its Other," modernity and antimodernity. The implications are that obsession with *one kind of modernity* can lead to repressing *another kind of modernity*, and that those who construct "the Others of reason" in dualistic terms often fail to appreciate that some of those with whom they disagree are advancing *different versions* of rationality and modernity.

In a similar spirit Andrew Bonnell examines the role that such themes as "enlightenment" and "the Other(s) of reason" played in German politics between 1890 and 1914. Bonnell argues that the belief that the German Social Democratic Party was the heir to, and the true representative of, the Enlightenment tradition in a society that still fell short of Enlightenment ideals was very important to the self-image and morale of the German Social Democratic Party. Social Democrats saw the Imperial German state, with its appeal to premodern forms of political legitimation and its backward constitutional arrangements, as the "Other" of the Enlightenment. According to Bonnell, the German Social Democrats hoped that the Enlightenment tradition of critique, rationalism and emancipation would be able to counter the Wilhelmine state. In their optimism they seriously underestimated the limitations of a narrowly conceived rationalism, and also failed to comprehend the relevance of a complementary "Other of reason." In this way, Bonnell illustrates how the debates about "reason and its Other" may lead to specific interpretations of modern German political history.

It is possible, however, that the terms of the debate over "reason and its Other" are themselves too unhistorical. In support of this view, Reinhard Alter explores the connections between irrationalism, expressionism, and the conflict of generations. In the case of German Expressionism, Alter argues that any simple antinomy between "reason" and "its Other" is inadequate as a basis for analysis. Instead, Alter offers a generational analysis, indebted to Karl Mannheim's famous essay on "The Problem of Generations." In place of the standard dualistic contrast between rational Wilhelminian fathers and their irrational sons, Alter attributes a definite modernity to those who revolted against Wilhelminian culture's attempt to reconcile modernity and tradition. In his essay Alter considers the controversial case of Gottfried Benn, which subverts the simplistic identification between bourgeois irrationalism, expressionism and fascism proposed by Lukács and Alfred Kurella. Benn's position, he argues, cannot be understood in terms of Ernst Bloch's distinction between "authentic" and "inauthentic" irrationalism, or in terms of any simple clash between "reason and its Other." Because Benn sympathized with National Socialism from a promodern, heroic modernity standpoint as an alternative to the liberal bourgeois nineteenth-century world, he did not share the Nazis' antimodernism, and defended modernist attacks on bourgeois culture. By means of such considerations, Alter illustrates how concrete analyses may call into question distinctions drawn in the course of theoretical debates.

## III

By way of conclusion, it may be useful to relate some outcomes of the debates about reason and its Other to wider controversies about the contemporary status of philosophy. One important outcome of the debates about reason and its Other has been to problematize modern understandings of "reason." The claim that modern reason excludes many aspects of reality from itself and then oppresses them is an important one. Certainly, attempts to exclude the body, desire, fantasy and nature from "reason" have been plentiful, and have led to oddly one-sided, indeed dualist, views of all four areas. There is also merit in the claim that modern understandings of reason tend to inflate reason into "Reason," and then to make claims for "Reason" as if it were the whole of reality. Clearly the precise processes that lead to such results need more exact study, and talk of "modern," "reason," and "Enlightenment" is really shorthand for research programs that need to be undertaken.

It is also fair to concede that new figures of reason may be called for. Certainly the Kantian figure of reason sitting in judgment over validity claims is now controversial, and this has crucial political implications, as ethnic groups and feminists, among others, insist. The Böhmes are also probably right to insist on the need for less homological, more differentiated perspectives that recognize the importance of various kinds of experiences, including experiences that "remain excitements without an object."

The issues raised by the debates about "reason and its Other" also problematize the Eurocentric self-understanding that has prevailed in twentieth-century German, and indeed European, philosophy. Paradoxically, they strike at the cultural authority of the discourse and its institutional location in which they are advanced. Once the historically specific character of *modern European*, and not merely *modern*, reason is researched in comparative terms, it becomes much harder to accept Weber's account of rationality, on which Habermas by and large relies, or to deny that the pretensions of European rationality to be universalist and neutral are open to challenge. In the same way the European Enlightenment turns out to have no right to legislate enlightenment in general, and the universal and transcendental claims of the former appear as historically conditioned, and also specific to one civilization at a certain moment of its reorganization. Likewise, that it is hegemonic to attempt to impose eighteenth-century European homological notions of "Reason" on the rest of humanity, let alone *Aufklärung* notions as opposed to notions deployed in Italy in the *Illuminismo* or in Holland in the *Verlichting*, is obvious. None of the above implies that either historicism or relativism is true. Nor does it deny that universalizing claims for rationality may have their uses. It is not that grand questions asked by Kant at the end of the eighteenth century should now be answered in the negative. Rather, the point is that the discursive and institutional site of those questions has become problematic. The issue today is whether such high talk illuminates the matters in issue, or whether more modest discourses, which specify, for example, local partialities as to metaphor and ranking, may not deliver more effectively over a range of contemporary issues.

Many of the issues raised in the debates about reason and its Other revive questions raised by the crisis of historicism in German thought after the First World War. There are also significant parallels with the "crisis of reason" debates in Italy in the 1970s, in which once again, the question of the historical determination of reason was central. There are also structural links with earlier waves of historicism, and with the work of Ortega y Gasset and his followers in particular. That Ortega returned from a German university education to Spain to write a stream of books exploring "vital reason" and the historicity of reason suggests directions that a neo-Kantian conception of philosophy may take, once there is a loss of faith in its transcendental status and a radical opening to nonintellectualist and historicist perspectives.

Similarly, the link between the "green philosophy" that appears in the debates about reason and its Other and the wider turning to aesthetics in contemporary German philosophy point back not only to Adorno, but to the early German Romantics. A comparison between these Romantics, contemporary French thinkers alleged to be "neo" or "post" structuralist, and contemporary German philosophers is striking. Many of the *topoi*, and even some of the outcomes, are the same. Apart from the obvious issue of influence (pervasive debts, for example, to Surrealism, the continuation of Romanticism in France), there is also evidence for transperiodal organizational logics that subvert the localist and skeptical conclusions by which the philosophers who adopt them are tempted. Such losses point to the possibility that the debates about reason and its Other really signal a transition away from, and not toward the important intellectual terrain to which these debates draw attention.

Another outcome of these debates has been to underline the need to reread the classic texts of German Idealism: to return to key insights of Hegel, Fichte, Schelling and Schopenhauer that turn out not to have been adequately assimilated. Here there is a crucial parallel with the issues thrown up by the French philosophy mis-called "poststructuralist." E.g. Fichte's insight that consciousness knows that it cannot grasp its origin and that it is therefore necessary to posit a nonconscious identity and singular account of reason. In the same way, the Kantian differentiations of reason (formal reason, theoretical reason, practical reason) imply a political order, a triumvirate, which can no longer be imposed on citizens of a republic by some master discourse called "philosophy."

The debates about reason and its Other also raise important issues for contemporary controversies about the future of philosophy. Specifically:

(1) the claim that reason is not one; and (2) the claim that reason is not ahistorical, pure, autonomous and closed. Insofar as such discussions assume implausible levels of voluntarism and plasticity, they perhaps underestimate serious issues which any philosophical account of rationality has to face. Like Nietzsche, they take up radical positions without recognizing the preconditions for such option-taking. On the other hand, such debates are part of a wider movement to respace philosophy. Certainly many philosophers now accept greater degrees of contingency, inconsistency, and the existence of irreducibly heterogeneous materials than was the case before these debates took place.

The long-term consequences of such reassessments are harder to predict. Thus there are moves away from the ethnocentrism that used to characterize European philosophy, but no single outcome has emerged. Here it is useful to note contemporary attempts to globalize philosophy, to take account of non-Western philosophical traditions, and to encourage comparative philosophical studies.[14] Such research paradoxically provides some support for rather traditional rationalist claims, because it shows transcultural organizational logics that do not depend on the language or culture in which they are articulated. But the same research subverts the "old European" tendency to confuse "reason" with what European philosophers have written about it, and the related tendency to assume that all major developments have occurred in Western Europe since 1400, or in cultures dependent upon frameworks provided by Western Europe. Here it is fascinating to consider the work of the Japanese philosopher Tanabe.[15] Tanabe advances a metanoetic in the context of claims that reason is historical in principle, finite and relative. Yet despite his debts to Western influences, the way he develops such issues is strikingly Japanese and actually illuminates classic Western debates.

To this extent, the debates about reason and its Other may be *contributions to communication processes that tend to provoke changes of frame not intended by the contributors*. The success of the doubts raised has not been to enforce the alternativist agenda advocated by the Böhmes, but to open minds to the possibility that the same doubts turned into research programs would force *different alternative programs*. Thus it is not "the body," but the historically and culturally specific gendered body which has moved to the center of contemporary concern, just as it is not carnality that has been rehabilitated, but the need to research historically and culturally specific constructions of human sexuality. It is also important to note that the

14. See J. C. Plott et al., *Global History of Philosophy*, Delhi, 1963, 1979, 1980, 3 vols, and J. R. Burr, *Handbook of World Philosophy: Contemporary Developments since 1945*, London, 1980.

15. See, in English translation, H. Tanabe, *Philosophy as Metanoetics*, Berkeley, 1986.

debates about "reason and its Other" raise, but do not satisfactorily resolve, the problem of the relationship between philosophy and particular legal regimes.

Put more positively, the outstanding merit of the debates about "reason and its Other" is that they signal the need for major changes in the vocabulary of philosophy that, in turn, lead to still other changes. Such debates occurred within one, admittedly extremely important European culture, the German. But their impact and effective history (*Wirkungsgeschichte*) are matters of international importance. Given the outstanding political changes that have occurred since those debates began, it may be that the political context to which they need to be related is that of a planet undergoing globalization and seeking new political forms. To this extent, the historical revivalism present in such debates may strike a chord as a united Germany seeks to define and celebrate its "classics." But, in the longer term, the "classics" of other nations and cultures will have to be taken into account as well. In the process Weber's insistence on the singularity of the West is likely to be confirmed, as against any uncritical pluralist cult of "difference." But precisely those outside of Europe, but indebted to it, are likely to redraw the terms of the debate in ways that lead it away from the cultural, and even the sociopolitical, horizons of those who, to their credit, helped get it underway.

# –2–

# The Challenge of a Totalizing Critique of Reason and the Program of a Philosophical Theory of Rationality Types

## KARL-OTTO APEL

## I. Exposition

I cannot, at the very beginning of my deliberations, give a sufficiently detailed characterization of the complex phenomenon or syndrome of contemporary philosophy I would like to define as a "totalizing critique of reason." At this point I can only introduce it by asserting its existence and its symptomatic significance. And perhaps I can give you a rough idea of what I have in mind by drawing your attention to the currently fashionable talk about "putting modernity into question" or "transcending modernity through postmodernity."[1] The following philosophers are usually named as precursors of postmodern thought: Nietzsche, Heidegger, and French poststructuralists such as Foucault and Derrida. Occasionally, the impact of Heidegger's philosophy is associated with the hermeneutical philosophy of Gadamer and, as a further development of hermeneutics, the "neopragmatic turn" of American philosophy as it is represented, for example, by Richard Rorty. Finally, one can see certain affinities with postmodernism in the deeply pessimistic consequences that Horkheimer and Adorno drew from their reconstruction of the "dialectic of Enlightenment."

---

1. See J.-F. Lyotard, *La condition postmoderne: rapport sur le savoir*, Paris, 1979; Lyotard, *Le différend*, Paris, 1983, G. Vattimo, *Le avventure della Differenza: Che cosa significa pensare dopo Nietzsche e Heidegger*, Milan, 1981; Vattimo, *La fine dela modernitá: nichilismo ed ermeneutica nella cultura post-moderna*, Milan, 1985; J. Habermas, *Der philosophische Diskurs der Moderne*, Frankfurt, 1985; R. Rorty, "Habermas, Lyotard et la post-modernité," in *Critique* 442, 1984, pp. 140–149; A. Villani, "Le 'chiavi' del postmoderno. Un dialogo a distanza," in *Il Mulino* XXXV, no. 303, 1986, pp. 5–22.

When I speak of the challenge of a *totalizing critique of reason* I do not, by any means, have in mind just any attempt at a self-criticism of reason. Even less do I think of the attempts at a critique of the kind of *scientific rationality* that has dominated the modern age in Europe. Since Kant's "Critique of Pure Reason" (understood as a critique *of* reason as well as a critique of reason *by* reason) such critiques of reason have been regarded as a legitimate concern of philosophy. In fact, self-criticisms of this kind can be seen as part of its permanent tasks. A critique of the scientific rationality that has dominated the modern age (in the sense of an all-encompassing interest in a value-neutral control of facts for the purpose of their technological use) has indeed been one of my own long-standing concerns, a concern that can definitely be understood as situated within a *hermeneutical* philosophy originally inspired, among others, by none other than Heidegger.[2] As a matter of fact, in the presence of the global crisis, both in ecological terms and in terms of the proliferation of nuclear armament and strategic developments, one could be inclined to launch a critique not only of the technologico-scientific rationality of European modernity, but of the concomitant rationality of *homo faber* as it has evolved since the beginnings of human history. Because of man's technological intervention in the delicately balanced systems of nature, one could be tempted, along with Arthur Koestler, to denounce humankind as an "Error of Evolution."[3]

One would assume, however, that any such critique, if it was to be meaningful and legitimate, would have to presuppose, and claim as valid, the idea of an intersubjectively binding form of reason (in a sense, of course, that needs too to be specified further). Yet this is exactly what the present critique of reason seems to overlook or what it even deliberately ignores. This impression appears inevitable when one is confronted with the following theses:

The *Will to Truth* and as such the *claim to intersubjective validity* that reason brings to public expression and acknowledgement in an argumentative discourse – this will or this claim is said to be nothing other than the *Will to Power*.[4] To engage in argumentation – and presumably this applies to the argumentation of the critic of reason as well – is nothing more than the rhetorical practice of self-assertion through exercising power. On this view the *formation of a consensus* through an argumentative dialogue would be no more than the subjection of individual spontaneity and autonomy to

2. See K.-O. Apel, *Transformation der Philosophie*, 2 vols, Frankfurt, 1973, *et passim*. Selected Engl. trans.: *Towards a Transformation of Philosophy*, London, 1980.
3. A. Koestler, *Der Mensch als Irrläufer der Evolution*, Berne and Munich, 1978.
4. See M. Foucault, *Die Ordnung der Diskurse*, Munich, 1974, p. 14f.; Foucault, *Überwachen und Strafen*, Frankfurt, 1978, p. 195. Horkheimer and Adorno, too, do not doubt Nietzsche's "pitiless doctrine of the identity of power and reason." See *Dialektik der Aufklärung*, Amsterdam, 1947, p. 59.

the claim to power of a social system, and hence a form of self-alienation.[5] Lyotard's postmodernism seems to accord here, in its presuppositions, with Niklas Luhmann's systems theory, which tries to understand communication itself – including its own discourse as systems theory – in terms of the functionality of the social system.[6] It seems, however, that both Lyotard and Foucault are desperately trying to defend themselves against the claim to power by the social system. And they do so not by setting against this claim, as Habermas does, an appeal to an argumentative formation of mutual agreement free of coercion, but by the paradoxical demand for the formation of *dis*agreement. In Foucault's work this corresponds to the denunciation of universal moral principles, which – for instance in the shape of basic human rights – after all make political freedom and tolerance possible. Nonetheless, such principles are rejected as a means of a repressive normalization of individual forms of life.[7]

It appears, then, that the tenets of the radical critique of reason launched by postmodernism are by and large inspired by Nietzsche; and those tenets seem to be nothing other than variants of that peculiar type of a genealogical self-destruction of the argumentative claim to reason that had occurred already in Nietzsche through his complete reduction of the will to truth, and the intersubjective validity claims of reason, to the will to power.

The basic arguments that can be derived from the totalizing critique of reason, and from the critique of Western *logos* put forward by the later Heidegger, are more sophisticated and more difficult to grasp. In Heidegger's work, as is well known, Nietzsche's philosophy of the will to power appears as a manifestation – more precisely, as the last manifestation – of the *logos* of Western metaphysics, which, so the argument goes, is *a priori* designed to enable the domination of the world and the empowerment of the self.[8] The genealogical point and principle of origin that Heidegger pits against the *logos* of Western metaphysics is not the will to power concentrated in all beings, whether as subjects or objects of domination; rather, the origin of the world-historical reign of the ontical will to power – and hence the *logos* of metaphysics – is said to lie in temporal Being. The latter, because of the "ontic-ontological difference" between beings and Being, is

---

5. This is the only plausible way in which I can understand Lyotard's paradoxical polemic against the discursive formation of mutual agreement. See Lyotard, *The Postmodern Condition*, Minneapolis, 1984, p. 25 and p. 66.

6. See (most recently) N. Luhmann, *Soziale Systeme*, Frankfurt, 1984.

7. See M. Foucault in *Les Nouvelles littéraires* of 29 May and 28 June, 1984. I have addressed this issue in K.-O. Apel, "Der postkantische Universalismus in der Ethik im Lichte seiner aktuellen Mißverständnisse," in K.-O. Apel, *Diskurs und Verantwortung*, Frankfurt, 1988.

8. See M. Heidegger, *Nietzsche*, 2 vols., Pfullingen, 1961; also Heidegger, *Holzwege*, Frankfurt, 1950.

said to be distinguished from mere beings, and thus inaccessible to any form of thought directed at objects. At the same time, temporal Being, through the "epochal," that is to say simultaneously "disclosing and concealing" event (*Ereignis*) of a meaning-constitutive difference, is said to have "grounded" world history, and thus the hitherto "legitimate" sovereignty of the *logos* of Western metaphysics.

One could be inclined to think that in this Heideggerian conception a totalizing critique of reason involving a self-invalidation of argumentation might be avoided. This is suggested, in particular, by certain statements made by the later Heidegger according to which a mode of "thinking" is possible that is more rigorous than the *logos* of Western metaphysics, that is to say, more rigorous than that of science and philosophy.[9] The problem arising from this, however, is that Heidegger tries to ground the truth claim of assertions, and the corresponding concept of propositional truth as well as the Platonic-Leibnizian principle of the *logon didonai*, that is to say, the "grounding" of asserted propositions on the basis of intersubjectively valid reasons, in the *logos* of the "frame" (*Gestell*), i.e., the technological "framing" (*Stellen*) of objects in terms of a subject-object relation. The *logos* of occidental rationality as a whole is said to be nothing but an "epochal," and thus contingent, disclosure of the meaning of Being within the context of the history of Being, a "disclosure" that in this process simultaneously conceals itself. And it thereby conceals the possibility of a different meaning and a different form of thought. But how can Heidegger himself *know* that this is so, and how can he *assert* and *justify* his own claim to truth?

Heidegger cannot answer this question because he has construed the *logos* of statements and their justification genealogically, as part of the epoch of the "history of Being" that he wishes to destruct. In this sense, as in the case of postmodern thinkers, what we have in the work of Heidegger is a totalizing critique of reason in terms of a self-dissolution of the principles of argumentation. (As far as I can see, Jacques Derrida has adopted Heidegger's critique, in his own critique of "logocentrism," and in his thesis of the hidden activity of a meaning-constitutive "différance." In fact, as

---

9. See M. Heidegger, "Brief über den Humanismus," in Heidegger, *Platons Lehre von der Wahrheit*, Berne, 1947, p. 56f., and 110ff. In his late lecture "Das Ende der Philosophie und die Aufgabe des Denkens" of 1964 Heidegger says the following about Western reason: "What is *ratio, nous, noein*, listening? What is the meaning of ground and the principle of all principles? Will we ever be able to determine satisfactorily what this means without experiencing the Greek notion of *aletheia* as unconcealment and then – going beyond the Greek – to think of it as the 'clearing' of concealment? . . . Perhaps there is a thinking beyond the distinction between what is rational and irrational, more sober even than scientific technology . . ." (in *Zur Sache des Denkens*, Tübingen, 1969, p. 79).

far as the paradoxical nature of his own validity claim is concerned, he has, if anything, surpassed even Heidegger himself).[10]

I think we should take this self-destructive critique of reason as an internal challenge to contemporary philosophy, a challenge that is both a symptom and something that needs to be understood in terms of its external and internal motives. At the same time, it must be taken seriously, and therefore requires what might appear to be a somewhat pedantic refutation. The fact that the various types of totalizing critiques of reason we have so far encountered have been plausibly targeted at quite *different* aspects of reason or rationality contains, it seems, a formal indication of what any possible *consistent* critique of reason must be like: it obviously cannot be totalizing. This indication is reinforced by the fact that we can always find, within the philosophical tradition, a strategy of argumentation that is able to absorb, as it were, any external critique of reason: I mean the strategy of the reflexive self-differentiation of reason.[11]

Drawing on the traditional strategy of the self-differentiation of philo-

10. See J.Derrida, *L'écriture et la différence*, Paris, 1967; also Derrida, *De la grammatologie*, Paris, 1967; Derrida, *Marges de la philosophie*, Paris, 1972; and Derrida, *Positions*, Paris, 1972. In line with the spirit of Heidegger, he wants to transcend Heidegger and "deconstruct" the thinking of the truth of being as "logocentric." He thus regards Heidegger's thought as still belonging to the "metaphysics of presence" and therefore committed to the idea of a subject-object relation: "La pensée du sens ou de la vérité de l'Etre, la determination de la différance en différence ontico-ontologique, la différence pensée dans l'horizont de la question de l'Etre, n'est-ce pas encore un effet intra-metaphysique de différance?" (*Marges*, p. 23). The activity ("mouvement," "déploiement") of "différance" that Derrida attempts to think "n'est pas précédée par l'unité originaire et indivise d'une possibilité présente que je mettrai en reserve" (*Positions*, p. 17). Rather, what he is concerned about is a kind of thinking that "ne veut rien dire," which, as "écriture," is nothing but the trace ("trace") of a lost "archi-écriture": "pure signifiance sans signifié originaire." Yet how is it possible to think this, that is to say, how can its validity in terms of its meaning and its truth be claimed? It is this question that provides the starting point for my metacritique of the deconstruction of the *logos* of Western philosophy.

11. See, for example, Kant's distinction between "understanding," "reason," and "judgment" and Hegel's distinction between ("abstract") reason and global ("speculative") "reason." As far as the theory of different types of rationality is concerned, which I will develop in what follows, one thing is clear. It is the Kantian notion of understanding and Hegel's abstract reason alone that, according to both thinkers, correspond to that type of value-neutral (logico-mathematical, technologico-scientific and strategic) rationality that can perhaps be equated with Heidegger's *logos* of the "frame" (*Gestell*) or the process of occidental "disenchantment" identified by Max Weber. Reason, however, (and "judgment," which stands in its service) is neither value-neutral nor does it serve the "Will to Power." Instead, it corresponds *a priori* to its own "interest in reason." In Hegel this interest in reason is identical with the interest of the world spirit (*Weltgeist*), and thus guarantees the necessary evolution of world history, which constitutes a return to an emphatic notion of metaphysics. In Kant, however, the interest in reason is only capable of a "moral teleology" of "regulative principles" and "postulates." The latter conception can, in my view, form the basis of an ultimate transcendental-pragmatic justification through a rigorous reflection on the inescapable conditions of argumentation.

sophical reason, I would like to develop, in what follows, a program of a philosophical theory of rationality. In doing so I would also like to make heuristic use of the current motives underlying totalizing critiques of reason.

The heuristic use of the external motives of contemporary critiques of reason will serve the function of correcting, to some extent, the reflexive self-differentiation of reason. It is with regard to this corrective function of an external heuristics, and thus in a merely preliminary and fallible sense, that the reflexive self-differentiation of reason should take the shape of a theory of rationality types.[12]

## II. The Program of a Philosophical Theory of Rationality Types

### II.1 Preliminary Considerations: The Idea of an Ultimate Transcendental-Pragmatic Justification of a Philosophical Rationality as Discursive Rationality

The program of a theory of rationality types I envisage is conceived as an answer to the contemporary challenge to reason as it manifests itself in totalizing critiques of reason. Such an attempt at a response presupposes, in my view, a methodological conception of philosophy that is contrary in several respects to that propagated by postmodernism. For example, it is incompatible with an entirely undifferentiated rhetorical and literary conception of philosophical discourse. More precisely, it is incompatible with a conception that does not distinguish between fictional language and a language expressing truth claims, between persuasion through insinuation and persuasion through argumentation, and perhaps even between negotiation and argumentative discourse.

On the other hand, the aim is not to disregard entirely any literary and rhetorical forms of language, and to renew the heroic attempts made during the era of Carnap and Tarski to restrict the language of philosophy to a formalized construct purified from all subjective pragmatic dimensions of context-relative speech. This is impossible because the attempt at a reflexive self-differentiation of reason has to make use of precisely those dimensions of natural language that were considered troublesome by the proponents of formal semantics because they led to semantic paradoxes, namely, the transcendental-pragmatic dimension of the self-reference of situated speech acts. This reflexive dimension of speech, which is not immune *a priori* against semantic antinomies, makes natural language the pragmati-

12. For a first attempt in this direction see K.-O. Apel, "Types of Rationality To-day: The Continuum of Reason Between Science and Ethics," in T. Geraets (ed.), *Rationality Today*, Ottawa, 1979, pp. 307–340. In the meantime, J. Habermas has set new standards for a theory of rationality types in his *Theorie des kommunikativen Handelns*, 2 vols, Frankfurt, 1981.

cally ultimate metalanguage. The existence of a natural language is presupposed by all artificially constructed languages, and it is necessary even for the formalization and logical reconstruction of arguments. As such, natural language, with all its metaphorical and context-sensitive (for example indexical) elements, is therefore the language no philosophy can do without.

Now because of the fact that a philosophical theory of rationality – more than any other form of philosophical theorization – is dependent on the reflexive dimension of language, it must take care to avoid, at any cost, what we might call a *performative self-contradiction*. It assumes, for example, that the paradox of the liar does not occur because of the self-referential use of language alone as it manifests itself in statements such as "All men lie" or "I always lie" or "I am now lying." Such statements are paradoxical also because, in making such statements, the speaker simultaneously denies, and therefore cancels, his claim to truthfulness and thereby also his claim to speak the truth. We should note also that the rule that forbids the commission of a performative self-contradiction is not introduced, like the principle of noncontradiction, as an axiom of propositional logic. Rather, it is the result of a reflexive insight: i.e., the insight that the introduction of any conceivable theory or any conceivable set of axioms already presupposes the performative self-consistency of speech. The postulate of self-consistency thus does not rest on a pure positing or a decision: it is a condition for the possibility of any kind of meaningful positing or decision making. Performative self-consistency is thus a requirement of thinking and argumentation that cannot be side-stepped. It follows that the rule prohibiting performative self-contradiction cannot be *grounded* if by "grounded" we mean – as is customary in the tradition of logic – the process of deductive or inductive inference from final premises. Any such grounding would have to presuppose as valid what it wishes to ground and therefore commit a *petitio principii*. But becoming aware of this fact means, at the same time, that we realize that our principle provides us with a philosophically satisfactory justification since it is obvious that any kind of objective logical justification is always already dependent on it. I have called this the ultimate transcendental-pragmatic justification of philosophy. And taking my point of departure from the inescapable presupposition that pragmatic or performative self-contradictions are to be avoided, I have proposed the following criterion for a philosophical, that is to say transcendental-pragmatic, foundation of the principles of both theoretical and practical philosophy:

> We are justified in regarding those presuppositions of argumentation as ultimate principles which we cannot deny without, in the process, committing a

performative self-contradiction but which cannot, for the same reason, be logically deduced without involving us in a vicious circle (petitio principii).[13]

I would like to call these ultimate presuppositions of argumentation the principles of a philosophical rationality of discourse; in short: the principles of reason or the *logos*. At this point I can only assert that what we are dealing with here are principles sufficient for a grounding of both theoretical and practical reason, thus including the principles of ethics. The previous deliberations have provided us already, it seems, with at least a preliminary characterization of the type of philosophical rationality that we indicated earlier. This has been achieved not so much on the basis of the content of our deliberations, but on the basis of the methods we employed when we tried to reconstruct the principles of a discursive rationality. We did not introduce the primary and fundamental type of rationality within our theory of rationality types in an axiomatic fashion. Instead, we asked ourselves what kind of rationality would have to be presupposed by any theory of rationality whatsoever. And this is precisely the rationality that governs argumentative discourse.

The nature of this type of rationality can best be illustrated by distinguishing it clearly from the type of rationality underlying formal, apodictic logic. I was alluding to this difference before when I referred to the different relation in which both types of rationality stand to the self-reflexive nature of speech. The type of rationality that characterizes formal and mathematical logic owes its maximal precision to the fact that, unlike the discursive rationality we introduced above, it abstracts away from the situated self-reflection of concrete argumentation. In my view, this difference suggests that we are confronted here with the most profound distinction between possible types of rationality.

The import of this distinction, however, seems to remain invisible to the participants in contemporary philosophical debates because of two prejudices: (1) the confusion of the self-reflection built into argumentation with a psychologico-anthropological or metaphysically relevant type of self-knowledge; and (2) the confusion of self-reflection with the possibly infinite metalogical thematization of argumentation through a hierarchy of metalanguages.

The first confusion contains the misleading suggestion that the self-reflection of thought as argumentation must lead to ontologico-metaphys-

13. See K.-O. Apel, "Das Problem der philosophischen Letztbegründung im Lichte einer transzendentalen Sprachpragmatik," in B. Kanitscheider (ed.), *Sprache und Erkenntnis*, Festschrift für G. Frey, Innsbruck, 1976, pp. 55–82, (English transl. in *Man and World* 8, 1975, pp. 239–275; Spanish transl. in *Dianoia* XXI, 1975, pp. 140–173; French transl. in *Critique* 413, 1981, pp. 895–928). See also W. Kuhlmann, *Reflexive Letztbegründung: Untersuchungen zur Transzendentalpragmatik*, Freiburg and Munich, 1985. Also D. Böhler, *Rekonstruktive Pragmatik*, Frankfurt, 1985.

ical insights (so Descartes and his critic Nietzsche) or else must be irrelevant because it is only of psychological interest (Frege). The second confusion suggests that the transcendental reflection on the conditions of the possibility of argumentation can be replaced by a metalogic in such a way that the potentially paradox-engendering self-reflection of language is replaced by a successive objectification of the dimension of reflection through a series of metalanguages. But our introduction of the principle that prohibits performative self-contradictions has already indicated that a theory of metalogic cannot thematize that which makes such a logic possible in the first place. The language concerned with a reflection on philosophical argumentation is not a metalanguage in the sense of an indefinite series of formal languages. Rather, the language of reflection is the language that allows us to formulate the insight that the sequence of metalanguages is infinite and thus cannot be brought to a closure.

We need to ask, then, what the relationship is between the type of rationality associated with discursive self-reflection and the concept of rationality, *logos*, or reason presupposed in the contemporary forms of a totalizing critique of reason.

## II.2 The Main Theses of the Totalizing Critique of Reason of Postmodernism

The best way of answering this question is perhaps by setting specific traits and forms of argumentation of the postmodern critique of reason in relation to the approach taken by the transcendental-pragmatic theory of rationality outlined above. And I would also like to include in my discussion Max Weber's still widely discussed thesis of the occidental process of rationalization and disenchantment. Let me focus on the following theses and suggestions:

1. *The Global Thesis of Postmodernism* (in Heidegger's sense): Reason (*logos*) is only the subject-related correlative of a contingent, epochal disclosure of meaning within the wider context of a "history of being." The epoch characterized by the *logos* of metaphysics must be overcome (*verwinden*) so that it can open itself up to the Other, an Other inaccessible to *logos*. In accordance with Derrida, the global thesis could be formulated thus: we need to overcome Western "logocentrism" because it conceals the meaning-constitutive activity of "différance."

2. *A Specific Thesis Concerning the Logos of Metaphysics* (in Heidegger's sense): Since Plato and Aristotle, the *logos* has been conceived of as the "apophantic" expression of beings in their "presence," that is to say in their being or their essence (*essentia*). In this sense, temporal Being, by virtue of its difference from what is present and what is conceived as the essence of beings, is inaccessible to the *logos* of metaphysics.

3. *A Specific Thesis Concerning the Logos of Science and Technology* (in Heidegger's sense): The subject-object relation underlying the natural sciences is prefigured in the apophantic *logos* of classical metaphysics. Transcendental consciousness conceives of the world and human beings as objects of investigation and technologico-strategic use, a form of objectification that today undergoes its final transformation, for example in a microphysics that no longer allows the use of models accessible to concrete intuition. Instead of the "representation" of "objects," we find the mere "computation" of "physical states." In short: what is built into the occidental *logos* is the "frame" (*Gestell*) of modern technology and its concomitant laying to waste of the world (*Weltverwüstung*) and the self-manipulation of man.[14]

4. *A Specific Thesis Concerning the Occidental Process of Rationalization* (in Max Weber's sense): The highest form of modern rationality is a means-ends rationality, which is supported, as an "objective rationality of ends," by the rationality of the modern natural sciences. This rationality manifests itself in causal analysis and technologically useful prediction. Compared to this form of rationality, the rationality of values (*Wertrationalität*) and its orientation toward the intrinsic value of actions regardless of their consequences is, in principle, regarded as less rational, since it has to resort to subjective final decisions made in the light of axiomatic values. All this is a result of the occidental process of rationalization and disenchantment.[15]

*II.2.1*    As far as the global thesis of postmodernism is concerned, I would like to offer the following answer. The type of *logos* or reason intended here cannot, on pain of a performative self-contradiction, be identical with the type of *logos* or reason presupposed in the validity claim made by the global thesis. As an object of a relativizing history of Being only a restricted notion of reason, that is, a certain abstractive type of rationality, can be meant. The *logos* presupposed in the validity claim of the global thesis, however, has already become visible as the type of self-reflexive rationality of discourse outlined above. This can be supported by the following consideration.

Heidegger's "ontic-ontological difference," and thus the difference

14. See particulary M. Heidegger, "Die Frage nach der Technik," in *Vorträge und Aufsätze*, Pfullingen, 1954.

15. See W. Schluchter, *Rationalismus der Weltbeherrschung. Studien zu Max Weber*, Frankfurt, 1980; also Schluchter, *Die Entwicklung des okzidentalen Rationalismus. Eine Analyse von Max Webers Gesellschaftsgeschichte*, Tübingen, 1979; J. Habermas, *Theorie des kommunikativen Handelns*, vol. 1, chapter II; K.-O. Apel, "Läßt sich ethische Vernunft von strategischer Zweckrationalität unterscheiden? Zum Problem der Rationalität sozialer Kommunikation und Interaktion," *Archivio di Filosofia* LI, 1983, pp. 375–434, particularly p. 378ff.

between temporal Being and mere beings, can only be investigated because this difference can be thematized in language, and thus made an "object" of true or false statements. This is not to deny that we must reckon with a simultaneously "revealing and concealing" process of world disclosure of an originary linguistic nature, a disclosure which, as an ongoing historical event, is not at our disposal. In this sense, the possibility of true or false judgments concerning phenomena within our world is indeed dependent on a prior disclosure of meaning (*aletheia*). But this disclosure, as an "event" within the history of Being, cannot be regarded as constituting, in its entirety, the *logos* of philosophy. Rather, the meaning-differentiating power of the history of Being must be seen as matched by the reflexive power of self-transcendence. Furthermore, we must presuppose that the communicative ability to come to a mutual agreement about meanings that is mobilized in argumentative discourse is on a par with the meaning-disclosing power of language and its vast richness.

However, in spite of this assurance of the complementary and co-extensive and co-intensive power of temporal disclosure of meaning, on the one hand, and of self-reflexive discursive *logos* on the other, the following question remains open. Are we not confronted by a primacy of an a-rational fate of an historical constitution of meaning, in spite of all our attempts at philosophical and scientific theorizing? Is it not the case that this theorizing, insofar as it needs the support of empirical evidence, remains, in the end, dependent in its selection and interpretation on the historical and fateful process of meaning-disclosure, a disclosure that is at once a concealment of meaning? Must we not restrict our claim to a progressive discovery of the truth to a limited horizon of meaning? For example: on a paradigm-dependent "normal science" in the sense of Thomas Kuhn?[16] And must we not give up the notion of any possible progress in the field of ethics as well as the supposition of universal ethical principles?

In my view, the answer to these suggestions, which are characteristic of postmodernism, must be a twofold one:

1. First of all, we need to point out that the relation of dependence between truth as the validity (and coherence) of judgments, on the one hand, and the disclosure of the world through language on the other, is not as one-sided as Heidegger and, in a similar way, the later post-Wittgensteinian theories of linguistic "frameworks" suggest.[17] All learning processes, in fact, that are supported by the confirmation of hypothetical assump-

16. See T. S. Kuhn, *The Structure of Scientific Revolutions*, Chicago, 1962.
17. See also Heidegger's correction of his earlier views in his *Zur Sache des Denkens* (p. 76ff.) according to which his notion of "*aletheia*" is not a more originary concept of truth, but refers to the disclosure of meaning in the sense of a "clearing" (*Lichtung*) that is prior to any possible truth (or correctness) and falsity of judgments.

tions, put into question the idea of the a-rationality and fatefulness of the disclosure of meaning. To be sure, they are made possible, on the one hand, by the linguistic horizon of an epochal disclosure of meaning, but on the other hand they are also capable, on the basis of their confirmation through empirical (i.e., ontical) evidence, of co-determining the future development of the process of the disclosure of meaning. Thus the variously weighted disclosure of meaning of sensory experiences represented in the languages of Polynesians, Arab desert tribes and Eskimos, for example, is apparently determined by the successful deployment of the results of quite different but vitally important learning processes. This is witnessed by such feats as the navigational discovery of the vastness of the Pacific ocean in small outrigger canoes, the survival of the Bedouins in the North-African deserts, and the hunting of whales and seals by Eskimos in a harsh Arctic environment of ice, water and snow. From a different perspective, according to Ernst Cassirer, the structural evolution of world-disclosing language can be reconstructed in terms of a transition from a phase of "imaginative expressions" referring to spatio-temporal relations, via a phase that allows the expression of more "abstract concepts" (for example the concept of taxonomical classes), to a final phase characterized by the ability to express "logical relations."[18] Also, this structural evolution, which could be seen as a prefiguration of the scientific mastery of the world through technologically useful knowledge (*Arbeitswissen*), can be understood as a result of learning processes whose occurrence could be rationally expected.

It is thus misleading to interpret the phenomenon of the disclosure of meaning exclusively, as the late Heidegger did, as the fate (*Zuschickung*) of temporal Being – as if the temporalization of time that we indeed experience as a-rational were identical with the origin of meaning or even with truth in the sense of "*aletheia.*" Heidegger was in fact much closer to the truth when in *Being and Time* he tried to determine the structure of the disclosure of the world in terms of the "hermeneutical circle," a circle that the philosopher only had to get into in the right way.[19] We need to note, however, that even then, as in Gadamer's hermeneutical philosophy, the question remained unanswered how exactly the philosopher is able to enter the fruitful circle of an explicative understanding of the world; whether, for example, there are any normative criteria apart from contingent projections or temporal fate. This is where the second, supplementary answer to the problem we have raised must be sought.

2. Even when starting out from the phenomenon of the successful

18. See E. Cassirer, *Philosophie der symbolischen Formen. Erster Teil: die Sprache*, Oxford, 1956.

19. See M. Heidegger, *Sein und Zeit*, 5th edition, Halle, 1941, p. 153 and 324f.

deployment of knowledge in learning processes, the question remains what the criteria are by which cognitive innovations at the level of cultural evolution are selected. It is well known that there are learning theories that suggest that what happens here is nothing but a further extension of biological processes of adaptation in the interest of the survival of a population, more precisely, in the interest of "the proliferation of genes." In this case truth and cognitive success could be reduced, in the manner of a social Darwinism, to adaptation and selection. There would be no normative culture-specific criteria for cognitive success, not to mention normative criteria for the selection of rules of behavior in the sense of moral learning processes. Cynics could be inclined to say: for the sobering gaze of science this would be the external appearance of what the postmodernists, following Heidegger, experience as the fateful disclosure and concealment of the meaning of Being. For what is it that could function as the objective and practically relevant criterion for differentiating between the two perspectives? Are they not both manifestations of a nihilism embodied in the philosophy of culture and history?

At this point in our discussion I would like to bring to the fore the normative criteria of understanding, that is to say, the criteria of the rational reconstruction of cultural learning processes. These criteria are "always-already" contained in the *logos* of discursive rationality. What we find here are, in my view, the (transcendental) constituents of the fore-structure of "Dasein," and that means the constituents of the "being-with" other subjects in the world or "being-in-the-world" that Heidegger failed to analyze in *Being and Time*: constituents that he overlooked when he engaged in a quasi-reflexive analysis in the sense of a forgetting of the *logos*. Instead, his analysis was an attempt to show the dependence of understanding on the "thrownness" of "Dasein." Later he conceived of the contingency of this "thrownness" as the fate (*Zuschickung*) of Being.[20]

---

20. See my discussion of Heidegger and Gadamer in K.-O. Apel, *Transformation der Philosophie*, Frankfurt, 1973, vol. 1, "Einleitung," p. 38ff.

In the meantime I have come to the conclusion that Heidegger's and Gadamer's analysis of the "fore-structure of understanding" needs to be revised even more radically. If the task is to overcome Husserl, who was the last classic philosopher of a "prelinguistic" and "prehermeneutical" transcendental philosophy of consciousness (or the subject), in order to transform this philosophy by situating it within a "postlinguistic" and "posthermeneutical" philosophical paradigm, then a more profound solution to the problem of the *a priori* must not only be sought in the direction of the prereflexive presuppositions of the facticity of our being-in-the-world, that is to say, in the direction of the *a prioris* of the contingent life world. Although we can see that the *a priori* of the historically contingent life world is identical with the *a priori* of the constitution of meaning over which pure consciousness has no power, consciousness is still the *a priori* site at which a reflection on the validity of normative claims to truth and rightness takes place. For this reflection is capable of transcending the power of the *a priori* of the historically contingent life world. It is this forgetting of the power of the *logos* that characterizes Heidegger and Gadamer (and of course the whole of postmodern thought).

The normative criteria for the rational reconstruction of culture-related learning processes we are discusing here are, in my view, contained within those noncontingent constituents of the fore-structure of a hermeneutical "being-in-the-world." And these constituents are the conditions for the possibility of a philosophical analysis of our "being-in-the-world."[21] Among these we find, for example, the four universal validity claims of human speech specified by Habermas: the claim to speak intelligibly, the claim to truth, the claim to speak truthfully, and the claim to perform an ethically and normatively acceptable speech act in the sense of a set of always already presupposed norms of an ideal community of communication. Furthermore, we find the presupposition that the four validity claims (with the exception of the claim to be truthful) can be redeemed, in principle, though rarely factually, in accordance with a discursive rationality.[22] Indeed, this last presupposition must, in the case of actual argumentation, take on the character of a counterfactual anticipation of the ideal formation of a consensus. Any participant in a discussion testifies to this, willy-nilly, even if he or she states the exact opposite.

Now the necessary conditions of argumentation contain the normative criteria for a rational reconstruction of cultural learning processes insofar as they provide them, in a formal sense, with an intrinsic goal of all such processes. Alongside strategies of survival, this is a goal that must play, at the very least, the role of a regulative principle governing both ontogenetic and phylogenetic processes of cultural learning. What we are dealing with here is not a *telos* in the older metaphysical sense of the word, but it is nonetheless a teleological principle whose validity must be presupposed by any attempt at a rational reconstruction of human evolutionary processes. Anyone engaged in such an attempt must, in order to make sense of his or her endeavor as a result of an evolutionary process, appeal to his or her own reconstructive competence as a standard (i.e., the *logos* of discursive rationality) that also underlies the learning processes he or she wishes to recon-

---

It can be shown, however, that the transcendental self-reflection of the *ego cogito* on the conditions of its own validity is in need of a "postlinguistic" transformation, a transformation that does not lead back to the solitary consciousness of the "I think" in the sense of the methodological solipsism of Descartes and Husserl, but which remains within the framework of a linguistically mediated self-understanding and its publicly valid articulation. In short, it leads us to the *a priori* of argumentation and its *logos*, a *logos* that cannot be transcended, even by the fate of Being.

21. See the reflexive turn taken in K.-O. Apel, "La razionalità della comunicazione umana nella prospettiva transcendentalpragmatica," in Umberto Curi (ed.), *La Comunicazione Umana*, Milano, 1985, pp. 158–176.

22. See J. Habermas, *Theorie des kommunikativen Handelns*, Frankfurt, 1984, chapters 2 and 8; also K.-O. Apel, "Zwei paradigmatische Antworten auf die Frage nach der Logos-Auszeichnung der menschlichen Sprache: die philosophische Relevanz der Sprechakt theorie," in H.-G. Bosshardt (ed.), *Perspektiven auf Sprache*, Berlin and New York, 1986.

struct. I have called this the postulate of the self-recognition of rationality (*Selbsteinholungs-Postulat*) characteristic of reconstructive sciences.[23]

A particularly fruitful and promising attempt in the sense of a realization of the reconstruction of learning processes has been made, in my view, by Jean Piaget and his cognitive developmental psychology, as well as the theoretical reconstruction of the development of the competence of moral judgment as it has been developed by L. Kohlberg and his collaborators on the basis of Piaget's work.[24] These theories try to mediate, as it were, between the ideal *telos* of the rational redemption of the universal validity claims of the *logos* and the biological *telos* of the adaptation of individuals for purposes of human survival. This mediation is conceived as a hierarchy of developmental stages aiming at the progressive realization of an equilibrium between the formation of an ability to pass rational judgments and the vitally necessary adaptation to a natural and social environment. Since the realization of the learning processes (in terms of an ontogenetic development of our consciousness) investigated by Piaget and Kohlberg is not only dependent on natural but also on socio-cultural environmental conditions, it is necessary to presuppose the possibility of a progress through learning in this area as well. It would be a form of learning aimed at the progressive realization of the *telos* of a rational redemption of universal validity claims. This dimension of learning has also come under investigation in terms of theories concerning the acquisition of rational cognitive structures.[25]

I can now conclude and summarize my answer to the global thesis of postmodernism as follows:

1. *Logos* or reason as such cannot be understood as the contingent and epochal result of the history of Being since such a thesis would thereby cancel its own validity claim.

2. The *logos* of discursive rationality, as it is presupposed in any genuine argumentation, contains within it the *telos* of a rational reconstruction of cultural learning processes. These processes constitute a counter-

23. See K.-O. Apel, "Die Situation des Menschen als ethisches Problem," in G. Frey (ed.), *Der Mensch und die Wissenschaften vom Menschen.* Die Beiträge des XII. deutschen Kongresses für Philosophie, Innsbruck, 1983, pp. 31–49; also in Apel, *Diskurs und Verantwortung,* see note 7.

24. In particular, see L. Kohlberg, *The Philosophy of Moral Development,* San Francisco, 1981; on this topic see J. Habermas, *Moralbewußtsein und kommunikatives Handeln,* Frankfurt, 1983, chapters 2 and 4; also K.-O. Apel, "Die transzendentalpragmatische Begründung der Kommunikationsethik und das Problem der höchsten Stufe einer Entwicklungslogik des moralischen Bewußtseins," in Apel, *Diskurs und Verantwortung.*

25. See K. Eder, *Die Entstehung staatlich organisierter Gesellschaften,* Frankfurt, 1976; also Eder, *Geschichte als Lernprozeß,* Frankfurt, 1985; K.-O. Apel, "Weshalb benötigt der Mensch Ethik?" in K.-O. Apel, D. Böhler, K. Rebel (eds.), *Funkkolleg: Praktische Philosophie/Ethik, Studientexte,* Weinheim and Basel, 1984, vol. 1, pp. 13–156.

argument against the conception of the dependence of all cognition on an a-rational fateful disclosure and simultaneous concealment of the meaning of Being. There is no reason to abandon the idea of progress in the sense of a possible progress toward truth and moral competence. Rather, this idea is presupposed by all attempts at a reconstruction of human learning processes, even though it is to be distinguished from the speculative teleology of traditional metaphysics.

*II.2.2*   In discussing the second and third of Heidegger's theses (concerning the *logos* of metaphysics or of modern science and technology) I can, for the first time, accommodate some aspects of the postmodern critique of reason. This can be done in the context of the program of a critical self-differentiation of reason, a program that is both possible and necessary today.

Thus we can show that the apophantic *logos* of classical metaphysics had already, in Plato and Aristotle, been restricted to the propositional representation of states of affairs by abstracting away from the pragmatic dimension of speech. Those functions of dialogic speech that were not representational because of their pragmatic nature were deliberately separated, in a fragment on the *logos* attributed to Theophrastus, from the apophantic *logos* of philosophy and relegated to the fields of rhetoric and poetics. What had thus been separated off were the communicative and self-expressive functions of speech, including the internally related function of the reflection on the concrete validity claims of argumentation.[26]

This successive restriction of the *logos* of language in the tradition of a logic-oriented philosophy of language reflects, indeed, a corresponding development of the *logos* of metaphysics toward the technologico-scientific *logos* of the "frame" (*Gestell*) in Heidegger's sense. This development manifests itself, in particular, in the foundation of logical semantics in Frege and Tarski, a development that had already been anticipated in a more speculative way by Leibniz. Frege not only eliminated the semantic indicator of an assertion from the notion of a propositional statement as a merely psychological and subjective moment (cf. the Stoics' notion of the *lecton*). He also, for the first time, conceived of the statement as modelled on the idea of a mathematical function. Tarski, in a similar fashion, regarded propositions as special cases of sentence functions, that is, as "instantiated" sentence functions. This meant that the *logos* presupposed by modern science and technology had reached its full development, at least at the level of the philosophy of language. It had become the *logos* of the *calculus ratiocinator* (Leibniz) or, in Heidegger's terminology, the *logos* of the "compu-

26. On this, and what follows, see K.-O. Apel, *Die Idee der Sprache in der Tradition des Humanismus von Dante bis Vico*, 3rd edition, Bonn, 1980, chapter 5; also Apel, "Die Logosauszeichnung der menschlichen Sprache," note 22.

tation of the world," which excludes all evaluative understanding of the subjective and communicative dimensions of the world.

If this is admitted as a confirmation of Heidegger's thesis, it is necessary, at the same time, to present a counter-argument in terms of a completion of the reconstruction of the differentiation of rationality types adumbrated earlier. What is required is in fact a completion of the characterization of the technologico-scientific rationality type as well as its supplementation by a complementary type of rationality.

First of all, I would like to correct an inaccuracy. It lies in the fact that the logical genealogy of the *logos* of the "frame" sketched above does not take into account the difference between logical and technologico-scientific rationality. This difference can be conceived, in Kantian terms, as the difference between the purely analytical determinations of logic and the synthetical *a prioris* of the construction of the world of objects in terms of the categories of "pure understanding" and the forms of intuition of "pure sensibility." From the point of view of a transcendental-pragmatic transformation of Kant's theory of knowledge we can say, however, that the constitution of an objective world of nature in physics – or, more precisely, in protophysics – presupposes not only forms of intuition and categories of understanding, but also a specific knowledge-guiding interest and certain correlative forms of manipulative interference in the world in the sense of a Heideggerian "framing" such as measuring, for example. Paul Lorenzen and his disciples have shown that within protophysics this applies to processes of spatial and temporal measuring.[27] Drawing on G. H. von Wright, I would like to emphasize, in particular, that our protophysical expectations with regard to necessary causal connections between events always already presuppose the firm belief that through a manipulative interference in nature we can bring about something that would not otherwise occur.[28]

If one takes into account the transcendental-pragmatic conditions of the possibility of a protophysical constitution of the world as it has just been adumbrated, the intrinsic, that is to say noncontingent, connection between an experimental causal analysis as it is practised in the natural sciences, and the instrumental manipulation underlying technology, becomes intelligible. This intrinsic connection also allows us to gain a clearer con-

27. See P. Lorenzen, *Methodisches Denken*, Frankfurt, 1968, particularly p. 120ff.; also Lorenzen, *Grundbegriffe technischer und politischer Kultur*, Frankfurt, 1985, chapter II, "Technik"; and P. Janich, *Protophysik der Zeit*, Frankfurt, 1980; on this see G. Böhme (ed.), *Protophysik*, Frankfurt, 1976.

28. See G. H. von Wright, *Explanation and Understanding*, Ithaca, 1971, chapter II. I refer to this in K.-O. Apel, *Die Erklären:Verstehen-Kontroverse in transzendentalpragmatischer Sicht*, Frankfurt, 1979, p. 97ff. (Engl. trans.: *Understanding and Explanation. A Transcendental-Pragmatic Perspective*, Cambridge, Mass., 1984.)

ception of the type of rationality that lies at the basis of what Heidegger called the *logos* of the "frame," particularly if we also take into account the presuppositions of the logico-mathematical type of rationality and its further extensions. What we are confronted with here is, in my view, a type of rationality that rests on the *a priori* interdependence between the capacity for successful instrumental action and the capacity for the causal or statistical explanation, and thus prediction, of events. And the interdependence between these two capacities must be understood in transcendental-pragmatic terms. One could call this capacity for the cognitive and practical control of the world the technologico-scientific *logos*. But it is also possible to distinguish between the *logos* of the nomological sciences and of instrumental technology, depending on whether we look at this question from the point of view of the purely cognitive or a practical interest. Nonetheless, in making such a distinction between "theory" and "practice," one should keep in mind the internal, i.e., *a priori*, connection between the constitution of a meaningful world enabled by the language of science (i.e., the "setting free" or "disclosure" of the meaning of Being) and its correlative technologico-practical knowledge-guiding interest. For the disenchanted relationship, characteristic of the modern age, between the "theoretical" and the "practical" aspect of the "frame" apparently consists in the fact that the technologico-practical interest subjects itself, without any restrictions, to the value-neutral interest in a description and explanation of events in order to triumph, all the more successfully, over other possible interests as the originary interest in a technological control of the world in line with Francis Bacon's tenet: *natura non nisi parendo vincitur.*

Even after this supplementation of our reconstruction of rationality types in the sense of a differentiation between the logico-mathematical and the technologico-scientific type, it is possible to see this reconstruction as a confirmation of Heidegger's notion of the "frame" as the *logos* of Western natural science and technology. On the other hand, this reconstruction does not, I believe, exhaust the potential of the *logos* as such in the sense of an "occidental process of rationalization."

What needs to be done now is to establish, in the light of a reconstruction of a discursive rationality, the historical link between the rationality of human dialogue discovered in ancient Greece and the *logos* of the hermeneutical sciences conceived in the broadest possible sense.[29] What, then, is the *logos* of the hermeneutical sciences of understanding (*Verständigungswissenschaften*) insofar as it differs from that of the technologico-scientific *logos*? It is no coincidence that the difference between the two has in fact been denied quite frequently from both the scientistic perspec-

---

29. In K.-O. Apel, *Die Idee der Sprache*, see note 26.

tive of the program of the unity of (nomological) science, as well as from the Heideggerian perspective of the critical and global reduction of the *logos* of occidental science to the *logos* of the "frame."

Against this reduction, I would like to characterize and render intelligible the specificity and the normatively binding autonomy of the hermeneutical *logos* in terms of a process of coming to an intersubjective agreement about reasons and validity claims, bearing in mind that the hermeneutical *logos* is both a presupposition and a supplementation of the technologico-scientific *logos* of the subject-object relation. In accordance with what I have elsewhere called the thesis of complementarity,[30] I can then link the restriction of the concept of the *logos* in the tradition of formal semantics with the one-sidedness of the technologico-scientific subject-object relation.

In both cases the reason for my critique does not lie in the fact that the representatives of these traditions, in the interest of the logico-semantic representation and the technological control of what is or will be the case, increasingly abstracted away from the intersubjective dimensions of dialogical and referential speech. The reason for my critique is rather based on the fact that they failed to engage in a radical philosophical reflection on the nature and consequences of this abstraction. Instead, they either completely forgot about these neglected dimensions of speech, or understood them as something that had not yet been made an object of a potential empirical investigation and scientific control. Post-Cartesian scientism could thus assume that one could, in principle, regard as a value-free object for consciousness not only what had hitherto been represented and brought under control, but the whole of the external world, including other subjects and even oneself. It was no longer realized that even the most radical cognitive distanciation in the sense of the subject-object relation necessarily presupposes a linguistic understanding of the self and the world, and therefore also a subject-co-subject relation concerned with intersubjective communication, a relation that is complementary to the subject-object relation. It was assumed that each subject was capable of the cognition of objects, even under the condition of a total objectification of the world, i.e., as a *solus ipse*.

This assumption of the legitimacy of methodological solipsism in relation to the Cartesian subject of knowledge is, in my view, the reason for the "scientistic" inability to acknowledge the hermeneutical presuppositions of the natural sciences and technology, and thus the complementary function and methodological approach of the hermeneutical sciences. Furthermore, this assumption is also the basis of the post-Humean notion that

---

30. See K.-O. Apel, *Transformation der Philosophie*, Frankfurt, 1973, vol. II, p. 96ff., and Apel, *Die Erklären:Verstehen-Kontroverse*, note 28, p. 268ff.

the subject of knowledge, after having objectified the world, must deduce the norms of ethics from value-neutral facts, provided this is considered possible at all. Against this notion, the thesis of complementarity can point out the following. The natural scientist who, within the framework of his *logos*, turns the world into objects of value-neutral explanation, must himself be a member of a community of mutual communication. As such, he cannot take up a purely objectifying relation to his human environment, but must always already have acknowledged certain moral norms, namely, the norms that govern the formation among equal partners of a consensus free from coercion. In other words, the *logos* of value-neutral natural science and technology presupposes the hermeneutical *logos* of intersubjective communication, and thus the *logos* of an ethics of the community of truth seekers. The complementarity of these different forms of the *logos* consists precisely in the fact that they differ from, and supplement, each other, so that they cannot, either now or in the future, be reduced to one another, but stand or fall together.

*II.2.3* The thesis of complementarity and its relation to the *logos* of science makes it obvious, in my view, that the identification of the occidental process of rationalization with the *logos* of the technologico-scientific and instrumental rationality, as suggested by Heidegger and, in a somewhat different form, by Max Weber, is a rather crude simplification and falsification of the real situation.

To be sure, our reconstruction of the evolution of rationality in the West is in agreement with Heidegger insofar as this reconstruction does indeed confirm the fact that the dialogical *logos* has been ignored in favor of the "framing" of the world. Our reconstruction thus also confirms, in part, Weber's notion of the occidental process of rationalization and disenchantment. For we cannot doubt that since the beginning of the modern age, during the emergence of political systems based on the idea of the "reason of state" (*Staatsräson*) and of capitalist economies from an earlier medieval society based on the idea of a metaphysico-theological *ordo*, the technological and scientific as well as the instrumental and strategic forms of rationality have emancipated themselves from the political and moral obligations and claims of a metaphysically and theologically grounded view of the world. These claims were pushed aside as rationally problematic and even obsolete. It might appear, then, that what we find here is a uniform situation of the monopolization of the "frame" or a means-ends-rationality.

But if we take a closer look we will realize that the occidental process of rationalization has been co-determined, on the whole, by the complementary types of rationality presupposed in the "framing" of the world and in instrumental action. This is true, even if one has to admit that those complementary types of rationality have misunderstood their own role and nature by associating themselves with the perspective of the "frame" and of a rationality of means and ends.

Notwithstanding Max Weber's attempts to conceive of the rationality of *Sinnverstehen* primarily on the basis of a reconstructive understanding of purposive-rational actions, it has never been possible to account for the hermeneutical transmission of theological, juridical and humanistic literary traditions in terms of the categories of scientific or technologico-instrumental rationality. Weber could not avoid the use of the category of "value relation" in his *verstehende* sociology. Nonetheless, in his endeavor to understand sociocultural facts, he only wanted to make a value-free use of the different heuristically conceivable "value relations." It is more important, however, to show that the process of the rationalization of the legal system in modern European states cannot be made intelligible exclusively in terms of a logical systematization, a means-ends rationality and, in addition to that, a value rationality (*Wertrationalität*) – that is to say, a process that would account for the relation of the people to religious and metaphysical world views only at the level of subjective plausibility. It is by no means the case that in the modern age the rationalization of the legal system has only taken place at the level of a logical and instrumental-strategic rationality, with the necessary normative basis of society remaining unchanged within the realm of religious doctrine. Rather, it is precisely in the area of the development of universally valid principles of what have traditionally been called "natural rights" that a rational emancipation from the dogmatic presuppositions of religious and metaphysical world views has taken place. The universal *logos* of justice that had emerged had in fact been given an almost satisfactory foundation in Kant's rational and ethical justification of the "moral law" (*Sittengesetz*) on the basis of the autonomy of practical reason.

At this point in our reconstruction of the rationality types complementary to the "frame" we must pause for a moment and engage, for the last time, in a systematic discussion of the totalizing critique of reason put forward by postmodern thinkers. For the statements I have just made regarding the rationalization of the legal and moral dimension of the modern occidental process of civilization will indeed be contradicted by almost all proponents of contemporary philosophy. Not only legal positivists and Max Weber reject, as a dogmatic illusion, the idea of the possibility of an ethical and rational justification of natural rights. The later Heidegger as well sees in the *logos* of Kant's transcendental philosophy nothing but a stage in the epochal disclosure of the metaphysical *logos* of subjectivity, that is to say, of the "frame" – a stage within an overall development that ends, predictably, in Nietzsche's "Will to Power." How are we to respond to these theses?

*II.2.4*   I would like to begin with the following historical thesis. What has traditionally been called "natural law" has in fact provided, in the modern age, the universalistic justification of the idea of "human rights," and as such the legitimation for the various revolutions of the bourgeoisie. Nonetheless, I do not think that the idea of natural law can be taken as a rational and nonmetaphysical complement of the rationality of the "frame" in such a way that one could, on the basis of such an idea, convince a proponent of the value-free technologico-scientific and instrumental rationality that he must always already have acknowledged a rational principle of justice. This could only be done once we have provided an adequate reconstruction of the idea of natural law in the light of a transcendental philosophy. Even Kant did not really succeed in his attempt to legitimize natural law on the basis of the autonomy of law-giving reason. Let us look at this issue a little more closely.

It is surely entirely mistaken and one of the most astounding of Heidegger's and the postmodernists' misrepresentations and distortions, to characterize Kant's philosophy of the transcendental subject as a prefiguration of the philosophy of the "Will to Power" – for example through Foucault's identification of the "Will to Truth" or of Fichte's "Will to Reason" with the "Will to Power." The enormity of this distortion can be seen in the fact that Kant's transcendental subject is, at least in part, the representative of the universal validity claims that can only be redeemed in a sphere of argumentation free of coercion. Nietzsche and Foucault could only reduce these validity claims to a mere "Will to Power" on pain of a performative self-contradiction.[31]

On the other hand, it must be admitted that Kant's transcendental subject is also the subject that "frames" nature in terms of the technologico-scientific control of the world. It is the subject that "frames" nature, not only in the vague sense of the subject-object relation that is in general characteristic of post-Cartesian philosophy of consciousness, but in the more precise sense of a technologically relevant "framing" of nature through experimentation: a "framing" through which we force nature to answer our questions. It is exactly this that Kant has in mind when he refers to the "Copernican revolution" in philosophy.[32] Behind the inquisitive encounter of the transcendental subject with the world, there is not just the will to truth in general and the corresponding validity claim – in itself

31. See J. Habermas, *Der philosophische Diskurs der Moderne*, chapts. IX–XI; see note 1.
32. See Kant's "Vorrede zur zweiten Auflage" of the *Kritik der reinen Vernunft*, Akademie-Textausgabe, III, particularly p. 10.

this will to truth could not conceive of the world as meaningful and relevant to our concerns – but the particular knowledge-guiding interest that is indeed the hallmark of the *logos* of the "frame."

It will be of the greatest importance, then, to distinguish analytically between the dimension of the human will to power built into the technologico-scientific interest in knowledge on the one hand, and the dimension of the claim to truth on the other, which, as a universal validity claim, is dependent on intersubjective agreement about meanings and the formation of a consensus. Such a distinction could not be thought, however, at the level of a transcendental philosophy of the solitary subject and its consciousness. More precisely, since Kant was not yet able to take into account, as transcendental conditions of valid thought and knowledge, the linguistic and communicative conditions of the possibility of intending and referring to something *as* something (that is to say, of the whole dimension of our communicative exchange with other subjects), he also therefore could not provide a transcendental legitimation of the hermeneutical sciences concerned with "historical and social reality" in Dilthey's sense. Dilthey himself, we might note, did not really succeed in delivering such a legitimation in terms of the transcendental conditions of intersubjective agreement because he was too much under the influence of the subject-object paradigm. Furthermore, Kant, because of the Cartesian limitations of his transcendental reflection on the foundations of intersubjective validity as they are conceived by the solitary subject, could not develop a genuine legitimation of ethics and thus the traditional idea of "natural law."

More precisely: Kant's ethical intuitions were strong enough to discover, in the "categorical imperative," the universalizing principle that we understand today as the principle of the mutually and necessarily binding nature of all rights and duties. In accordance with his basically sound intuition, he even postulated something like the regulative principle implied in the dimension of intersubjective communication about rights and duties, namely, the idea of an ideal community open to the future. He conceived of it as a metaphysical "realm of ends" inhabited by rational beings guided by ends rather than means. But this did not, as yet, amount to a discovery of the real community of communication, including the ideal community counterfactually implied in the real, as a transcendental condition of the possibility of valid thinking in terms of linguistically mediated processes of understanding concerning others and oneself. Had Kant discovered, in the principle of the *cogito*, the principle of discursive rationality, and thus the principle of the rationality of ethics, then the legitimation of theoretical and practical philosophy that he aimed for could have been provided from within a common origin. He could then have avoided the necessity of breaking off, prematurely, the intended grounding of the validity of the moral law on the basis of our free will to reason. He was forced to abandon this attempt because he could not, by transcendental deduction, demonstrate the existence of human freedom.[33] A nondeductive legitimation of the existence and validity of an autonomous principle of ethics is indeed possible, however, on the basis of a transcendental reflection on that which we have always already freely acknowledged in genuine argumentation – or even when we seriously raise a question.[34]

In completing our attempt at a typological self-differentiation of reason, and our discussion of the totalizing critique of reason within postmodernism, we have now come back to our starting point, i.e., the ineluctable presupposition of a discursive rationality. In conclusion, let me summarize once more the typological result of my programmatic attempt and thereby clarify the methodological approach of a self-differentiating investigation of reason by reason itself. This constitutes an alternative to the totalizing critique of reason by postmodernism, a critique that cannot reflect on its own validity claim.

*II.2.5* We began by distinguishing the *logos* of reason as such, i.e., the self-reflexive *logos* of argumentation or of discursive rationality, from the nonreflexive "abstract" *logos* of logico-mathematical rationality. In doing this we were confronted with the most profound difference and the greatest tension within a typological self-differentiation of reason. For the logico-mathematical type of *logos* is, as analytic *logos*, minimally informative. This is why it is unsuitable for an ultimate philosophical grounding. Its criterion of the prohibition of the logical contradiction "a and non-a" is merely formal and dependent, for any content, on the semantic filling in of the variable "a." As a formal and abstract criterion it cannot be used to demonstrate definitively that the ultimate presuppositions of argumentation cannot argumentatively be denied. Its application is always dependent on axiomatic premises that are themselves in need of justification. Every justification through logical inference, however, (i.e., deduction and induction) necessarily leads into the trilemma whose alternatives are infinite regress, *petitio principii*, or the dogmatic insistence on the truth of the premises.[35]

In contradistinction to the criterion of the logico-mathematical *logos*, the criterion of the self-reflexive *logos* of argumentation (i.e., the principle of the prohibition of a performative self-contradiction), can indeed fulfil

33. See Kant, *Kritik der reinen Vernunft*, Akademie-Textausgabe, vol. V, p. 46f.

34. See the following essays of mine: "Das Apriori der Kommunikationsgemeinschaft und die Grundlagen der Ethik," in *Transformation der Philosophie*, vol. II, p. 358ff., see note 2; "Das Problem der Begründung einer Verantwortungsethik im Zeitalter der Wissenschaft," in E. Braun (ed.), *Wissenschaft und Ethik*, Berne, 1986; and "Die transzendental-pragmatische Begründung der Kommunikationsethik," see note 24.

35. See H. Albert, *Traktat über kritische Vernunft*, Tübingen, 1968, p. 11f.

the function of an ultimate justification. For its application in terms of the self-reflection of any participant in an argumentation is informative in the sense that it gives us a reflexive insight into undeniable presuppositions of argumentation. This criterion forces us to exclude propositions that are incompatible with the inevitable performative validity claims of argumentation. As I have tried to demonstrate, this leads to a *reductio ad absurdum* of virtually all of the theses of the totalizing critiques of reason advanced by postmodernism that have attracted such widespread attention. On the other hand, our criterion allows us to justify contemporary and entirely plausible critiques of attempts to absolutize abstractive types of rationality. These are types of rationality that are situated between the extreme abstraction of the logico-mathematical type and the integrating power of the self-reflexive rationality of discourse.

Thus, apart from the logico-mathematical *logos*, we have tried to reconstruct the taken-for-granted technologico-scientific *logos* of the modern age in the light of Heidegger's notion of the "frame" (*Gestell*). But we have also pointed out the possibility and necessity of a sublation of the abstractive absolutizing of the *Gestell* through a reflection on the complementary types of rationality presupposed in this *logos*. In this process of reconstruction we became aware of the discursive rationality without which such a reconstruction would indeed be impossible. We also pointed out the tripartite *logos* of dialogue as a complementary transcendental-pragmatic presupposition of the semantic and representational function of propositions. In addition, we revealed, as a complementary presupposition of the technologico-scientific *logos* of the modern age, the subjective/intersubjective *logos* of the communicative formation of a consensus which is always already presupposed in any scientific objectification and control of the world. Finally, as a further extension of the self-differentiation and self-recognition of discursive rationality, we uncovered the *logos* of the critical hermeneutical sciences and the *logos* of an ethics based on communication presupposed in these sciences.

Our sketch is incomplete insofar as we would have had to engage once more in a discussion of instrumental or means/ends rationality at the level of a communicative ethics. This discussion would have had to focus on the difference between and the mediation of, in the sense of an ethics of responsibility, consensual-communicative and strategic rationality. A context-sensitive mediation of these two forms of rationality would, in turn, be subject to a regulative principle that, as a principle open to consensus, must be able to be legitimated in the argumentative discourse of philosophy.[36]

36. See K.-O. Apel, "Läßt sich ethische Vernunft von strategischer Zweckrationalität unterscheiden?" note 15; also Apel, "La razionalità della comunicazione umana," note 21.

I would hope that the argumentative strategy of the proposed philosophical theory of rationality has become clear. Perhaps there is even something postmodern about it; postmodern, however, not in the sense of a totalizing critique of reason, but in the sense of a critique of the modern philosophy of the subject-object relation of consciousness. For this philosophy was characterized by a forgetting of the *logos* that manifested itself in the refusal of this philosophy to reflect on its own linguistic and communicative presuppositions.

*Translated by Dieter Freundlieb and Wayne Hudson*

# –3–

# Observations on Rationality and Language

## HERBERT SCHNÄDELBACH

The program of a "transformation of philosophy" by transcendental-pragmatic means requires that the critique of pure reason be replaced by the critique of linguistic reason. Then the analysis of the conditions for communication in language, which Kant had always assumed to be fulfilled, will prepare the way for the examination of conditions for the possibility of knowledge, which at the same time can be regarded as the conditions for the possibility of objects of knowledge. The critique of knowledge is rendered complete – indeed it is only made possible in the first place – once the skepticism of the critique of sense has placed in question the traditional foundations of the critique of knowledge. But precisely this transforms Kant's pure reason into linguistic reason, for the "synthetic unity of apperception," which appeared to him as "the understanding itself," and therefore as "that highest point to which we must ascribe all employment of the understanding, even the whole of logic, and conformably therewith, transcendental philosophy,"[1] is now to be understood as the "transcendental synthesis of linguistically mediated interpretation understood as the unity of our coming to an agreement about something in a community of communication."[2]

An important step in the implementation of this program is the transformation of the traditional concept of reason itself. If one wishes to explain "reason" as a fundamental transcendental-pragmatic term, then one can no longer, as Kant did, pursue the mentalistic paradigm of an introspective psychology of faculties and let formal logic take care of the rest. That new approach in the critique of reason from the outset places the

1. Kant, *Kritik der reinen Vernunft (KrV)*, B 134.
2. K.-O. Apel, "Der transzendentalhermeneutische Begriff der Sprache," in *Transformation der Philosophie* (henceforth *TdP*) II, Frankfurt, 1973, p. 354.

object of criticism into the realm of linguistically mediated intersubjectivity; it is a matter of examining communicative competence,[3] not the faculties of consciousness. The orientation toward formal logic is inadequate because linguistic communication in its syntactical, semantic and pragmatic aspects has become the "medium of transcendental reflection,"[4] and these aspects are simply not comprehensible with the aid of logic alone. This medium of transcendental reflection is then simultaneously its central "theme," because in the critique of reason based on the Kantian model, theme and medium necessarily coincide. Criticized reason is no different from criticizing reason, because the communicative competence that it is important to secure in terms of the criticism of sense must of course itself also be called upon in this business. Therefore that which is to be explained under transcendental-pragmatic conditions as reason relates precisely to the communicative competence that the transcendental pragmatist, in his attempt to analyze it, has already to have granted himself when he begins with the implementation of his analysis. This seemingly paradoxical structure distinguishes his "research programme" from that of the linguist and the ethnologist; only in this way does he have in view not somebody else's but his own reason.[5]

Today reason is discussed under the heading "rationality." In part, the reasons for this are to be found in the history of philosophy. The tradition of logical empiricism, which in its late theoretical phase became aware of the scandal of the "rationality gap" – a gap that came to light in the course of its attempt to achieve a rational reconstruction of science as the modern paradigm of rationality *per se* – preferred to leave the term "reason" to other intellectual tendencies. For the logical empiricists it smacked of metaphysics. Apart from that, rationality had become a topic for the social sciences, since at least Max Weber, and, most recently, the post-Wittgensteinians had taken it up in the same sense.[6] Via this detour it finds its way back into philosophical discussions today. But there is also a more content-based justification for that change in terminology. The term "reason'" can lead to "substantialist" misunderstandings, and although Kant himself strenuously confronted them with his doctrine of reason as the supreme

3. See *ibid.*, p. 352ff., also Apel, "Noam Chomskys Sprachtheorie und die Philosophie der Gegenwart," in *TdP*, p. 264ff., esp. 293ff.

4. See K.-O. Apel, "Sprache als Thema und Medium der transzendentalen Reflexion," in *TdP* II, p. 311ff.

5. The strict reflexivity of a critique of communicative competence is in my opinion the only feature that distinguishes Apel's transcendental-pragmatic program from the universalpragmatic program of Habermas; for both authors it leads, however, to a clearly different type of theory: see K.-O. Apel, "Noam Chomskys Sprachtheorie..." pp. 305f. and footnote; also 355ff.; as against that see J. Habermas, "Was heißt Universalpragmatik?" in K.-O. Apel (ed.), *Sprachpragmatik und Philosophie*, Frankfurt, 1974, p. 174ff., esp. 198ff.

6. See B. R. Wilson (ed.), *Rationality*, Oxford, 1979.

cognitive faculty and with his critique of the paralogisms of pure reason, reason in Kant is sometimes difficult to distinguish from *res cogitans*. Reason understood as a property, and not as a substance or fact, is "reasonableness" (*Vernünftigkeit*), and then one might as well say "rationality." A further advantage of this terminology is that it is much less prejudiced than talk of reason, which carries the burden of all sorts of traditional connotations: for example of the antithesis of reason and understanding (*Vernunft* and *Verstand*) or the etymological association of *Vernunft* (reason) with *Vernehmen* (perception). On the other hand, we will have to accept that "rationality" is usually associated today with a "means-ends rationality" (*Zweckrationalität*) and thereby with "instrumental reason" (*instrumentelle Vernunft*), and as a result often becomes the target of a general critique of reason. Usually a differentiation between types of rationality[7] based on examples is sufficient to prevent any misunderstandings. And this seems to be the most significant advantage of the term "rationality": its associated semantic field offers less resistance to an internal differentiation of what is meant by it than would be the case with any comparable term. If this is true and we wish to make use of that advantage, then the Kantian model of the philosophy of reason will have to be replaced by a transcendental-pragmatic theory of rationality whose basic outline is now becoming clear, but which by no means can be regarded as a program that is indisputable in every respect.

The following is intended as a contribution to this program in the form of some broad observations on the problem: how is it possible to represent rationality in language in a transcendental-pragmatic way? What is the significance for our understanding of rationality of the repetition of the critique of reason as the critique of linguistic reason in the medium of transcendental pragmatics? After a few intuitive thoughts on the predicate "rational" I would like to put forward three theses:

1. The critique of linguistic reason as the preparatory component of a transcendental-pragmatic theory of rationality must proceed from Kant's broader understanding of reason, that is, it must bear in mind the entire range of that which Kant divided up into understanding (*Verstand*), judgment (*Urteilskraft*) and reason (*Vernunft*).

2. From the conditions prevailing after Kant, to which the transcendental-pragmatic program is also subject, there arises the impossibility of representing rationality completely in principles, rules or norms. As a result, the difference between the rationality that we must always assume we are capable of and that which we can explicate as our actual

---

7. See K.-O. Apel, "Types of Rationality Today: The Continuum between Science and Ethics," in T. F. Geraets (ed.), *Rationality Today*, Ottawa, 1979, p. 307ff.

*Herbert Schnädelbach*

rationality cannot be transcended in principle; "rationality" is an open concept.

3. A consequence of this is the "historicity of reason" and an ineradicable moment of "decisionism" (*Restdezisionismus*) in ethics. There is no transcendental-pragmatic "First Philosophy" and therefore also no equivalent in a communicative ethics to Kant's "fact of pure practical reason."

# I

Considered intuitively, the predicate "rational" stands at the intersection of two distinctions: its use can be descriptive or normative, and it can be meant nondispositionally or dispositionally. In the first case we often consider rationality to be an attributable quality,[8] and only in this way can it be explained how it could become a topic of value-free social science. At the same time, by using the predicate "rational" we are also often adopting a normative or evaluative position toward that which we refer to by this term. And on this point, since at least Schopenhauer, we no longer take for granted that the rational is normatively superior. The traditional consensus that did assume such a normative superiority was totally shattered by the philosophy of life movement (*Lebensphilosophie*), and certainly can no longer be maintained in an age characterized by defeatist attitudes towards reason. Whoever uses the word "rationality" provokes normative dissent, and this would not be possible if the predicate "rational" allowed no normative usage. Presumably, the normative sense of "rational" is also the reason why the rational justification of norms in the tradition from Kant to Hegel was always considered possible and promising. The objection that Kant fell into a naturalistic fallacy[9] runs the risk of ignoring this; it is characteristic of our present situation in the history of philosophy (but not that of German idealism) that we can no longer claim without argument that reason and rationality represent the good, the exemplary, the binding. That reason and the will to reason, reason and the interest in the reasonable,[10] were at one time regarded as identical is evidenced even as recently as the work of Max Weber. For Weber the imperatives of rationality represent cultural values that he is not prepared to abandon – even if there is no ultimate justification for them.[11]

8. On this point see J. Bennett, trans. R. Kruse, *Rationalität. Versuch einer Analyse*, Frankfurt, 1967.

9. K.-H. Ilting, "Der naturalistische Fehlschluß bei Kant," in M. Riedel, *Rehabilitierung der praktischen Philosophie I*, Freiburg, 1972, p. 113ff.

10. See J. Habermas, *Erkenntnis und Interesse (Mit einem neuen Nachwort)*, Frankfurt, 1973, p. 234ff.

11. See M. Weber, "Wissenschaft als Beruf," in Weber, *Gesammelte Aufsätze zur Wissenschaftslehre*, 4th ed., Tübingen, 1973, p. 582 ff., esp. 603ff.

The second distinction between a nondispositional and a dispositional sense of "rational" can be based on the observation that whenever we consider actions, statements, solutions, institutional regulations, etc., to be rational – and these are all examples of nondispositional predications – we view what we consider in this way to be actualizations of a potential for rationality that we attribute to people, whether as individuals or as a collective. The dispositional use of "rational" in the main expresses the attribution of such a potential for rationality with regard to potential subjects of action. That means that "rationality" normally belongs to the language of persons and actions. The talk of "system rationality,"[12] then, is a category mistake in Ryle's sense. Hence, it is replaceable with "system functionality" because it is no longer distinguishable from it: the price of reducing rationality to a thing-structure-event language is the complete congruence of rationality and functionality.[13] The intuitively plausible correlation of rationality and the subjectivity of action also makes it clear why the whole metaphysical tradition placed the "objective reason"[14] of the intelligible structures of the world in a causal relationship with a divine *nous*; and this pattern also holds for the plausibility of the doctrine of the primacy of practical reason, in the modern philosophy of subjectivity. A further consequence of the capacity/action model underlying our intuitive understanding of rationality is that we sometimes believe that we can appeal to rationality: one cannot appeal to facts or structures, but only to capacities – i.e., demand their actualization – and the dispositional sense of "rational" provides the grammatical evidence for this common-sense conviction.

If one examines a little more closely the dispositional predicate "rational" in the context of intuitive considerations, it becomes apparent that it cannot be a simple dispositional predicate of the same type as "soluble" or "flammable." The person who continually demonstrates precisely the same predictable reaction under the same conditions is not, without any additional information, called rational but compulsive, even if we approve of the way he or she reacts. The only ones who are rational are the ones who fully control the realization of their own behavioral potential; reason is inconceivable without the rational use of reason.[15] Rationality is at least a metadisposition, if not a disposition of a higher level.[16] This means, as a

12. See N. Luhmann, *Zweckbegriff und Systemrationalität*, Frankfurt, 1973, esp. p. 14ff.
13. See J. Habermas, *Theorie des kommunikativen Handelns*, vol. 2, "Zur Kritik der funktionalistischen Vernunft," Frankfurt, 1981, e.g., p. 453ff.
14. See M. Horkheimer, "Zum Begriff der Vernunft," in Horkheimer/Adorno, *Sociologica* II, Frankfurt, 1962, p. 193ff.
15. See H. Schnädelbach, "Against Feyerabend," in Schnädelbach, *Vernunft und Geschichte*, Frankfurt, 1987, p. 263ff.
16. See J. Bennett, *Rationalität*, p. 24ff. and 116ff; also C. G. Hempel, "Rationales Handeln," in G. Meggle (ed.), *Analytische Handlungstheorie* I, Frankfurt, 1977, p. 400f.

Herbert Schnädelbach

rule, that we speak of reason only when the accomplishment of what is to be called rational could also have been left undone; the distinction between nature and reason and the thought of its fallibility,[17] but also the linking of rationality with freedom and responsibility, have their roots here. (Whoever rejects *all* responsibility is not considered reasonable but of unsound mind, except if we also make that person responsible for rejecting any responsibility.) As soon as we can no longer attribute rationality to an objective, superhuman subject – whether it be God or "History" – we are also always implying by the attribution of rationality that potentially rational beings are responsible for themselves; that is, we are implying our own responsibility.

## II

Kant in his philosophy of reason followed such intuitions very precisely; one can comprehend his doctrine of the spontaneity of the understanding and of practical reason as an attempt at conceptual analysis and argumentative justification. The metadispositional character of rationality in Kant appears in the context of his doctrine of judgment. Understanding is the "faculty of rules," reason that of "principles," which are nothing more than a particular kind of rules, namely synthesising rules for the rules governing concepts of understanding, and therefore meta-rules.[18] (Therefore in the following I shall make no use of the distinction between rules and principles). Judgment, on the other hand, is the ability "to subsume under rules"[19] and therefore the capability of a particular *use* of rules. If we must intuitively count the reasonable use of reasonable rules as rationality, then in the transcendental-pragmatic reconstruction of reason we cannot confine ourselves to what Kant says explicitly about understanding and reason. Rather, we must also take judgment into account. The result of this is that in the process, and beyond understanding and reason in general, a fundamental link between rationality and the particular enters the equation, because judgment is "the ability to conceive of the particular as contained in the general,"[20] taking into account that Kant then, of course, distinguishes between "determining" and "reflecting" judgment, depending on whether the general is already given or whether it must first be conceived. But the capacity for the reasonable use of rules and that for subsumption, "that is, [the faculty] of distinguishing whether something does or does not

17. As early a figure as Thomas Hobbes speaks of the "priviledge [sic] of Absurdity," which only humans enjoy; see *Leviathan* I, Harmondsworth, 1968, chapter 5, p. 113.
18. See Kant, *KrV*, B 356ff.
19. *Ibid.*, B 171.
20. Kant, *Kritik der Urteilskraft*, B xxv.

stand under a given rule (*casus datae legis*),"[21] is the same ability, because every use of rule occurs in an individual case. Through the indication of formal characteristics, Kant's theory of judgment allows us to reinterpret the Aristotelian list of dianoetic virtues (*techne, episteme, phronesis, sophia, nous*) that are offered together as the answer to the question of the meaning of rationality in the *Nicomachean Ethics*.[22] Because production and action always aim at something particular, which cannot be reached *a priori* and deductively from a general level, the corresponding dianoetic virtues "Art" and "Practical Wisdom" require an association of general knowledge with particular know-how, which Kant, at the end of a long tradition, assigns to judgment.[23] Art as "a state concerned with making, involving a true course of reasoning" and Practical Wisdom as "a reasoned and true state of capacity to act with regard to human goods,"[24] despite their fundamental link with the particular, are faculties of reason that Kant, with equally self-evident recourse to the tradition, understands as a cognitive capability.

Opposite them stand Scientific Knowledge (*episteme*) and Intuitive Reason (*nous*) as well as the combination of both, which Aristotle calls Philosophic Wisdom (*sophia*), because in them, as the virtues of the knowledge of the general, the link with the particular appears inessential. It is true that we subsume in logic and in the sciences, but according to Kant, logic as the organon of the sciences contains no rules of subsumption.

> General logic contains, and can contain, no rules for judgment. For since general logic abstracts from all content of knowledge, the sole task that remains to it is to give an analytical exposition of the form of knowledge [as expressed] in concepts, in judgments, and in inferences, and so to obtain formal rules for all employment of understanding. If it sought to give general instructions how we are to subsume under these rules, that is, to distinguish whether something does or does not come under them, that could only be by means of another rule. This in turn, for the very reason that it is a rule, again demands guidance from judgment. And thus it appears that, though understanding is capable of being instructed, and of being equipped with rules, judgment is a peculiar talent which can be practised only, and cannot be taught. It is the specific quality of so-called mother-wit; and its lack no school can make good.[25]

Kant then says in a famous footnote: "Deficiency in judgment is just what is ordinarily called stupidity, and for such a failing there is no remedy."[26] Terminologically he also establishes a close link between judgment

21. Kant, *KdV*, B171.
22. On the following see the sixth book.
23. On the history of the concept of judgment [Urteilskraft] see H.-G. Gadamer, *Wahrheit und Methode*, 2nd ed., Tübingen, 1965, p. 27ff.
24. Aristotle, *Nikomachische Ethik*, 1140a, 20f, and 1140b, 20f.
25. Kant, *KdV*, B 171f.
26. *Ibid.*, B 173.

and the opposite of stupidity: "Whoever shows judgment in business is sensible (*gescheit*). If in the process he shows wit (*Witz*), then he is called clever."[27] But the connection between judgment and cleverness, which identifies Kant here as a late Aristotelian,[28] is according to him also to be related to the theoretical sphere, and this distinguishes him from Aristotle. General logic, which can only contain rules but no rules for the application of rules, has to leave its own application open; it provides no doctrine of judgment because it is only a canon and not an organon of understanding and reason. Kant's interpretation of applied logic then also implicitly brings together judgment with the Aristotelian *techne*. At first he criticizes the traditional division of logic into theoretical and practical logic:

> General logic, which as a mere canon is abstracted from all objects, can have no practical component. This would be a *contradictio in adiecto*, because practical logic assumes the knowledge of a certain form of objects to which it is applied. General logic, considered practically, can therefore be nothing more than a technique of learning in general, an organon of the school method.

And as Kant then puts it, "methodology" as "logical art," wanting to teach independently from the knowledge of the sciences and their objects, is not merely "in vain" but even "harmful."[29]

With his doctrine of judgment as the integrating component of the faculty of "reason" in the broader sense, Kant affirms the Aristotelian view that even the "technical" and "phronetic" abilities of humans to relate "dianoetically" to the individual, without having to provide general rules for doing so, constitute an indispensable aspect of their rationality. The post-Kantian Aristotelians (from Hegel to Gadamer) have again and again attempted to remind the abstract principle-theorists of that. Formal logic with its stock of general rules can therefore never completely represent that which justifiably is called rational, because it cannot provide the rules of art and wisdom for the application of rules; the art and wisdom of the application of rules cannot be taught in a doctrinaire manner, but have to be practiced exemplarily against the background of a general canon that, as a "cathartic of common understanding," excludes certain cases.[30] Kant's problem, and that of all the transcendental philosophers after him, then is this: In what terms should an all-embracing concept of rationality be explicated if it cannot be explicated in terms of formal logic? How does one

27. Kant, *Anthropologie* I, section 46.
28. The similarity with Aristotle extends as far as the examples: see B 173f. and Aristotle, e.g., *Metaphysik* I, 1 and *Nikomachische Ethik* VI; it is always a matter of the relationship between the knowledge of rules and experience.
29. Kant, *Logik*, A 13; "Technique" here is still – as the context shows – understood essentially in terms of *techne* or *ars*. See Kant, *Logik*, A 13ff.
30. Kant, *KrV*, B 78.

integrate the equivalents of judgment, in relation to which there can be only a critique but no specification in terms of the systematics of transcendental philosophy,[31] into the transcendental theory of rationality, and at the same time affirm its *a priori* character, which necessarily appears to exclude from it the area of application? How can one represent rationality in *a priori* rules, when after all it is obvious that for the application of rules, which is part of rationality, there can be no *a priori* rules?

# III

Kant's answer to this question consists of a shifting of levels and a thesis; he switches over from formal to transcendental logic and says,

> Transcendental philosophy has the peculiarity that besides the rule (or rather the universal condition of rules), which is given in the pure concept of understanding, it can also specify *a priori* the instance to which the rule is to be applied. The advantage that in this respect it possesses over all other didactical sciences, with the exception of mathematics, is due to the fact that it deals with concepts that have to relate to objects *a priori*, and the objective validity of which cannot therefore be demonstrated *a posteriori*, since that would mean the complete ignoring of their peculiar dignity. It must formulate by means of universal but sufficient marks the conditions under which objects can be given in harmony with these concepts. Otherwise the concepts would be void of all content, and therefore mere logical forms, not pure concepts of the understanding.[32]

In the context of transcendental logic, therefore, there *is* according to Kant a doctrine of judgment as an organon – the "transcendental doctrine of judgment;"[33] it is the "advantage"[34] of transcendental philosophy over all other disciplines. It means that whoever has transcendental rules at his disposal at the same time should have available *a priori* rules regarding the application of rules, without requiring further rules for the application of these rules of application and therefore slip into an eternal regression. By analogy this applies also to "pure practical judgment."[35] But conversely, of course, it is true that without such *a priori* rules for the application of rules that exclude the *regressus in infinitum*, no transcendental philosophy in the traditional sense would be possible; it would then divide again into a pure and an applied component and would *not* be able to show that "the conditions for the possibility of experience in general are likewise conditions of the possibility of the objects of experience" and possess therefore "objective

---

31. See Kant, *Kritik der Urteilskraft*, B XXIff.
32. Kant, *KrV*, B 174f.
33. *Ibid.*
34. Kant, *KrV*, B 175.
35. Kant, *Kritik der praktischen Vernunft*, A 119f.

validity in a synthetic *a priori* judgment."[36] The *a priori* rules for the application of rules are the test-case in which it is decided whether transcendental analysis is also really able to encompass *a priori* the entire sphere of rationality, which Kant, on the basis of the central theme of logic, had interpreted as the field of operation of the understanding, judgment and reason.[37]

My thesis, then, is that it is precisely the linguistically oriented transformation of transcendental philosophy into transcendental pragmatics that fundamentally excludes the complete representability of rationality in rules – and thereby in principles and norms. The transcendental pragmatist can reply that Kant himself did not measure up to this goal, and in support of this can cite the rationality of the critical activity, that is, criticizing reason itself does not appear on the side of criticized reason. Indeed, the "transcendental reflection" of the amphiboly chapter in the *Critique of Pure Reason*, which at least in part deals with the method of the critique of reason itself,[38] does not depict that which in the transcendental dialectic appears as the *proprium* of reason. Critical reason is simply not restricted to the logical and transcendental use of reason; in truth, the reflecting judgment itself is the organon of the "critical business,"[39] and thus the mere existence of the *Critique of Judgment* expresses the systematic surplus of critically-reflecting reason over "doctrinal" reason.[40] That this is not just a contingent shortcoming of the Kantian system that can be regarded as overcome by Fichte or Hegel is made clear by arguments of principle that are raised even in the early part of the hermeneutic turn of transcendental philosophy to language against the complete representability of reason in rules. Thus Dieter Henrich has indicated that any reflexive explication of reason on the basis of its reflexive structure is obsolete in principle.[41] Gerhard Frey has added Gödel's theorem to the argument.[42] Neither of these arguments, however, will be used here; instead, I would prefer to show that even in the confined realm of theoretical reason, which Kant believed he had thoroughly criticized, the complete representability of rationality in

36. Kant, *KrV*, B 197.
37. See Kant, *KrV*, B 360.
38. See H. Schnädelbach, *Reflexion und Diskurs. Fragen einer Logik der Philosophie*, Frankfurt, 1977, p. 90ff.
39. See G. Schönrich, *Kategorien und transzendentale Argumentation. Kant und die Idee einer transzendentalen Semiotik*, Frankfurt, 1981, p. 225f.
40. See W. Bartuschat, *Zum systematischen Ort von Kants Kritik der Urteilskraft*, Frankfurt, 1972.
41. See D. Henrich, *Fichtes ursprüngliche Einsicht*, Frankfurt, 1967; Henrich, "Selbstbewußtsein," in Bubner, Cramer, Wiehl (eds.), *Hermeneutik und Dialektik* I, Tübingen, 1970, p. 257ff.
42. See G. Frey, *Sprache – Ausdruck des Bewußtseins*, Stuttgart, 1965, p. 38ff.; Frey, *Theorie des Bewußtseins*, Freiburg/Munich, 1980, p. 69ff.

rules and in rules for the application of rules is unachievable, and this solely on the basis of the linguistic orientation of transcendental analysis in the context of transcendental pragmatics. According to Apel, one should label "transcendental pragmatic" any analysis that does not deal with communication *per se* in a quasi-objective respect, but with communication exclusively as a condition for the possibility of philosophical reflection and thereby of a very specific type of discourse.[43] Such an analysis examines the conditions that those who philosophize critically – that is, those who question the possibility of reasonable understanding, cognition and action – must necessarily have already assumed to be fulfilled in order to ask any questions at all.

Kant's claim of completeness can only be defended if formal logic as a self-contained theory is workable as the central guide in the analysis of the use of the understanding and reason; furthermore, this requires the feasibility of a transcendental deduction of pure concepts of understanding that were reconstructed according to this central guide. If both preconditions are fulfilled, then the "transcendental doctrine of judgment" and the dialectic of pure reason can be achieved in analytic steps. If one now attempts to repeat this program with transcendental-pragmatic means and tries to cover, as Kant did, the whole area of theoretical rationality in order to make scientific knowledge possible, then that goal of completeness fades into the unreachable distance: for language is *impure* reason, that is, reason affected by the empirical and afflicted with contingency.[44] One cannot represent language in rules of formal logic, and no transcendental deduction of impure concepts of the understanding is possible; therefore there can also be no transition to a "transcendental doctrine of judgment," which would allow one to formulate *a priori* rules on the application of rules of linguistic reason. The result is: linguistic reason is, at most, limited by rules that can be spelled out. However, it can never be comprehensively expressed by them.

This line of argument, however, still cannot satisfy us, because it appeals only to the antithesis of pure reason and language, without detailing more precisely what exactly is meant by "language." The transcendental-pragma-

43. See Schnädelbach, *Reflexion und Diskurs*, p. 366ff.

44. Hamann, in his *Metakritik über den Purismum der reinen Vernunft* (1784), was probably the first philosopher who linked the business of critical reason to language and thereby introduced the hermeneutic turn in the critique of reason; the dependence of all achievements of reason on the successful linguistic achievements of understanding is a key theme as early as the work of Schleiermacher, who to this day is misinterpreted as the proponent of a "psychological" hermeneutics. (See Manfred Frank, "Einleitung" in Schleiermacher, *Hermeneutik und Kritik*, Frankfurt, 1977). The hermeneutic turn to language under the conditions of the late nineteenth century is then experienced as the intrusion of psychologism and historicism into the realm of reason, an intrusion that needs to be contained through a neo-Kantian "purity."

tist also does not simply speak sweepingly of "language" but of "communicative competence," and it seems as if rationality would now allow itself to be represented as a central stock of rules of communicative competence; apart from that, the transcendental-pragmatic perspective is adopted in that, in the examination of this question, it is only a matter of the competence that the researcher must already have attributed to himself or herself in order to carry out the examination. After this double limitation of the field of research everything in a transcendental-pragmatic theory of rationality depends on the concept of competence. Chomsky had introduced it in his *Aspects of the Theory of Syntax* (1965) in the context of his competence-performance distinction: "competence" there was defined as an ideal speaker-hearer's knowledge of the rules of his language and his ability to avail himself of them; if one then disregards certain marginal conditions that are irrelevant for linguistics, "performance can be understood as the direct reflection of linguistic competence."[45] Without going into detail[46] one can say that this concept of linguistic competence has experienced at least two extensions as a result of its reception by Habermas and Apel. Firstly, the transition from the purely linguistic competence in the generation of grammatically correct linguistic entities to communicative competence leads here to the integration of the dimension of action into the linguistic theory: communicative competence is essentially competence in communicative action.[47] Secondly, the competence that makes communication possible must also – as Apel and Habermas have shown – already contain within itself metacommunicative competences, because communication in natural languages always presupposes the ability to come to an agreement about language itself.[48] Both extensions have extremely far-reaching consequences for the theory of rationality.

Linguistic competence can be conceived of as a computer program that under ideal conditions also effectively generates the performance that can then be regarded as a "direct reflection of linguistic competence." However, as an explication of communicative competence this model is inadequate because of the fact that performance is grounded in human action, something the transcendental pragmatist insists upon. Here the actualization of competence can by no means be understood according to a stimulus-response model as a quasi-mechanical process that under certain antecedent conditions ideally always takes place in the same manner. This

45. N. Chomsky, *Aspekte der Syntax-Theorie*, Frankfurt, 1969, p. 14.

46. See the article "Kompetenz," in J. Ritter (ed.), *Historisches Wörterbuch der Philosophie* 4, col. 918ff.

47. This as early as in J. Habermas, "Vorbereitende Bemerkungen zu einer Theorie der kommunikativen Kompetenz," in Habermas/Luhmann, *Theorie der Gesellschaft oder Sozialtechnologie?* Frankfurt, 1971, p. 101ff.

48. See K.-O. Apel, "Noam Chomskys Sprachtheorie . . .," p. 297ff.

view would be compatible with Chomsky's theory of linguistic competence because it after all only defines which linguistic entities are generated
when speech occurs. But if communicative competence is considered as
competence in communicative action, then not only the how but also the
whether of action is placed in the hands of the competent speaker. Therefore, at least for the reason that even nonaction can be regarded as action,
communicative competence cannot be merely a capability to follow rules,
but must be a capability to have rules at one's disposal. But whoever can
remove rules from use must also be thought to have the capability to deliberately break rules or to creatively modify them. But precisely these – as is
intuitively obvious – are structural characteristics of rationality as a higher-
level dispositional predicate, which has no counterpart in Chomsky's version of competence. To this one can immediately add the other extension
of the competence concept carried out by Apel and Habermas. He or she
who not only follows the communicative rules but also, and at the same
time, has them in principle at his or her disposal must also be in a position
to explicitly talk about these rules; only in this way is "rule-changing cre-
ativity"[49] more than a purely naturalistic event. This means that metacommunicative elements cannot be labelled as dispensable components of
communicative competence, and that they are the linguistic basis for the
doctrine of original reflexivity in mentalist theories of consciousness.[50] If
one now asks what sort of reasons competent speakers could have for creatively modifying the rules, the point becomes visible at which the extended competence theory comes in contact with the tradition of hermeneutic
philosophy. It is a basic concept of hermeneutics that the application of
rules and our experience thereof possess constitutive significance for the
body of rules, that rules change in the course of their application and therefore themselves cannot be defined without the simultaneous specification
of their conditions of application; but changed rules again generate a new
application, and so on. This "feedback" between rule and application of
rule is only a special instance of the hermeneutic circle connecting whole
and part, general and individual, foreknowledge and actual understanding,
which is only then not merely an empty or "vicious" circle if that which is
rotating in this circle – to express it in modern terms – represents a "self-
learning" system. For the theory of rationality this means that it is insufficient to unify, as Kant does, understanding, reason and judgment in an
extended concept of reason; rather, if one operates with the model of communicative competence in the suggested sense, one must construct rationality as a complex unity of rule-possession and rule-application characterized
by the interaction of its elements, in which there is no space for a one-sided,

49. See *ibid.*, p. 306.
50. See Schnädelbach, *Reflexion und Diskurs*, p. 142 f.

*a priori* deductive relationship between understanding/reason and judgment, competence and performance. Considered in this way, rationality is to be seen at least as an open system of communicative competence, i.e., one that is not entirely capable of representation in rules. It may be limited by rules, but at the same time by rules that in principle allow themselves to be changed, even intentionally, by being competently obeyed. We cannot, on the one hand, reject Chomsky by conceiving of our linguistic capability as an open system of rules and, at the same time, from the same perspective, confine our reason to unchangeable universal rules; because of the hermeneutic implications of this viewpoint, a theory of rationality will have to bid farewell to the ideal of fixed communicative rules and rules for the application of rules.

## IV

And so the result is the "historicity of reason": rationality, too, is then always something empirical, contingent, changeable.[51] If the actual application of rules really reacts upon the body of rules as the hermeneuticists claim, then there is no reason to contemplate any form of competence-dogmatism. I do not see how the absolute stability of the communicative body of rules that the well-known competence-performance distinction suggests can seriously be put forward without strong nativistic premises.[52] The alternative is at least a general suspicion of historicity with regard to everything that, from a transcendental-pragmatic perspective, falls under the body of rules for our communicative competence and thereby the core of our rationality. This suspicion, however, is suggested not only by the mistrust of nativism but also by the two considerations that came to the fore concerning the "costs" of the hermeneutic turn in the critique of reason: the fact that it is impossible to fully set out the application of linguistically expressed rules of reason in rules has as a consequence that the difference between that which we have always claimed as our rationality and that which we can explicate as our rationality can never be regarded as fully resolved in principle. Furthermore, if we do not wish to be nativists, we must take into account the changeability of rules of rationality in the course of their application. From a transcendental-pragmatic perspective this result has the epistemological consequence that claims about the universality of rules representing rationality can always only possess a hypothetical and never an apodictic character. Since the historicity of rules of

51. On this point see H. Schnädelbach, "Zur Dialektik der historischen Vernunft," in Schnädelbach, *Vernunft und Geschichte*, Frankfurt, 1987, p. 47ff.
52. See N. Chomsky, *Sprache und Geist*, Frankfurt, 1970; Chomsky, *Regeln und Repräsentationen*, Frankfurt, 1981, e.g., p. 11ff.

rationality cannot be totally excluded, such rules only permit the theses about universality associated with rationality in a quasi-empirical sense; one must do without the transcendental predicate "necessary." The reasons for this become clear when we compare Kant's method with that of Wittgenstein. Both assume that we cannot identify rules independently of their use. For Kant, the "logical use" of concepts of the understanding and reason – that is, their "logical function" in judgments and conclusions – is the "guiding thread" whereby the rules of understanding and the principles of reason must be sought out. For Wittgenstein, the inseparability of rule and application of rule is the basis of what one has become accustomed to calling the "use theory of meaning"; this "theory" is then also the key to explicating the "concepts of understanding, meaning and thinking."[53] The difference between Kant and Wittgenstein is only that Kant considers for-mal logic, which is interpreted as a final and completed theory, to be the guiding thread whereby *a priori* rules of the understanding can be identi-fied independently of their empirical use and then can be transferred to their transcendental interpretation, whereas Wittgenstein, in his *Philosoph-ical Investigations*, begins by relegating the question about thinking and its rules to the actual use of the terms "understand," "mean" and "think" in a nonideal language. And the use of these terms can only be identified empirically – ideal languages and ideal rules of communication are at best a mental construction.[54] The rationality incorporated in nonideal, contin-gent, changeable rules of communication is historical rationality also for the reason that language, as far as it is "the sole, the first and the last crite-rion of reason," must get by "without another support but tradition and use."[55] Therefore, in the theory of rationality one cannot affirm the Kant-ian-Wittgensteinian inseparability of rule and rule application, join in the linguistic turn and, at the same time, proclaim a strict apriorism in the sense of the Kantian completeness thesis. Not only does the possible con-tingency of the rules of rationality themselves lead to this consequence, but so does the impossibility in principle of being able to identify reconstruc-tively such rules after the hermeneutic turn in transcendental philosophy, independently of an empirical use of language. But if the reconstructed reason of transcendental-pragmatics is always merely historical reason, then there is no transcendental-pragmatic First Philosophy.

In ethics such considerations have analogous consequences. In commu-nicative ethics there is no place for "pure practical judgment," which

53. Wittgenstein, *Philosophische Untersuchungen*, section 81; his use "theory" is: "For a *large* class of cases – though not for all – in which we employ the word 'meaning' it can be defined thus: the meaning of a word is its use in the language" (section 43).

54. See section 81.

55. Hamann, *Metakritik über den Purismum der reinen Vernunft* (1784), in J. Simon (ed.), *Schriften zur Sprache*, Frankfurt, 1967, p. 222.

would have to be interpreted as the capability of purely *a priori* norms in the application of norms. Karl-Otto Apel, in responding to Habermas's objection that in Apel's foundation of ethics there existed an "unresolved problem of decisionism," reminded Habermas of the distinction between a decision as the justification of norms (or their replacement) and the decision to apply norms; and in the second instance he defended the freedom to decide as an inalienable component of our self-respect as human beings.[56] This must be accepted, but at the same time it must be asked how it is possible under transcendental-pragmatic premises to distinguish between the justification of norms and the application of norms in such a way that the remaining element of decisionism in the application of norms does not encroach on the justification of norms. It lies in the nature of the concept of the norm that one can factually deviate from it, just as it lies in the nature of the concept of the rule that exceptions are permitted; thus the factual deviation is not the problem. However, when we become serious with transcendental pragmatics even in ethics, then, because of the inextricable linking of communicative-ethical rules with their empirical-historical application, there can be no justification of morals in the Kantian style: practical reason – i.e., reason that brings forth the "determining grounds of the will"[57] – as communicative reason is also impure reason. Thus it always necessarily also contains culturally specific conventional and decisionistic elements: there is no "fact of pure practical reason" but at best a "fact of historical and practical reason" – which itself is a historical fact. Human dignity therefore does not consist merely – as Apel says – of our being the targets of an obligation from which we can withdraw ourselves if we so wish; it consists simultaneously of the burden of being responsible for the principles of obligation to which we find ourselves subjected, because their content is also fundamentally dependent on our contingent life as moral beings.

This impure character of practical reason at the same time means that the field of rationality is broader than that of morality. That we remain reasonable human beings even when we withdraw from justifiable moral claims was expressed by Kant in his doctrine of the "radical evil" (*das Radikal-Böse*), which according to him exists in the free reversal of the moral order of the motivating forces "self-love" and "respect for the law" in the affirmation of maxims of action.[58] The remaining element of decisionism in Kant exists in the thesis "that the ultimate subjective ground of the adoption of moral maxims is inscrutable," for

> since this adoption is free, its ground (why, for example, I have chosen an evil and not a good maxim) must not be sought in any natural impulse, but always

56. See Apel, "Types of Rationality Today," p. 334.
57. Kant, *Kritik der praktischen Vernunft*, A 29.
58. See Kant, "Die Religion innerhalb der Grenzen der bloßen Vernunft," B 34.

again in a maxim. Now since this maxim also must have its ground, and since apart from maxims no *determining ground* of free choice can or ought to be adduced, we are referred back endlessly in the series of subjective determining grounds, without ever being able to reach the ultimate ground.[59]

The freedom of that "adoption" – and it is only this freedom that allows us to hold someone responsible – is the privilege of reasonable beings, which even remains in the case of the radically evil. Kant's argument, in truth, is directed against his own thesis of completeness in the context of ethics; the freedom to choose a maxim that perhaps does not render invalid the categorical imperative as a moral supernorm but certainly cancels its application, prevents this supernorm based on the model of the "transcendental doctrine of judgment" from taking care *a priori* of all cases of application. The surplus of rationality over morality created in this way is increased in dramatic fashion from within a transcendental-pragmatic perspective, because here, in addition to that freedom of the "acceptance" of a set of norms, one must reckon with the effect of the lived application of norms upon the set of norms itself, an effect that is in part constitutive of those norms. It is thus true of practical rationality as well that it cannot be fully represented in practical rules, i.e., norms. It is not permissible to define it in terms of a fixed set of rules and to exclude the application of norms as prerational or arational. The application of norms is not completely determined by that set of rules, and apart from that it is limited by it in a changeable way and in a way that changes the set of norms itself. Also, since practical rationality embraces all this, the categorical imperative, reformulated along transcendental lines, cannot be the fundamental norm of rationality *per se*.

## V

It seems that in the theory of rationality historicity is the final word and that relativism is inevitable, but this is not the case.[60] Rationality is an assumption that from a transcendental-pragmatic perspective is necessary and inevitable in the form of the presupposition "I am reasonable." That it may have been wrong in individual instances is no valid argument against it, because in order to be able to establish this I already have to make claim to it again. Even to become aware of our unreason we need first to have thought ourselves capable of reason. On the other hand, what we credit ourselves with as our rationality, beyond the mere "That" of reason, stands under the suspicion of historicity that cannot be removed *a priori*. If from

59. *Ibid.*, B 7 footnote.
60. On the following see H. Schnädelbach, "Zur Dialektik der historischen Vernunft."

the beginning we wish to escape from this suspicion we can no longer grant ourselves anything more than the naked That of rationality without being able to say, at the same time, what we have actually granted ourselves. If we believe that we can pass immanently and purely *a priori* from the That of the presupposed rationality to the What and to the self-identification as rational beings, then we are being taken in by a false conclusion analogous to Kant's critique of the transition from "I think" to the *res cogitans* as the "paralogism of historical reason." Nevertheless there is no reason to lay down one's arms before the spectre of historicity. The philosophy of reason, which today must appear as the theory of rationality built around the central theme of language, may not wish indeed to exclude historical elements from itself, but this is no reason for defeatism. Rather, it must ask itself how we can combine rationality and historicity in thought, and do so without dogmatic premises and relativistic consequences. This much is required of us by the transcendental-pragmatic "theme and medium of transcendental reflexion," i.e., language itself, in which rationality and historicity have always been united. It remains to be shown in what way this is the case.

*Translated by Peter Monteath, Dieter Freundlieb and Wayne Hudson*

# –4–

# Two Centuries of Philosophical Critique of Reason and Its "Postmodern" Radicalization

## MANFRED FRANK

The concept of a critique of reason has always been so much a part of any philosophical endeavor that for centuries philosophizing itself has been understood as an attempt to make the world more rational. This self-image of philosophy reached its peak in the epoch that proudly called itself "the Enlightenment." As Starobinski has pointed out,[1] a long process of philosophical praxis was thus given a splendid emblematic representation through metaphors of light and illumination. "Enlightenment" means to transform anything merely posited, anything merely believed, into objects of secure knowledge. These objects include all forms of living whose only justification rested on tradition, as well as any authority based on the supersensible. The positivity of natural phenomena seemed to have been abolished as well. Their mythical spell was dissolved into elementary particles obeying natural laws. Human reason no longer regarded the law-like connection between these elements as its "Other," but as its own product. In other words, nature has its ultimate truth in spirit. Its three fundamental qualities are: its conformity to thought, its generality, and its lawfulness. The same applies to human practice: it is self-determined, that is, in conformity with reason, insofar as it follows self-given laws which, as laws, are binding for all.

Today something has happened that would have been inconceivable from the perspective of the seventeenth and eighteenth century: reason and rationality as such have been brought to court, and their legitimacy has been put into question. But to question the legitimacy of rationality means no less than to regard with suspicion that which hitherto formed the basis of any legitimacy.

1. J. Starobinski, *Die Embleme der Vernunft*, Munich, Paderborn, Vienna, 1983.

Indeed, today it is rationality, as well as the whole of philosophy, that together have to face an imaginary court that demands of them a justification for their existence. Philosophy, to be sure, has traditionally been the custodian of the universal, and the philosopher, according to a well-known dictum of Sartre's, is "le spécialiste (ou bien technicien) du savoir pratique" and "le gardien de l'universel."[2] The politics of reason of the ancient Greeks regarded those who concerned themselves with the particular, in the sense of the private, as *idiótäs*, i.e., as idiots. Sartre's great study of Flaubert, *L'idiot de la famille*, is about the sustained rationalist devaluation of the particular to be found well into the nineteenth century, a devaluation that regarded the particular as bearing the stigma of feeble-mindedness. Since then, along with the waning of the unquestioned dignity of the "universal" – the idea that there is a trans-individual and trans-historical Truth – philosophical rationalism has come under increasing pressure to justify itself. Under the somewhat mocking title of the "maîtres penseurs" the so-called "essential thinkers," as Jaspers and Heidegger had called them, following an established European tradition of philosophical pathos, have been mercilessly put on trial. Not only Plato, Hegel and Marx, but even Kant and the idea of a universal enlightenment are being interrogated by Foucault and his successors, by the "nouveaux philosophes," and, more recently, in Anglo-Saxon philosophy by philosophers such as Richard Rorty and Paul Feyerabend. The accusation made against them is a serious one. The master thinkers are said to have justified, in the name of rationality, the use of physical and political force, as well as a coercive methodology.

From behind the allegedly presuppositionless and value-free project of a pure *philosophia*, i.e., the will to truth, there emerges the will to power. The will to truth, it is argued, reveals itself as a sublimated, and – because of its disguise – particularly insidious, form of a will to conquer nature, including human nature. Contrary to its own self-understanding, enlightenment rationalism does not reach its final aim in democracy (unless one takes this to mean the social Darwinism characteristic of liberal competitive societies), but in political totalitarianisms of all kinds. The process of Western rationalization is thus said to lead to a pathology of modernity. Faced with the experience of fascism, Hegel's dictum according to which "the whole is the true"[3] was cynically reversed by Adorno: "the whole is the false."[4] Since Hegel's project of a totally self-enlightened spirit and a complete state, conceptualizations of society in terms of totalities, so the argu-

2. J.-P. Sartre, "Les Intellectuels," in *Situations VIII*, Paris, 1972, pp. 371–455.

3. G. W. F. Hegel, *Phänomenologie des Geistes*, ed. J. Hoffmeister, Hamburg, 1952, p. 21. (*The Phenomenology of Mind*, p. 81)

4. T. W. Adorno, *Minima Moralia*, Frankfurt a. M., 1969, p. 57. English translation: *Minima Moralia. Reflections From Damaged Life*, London, 1974, p. 50.

ment goes, have shown their true colors. A critical analysis of the rationalist vocabulary unmasks the true aspirations of the master thinkers. Their dreams are dreams of exploitation, unmasking, subjection, division, conquest, expropriation, and "*grasp*"(a metaphor whose original meaning is still visible: "saisir avec les *griffes*," to seize with talons). In one of his interviews Foucault reduced this new form of rationality critique to the formula: "La torture, c'est la raison."

To be sure, this is a brand of criticism predominantly found among the younger generation of philosophers over the last decade, particularly in Paris. I am inclined to take it seriously, however, not least because it finds much favor with the young generation. This critique of reason may be weak argumentatively, but it seems to reflect very accurately the current disaffection with government and national politics, as well as a certain weariness with civilization. The skeptical attitude toward rationality is in fact nothing but a particular manifestation of a much more widespread discontent experienced by many in the emotional climate of the whole of the Western world.[5]

The skeptical attitude toward reason is by no means a very recent achievement. The philosophical critique of the totalitarianism of rationality found its most prominent expression as long as forty-three years ago in Adorno and Horkheimer's famous book, *Dialectic of Enlightenment.* We all remember their introductory statements, which already point to the heart of the matter:

> In the most general sense of progressive thought, the Enlightenment has always aimed at liberating men from fear and establishing their sovereignty. Yet the fully enlightened earth radiates disaster triumphant.[6]

Originally developed in order to tame a hostile nature through an imposition of order, rationality has since become a second nature – and a much worse one at that – that has turned against the human species. The order of reason has used its rigor and its absolute claim to validity with devastating force and effect against the will of the subject, which it was initially meant to serve. In the meantime – with the anxiety caused by the destructive machinery of National Socialism still vivid in our memory – we live again in fear at the prospect of a world of technology and a complex of forces of military destruction beyond our control, whose inhuman rationality Adorno and Horkheimer analyzed so tellingly as early as 1944.

The question of the legitimacy of reason, however, is much older than

---

5. See M. Frank, *Was ist Neostrukturalismus?* Frankfurt a. M., 1983.

6. M. Horkheimer and T. W. Adorno, *Dialektik der Aufklärung. Philosophische Fragmente,* in T. W. Adorno, *Gesammelte Schriften,* Frankfurt a. M., 1981, vol. 3, p. 19. English translation: *Dialectic of Enlightenment,* London, 1973, p. 3.

the Frankfurt School. Dozens of thinkers have addressed this theme since the second half of the nineteenth century. The most influential among them was no doubt Friedrich Nietzsche. In fact, if we look at the contemporary French scene, he might seem to be still alive. Nietzsche was particularly tenacious in asking the crucial question about the "genealogical" foundation of rationality. We all know what his answer was. Rationality is not in itself a form of rational behavior, but an evolutionary necessity of the human species formed as an adaptation to a hostile environment in order to ensure the survival of the masses. Rationality, or as Nietzsche put it, the will to truth, is aiming at a state of equilibrium between the human and the natural economy. This equilibrium is interpreted, in a fictitious manner, as the rule of natural laws that, in turn, presupposes an expectation that they will always remain the same. It makes possible a stable language, as well as social order and human intercourse.[7] Nietzsche sees this as a danger. The social aspect of the will to truth (which he despises as its "consideration of the herd" in terms of the "far too many") seems to him to contradict that other force of life that he characterizes as the will to overpower, the wish to enhance life, to transgress each state of equilibrium, and to take advantage of the weakness of others. From the perspective of the will to power the social, that is to say the universalistic component of rational behavior, appears as counter-productive and "bio-negative," i.e., as a symptom of "decadence," of a weakened will to live that celebrates its powerlessness against a competing predator (meekly titled "'fellow man") in the name of "morality." If decadence is left uncontrolled, Nietzsche argues, European civilization will perish in nihilism. Cut off from the roots of life, no value can be envisaged any longer by this civilization. If asked about the value it embodies, the world, as it is interpreted and dissolved by analytical reason, will increasingly answer: there is no value. This feeling of a general lack of meaning is spreading. Ever since the point at which rationality turned against the forces of life and of sensuality, without ensuring the survival of a transcendent source of value – that is, ever since Kant – only life itself has remained as the last and sole value. But this value is asocial.

The impact of Nietzsche's version of a critique of rationality was tremendous, partly perhaps because of its contradictoriness. On the one hand, it enabled us to question the deceptive objectivism of a scientific attitude toward the world by reminding us of its genealogical origin. In fact, as a critic of objectivism of every kind Nietzsche has influenced both Critical Theory and poststructuralist thought. On the other hand, Nietzsche's deconstructive thinking remains within an epistemological framework characterized by a vitalism and social Darwinism specific to the time,

---

7. See Frank, *Was ist Neostrukturalismus?*, Lecture 13.

welcomed, in particular, by the so-called "irrationalists" (from Klages to Spengler and Alfred Baeumler), and the extreme right (from Gentile to Rosenberg, and even the "Nouvelle Droite" of today).[8]

It was one of the achievements of Martin Heidegger's "new beginning in philosophy" to have given Nietzsche's critique of rationality a deeper epistemological foundation. This new and deeper foundation makes it possible to relativize and question (*hinterfragen*) even Nietzsche's own basis, the idea of a "will to power" as a late historical expression of a global occidental interpretation of "Being." "Metaphysics" is the title given by Heidegger to the entire set of answers that Western thought has provided to "the most fundamental and most radical of all questions," i.e., the question of Being. Being as metaphysics appears in different guises, but it does so within a process of continuous development, and it is interpreted as "presence" and what is "present-at-hand." From Parmenides to Hegel, the only aspect of Being that had been of interest was the extent to which it was sensorily, intellectually or practically given and exploitable. The most recent manifestation of this interpretation of Being is modern technology and the natural sciences that go along with it. These are allegedly value-free but, in truth, provide a form of knowledge intrinsically associated with domination and control. What Nietzsche had taken to be an invariant structure of life – the will to power – is now unmasked in Heidegger's interpretation as something that is itself historical, as the continuing effect of an original unfolding of the "meaning of Being" for which Being itself is responsible rather than human beings. It is this more fundamental interpretation with which Heidegger's "essential thinking" is concerned, a form of thinking that can no longer be called "scientific." Each horizon of meaning, each linguistically determined world view, defines the conditions under which something can be identified as something and under which communication with others is possible. But since our thinking and speaking only becomes possible *within* the horizon of a semiotic order, we cannot regard ourselves as the originators of this order. Truth – conceived as an intersubjectively valid state of affairs – is thus in itself something derivative. Such a truth can only be discovered within the framework and under the conditions of a discursive order that has been instituted by Being. For example: the order of rationality. This is the meaning of Heidegger's famous and seemingly absurdly arrogant statement that "science does not think." According to him, the intellectual methods by which the purely rational sciences operate are "derivative." They are derived from a more fundamental interpretation, which, prior to any scientific endeavor, sets the conditions under which something can be known as true or false, as advisable or inadvisable.

8. See M. Frank, *Der kommende Gott*, Frankfurt a. M., 1982, p. 28ff.

Presumably, Heidegger's relativization of the validity of "rationality" in terms of a history of Being would have been less successful had the way not been paved by the systematic work of someone who can hardly be accused of irrational inclinations and a distaste for methodologically disciplined thought. I mean, of course, Max Weber's grandiose sociological reconstruction of what he called, among other things, "occidental rationality." A close look at his basic ideas will also provide us, for the first time, with an opportunity to *define* the meaning(s) of expressions such as "rationality" and "rationalization." The reader will be familiar with Weber's diagnosis of a "disenchantment" of the world that began several millennia ago and is now reaching its final point of destiny. The term "disenchantment" is virtually synonymous with "rationalization". This latter word is used in three distinct, yet closely linked, senses.

First, "rationalization" means the capacity to control objects through their reduction to the laws governing their behavior. In this sense, it is identical with *scientific technological* rationality. Second, "rationalization" means the systematization of relations of meaning. If used in this sense, it operates in accordance with an "intrinsic necessity" when the member of any culture conceives of the world as a meaningful whole; it also allows him to set himself in a meaningful relation to the world. This is *metaphysico-ethical* rationalism. Finally, rationalism means "the formation of a methodical practice of living. As such, it is a *practical* rationalism in the widest possible sense."[9] According to Weber, these three varieties of rationalism are related to each other differently at different historical conjunctures. What is decisive, however, is the way in which, in each case, the practical forms of life are determined by the historically given forms of scientific and ethical rationalism. Only in an already meaningful world, and a world that has already been interpreted epistemically, can humans live with dignity and work scientifically. This is a conviction Weber obviously shares with Heidegger.

Where Weber differs from Heidegger's history of Being is in the story he tells us about the disenchantment of religious and value-forming beliefs in the course of occidental rationalization. In Weber's view, what is fatal about the process of disenchantment is that through it the social consensus about the highest values of human existence and social life become uncoupled from the other two spheres of rationality, i.e., the sphere of science and the sphere of practical everyday conduct. As a consequence, to put it very pointedly, science and everyday life become as meaning-less and un-holy as the world itself, the control and exploitation of which formed the aim of both science and everyday life. What is left, in the end, are secular

9. W. Schluchter, *Rationalismus der Weltbeherrschung. Studien zu Max Weber*, Frankfurt a. M., 1980, p. 10.

ascesis and the instrumental control of nature as tools for an ideology of self-redemption without any transcendence. According to Weber, this is the stage reached by capitalism: the perfectly value-neutral and rational form of economy. It is the beginning of the "world domination of unbrotherliness."[10] The metaphor of the "cold heart" begins to spread and turns into the central symbol of the European emotional climate under the conditions of cultural and economic modernity.[11]

The *leitmotif* of the aporetical deliberations in which Weber engaged when he addressed this problem is embodied in the concept of charisma and the idea of the charismatic personality. No doubt, the personal influence of the circle around Stefan George and the critical analysis of neomythological or neoreligious "world views" in the prefascist era played a crucial role here.[12] The attraction these irrationalisms held for the broad mass of the German (and not only the German) population needs, of course, to be investigated sociologically. The fact that the widespread talk about problems of legitimation and crises of meaning originated and was first articulated by the political right was, as Ernst Bloch tells us, a hard lesson for the left. Over and above what can be seen from Max Weber's perspective, the legitimation crisis of modern society brings to consciousness the counter-productive consequences of a totalizing rationalism (i.e., a rationalism that excludes everything else, and that quite literally leaves no room for hope and consolation). In the end, this global rationalism claims even the highest values of human solidarity as its victims. Rationalization becomes pathogenic.

Right from the beginning, this indictment was the perspective on rationalism taken by early German romanticism. It described modern rationalism as an abstractive analytical mentality and simultaneously identified it more concretely in sociological terms. Literally translated, "analysis" means dissolution and decomposition. That is to say, it is aimed at anything synthetic, and it tries to demonstrate that synthesis is not an original state, but something that can be decomposed into its atomic elements. Analysis is the articulation of the interests of the ascending class of the bourgeoisie. The tool of analysis that proved to be so successful in the natural sciences, particularly in chemistry, allowed the bourgeoisie to besiege untenable religious certainties, above all the certainties on which feudalism rested, such as the divine right of kings. Everything was analyzed and taken apart, including the human mind, which revealed itself as a mechanical ensemble

10. M. Weber, *Gesammelte Aufsätze zur Religionssoziologie*, Tübingen, 1920/21, vol. I, p. 571 *et passim*.
11. I have dealt with this issue in more detail in M. Frank, *Das kalte Herz*, Frankfurt a. M., 1980, p. 28ff.
12. See A. Mitzman, *The Iron Cage: An Historical Interpretation of Max Weber*, New York, 1979, p. 253ff.

of elementary sensory impressions and elementary ideas, that is to say as a highly complex but nonetheless exactly analyzable machine. The state, too, i.e., the juridical organization of bourgeois society, could be conceived as the mechanical interaction of monadic individuals. The bond of brotherliness was nothing but a veil hiding the true state of isolation of the citizens whose function, like that of bolts and cogwheels, was to keep the machine of the state running.

Such descriptions can be found again and again in the earliest programmatic writings of German idealism. The historical preconditions of this anti-analytical and antimechanical spirit can be dealt with here only in very simple terms. From the second half of the eighteenth century the voices that characterize the process of rationalization as destructive begin to multiply. Herder is one of the more important among them. The faculty of imagination is said to have a synthetic capacity that defies analysis, and Herder argues that this capacity is at work in language as well. To speak means to create a vision of the world. What was called reason by the Enlightenment is none other than an abstraction of the regularities at work within language. "Reason [itself] is thus formed through *fictions*," as Herder insisted.[13] Given its dependence on the synthetic power of a linguistically determined world view, reason cannot simultaneously claim to be the originator of this world view. This means that the axioms underlying the structure of a world view cannot be explicated by means of this structure. If the entirety of what can be communicated and brought before our consciousness by means of an existing "symbolic order" is called a body of knowledge, then the principle on which this knowledge is based – the hermeneutical "seed" from which this knowledge sprang forth – is in itself something unknowable, something that could therefore be called an object of belief rather than of knowledge. As Sartre has put it: "L'analyse est, en elle-même, une entreprise synthétique."[14]

This marks the birth of romantic hermeneutics: the Western conception of a timeless and general rational order that is *a priori* valid for all rational beings is reminded of its linguistic, historical, economic, national, epistemological and similar conditions of its birth. In short, it is reminded of its "historical *a priori*." The allegedly universal character of the *one* rationality reveals itself as an *individual universal*.[15] That is to say, a universal insofar as it still ensures social intercourse and human communication, and thereby the possibility of intersubjectively valid rules of thought, action and speech. But it is also individual insofar as this universality is no longer

13. J. G. Herder, *Sämtliche Werke*, ed. B. Suphahn, Berlin, 1877ff., vol. 18, p. 485.
14. J.-P. Sartre, *L'Idiot de la Famille*, Paris, 1971/72, vol. I, p. 471.
15. See M. Frank, *Das individuelle Allgemeine*, Frankfurt a. M. 1977, 2nd edition 1985.

based on a logical *a priori*, but is founded on synthetic interpretations of the world undertaken by individuals transcending their own identity in future-oriented projections. It is thus the individual who makes possible the intersubjectivity of meanings exchanged in communicative acts, while at the same time preventing the given communicative system from becoming truly universal, in the sense that all meanings would become strictly determined and exhaustively definable. Thus reason opens out to history, and no *terme final* can be envisaged.

One might be inclined to believe that the discovery of what Friedrich Schlegel in 1789 called the "historical transcendental"[16] would long ago have been identified as nothing more than itself an historical fact, and hence regarded as superseded, and as a "romanticism" in the vulgar sense.[17] In order to emphasize the continuing relevance of Schlegel's discovery, I would like to remind the reader that contemporary postempiricist philosophy of scinece still insists on this misleading view. Without mentioning any names, let me just give you a brief sketch of the basic features of the theory itself. It is assumed that the elementary forms of rationality prove their validity, firstly, in the use of clear and well-defined concepts; secondly, in the justification of the grounds for a statement or an action, be they of a logical nature (i.e., through an appeal to an already acknowledged proposition or a norm), or an empirical nature (i.e., through pointing to an established fact or a rule of action). Thirdly, operational or instrumental explications are called rational if they set out a procedure that is to be followed if a certain end is to be achieved (e.g., a knitting pattern or a procedure described in a manual for a tradesman's tool). Fourthly, norms are rationally justified in the sense that one can demonstrate the conformity of certain actions or practices with accepted ends, norms or customs. All four forms of rational behavior have in common – and this is how the romantic heritage proves its validity in contemporary philosophy of science – that they ultimately appeal to the criterion of intersubjective reproducibility. Each participant in a rational discourse, in order to fulfill the first condition of rationality, must be able to refer to the same state of affairs as the others, using the same concepts and statements. One could call this, in Karl Hübner's words, the criterion of semantic intersubjectivity. Furthermore, the explanation or justification provided must, in each case, be generally acceptable.

One could differentiate here between intersubjectivities on the basis of logical, empirical, instrumental, and normative claims. Nonetheless – and

16. F. Schlegel, *Kritische Ausgabe seiner Schriften*, ed. E. Behler et al., Paderborn, 1958, vol. 18, p. 101, no. 863.
17. See for example K. Hübner, *Kritik der wissenschaftlichen Vernunft*, Freiburg, 1979. Also H.-P. Duerr (ed.), *Der Wissenschaftler und das Irrationale*, two vols, Frankfurt a. M., 1981.

this is the point of tracing back all possible forms of rationality to the idea of semantic identity – there is no *a priori* criterion that ensures that everyone means the same thing by the same word or sentence. Such a criterion would only be conceivable under the condition that certain words or propositions directly, and in a controllable way, refer to sensory experience or to *a priori* valid ideas. Since we know that language is not a "nomenclature" mirroring ready-made states of affairs or conceptions of states of affairs, in short, since we know that the paradigm of re-presentation is no longer viable, we also know that our understanding of something as something must appeal to a systematic disclosure of the world, that is, to a linguistic system that is prior to, and enables, each act of understanding. If that is correct, it follows immediately that the justification of a law (whether it be scientific or moral) presupposes the hypothetical validity of an axiomatic system that allows us to verify or falsify any statement that might be made. (For example, it is necessary that the values "true" and "false" must have a definite meaning, something that is not a natural or logical necessity for every kind of orientation in the world. Other similarly fundamental distinctions are conceivable in different linguistically possible worlds). The axiomatic system that *a priori* comprises the sphere of rational propositions cannot itself be subjected to a rational justification, unless at the price of an infinite regress. One either has to remain satisfied with an already established but preliminary axiomatics, which functions as a condition of the intelligibility of the world, or one is confronted with the prospect of an unending process of justifications of justifications, etc., of a given historical *a priori*. It could thus be said that each point of origin for the rational justification of a totality of propositions or statements is in itself nonrational (which, to be sure, does *not* mean that it is irrational). To put it another way, the scientific attitude is founded on something that, in itself, is not scientific. It is based on a prior interpretation of the world sedimented in a shared semiotic order, which provides the historical *a priori* for any rational explanation, that is, for any explanation seeking intersubjective validity.

But let us return to our historical context. We have stated that the romantics made a discovery according to which every rational explanation of something resulting in a valid conclusion must appeal to an axiomatics that, in the last instance, is an already disclosed and semiotically articulated view of the world. But apart from this hermeneutics of the world, there had to be another important discovery before the bastion of the analytic spirit could be lastingly shaken in the way in which this was seen as the achievement of Romanticism by Foucault, Sartre, and Koselleck, in their different fashions. What I have in mind are the consequences of Kant's critique of reason, which, as its title indicates, had corrected in a similar way the dreams of unlimited power of a sovereign rationality by turning the torch of rational critique against reason itself. What this critique revealed was that all the achievements of analytical reason originate in a primordial synthetic act, i.e., in self-consciousness. It is the unity of this self-consciousness that founds the unity of our intuitions and our experience of the world, just as its laws in the moral world prescribe and enable rational human conduct. More importantly, Kant had also questioned the *mechanical* conception of nature by demonstrating that certain natural phenomena cannot be explained in terms of mechanical processes. They can only be understood if their mechanical operation is conceived of as functioning teleologically, i.e., under the guidance of an Idea. Kant called such entities *organisms*.[18]

These two epistemological innovations provide the historical field on which early romantic thought could grow. Put very simply, the basic conception is that each process of analysis whose laws are revealed by the understanding is grounded in a synthesis that cannot be circumvented. Something nonrational constitutes the basis of rationality.

In applying this to the concept of reason and to the Enlightenment concept of the state, the romantics made the following claim: the emancipatory mission of the Enlightenment results in a new cult of rationality as soon as rationality declares itself autonomous and self-sufficient, that is, when it fails to reflect upon the synthetic acts on which it is based. The process of reason, if left to its own devices, resembles a self-regulated machine whose function no longer serves a particular end. By rejecting the notion of ends and of justification on the basis of "Ideas," analytic rationality, in its most pointed form, simultaneously completely abolishes the notion of legitimation as such by way of a rejection of all positivities ("undermines itself to the point of self-destruction"[19] is the phrase used by Friedrich Schlegel). From then on rationality is suspected of being illegitimate. At the least, it remains doubtful whether it can legitimate itself through its own means. This situation, however, poses a great danger, a danger that becomes even greater if one proposes that any doubts about the legitimacy of a rationality-based social order should be suppressed by reducing the question of legitimation to that of legality. This is the position taken by the political right from Carl Schmitt to Niklas Luhmann. Not only does it have no cogent criterion by which to distinguish between legal but unjust systems of power, and the legitimate power of the constitutional state; it also cannot adequately interpret the crisis of meaning that poses a permanent threat to late capitalism, a crisis of meaning experienced particularly by the young generation.

18. See Frank, *Der kommende Gott*, pp. 153–188.
19. Schlegel, *Kritische Ausgabe*, vol. 3, p. 89.

Max Weber had clearly foreseen these problems. He calls the final stage of scientific and political rationalism "a procedure uncritical toward itself"[20] because it fails to critically analyze the conditions of its own positivity. In a very similar way, Karl Marx had accused the bourgeois revolution of having dissolved social life "into its parts, without *revolutionizing* these parts themselves and subjecting them to criticism."[21] Thus the hoped for political emancipation leaves unanswered the question of the grounds and the ends of the whole endeavor; that is to say, it tends to become meaning-less. On the one hand, it suppresses and destroys the meaning potential of synthetic, and particularly of religious, world views. On the other hand, it does not know how to replace this loss of meaning. This is the destructive and most recent aspect of Western rationality, which we face with a feeling of increasing perplexity.

In this situation – a situation in which "rationality" tends to become a synonym for a technology of terror outside of human ends – the public is disturbed and frustrated by philosophy. Where philosophy is not itself affected by the traces of rationalization and has deteriorated into a particularized technical discourse, or become a highly specialized discipline (as in the case of philosophy of science, formal logic, or positivist history of ideas), contemporary philosophy, under the weight of the demands made upon it, feels as much overtaxed as the public it ought to address. One reason for this is, of course, the fact that philosophy itself emerged within the tradition of a rational interpretation of the world, and is thus, in part, responsible for reducing it to the model of instrumental action. The attempts of contemporary philosophy to escape the "network of delusion" of a rationally ordered world without abandoning the idea of intellectual legitimation are modest, but deserve serious attention. In France, it was particularly the life work of Jean-Paul Sartre that unmasked the destructive effects of a conception that reduced reason to an "esprit d'analyse" no longer in the service of a practical and teleological totality.[22] In Germany it was the Critical Theory of the Frankfurt School that tried to do something very similar. If today the younger generation in the universities begins to turn away from both these traditions, and embraces the much more radical, so-called "postmodern," critique of rationality practiced by neostructuralism, then this, again, is a phenomenon that needs to be understood. It can be understood, initially, as a reaction to the failure of both the existentialist and the neo-Marxist critique of ideology. I can offer only an educated guess as to the reasons for their failure, and, in conclusion, open up a

20. M. Weber, *Gesammelte Aufsätze zur Wissenschaftslehre*, Tübingen, 1968, 3rd edition, p. 167.

21. K. Marx, "Zur Judenfrage," in *Marx/Engels Werke*, vol. 1, p. 367.

22. See Sartre, *Situations*, vol. 2, Paris, 1948, p. 16ff.

perspective on the area in which philosophy might be able to regain some ground in contemporary society.

Let me begin with some comments on the reasons for the failure of existentialism and Critical Theory. Their failure, it seems, is due to the fact that both insisted on a universalist morality under the conditions of a total loss of *a priori* values. Thus this kind of philosophy reenacts a dilemma already inherent in romantic thought. For the two objections put forward by the romantics against the analytic spirit do not always lend mutual support to each other. On the contrary, they sometimes conflict with each other. The first objection (i.e., the hermeneutical one) insists that each construction of a world view is historical and thus relative. The second objection says that a discursive order that does not refer to a *telos* (i.e., to a final goal that is not itself relative) cannot be legitimized and becomes meaningless. What is demanded by the second is denied by the first. On the one hand, an absolute meaning is postulated as a reference point (i.e., an Idea in the Kantian sense as ultimate legitimation). On the other hand, every value-conferring absolute is historicized and relativized by hermeneutics. No order can be self-justifying, but at the same time our belief in a transcendent principle that could validate it has become discredited and is no longer available.

Given these conditions, how can we develop a normative theory of society? Neither Sartre – who spent a lifetime to work out a moral system, but lacked a founding origin – nor Adorno and Habermas were able to deduce their humanist political commitment from an ethical principle. Or, to put the point more decisively, we can sympathize with the ethics they practice, but their ethics does not follow necessarily from the premises of the contemporary historical *a priori*.

How then should we account for Habermas's warning that "among modern societies only those that manage to integrate into the realm of the profane essential features of their religious traditions, i.e., elements that transcend the merely human, will be able to preserve what is substantially humane"?[23] To save the substance of religious legitimation under a-religious conditions can only mean to maintain religion's function without accepting its traditional form. Yet the function of religion seems to be to protect human reason from the unfulfillable demand of a pure self-justification. Religion appeals to an "*extra nos*," which is not necessarily something transcendent and superhuman, as the experience of hope and obligation can teach us. The experience of hope, which motivates us to prefer life to death under all circumstances, is a force, inscribed implicitly in every human act, that anticipates the success of our actions: "je ne peux entre-

---

23. Paper presented on the occasion of G. Scholem's 80th birthday, *Merkur* 1, 1978..

prendre une action sans compter que je vais la réaliser." This anticipation is not open, of course, to demonstration or proof. He who lives in hope can be discouraged, but not refuted.

Similar things apply to the realm of obligation. It transcends the real and makes me conscious of an internal necessity ("une sorte de constrainte intérieur") without, however, originating in my own consciousness. In one of his last interviews (with Bernard-Henri Lévy), Sartre proposed to interpret this inner necessity as the voice of the other-in-me ("autrui-en-moi"), reminding me that I share the world with others, and that my actions will always have implications for the future of other agents. This awareness opens up in a new way the moral dimension of life, but in an entirely un-Kantian fashion.[24] It is an essential part of the nature of an obligation that, unlike a predilection or an idiosyncratic inclination, it is never valid for just one person. This is what it shares with a value. The religions interpret the unity of the community of believers as reflecting the trans-individuality of the divine imperative situated above the highest human values and obligations. Today this path is no longer viable.

But could we then not (following Musil) restore the binding force of values inductively, as it were, by creating the conditions for brotherliness and unity among human beings themselves, thus preparing the ground for a coming god and paving the way for his advent?[25] Put in a less literary language, could we not work toward a restoration of forms of social conduct between the alienated members of society that would, counterfactually, bear within themselves the *telos* of mutual understanding, and thus oblige each member to aspire to this *telos?*

This conception bears a strong resemblance to the basic ideas of the social contract (*contrat social*) that Jürgen Habermas has always held on to as the ideal of a practical and communicative rationality. The specifically bourgeois universalism acquires its posttheological rationality precisely from the idea that the lack of a transcendent principle (God, the Absolute) directs human societies to the long and arduous task of mutual agreement and understanding. Mutual understanding is inscribed as a *telos* in each concrete act of communication, and serves as a practical criterion of the rationality of our endeavors.

Still there are serious objections to the attempt to found obligations and social unity in a theory of communicative consensus. Each normative concept of community that aims at universal validity has the potential to become a reified force – a "total network of power" – acting against the individuals as participants in a consensus-oriented community. The idea of mutual agreement and understanding, if subjected to the categorical

24. *Nouvel Observateur*, 10 March 1980, pp. 59–60.
25. See R. Musil, *Gesammelte Werke*, ed. A. Frisé, Reinbek, 1978, vol. 3, p. 1022.

imperative of a comprehensive unifying force that allows no exception, tends to become totalitarian.

Proponents of classical structuralism argued, above all, that a universalist morality really served the cause of Eurocentrism and thus of imperialism. So-called primitive cultures (e.g., American Indian cultures) were completely exterminated in the name of the universal nature of man, an idea that, in truth, only stood for attributes typical of European culture. Even today, the allegedly universal nature of man tends to justify economic and military genocide.

A second argument, which could be seen as originating in Adorno as well as Derrida, points to conceptual difficulties within Habermas's communicative universalism when it comes to setting it apart from the alternative conception of an already existing conformity with the ruling unreason that inescapably forces itself upon us. Schleiermacher already warned of this when he said, "Linguistically mediated tradition cannot be considered as truth."[26] Anyone who disputes this would confound consensus with conformism, that is with the subjection to the reigning evil as long as everyone is practicing it. Participation in whatever happens to be the dominant discourse can be widespread, without thereby being legitimate. Adorno believed that the only way to escape from this was by choosing the solitude of a philosophical reflection that could regain for philosophy the truth that had been veiled by the collective consciousness. He even regarded the totality of the factually existing consensus within society as a "collective network of delusion," which one could only evade by radically rejecting the evil of bourgeois society that is now the norm.

But there is a third decisive reason for being skeptical about the universalist aspirations of the consensus theory. It argues that each consensus that makes claims to universal validity levels and neutralizes the rights of those whose claims it was originally designed to provide with a general legitimacy, that is, the rights of the individual. In this context, we need to remind ourselves that it was precisely in the name of an irreducible *individuality* of meaning that romantic hermeneutics acted when it uncovered the shortcomings of an analytically understood conception of universality, i.e., the notion of universality developed by the bourgeois Enlightenment. For what prevents a general order from becoming subsumable, once and for all, under a definitive (Hegelian) concept must be that which cannot be reduced to the status of an element of this order. This is precisely what I mean by the *individual.* In order to understand its specific eccentricity, it has to be distinguished rigorously from the *particular,* even though the

---

26. F. Schleiermacher, *Dialektik,* in *Sämtliche Werke,* vol. III, 4/2, Berlin, 1893. See also *Dialektik,* ed. Odebrecht, Leipzig, 1942, p. 374: "So there is error and truth in language as well; incorrect beliefs can be shared, too."

dominant philosophical terminology tends to neglect this distinction. The particular is always an element within a system, or something that can be subsumed under a general law or rule. It is completely controllable by a superordinate concept, and as a *type* it is indistinguishable. This is why the particular cannot bring about any changes with regard to the general. My contention is that a universal consensus tends to subsume its participants as particular elements and to treat them as indistinguishable. In contrast to the particular, the singular or the individual is an element or a part that can never be derived logically from a universal concept in a finite number of steps. Individuals cannot be deduced from a concept (a structure, a code, a system, etc.) because it is in *them* that the concept of a whole first originates. To put it differently, the meaning of a whole has no existence outside the consciousness of individuals who internalize the universal in their specific and unique ways, and who return it to a state of public accessibility by their actions. Two implications follow from this. Firstly, through the intervention of the individual the universal concept is split within itself, that is to say, it loses its semantic and normative identity (in other words, a singular interpretation fissures its identity). Secondly, the universal concept does not exist in only one interpretation, but in uncontrollably many (i.e., as many as the number of individuals within a speech community). Each interpretation can incorporate any other only by means of a hermeneutic "divination," and each divination bears an index of uncontrollability. None attains to the status of objective knowledge.

For a consensus theory that holds on to the ideal of the universal, i.e., to the necessity of complete agreement, this is a necessary evil. But since this evil is the consequence of epistemological, and not just moral and political, conditions, it can hardly be overcome. It seems to me, moreover, that he who attacks it in the name of the consensus theory has lost sight of the founding motive of this theory. A consensus theory of rationality only makes sense if it puts an end to the rigorously nondialogical conception of the universal characteristic of the Enlightenment. For it is precisely the individual that prevents the closure of the general system and thus the constitution of the general as such. In other words, we must seek agreement because we cannot rely on the binding force of a preexisting framework of universal concepts, and because we are nonidentical singular individuals whose interpretations of the world do not coincide in a preestablished harmony or an Archimedian point. Neither language, nor a discursive order, nor the socioeconomic conditions under which we all live, will restore to us the lost absoluteness and reliability of a trans-individual body of knowledge and belief, because their application itself requires a hermeneutic, and thus individual, transcendence of these orders.

The concept of a rule that secures its correct application through further rules is contradictory and leads to an infinite regress. Such a regress can only be avoided if the freedom of the individual is brought into play. But to do this means to interpret the universality of the given and dominant forms of a consensus about meanings (be they social, academic, epistemological, or normative) as that which they truly are: hypotheses that motivate, but do not cause, individuals, capable of interpretive acts, to engage in actions. They cannot determine such actions because the meaning of actions only constitutes itself in the sense that it is created by an individual (which means that the individual, in applying an already given meaning, transcends and modifies it). A concept of generality (grammatical, logical, contractual, juridical, disciplinary, etc.) that tried to dictate, in advance, the conditions under which an attempt at coming to an agreement may be called true, would obviously bear the traces of a discursive coercion, an institutional disciplining power. Thus, under the guise of an interest in the intentions of another subject, its individuality – that is to say, its irreducible ability to constitute meaning anew, and in ways that differ from the ruling consensus – has been brought to heel. Instead of helping to draw the generalizable wishes of the individual to society's attention, the universal reduces them to the status of a particular case, that is, it forces them into a fatal submission to its own norm. But is it possible to instate the individual to its rightful position without restricting the rigorously obligatory character of moral rationality? I believe that inter-individual obligation can, in fact, *only* be brought about by acknowledging the full rights of the individual. For an inter-individual order can only be had through a social and cultural organization of life in which real individuals (and not just bearers of certain functions or representatives of certain types) can stand in for each other. Only *that* voice within my conscience, that is indeed the voice of this unique individual, obliges me to my fellow human being.

Only a society set up on the basis of this insight will succeed in achieving what Emile Durkheim, rather romantically, called "the transition from a mechanical to an organic solidarity." The individualization of the universal was only one of the two innovations by which romanticism transcended the analytic concept of rationality. The other consisted in providing the universal with a teleology. To be sure, the aim of forming a community can no longer be a trans-historical absolute, conceived as its ultimate justification, if we take the rights of the individual seriously. But it is precisely the mechanical concept of a universal consensus that is entirely unsuitable as a foundation for the formation of a community of individuals, for this concept cannot account for individuals other than as members of a set, i.e., as *êtres particuliers*. This is why it loses its legitimizing force, that is, its orientation toward an all-encompassing meaning. A society whose members would be true individuals, however, would only be conceivable as an *organism*, as a community of free and single individuals (*singuliers*), whose communicative acts would bear the *telos* of mutual understanding and agreement, but without this *telos* forcing them into a general conformism. Indeed, such a coercion can only emerge when the normally unstable consensus among the members of a society becomes rigorously codified, and henceforth operates as a hostile power directed against genuine individuality. In the case of an organic solidarity, on the other hand, a consensus conceived in terms of a Kantian Idea would preserve its counterfactual force. It would help to realize the truth contained in the inner core of the bourgeois social contract, though it would do this by strenuously contradicting the factually existing machinery of the bourgeois state and its "empty functioning."

This is the precious lesson we were taught by early romantic hermeneutics and social theory and its commitment to the freedom of the individual. Given, on the one hand, the threat that the "dispositifs" of power pose for the individual and, on the other hand, the spread of philosophical conceptions such as systems theory and radical forms of structuralism that give theoretical support to the already existing factual threat to the subject, the actuality of this commitment is evident. Philosophy could appropriate this commitment in order to align itself with a concept of rationality that would be immune against the forms of critique that have so far been launched against it.

As far as I can see, the widespread desire within the young generation for a decentering and a decentralization of power (manifesting itself in regionalism, epistemological and practical anarchism, alternative cultures, etc.) is largely a desire to save the individual; it is a return of romanticism. All the contemporary French conceptions that I subsumed under the catchword of neostructuralism propagate a "dissémination" of general concepts, institutions, and discursive or – more generally – intersubjective systems. Everywhere the dogma of semantic identity is being challenged, everywhere a battle is fought against the totalitarianism of models that intend to trap the human world in a web of codes, a network of orders, of control and of instrumental power. I do not believe that there is a general feeling of semantic and normative nihilism at work within the generation of people who read and are sympathetic toward such programmatic statements, a nihilism that wants to tear down the last remaining and subjectively binding "rational" universals. On the contrary, the battle is directed at the mechanistic and scientist universalism which, in the shape of an everyday power, wishes to normalize the last areas of individual freedom and to transform the singularity of the individual into a particular element of a system. The illegitimacy of this concept of rationality is a lived experience of this generation. But if "the whole" that Hegel claimed to be "the true" has been emptied of meaning, why should the attempt to regain the multiplicity of lost meaning through "dissémination," through the destruction of complex institutions, and through regionalization be considered wrong and misleading? I recognize in this process the "intuition embryonnaire" in which neostructuralism and the contemporary postmodern rationality originated. I am also of the view, however, that it systematically misunderstands its own knowledge-guiding interest when it cuts off the roots of the "subject." The subject, we are told, is the well-spring of all power and has always allied itself with the universalism of a discursive order. If this is true of the subject, it is *not* true of the individual, which withers away under the power of a rigorous universalization and rationalization.

To be sure, from a technological, bureaucratic or scientific point of view the idea of the irreducibility of the individual to any conceivable discursive order is not very important. The world will continue to exist without it. But as everyone knows, it is even easier for the world to continue without any human beings at all.[27]

*Translated by Dieter Freundlieb and Wayne Hudson*

27. See Sartre, *Situations II*, p. 316.

# Beyond the Radical Critique of Reason

## GERNOT BÖHME

### I. The Critique of Reason and the Enlightenment

When one speaks of the Enlightenment, who does not think first of all of Kant? This is perhaps because at university we got to know about the Enlightenment through Kant's short essay "An Answer to the Question: 'What is Enlightenment?'" (1784). No doubt, Kant's definition of enlightenment as man's departure from a state of self-incurred tutelage has shaped our perception of the Age of Enlightenment, just as Kant's towering figure has overshadowed the Enlightenment philosophers before him. But in what areas did Kant himself provide enlightenment? What feuds with the authorities did he engage in? What cultural, what politico-legal battles was he embroiled in? Such questions make it clear that Kant was a latecomer to the Age of Enlightenment. Even the discussion of the question "What is Enlightenment?" in the *Berlinische Monatsschrift*, to which Kant's essay belongs, indicates that in his time the Enlightenment had already become uncertain of itself. Kant enlightened reason about itself. In doing so, he belonged to the second phase of the Enlightenment – the first is characterized by names such as Thomasius or Pufendorf in Germany – to the phase in which the Enlightenment is already becoming self-conscious.

Just as one has to speak of a first and second phase of the Enlightenment, so one also has to employ the terms enlightenment and meta-enlightenment. This distinction would also help to end the fruitless argument between philosophers of the right and the left over whether the Enlightenment is a project that can be completed, a project after which we can return to our more immediate concerns. The Enlightenment had to contend with belief in witchcraft, superstition and mythologies, with debilitating authorities and circumstances, with false consciousness and with the repression it legitimized. Even today enlightenment has to do with all those things or with their modern-day counterparts. On this elementary level enlightenment is a process that cannot be brought to an end; rather, the task is set anew for every generation. Material human history is not a history of a progressive development but a process of constant turmoil. Again and again circumstances become independent of the people who produce them; again and again relations of dependence arise and are stabilized ideologically; again and again the power of images grows as our power over reality recedes. The speechlessness of our philosophers when confronted with the new fundamentalism or the objective insanity of the arms race rests on the illusion that humankind generally has learned what the philosophers as a profession have learned from the Enlightenment.

With Kant the Enlightenment becomes self-conscious. It begins to become aware of its ambivalence; reason (*Vernunft*) battles against monsters of its own creation. This ambivalence, or rather, as Horkheimer and Adorno would put it, this dialectic of the Enlightenment, had already been perceived by many Enlightenment philosophers themselves. For example, D'Alembert pointed to the shadows that were a by-product of the Age of Light: "New light, which was cast upon many things, new darknesses, which arose, were the fruit of this general fermentation of the intellects: just as the effect of the tide comes from washing new things onto the shore and taking others away."[1]

Kant understood this ambivalence of the Enlightenment as reason's over-estimation of itself. He recognized the new irrationalism as the mirror image of the exaggerated rationalism of his time. "Dreams of a Spirit-Seer" (1766) is the name of the treatise in which on the surface he appears to take to court the visionary, or, to put it more mildly, the seer and prophet, Swedenborg; but his true target is the great Enlightenment philosophers and metaphysicians before him. The dreamers of reason, says Kant, are related to the dreamers of sentiment; indeed, with their metaphysical castles in the air they even legitimize the latter's empirical enthusiasm. It can be shown that here, in the debate with Swedenborg, Kant's turning to critical philosophy occurs. Here he completes the transition to transcendental thinking, which is occupied "not so much with objects as with the mode of our knowledge of objects" (*Critique of Pure Reason*, B 25). From this point on, the business of the metaphysician is critique, and it is directed not so much toward such things as the soul, the world in general or God, but rather towards reason itself as a faculty of cognition.

With Kant enlightenment becomes reason's enlightenment of itself. The critique of reason indicates an enormous disillusionment or even humiliation, the loss of man's trust in his natural light. Kant's contemporaries such as Hamann, who called Kant the destroyer of all things, were

1. D'Alembert, *Eléments de Philosophie I; Mélanges de Littérature, d'Histoire, et de Philosophie*, nouvelle édition, Amsterdam, 1759, vol. iv, p. 6.

still well aware of what had happened. But it was rapidly covered up and suppressed by German idealism (a process, by the way, that has not been satisfactorily explained from a history of ideology perspective). Only with Nietzsche is the process rediscovered in all its radicality. God is dead. For Nietzsche that meant the loss of the great sun, of reason as something given:

> What did we do, when we unchained this earth from its sun? Where is it moving to now? Where are we moving to now? Away from all suns? Are we not perpetually falling? And backwards, sideways, forwards, to all sides? Is there still an above and a below? Are we not wandering as if through an eternal nothing?[2]

Through Kant reason becomes a project. It is not a human gift but a discipline. The human being is not an *animal rationale*, but an *animal rationabile*, an animal that must civilize, cultivate and moralize itself in order to become a human being. Reason is not a world soul that orders nature as a cosmos; rather, *we* impose laws on nature and consider it *as if* it had been created teleologically. Reason also is not God, because God is the highest good, an assumption that is supposed to bridge the gap between dignity and bliss.

Kant restricts reason to its disciplined usage as understanding. The land of truth that Kant thereby determines is indeed finite, but capable of extension. The regulative use of ideas of reason means precisely this transformation of reason into a project. The project of theoretical reason, accompanied by cosmological ideas, moves toward the extensive penetration of nature according to the rules of the understanding. Reason as a practical project proceeds under the idea of a realm of rational beings toward the complete establishment of laws governing human behavior. According to Kant, reason is the project of totalizing the powers of the understanding.

## II. The Radicalization of the Critique of Reason since Nietzsche

As sensitive to the dialectic of the Enlightenment as Kant is, his solution is not appropriate to it. After he identifies the danger in the effusive use of reason, he then wants to rescue reason by infinitely extending the powers of the understanding. As much as this solution corresponded to the actual course of history – August Comte interpreted this somewhat later as the transition from the metaphysical to the positive age – Kant did completely fail to recognize the psychological and the social dynamics in which the

2. F. Nietzsche, "Der tolle Mensch," in *Nietzsche Werke. Kritische Gesamtausgabe*, Berlin, 1973, edited by G. Colli and M. Montinari, fünfte Abteilung, vol. 2, "Die fröhliche Wissenschaft," book III, aphorism 125.

history of reason and ultimately also his transformation of reason into a project are embedded. Since Nietzsche the insight into this dynamic has led to a radicalization of the critique of reason that sets reason's dependence on nature and society against its autonomy, its functionality against its dignity, and that points out the costs associated with its benefits.

For Nietzsche reason is one of the conditions required by human life. Its origin is not power and abundance, but necessity and scarcity. It is a factor in the fight for survival and self-assertion. This naturalization of reason is expressed most strongly in Nietzsche's statement that truth is that form of error without which a particular species could not survive. Freud transfers this interpretation into the social sphere. According to him, being rational involves a form of discipline through which the individual achieves socially acceptable behavior, but as he explains in *Civilization and its Discontents* (1930), this is accompanied by a constant uneasiness. Should the opportunity arise, for example in war, this uneasiness can vent itself in catastrophic behavior. Freud reveals to the bourgeois individual, who has styled himself – or was forced to style himself – as an autonomous subject of reason, that he is not master in his own house. In Freud's theory the ego, once philosophy's *fundamentum inconcussum*, transcendentally the highest point, the peg on which the entire philosophy of reason was hung, becomes an epiphenomenon, an appendage to the larger unconscious mind, something that, far from being an authoritative power, is supposed to instantiate reason as the mediator of the demands of reality and society over against the surge of relentless drives.

Taking this as their starting-point, Horkheimer, Adorno, Elias, and later Foucault, have presented the phylogenetic and the ontogenetic development of the rational human being as the construction of inner compulsory mechanisms. In the analysis of the authoritarian personality Horkheimer and Adorno for the first time pointed to the costs of inaugurating reason. These costs are not simply restrictions, not just the renunciation of experiencing life directly and to the full, but rather the emergence of irrationality as a by-product. This idea was first extended by Horkheimer in his essay "The End of Reason" (1942) and then by Horkheimer and Adorno together in *Dialectic of Enlightenment* (1944) into the area of social psychology and politics. The experience of fascism and of "the American way of life" combined to persuade them that the progressive and thorough rationalization of society – accompanied by the simultaneous stultification of the subject's faculties – produces irrationality. "The new order of Fascism is Reason revealing itself as unreason."[3]

---

3. M. Horkheimer, "The End of Reason," *Studies in Philosophy and Social Science* 9, (1941), p. 387.

That reason, which after all had set out to control the irrational, produced its own irrationality, was something Kant already came across in the case of Swedenborg, although he did not arrive at a complete understanding of the phenomenon. In Germany this insight, born of the horrors of our century, was first gained in research into the century of the Enlightenment carried out by literary scholars.[4] In France it was gained by Foucault's philosophy proceeding along "archaeological" lines. Through his broadly based studies Foucault has shown how the realization of reason, that is, the emergence of rational institutions, has been achieved at the price of a simultaneous production of irrationality. Just as the establishment of certain discourses is inextricably linked with the production of the unspeakable (the irrational in a literal sense), so the progressive legal regulation of bourgeois life is linked with the creation of devices of surveillance and punishment and of normative vacuums beyond them. In the same way, the pervasive rationalization of everyday social existence and the reduction of human beings to calculable items is linked with exclusion, or, literally, with the definition of insanity. The process of the Enlightenment becoming self-conscious, which first of all raised the Enlightenment to a meta-level, now turns back upon its base: what began as the enlightenment of reason about itself again becomes the critique of institutions. The radical critique of reason has revealed that the realization of reason as the progressive differentiation and rationalization of areas of various forms of social life leads to the opposite of what the fathers of the Enlightenment had hoped for: namely, liberation from constraints, humanization of living conditions, intellectual maturity.

### III. On Revising the Project of Modernity

Enlightenment is a never-ending business, but meta-enlightenment, the enlightenment of reason about itself, could have an end if the philosophers integrated the radical critique of reason into their understanding of themselves. But just as after Kant the critical self-perception of reason was again obscured, and just as the Kantian attempt to delimit reason gave rise precisely to its fantastic expansion with Schelling and Hegel, so even today the chances of learning from the history of reason, partly through a renewed appeal for "comprehensive" reason, partly through an intensification of the project of reason, are being wasted. Meta-enlightenment is necessary as long as philosophy has not developed an understanding of reason in which reason incorporates a relationship with its Other. When one has learned

4. See W. Promies, *Die Bürger und der Narr oder das Risiko der Phantasie*, Frankfurt, 1966, and H. J. Schings, *Melancholie und Aufklärung*, Stuttgart, 1977.

from the radical critique of reason that reason is not independent of nature, that the rational human being is not autonomous, and that the realization of reason has its costs, one will give up wanting to achieve the goals of reason by approaching it in a straight line. Meta-enlightenment will only then be superfluous when reason will have become something like level-headedness (*Besonnenheit*), the Platonic virtue of *sophrosyne*. The everyday expression "be reasonable" is cause for hope.

After Freud a philosophy of consciousness such as that of Husserl had to appear naive. But if Husserl's recommendation of a transcendental phenomenology as a helpful contribution in his "Predicament of Our Time" (written at the beginning of the 1930s!) could still be excused by saying that even thoughts need time to take root, it is incomprehensible that Habermas today wants to invalidate attempts to call into question the project of modernity by calling for its completion. It is like answering the criticism of modern technology with the observation that present technology is not the final version. How is it possible that the reformulation of reason as communicative rationality bears no traces of the radical critique of reason that precedes it? How is it possible that Habermas believes he can render irrelevant the "philosophical discourse of modernity" (1985) by recommending the "paradigm of communication"? Was not the Frankfurt School precisely a birth-place of the radical critique of reason? And did not Habermas himself begin with an extensive philosophical reappraisal of psychoanalysis many years ago, albeit only from the external viewpoint of a philosophy of science perspective?

In Habermas's *The Philosophical Discourse of Modernity* Freud is no longer an issue. And as far as Adorno and Horkheimer's *Dialectic of Enlightenment* is concerned, the fact that one now speaks of a "New Frankfurt School" is justified not only because it constitutes itself through a historicization of the old one, but also, and more especially, because it distances itself from the *Dialectic of Enlightenment*. Allegedly Horkheimer and Adorno had underestimated the "cultural resources" of modernity. Unfortunately, what is apparent in this conclusion is not only a legitimate distancing from the previous generation, but also a fading of the historical experience that Horkheimer and Adorno wanted to impart to philosophy. The envisioned completion of modernity after the "linguistic turn" and under the "paradigm of communication" is indeed a continuation of the project of reason as the totalization of the powers of the understanding. What earlier seemed to succumb to "irrational" judgment, decisions and personal discretion now becomes accessible through the differentiation of the discourses of rationalization. What then had to be accepted as instinct, inclination, or need now requires justification. But there is no indication of the fact that differentiation also means particularization, and that ratio-

Beyond the Radical Critique of Reason

nalization has a double meaning. That a discourse free of domination requires a further increase in the individual's transfer of external pressures to within, is not mentioned. And it does not occur to Habermas that communication can only then really become communicative when it allows for the "irrational" behavior of the partner (otherwise one would be able to anticipate it and then one would not need the partner in discourse). And that rationality generally, or even communicative rationality specifically, has its roots in natural preconditions, that it belongs to the realm of necessity and not of freedom – this was never articulated by the Frankfurt School, except by Marcuse. The human relationship with nature, which is again suppressed in the communicative definition of rationality, is precisely the dimension in which today it is most questionable whether the concept of modernity was correctly conceived, and even more harshly, whether it is achievable at all.

A leap into irrationalism as a continuation of philosophy beyond the radical critique of reason is just as inappropriate as an expansion of the resources of reason. The "Kynic's" refusal to participate in discourse may well offer an individual solution; proclaimed with considerable verbosity in the book market, such a refusal can only contradict itself.[5] It is precisely the radical critique of reason that has taught us that one cannot do without rationality. The criticism of Kant[6] that always points out his blind-spots regarding the dynamics of reason as a project must not result in an abandonment of the project of reason as such. But the self-enlightenment of reason on the one hand, and the concrete experience of the project that humanity meanwhile has gathered on the other hand, force us to a basic review of the current state of this project. The design of this project as it has been handed down to us since the Age of the Enlightenment has to be fundamentally changed. Our understanding of ourselves, on the one hand, and our relationship with nature on the other have to undergo a thorough transformation. In philosophy this requires climbing down from the meta-level. This is necessary because work in philosophical anthropology and the philosophy of nature has to be undertaken.

Beyond the radical critique of reason, what matters is the overcoming of our understanding of ourselves as an *animal rationale*. It is a matter of turning away from the ideal of the autonomous rational human being. It is a matter of developing a knowledge of how to orient ourselves in our bodily existence and our dealings with atmospheres of feeling.[7] It is a matter of

5. Böhme is here alluding to P. Sloterdijk's *Kritik der zynischen Vernunft*, 2 vols, Frankfurt, 1983. English transl.: *Critique of Cynical Reason*, Minneapolis, 1987. [Editors' note.]
6. See H. and G. Böhme, *Das Andere der Vernunft. Zur Entwicklung von Rationalitätsstrukturen am Beispiel Kants*, 2nd ed., Frankfurt, 1985.
7. The term "atmosphere" is borrowed from H. Schmitz's monumental work *System der Philosophie*, 10 vols, Bonn, 1964 and later. [Editors' note.]

rehabilitating the imagination as a faculty of knowledge. It is a matter of overcoming Eurocentrism and an understanding of history that sees scientific-technological civilization as the ultimate goal of human development. It is a matter of the theoretical recognition and the practical realization of a plurality of human conditions.

Beyond the radical critique of reason, it is a matter of understanding what it means for humans themselves to be part of nature. It is a matter of acquiring a knowledge of nature that does not view nature as the nonhuman, the alien. It is a matter of regaining a new meaningfulness in our relationship with nature. It is a matter of acknowledging the independence of nature as an agency and of developing the awareness that humans rely on this independence. It is a matter of developing practical relations with nature based not on the idea of production but rather on the idea of the reproduction of both human beings and nature. It is a matter of overcoming the opposition of nature and society, and ultimately it is a matter of creating the space in which the discussion about a social evolution of nature can take place.[8]

Beyond the radical critique of reason, it is important to preserve the balance. A leap into the irrational is not what is required, and neither is the mobilization of new resources for rationality an answer to the "predicament of our time."

*Translated by Peter Monteath, Dieter Freundlieb and Wayne Hudson*

8. This sketch of a philosophy beyond the radical critique of reason is the author's own philosophical program. Parts of it, relating to a new understanding of nature, the sciences and humanity, have been published. See my *Anthropologie in pragmatischer Hinsicht*, 3rd ed., Frankfurt, 1991; *Für eine ökologische Naturästhetik*, Frankfurt, 1989; *Natürlich Natur. Über Natur im Zeitalter ihrer technischen Reproduzierbarkeit*, Frankfurt, 1992; and *Coping with Science*, Boulder, Colorado, 1992.

# –6–

# The Institution of a Common World and the Problem of Truth

## ALBRECHT WELLMER

The idea that the concept of truth – the distinction between "true" and "false," paradigms of the "right" and the "wrong," criteria of rationality connected with models of "good" or "bad" reasoning – is internally related to the institution of a common world is an idea shared by such different philosophers as Castoriadis, Wittgenstein, Habermas, and Rorty. The world opened up through language is essentially a *common* world, a common universe of meanings, of forms of praxis, modes of self-understanding, of need-interpretation, of valuation and reasoning. However, regarding the *interpretation* of this common premise, as well as the *conclusions* to be drawn from it, the different philosophers I have mentioned sometimes seem to be radically opposed to each other. I would like to discuss here – in a somewhat schematic way – a characteristic difference between the positions of Castoriadis and Habermas respectively.

Before I turn to some basic arguments of Castoriadis, I want to give a brief presentation of Habermas's ideas concerning "truth" and "rationality." Habermas has analyzed the idea of truth in terms of (a) an internal relationship between meaning and validity, (b) a dialectic of context-immanence and context-transcendence, and (c) a continuum between questions of truth *within* a language and questions concerning the "adequacy" *of* a language. As far as (a) is concerned, Habermas has expressed the internal connection between meaning and validity by the formula: "We understand a speech act when we know what makes it acceptable."[1] To know what makes an utterance (in particular, truth claims) acceptable is to know (be familiar with) the potential of reasons that might be brought forward for or against such a truth claim. This thesis certainly needs some qualification, but we may take it as a first approximation toward what a

1. J. Habermas, *The Theory of Communicative Action*, vol. I, Boston, 1984, p. 297.

"pragmatic" reformulation of a basic idea of modern truth-semantics would look like. As far as (b) is concerned, truth claims transcend the time and place of their utterance, although it is always only within specific contexts, by means of the arguments and criteria available in such contexts, that we can argue for or against them, that we can "redeem" or "falsify" them in an argumentation with others. The dialectic of context-immanence and context-transcendence signifies the internal relationship as well as the difference between "truth" and "rational acceptability." As far as (c) is concerned, although the concept of truth applies only to propositions *within* a language, the language we speak may prove inadequate for the expression of truth. In such cases we may have reasons to revise our language, to find a better language; and in this sense we might speak about a *language* as being "false" or "inadequate."

I deliberately omit other, more problematic aspects of Habermas's conception of truth, in particular his so-called "consensus theory of truth," because I want to present his position as strongly as possible. Since in what follows it might be objected that my reading of Habermas is very idiosyncratic, I shall, instead of talking about Habermas, talk about a synthetic figure called the "PPL" (the pragmatic philosopher of language). Of course, the position of the PPL is more or less my own; however, for the purposes of the exploration I am attempting here, I find it preferable to talk about him (i.e., myself, i.e., Habermas in my idiosyncratic reading) in the third person.

As far as the pragmatic conception of truth is concerned, which I have sketched above, the decisive difference between Castoriadis and the PPL seems to concern the third aspect. According to Castoriadis the basic conceptual scheme, the universe of meaning in terms of which a society interprets the world and itself, is determined by a "social imaginary," the "acceptance" of which cannot be thought of – cannot in principle be thought of – as being rationally justified or rationally motivated in a sense analogous to that in which the acceptance of a proposition *within* a language can be said to be rationally justified or rationally motivated. With respect to the universe of meaning that is instituted by a social imaginary, the question of truth or falsity, according to Castoriadis, does not make sense, since – so one might interpret Castoriadis – it rather defines the basic parameters on the basis of which not only questions of truth and falsity, but also questions of "right" or "wrong," "adequate" or "inadequate" might be raised in any possible sense. The social imaginary is a collective creation through which a historical society at the same time institutes and defines itself, interprets the world and its own being in the world. To be sure, after a closer look, the differences between Castoriadis and the PPL no longer appear as clear as they do at first sight. For Castoriadis would not deny that the world must "yield" to the conceptual distinctions constituted by a social universe of meaning, *and* that a social imaginary is not a *creatio ex nihilo*. On the other hand, the PPL would not deny that the world-disclosing and world-constituting dimension of language has a creative aspect, so that a rupture in the basic universe of meaning could not possibly be rationally motivated in the same sense as the acceptance of a logical conclusion, empirical evidence, or even a new scientific theory might be.

Furthermore, it seems that Castoriadis would acknowledge a continuum between the ordinary life of language (where we can speak of rationality and truth) and those creative innovations that concern a universe of meaning as a whole. He says, for example, that man can only exist "by defining him/herself as an ensemble of needs and corresponding objects" *and* by "constantly (!) transcending these definitions"[2] – which, as I understand it, means that the creation of new signifiers and new signifieds does not only occur at the dramatic moments of revolutionary rupture, but also, as it were, in the microstructure of historical life, in the everyday life of language and meaning. The PPL, on the other hand, would have to acknowledge that in what he calls communication and discourse an element of constant innovation, an element of world-disclosure through a change of linguistic meanings, through linguistic innovation, through redescribing and redefining the world and ourselves, is inscribed; a manifestation of what Kant called the faculty of imagination *within* communicative reason.

So far, therefore, the differences between Castoriadis and the PPL seem to be less dramatic than they might at first appear. The difference might actually be more terminological than substantive: while Castoriadis tends to reserve the term "rational" for the identity-logical dimension of language, (although he calls rationality in this restricted sense also "pseudo-rationality"),[3] the PPL tries to defend a wider conception of rationality. When he talks about rationality, his paradigm of rationality is a productive dialogue or a good deliberation rather than the rational necessity embodied in a logical demonstration. For the PPL, therefore, imagination, "phronesis," and the faculty of judgment would be constitutive of rationality in its more interesting manifestations, i.e., of communicative and deliberative rationality.

Of course, the question whether the concept of rationality or of rational discourse should be restricted to the identitary-logical dimension of language, or whether we should give it an extended use in the sense indicated above, is a question of the highest philosophical importance. I think, however, that so far the terms of the debate are not yet clear enough; I therefore

---

2. C. Castoriadis, *L'institution imaginaire de la société*, Paris, 1975, p.190. Unless otherwise indicated, the author is responsible for the translation of the various quotations.
3. *Ibid.*, p. 223.

now want to take a closer look at some of Castoriadis's basic arguments.

I would like to distinguish between three basic arguments of Castoriadis, which then might also be interpreted as arguments against a "strong" conception of truth and reason in the sense in which it is advocated by the PPL. The first argument concerns the creative aspect in the institution of a social imaginary and a corresponding universe of meaning. Castoriadis describes this creative moment in the institution of a common world as transcending – like the creation of artworks – the disjunction of the contingent and the necessary. The institution – or re-institution – of a common world is neither an unmotivated leap in the dark, a *creatio ex nihilo*, nor a collective act that could be explained as being rationally or causally necessitated. The institution of a social imaginary does not only *transcend* these disjunctions, it *precedes* them. It is, one might say, the condition of the possibility for these disjunctions to become operative.

The second argument concerns the "irreducibility" of the "signifying relationship." Castoriadis's analysis of the signifying relationship is in some sense quite close to Wittgenstein's analysis of the concept of meaning. Both Wittgenstein and Castoriadis claim that the signifying relationship, to put it in Castoriadis's words, "has no place in the traditional logic/ontology."[4] It is a relationship preceding all other relations – being their condition of possibility – and therefore irreducible to any of them. Although it is that relationship that constitutes identitary logic, makes it possible, it is always also beyond identitary logic: the idea of language, of *legein*, as a closed and formalized system is, as Castoriadis – very much in the spirit of Wittgenstein – says, "an incoherent fiction."[5] Castoriadis speaks of the signifying relationship also as of the "original institution" (*institution originaire*).[6]

The two arguments I have mentioned are obviously closely related. I have distinguished between them because they are, as it were, located on two different levels of generality. The signifying relationship as that which constitutes *legein* as such must be operative in any possible institution of a social imaginary, of a common world; it defines what makes a common world a universe of *meaning*.

The third argument concerns the essentially *practical* character of the institution of a common world. This institution is a self-institution of society also in the sense of a self-*creation*. Our definitions and self-definitions, our interpretations of the world and of ourselves in the world, are constitutive of what we *are* as social beings.

Given these three arguments Castoriadis seems to have strong reasons to

4. *Ibid.*, p. 338.
5. *Ibid.*, p. 360.
6. *Ibid.*, p. 338.

limit the applicability of the ideas of truth and rationality to the sphere of an *instituted* world, and to deny their applicability to its other side – to the "event" of its *institution*. Since, as I have already indicated, the dimension of instituting and self-instituting continues to remain a dimension even of the instituted world, and since on the other hand the institution of a social imaginary is not a *creatio ex nihilo*, but always occurs in a specific historical context (i.e., with a background of problems, conflicts, irresolvable incoherences, etc., and therefore as a "motivated," although not *necessary* social creation), we might also say that Castoriadis limits the applicability of the ideas of truth and rationality to language as institu*ted* in contrast to language as institu*ting*, where language as instituted and language as instituting signify two different dimensions of language that in *some* sense are always co-present in historical reality. Perhaps we could speak of a double character of language as being instituting/instituted; a consequence of this double character or two-sidedness of all *legein* would be an irreducible opacity of all language: not only is the idea of language as a closed formalized system an incoherent fiction, but also the idea of an ideal state of communication in which perfect understanding and complete truth would have been reached. As far as Habermas's conceptions of truth and rationality are based on such a fiction, one might say that Castoriadis's philosophy contains strong arguments against Habermas. However, I do not believe that a conception of communicative rationality *needs* to be based on such idealizing fictions (elsewhere I have extensively argued for this claim).[7] If this is granted, we might make a new attempt to state the possible disagreements between Castoriadis and the PPL.

I want to make three different attempts to pin down these (possible) disagreements. The three attempts focus upon the *creative*, the *holistic*, and the *practical* aspects of what I have called the institution of a common world. As far as the creative dimension behind and within *legein* is concerned, the difference at stake seems to be that Castoriadis would claim that there is no "rational link" connecting the old with the new, no rule or logical necessity that links them with each other. But, of course, a pragmatic philosopher of language (PPL) could concede this, and yet claim that the element of innovation, of imagination, of redescription that is characteristic of a good (i.e., productive) dialogue, is not a disruption of communicative reason, but its life-element. Rational argument involves the ability to move back and forth between theoretical perspectives, problems and experiences as well as between old and new theoretical perspectives. Otherwise it would be impossible to argue about new theories as, for example, Einstein's theory or Castoriadis's philosophy. At least I would

7. A. Wellmer, *Ethik und Dialog*, Frankfurt, 1986. "Was ist eine pragmatische Bedeutungstheorie?", in A. Honneth et al., (eds.), *Zwischenbetrachtungen*, Frankfurt, 1989.

suggest that we take as our paradigm of rationality not logical deduction or algorithmic calculation, but the rationality of a good dialogue where the new way in which an argument is presented may be constitutive of its force with respect to an old problem.

In talking about the creative dimension of rational dialogue, I have already touched upon the second aspect that I mentioned above, namely the holistic aspect of the instituting dimension of language. As is well known, even the rationality of natural science was questioned the very moment it became apparent that the progress of physics does not conform to a "procedural" or "algorithmic" or "criterial" conception of rationality. There is no possible formal proof that Einstein's theory is superior to Newton's, and yet today hardly anybody doubts that there are good arguments to believe this (that is, with the exception of some philosophers of science). Consequently, the holistic character of a theoretical innovation does not place this innovation outside the space of rational argument: even if no rational procedure could lead to the invention of a new theory, the new theory does not mean a *disruption* but an *extension* of the space of possible reasoning; or perhaps we should rather say: disruption and extension are two sides of the same thing.

If we turn to the third aspect of what I have called the institution of a common world, its practical aspects, things become more complicated. The change from Newton to Einstein, in spite of its holistic character, is still a *cognitive* change: i.e., a change of beliefs *within* the tradition of modern natural science, which may be characterized by a set of continuing goals, ideals of knowledge, criteria of success, and ideals of explanation – a set of parameters that might be understood as part of the social imaginary of the modern world. Kuhn falsely compared scientific revolutions within this tradition to *social* revolutions, after which, as he says, we live in a different world. However, if it comes to social revolutions, to a rupture in the social imaginary, it seems that we *do* live in a different world after the revolution. Such changes seem to be holistic in a more radical sense than the change from Newton to Einstein because they are *practical* changes in the sense in which I have explained this term above. A practical change would not just be a change of beliefs, but, via a change of self-definitions and self-interpretations, a change of a mode of being in the world. Not only people's beliefs change, but *people* change in such a process. By defining themselves anew, they invent, constitute themselves anew, become different kinds of beings with different priorities, different needs, a different self-conception. While in the case of a cognitive change that I have discussed above one might say that there is still a basic continuity concerning the cognitive goals – namely theoretical explanation, which is grammatically connected with an interest in prediction and control – in the case under consideration now, *all* the parameters may change so that, in as much as there are no common parameters left that would make a commensuration possible, one might argue that it does not make sense any more to say that the new form of life is – in some "objective" sense – "better" or more "authentic," or more "adequate" than the former one.

I think it cannot be denied that there is a real problem here, although I think that it should not be overdramatized. The real problem is that with respect to different cultures a genuine incommensurability does exist. The overdramatization of this problem would consist in our neglecting the fact that: (1) complete incommensurability is a myth (since in the case of complete incommensurability translation would be impossible; therefore we could not even be sure whether what we take to be a different culture *is* a culture at all); and (2) that the ruptures in the social imaginary that are part of our history are never *complete* ruptures; only retrospectively – seen from a great distance – do they appear as total ruptures. This means, however, that such ruptures might be more adequately characterized by an acceleration and intensification of changes and innovations, which under conditions of historical "normalcy" might occur much more slowly and less perceptibly. But then it becomes conceivable that even with respect to more radical changes in the social matrix of world interpretations and self-interpretations, critique and argument may play a decisive role, in a destructive as well as in a constructive sense. And, actually, Castoriadis leaves no doubt that this is the case: for instance, when he tries to show how the revolutionary project of an autonomous society is based on "the interpretation of a discourse which the present society conducts about itself."[8]

But even if this point is granted, Castoriadis certainly would be right in insisting that a fundamental change in a form of life can never by understood as the manifestation of a rational choice. However, I think it is not the term "rational," but the term "choice" that presents a problem here in the first place. No argument – except perhaps in the limiting case of formalized systems – can ever determine a choice in the sense of logical compulsion. The more a choice is likely to affect our whole life, the less it will correspond to a narrow model of rational choice. It is not only that we cannot know the future, so that every choice may turn out to be wrong. It is rather that in the case of fundamental choices our lack of knowledge of the future is more dramatic than in trivial cases. A simple choice may affect our whole future life, but it is impossible to know with any degree of certainty or precision *how* it will affect our life. There is an element of blindness in every major choice. In a sense we can only know retrospectively what we have chosen, and in a sense we can never know it – at least inasmuch as we

8. C. Castoriadis, p. 136.

do not know the consequences of an alternative choice. And yet all this does not, of course, invalidate the distinction between a blind and a well-deliberated choice, i.e., that distinction in terms of which choices may be more or less "rational."

Now, as I said before, the problem concerning far-reaching changes in a form of life does not so much concern the term "rational" as the term "choice" itself. I may know that I have to change my life, but even if I succeed in doing so, that change would be a complicated process over time that can hardly be understood in terms of a deliberate choice and its intended results. But if this is true even for individual actors, it is much more true for whole societies, i.e., for the reinstitution of a common world. A society is not a collective actor. To use the term "choice" for a revolutionary change of society, i.e., for its reinstitution, would therefore be rather misleading even if choices, including collective choices, and in addition arguments, public discourses, actions and deliberations, may play a crucial role in such changes.

I suppose that Castoriadis would agree with all this. But then the difference between Castoriadis and the PPL, who has already learned from Castoriadis, might in the end actually turn out to be more a matter of emphasis, terminology, focus and philosophical context. I am not sure about this. There is one point in Castoriadis's argument where I clearly disagree with him. Perhaps this disagreement, if correctly understood, could shed some new light on the remaining differences between Castoriadis and the PPL. The disagreement concerns the way in which Castoriadis opposes the project of an autonomous society to the social imaginary of existing Western (and Eastern) societies. Castoriadis first describes this project in terms that have an obvious affinity to a long tradition of thinking about freedom in the modern world, a tradition reaching from the theorists of natural right through Kant, Hegel, Tocqueville, Mill and classical anarchism to Arendt, Habermas, and Rawls. "Our conception of autonomy," says Castoriadis, "makes clear that on the one hand one can want autonomy only if one wants it for everybody, and that on the other hand its full realization is thinkable only as a collective project."[9] He then goes on to explain the idea of autonomy (a) in terms of collective self-determination and self-responsibility, and (b) in terms of social relationships in which the others are recognized and present as much in their selfhood as in their otherness.

I would say that this is a new variation on a grand theme that has occupied much of modern philosophy and political thought in the tradition I have mentioned. And not only that: this grand theme has been present in the great modern revolutions as well as in the social and liberation move-

9. *Ibid.*, p. 147.

ments of our days; not least has it been present as a "social imaginary" in the American revolution, as Tocqueville, an impressive social commentator, pointed out. This theme then signifies the tradition of modern democracy and modern liberal thought. Certainly one might see in Castoriadis's idea of autonomy a radicalization of the democratic idea, because of Castoriadis's emphasis on the collective and everyday aspects of democratic self-government, as well as of liberal thought, because of the emphasis not only on the equality, but also on the otherness of the other. In these respects Castoriadis's conception of autonomy is an important contribution to the rethinking of modern democratic and liberal universalism, a rethinking that today takes place in many different places, and the basic impulse of which perhaps is a critique of traditional European rationalism and scientism, of that part of the social imaginary of the modern world that has often and widely become operative at the *expense* of the democratic principle. The rethinking I am speaking about is a discursive, critical, even polemical interrogation of the modern spirit within the parameters of the modern spirit: an attempted self-transcendence of modern reason. In Castoriadis's case this interrogation is largely – explicitly or implicitly – also a "materialist" critique of the anti-institutionalist utopianism of the Marxist tradition, a critique of the idea of a fully transparent society without the need for institutional mediations, without the opacity of the symbolic and of the flesh. As far as this critical side of Castoriadis's conception of autonomy is concerned, I fully agree with him. The point where I disagree is where he claims that the idea of autonomy is the idea of a radically new self-institution of society that presupposes "a destruction of the known institution of society down to its ultimate foundations."[10] At this point, I believe, Castoriadis succumbs to a fallacy that was already the fallacy of classical anarchism, of the older Critical Theory, and ultimately also of Marxism. If the idea of autonomy, as I have claimed, is already – perhaps in a more or less distorted, incoherent, and undeveloped form – part of the social and political matrix of existing democratic societies, the idea of a radical revolution in the name of the idea of autonomy does not make sense. What is at stake – here as in the critique of modern rationalism – is rather an extension of the interior space of the modern spirit, of modern democratic institutions, of modern forms of collectivity, as well as of modern forms of individualism. Perhaps a qualitative change, the emergence of a second modernity, but not a radical rupture or a new self-institution of society. I rather believe that the rhetoric of a radical rupture is part of the romantic-anarchist-Marxist tradition that was already – partly *avant la lettre* – forcefully criticized by Hegel. Not that I want to defend Hegel's con-

10. *Ibid.*, p. 498.

ception of the modern state. Hegel, I think, was unable – for historical as well as philosophical reasons – to develop a conception of a modern democratic *Sittlichkeit* (ethical life). However, I think that Hegel was right in insisting on an irreducible element of "disunification" in any possible institutionalization of freedom in the modern world.[11] There is no space here to show how this Hegelian insight – which for Hegel meant the justification of a "pre-political" civil society – could be translated into a matrix of thought in which the ideas of autonomy and democracy in Castoriadis's sense would play a crucial role. However, I would like to propose that to achieve such a translation would be tantamount to showing that the project of an autonomous society could only be thought of as an internal radicalization of the modern project of democracy, a radicalizing self-extension of modern democracy, a self-extension that would amount to a democratic *taming* of capitalism and bureaucracy, not their radical abolition or overcoming in the romantic or anarchist sense of the word. In other words: I see the project of an autonomous society to be in *continuity* with the tradition of modern democratic and liberal thought; a continuity that has its own ruptures, revolutions, regressions and crises, but which, more importantly, also defines a space for possible radicalizations, for the self-transcendence of democratic institutions and practices. It is not the radical gesture of "going beyond" that I am opposed to in Castoriadis, but the dramatic rhetoric of discontinuity and rupture that I think conceals the fact that the project of an autonomous society has thousands of semantic, philosophical, and political links with the social imaginary of modernity. My reference to Hegel was an attempt to indicate how I would construe such links.

Now if my objections to Castoriadis at this point have any force, they might also shed some new light on the issues I have discussed above. For the emphasis of the PPL on universalist principles of human rights and on communicative reason as the medium in which democratic institutions can exist, grow, and be transformed, is an emphasis on the elements of continuity between the project of an autonomous society and the best paradigms of modern political thought and culture; elements that connect the project of an autonomous society with the "social imaginary" of the modern world. It is for this reason that the PPL would see public debate, philosophical and political discourse *already now* as an important medium of political change and transformation. The PPL would not deny the "voluntaristic" element in Castoriadis's philosophy its genuine place, a voluntaristic element that, for example, becomes manifest when Castoriadis says that "the overcoming of this self-alienation" is "*our goal, because we want it,*"[12]

11. A. Wellmer, "Models of Freedom in the Modern World," in *Philosophical Forum*, vol. XXI, No. 1–2, Fall-Winter, 1989–90.

12. C. Castoriadis, p. 498.

but he would object to opposing this voluntaristic element to the "rational" one. For although good reasons may not be able to move us to want something good, we may have good reasons to want what we want. And to find out whether what we want is clear, e.g., the idea of an autonomous society, and whether it is the right thing to want, we have to think it through, deliberate about it, expose it to the public forum of philosophical or political discourse. This, of course, is what Castoriadis himself has done in a marvellous way and for a long time in his philosophical and political writings. The force of many of his good arguments shows, I think, that the power of rational dialogue, even if indeed limited, reaches farther than he sometimes seems to be ready to admit.

# –7–

# Habermas's *The Philosophical Discourse of Modernity*

## WAYNE HUDSON

### I

Philosophical theater is by no means a thing of the past. The question of "reason and its Other" is very much one caught up in rhetorical, indeed theatrical contrasts. In Germany itself the role of such contrasts is obscured by a tendency to line up philosophers by schools or by political sympathies, without drawing enough attention to methodological tendencies common to thinkers divided by schools and politics. Here I signal this problem by means of a set of scruples about Jürgen Habermas's influential series of lectures published under the title *The Philosophical Discourse of Modernity* (1985).

Habermas is the most important philosopher writing in Germany today, and a peerless advocate of both discursive rationality and social democratic politics. One of his greatest achievements has been to continue the emancipatory intentions of Western Marxism, while struggling to break with its borrowings from German idealism in philosophy and its Romantic utopian political tendencies. My argument in what follows is that this process of methodological reform should be carried further. Specifically, I suggest that Habermas should make a clearer break with the partisan approach to the history of philosophy adopted by Western Marxists such as Lukács, Horkheimer, and Adorno: that he should adopt discursive practices that are more sensitive to historical contexts and to the thought of individual thinkers as they conceive it. Such self-denial is compatible, I suggest, with close attention to the political and social implications of philosophical ideas. It is also, in my view, likely to strengthen rather than weaken the impact of Habermas's substantive claims – claims that do not require or benefit from polemical discursive practices.

## II

Habermas's work is transitional between styles of thinking shaped by German Romanticism and Idealism and more analytical modes of discourse. As his lectures show, he has not entirely broken with the "comparative" and "history of the problem" modes popular with less analytically minded German philosophers, even though this mode puts the emphasis on reinterpreting the classic authors and the canonic texts of the German tradition rather than on rigorous clarifications of central theoretical terms. It encourages historical sloganeering, and the use of literary and rhetorical devices designed to strike the reader and enter subsequent discourse – of which "the Other of reason" is an excellent example – despite the fact that theoretical issues on which a debate turns may be obscured by the use of such striking devices.

In the case of *The Philosophical Discourse of Modernity* the context in which the lectures were given is important. Habermas detected conservative and irrationalist tendencies in both the United States and Germany of broadly "poststructuralist" derivation. In his lectures he sought to counter the influence of the French "poststructuralists," and also to point out the weaknesses of the "new critique of reason," associated in Germany with the work of Gernot and Hartmut Böhme.[1] In this context both the return to Nietzsche and the attractive allurements suggested by talk of "the Other of reason" seemed to Habermas politically as well as intellectually regressive. The dangers of both irrationalism and a flight toward the extraordinary seemed very real.

At the level of popular reception there was some basis for Habermas's judgements. It is probably true that the views of certain thinkers (Nietzsche, Heidegger, Derrida, Foucault), appropriately vulgarized, did at least for a time encourage irrationalist attitudes and inspire retreats from commitments to normative conceptions of reason. It is also the case that certain specific characteristics of the views of Nietzsche, Heidegger, Derrida, and Foucault facilitate such popular receptions, and that methodological reservations about the ways in which Nietzsche, Heidegger, Derrida, and Foucault present, explicate, argue for, and defend their views can be drawn accordingly, with implications for the procedural norms likely to facilitate rather than frustrate rational communicative practices in advanced technological societies.

Once this is said, however, problems remain about the discursive prac-

1. For Habermas's critique of the work of Gernot and Hartmut Böhme, see *Der philosophische Diskurs der Moderne: Zwölf Vorlesungen*, Frankfurt, 1985, translated by F. Lawrence as *The Philosophical Discourse of Modernity*, Oxford, 1987, pp. 301–5. I refer throughout to the English translation introduced by Thomas McCarthy, which is, and will continue to be, critical for the reception history of this aspect of Habermas's work.

tices by means of which Habermas responds to the intellectual as well as the political challenges involved. To suggest that Habermas's discursive practices need to be questioned in certain respects does not necessarily imply extensive disagreement with his substantive views. On the contrary, it is possible to agree with Habermas about the need not to retreat from high standards of discursive rationality, and the need not to give up the positive heritage of the European Enlightenment, while questioning the way in which he works out such stances in concrete engagements with the work of other thinkers, especially in politically sensitive contexts. It is also possible to respect and admire the way in which he attempts to get to the structural intellectual issues involved, while wishing that his structural contributions were more clearly presented and expressed in less ambiguous and less prejudiced language.

### III

One set of scruples relates to the way in which Habermas constructs issues around high terminology, often of a linear temporalist kind, which impedes rational analysis and prejudges central issues. Insofar as the issue is one of the ethics of the construction of critical cultural historical entities, it is only fair to emphasize that Habermas's procedures are shared by many other prominent German philosophical writers, from whom, in some cases, he takes over the constructions open to objection. Nor can Germans be singled out, as if international practice in this area was not problematic fairly generally.

My point, however, is that Habermas's own project is not furthered by such procedures, and might be furthered by breaking with them. In support of this, I give central examples that are crucial to the entire volume:

1. Irrationalism
2. Neostructuralism
3. The Philosophical Discourse of Modernity
4. The Enlightenment
5. The Dialectic of Enlightenment
6. A Critique of Reason
7. A Totalizing Critique of Reason
8. A Radical Critique of Reason

### 1. What "Irrationalism"?

Irrationalism is a key, if often implicit, term in *The Philosophical Discourse of Modernity*. For Habermas, like Lukács in *The Destruction of Reason* (1954), believes that it makes sense to talk of "reason" and "rationality," and that there is something called "irrationalism" which threatens "reason" and "rationality." Moreover, he also clearly believes, as his interventions in the recent *Historikerstreit* confirm, that "irrationalism," as Lukács claimed, was implicated in the catastrophe of National Socialism.[2] It is also evident that for Habermas, as for Lukács, irrationalism can be associated in Germany *inter alia* with the influence of German Romanticism and Nietzsche.[3]

Given that what Habermas claims here seems self-evident at one level, it is important to notice how this is not the case once one probes more deeply. This can be done by asking what is irrationalism and what is not, by demanding strict criteria of identification, and by conceiving of pluralities and heterogeneities rather than a homological field.

The problem is that the reification "irrationalism" catches too much, and obscures important distinctions and nuances. It may be that certain Xs are not rational. This can be expressed by saying that they are arational. To label them irrational, however, is to open up a range of assertions that need to be argued for separately. For the ir-rational is usually taken to stand (1) in a relation to "reason," and, more specifically, (2) in a negative or even an oppositional relation to reason, while neither may be true of the arational. Given that cultural phenomena that were irrational, and not merely arational, have played a major role in twentieth-century German cultural and political history – as Habermas, very importantly, keeps on insisting – it remains to be shown that specific phenomena in twentieth-century German cultural history were indeed irrational. The fact, for example, that certain philosophers have argued that arational considerations need to be taken seriously in diverse philosophical contexts does not make those philosophers or their views "irrationalist." Of course, duly vulgarized, popular receptions of the views of those philosophers may indeed encourage irrationalist attitudes, but that is another, albeit a related matter. Finally, even if "irrational" views can be identified, it does not follow that "irrationalism" can be used to characterize the views of those who hold *some* irrational views. "Irrationalism," in other words, cannot be invoked as a blanket characterization. If it is used at all, strict criteria for its identification and numeration are required. In *The Philosophical Discourse of Modernity*, however, Habermas comes close to implying that to take account of the arational is to truck with irrationalism.

## 2. What Neostructuralism?

There are also problems with Habermas's notion that recent French

---

2. See J. Habermas, *Eine Art Schadensabwicklung*, Frankfurt, 1987, chapter VI, and P. Baldwin, *Reworking the Past: Hitler, the Holocaust and the Historians' Debate*, Boston, 1990.
3. See Habermas, *The Philosophical Discourse of Modernity*, p. 412, footnote 3.

thought can be labelled "neostructuralism" or "poststructuralism,"[4] neither of which term is widely accepted in France. Habermas uses the label to imply that French thinkers of essentially different traditions can be lumped together for certain purposes and that their relation to "structuralism" is decisive. This saves him from working out the views of such thinkers in their detailed French context. He also deploys the label to attribute a common attitude to "modern forms of life." Indeed, he refers to poststructuralism's "wholesale rejection of the modern forms of life."[5] It is far from clear, however, that Derrida or the Paris-based Greek philosopher Castoriadis can fairly be said to subscribe to any such position. Once again an over-general construction impedes rational discourse and rigorous analyses.

### 3. What "Philosophical Discourse of Modernity"?

The assumption that it makes sense to refer to "the philosophical discourse of modernity" is fundamental to the whole volume. Once smuggled in, individual thinkers can be praised or blamed, depending on how their work allegedly relates to such a philosophical discourse of modernity. But what does Habermas mean by "the philosophical discourse of modernity"?

A naïve reader might suppose that Habermas might mean that there is an historical object "modernity" about which "a discourse" exists that is "philosophical." Three distinct identifications would then seem to be needed: (1) an identification of the alleged historical object; (2) an identification of the alleged discourse; and (3) an identification of the alleged sense of the adjective "philosophical." Habermas provides none of these identifications. Instead, he points to the work of certain European thinkers whom he interprets as addressing something called "the problem of modernity." As a result: (1) the historical object is unclear, since it could be "modernity" as an object constructed in certain texts, not "modernity" as a set of empirically identifiable social and cultural organizational changes, which is the relevant historical object; and (2) the "discourse" is indeterminate, since there is no way to know which texts by the writers mentioned are excluded, why other writers are not included, or by which technical attributes such "discourse" can be identified.

No doubt it is possible to pick out a body of literature that discusses "modernity," but it needs to be shown that there are methodologically sound reasons for positing "a discourse." The fact that those who contribute to such literature deal with some common themes and, in some cases, discuss and react to each others' views may not be enough, especially if the dependencies alleged were not those that the relevant writers them-

4. *Ibid.*, p. xix.
5. *Ibid.*, p. 327.

selves all had in view. Nor is it obvious that relevant discourses should be reduced to one. The sense of the adjective "philosophical" in "the philosophical discourse of modernity" is also unclear. Habermas provides no definition of this adjective, and what he says about it is hardly reassuring:

> The challenge from the neostructuralist critique of reason defines the perspective from which I seek to reconstruct here, step by step, the philosophical discourse of modernity. Since the late eighteenth century modernity has been elevated to a *philosophical* theme in this discourse. The philosophical discourse of modernity touches upon and overlaps with the aesthetic discourse in manifold ways. Nevertheless, I have had to limit the theme; these lectures do not treat modernism in art and literature.[6]

Habermas goes on to imply that the discourse he posits includes more than "philosophy." He also asserts that it is a discourse in which modernity has been elevated to a "philosophical" theme. But, if so, this would not make the discourse involved the *philosophical* discourse of modernity. The paragraph ends with a reference to modernism in art and literature, so that the relation between modernity and modernism is also uncertain. At the very least, Habermas appears to posit an aesthetic discourse that is *not* "the philosophical discourse of modernity," although it "overlaps with it." In short, the cuts that define the exact historical object of the pages that follow are fuzzy, or even incoherent.

That the critical cultural history entity Habermas has constructed is vague and under-defined can be seen from a passage such as:

> Since the close of the eighteenth century, the discourse of modernity has had a single theme under ever new titles: the weakening of the forces of social bonding, privatization, and diremption [divisive separation] – in short, the deformations of a one-sidedly rationalized everyday praxis which evoke the need for something equivalent to the unifying power of religion. Some place their hope in the reflective power of reason, or at least in a mythology of reason; others swear by the mythopoetic power of an art that is supposed to form the focal point of a regenerated public life.[7]

Nor are statements such as the following historically precise:

> The parties that have contended about the correct self-understanding of modernity since the days of the Young Hegelians all agree on one point: that a far-reaching process of self-illusion was connected with the learning processes conceptualized in the eighteenth century as "enlightenment." Agreement also exists about the fact that the authoritarian traits of a narrow-minded enlightenment are embedded in the principle of self-consciousness or of subjectivity, that is to

6. *Ibid.*, p. xix.
7. *Ibid.*, p. 139.

say, the self-relating subjectivity purchases self-consciousness only at the price of objectivating internal and external nature.[8]

Indeed, many of Habermas's historical claims appear both dogmatic and ethnocentric. Thus Habermas declares that Hegel "inaugurated the discourse of modernity," introduced the theme of its self-reassurance, and established the rules within which the theme can be carried on: "the dialectic of enlightenment." In the same *fiat* mode, he assures us that the philosophical discourse of modernity is characterized by the consciousness that philosophy is over.[9]

Of course, Habermas has a serious argument to develop. He seeks to retrace the path of the discourse of modernity and to draw attention to a path not taken: the path of determinate negation of subject-centered reason in favor of a theory of reason as communicative action. He attributes to Hegel the project of attempting to solve or overcome the diremption of modernity by expanding the rationality of the understanding (*Verstand*) that modernity recognized as its only obligation, into reason (*Vernunft*). Habermas then contrasts the good tradition of Hegel and the Young Hegelians, which recognized the problem of enlightening the Enlightenment by enlightened means but that failed to break with the philosophy of the subject, with the bad tradition of the critique of reason, deriving from Nietzsche, which exposes the problem of the subject, but flounders on a self-referential critique of reason, from which it attempts to escape by resort to the extraordinary.

There can be little doubt that Habermas's reading is a useful and a creative one. Habermas suggests that "the philosophical discourse of modernity" is defective insofar as it is based upon a subject-centered conception of reason. He claims that Hegel departed from his early interest in an intersubjective paradigm toward a subject-centered conception of philosophy, and that this conception was continued by his followers: by Nietzsche, by early Heidegger, and even, in a covert way, by Derrida. As a result a variety of problems could not be resolved satisfactorily, whereas a communicative concept of reason produces much more satisfactory alternatives. This enables Habermas to accept some of the alleged French critique of the subject and then to press the French at one of their weakest points: their failure to develop a satisfactory account of social interaction or intersubjectivity.

The problem is that he develops this argument in terms that slide over crucial discriminations and evade rather than sharply confront key historical and philosophical issues. In Habermas's usage, for example, the term "modernity" is far from unambiguous. Indeed, Habermas seems unclear

8. *Ibid.*, p. 55.
9. *Ibid.*, pp. 54 and 57.

about the exact relationship between "the modern age" and "modernity."
At times, he even inverts their relationship, making a period beginning
circa 1400 proud of developments apparent centuries later:

> Neither Hegel nor his direct disciples on the Left or Right ever wanted to call
> into question the achievements of modernity from which the modern age drew
> its pride and self-consciousness.[10]

Similar considerations vitiate statements such as that

> Certainly, in the course of a critique of tradition that integrated the experiences
> of the Reformation and the Renaissance and reacted to the beginnings of mod-
> ern natural science, modern philosophy from the scholasticism until Kant had
> already expressed the self-understanding of modernity.[11]

Likewise, it is impossible to establish the cut that allows Habermas to assert
that

> The discourse of modernity, which we are still conducting down to our own
> day, is also marked by the consciousness that philosophy is over, no matter
> whether this is presented as a productive challenge or only as a provocation.[12]

## 4. What "Enlightenment"?

Habermas refers throughout to "the Enlightenment." But it is not clear
that there was one Enlightenment, or that developments in France, Austria
and Italy, let alone in the rest of Europe, Latin America, and Japan can be
construed in terms of parameters used for the German *Aufklärung*. Habermas, however, takes these parameters as adequate for the Enlightenment
generally. This is surprising, given that this is an approach rejected by the
best contemporary scholarship on the Enlightenment, to which he significantly fails to refer.[13] Of course, he does not intend to confine the Enlightenment to Germany, or to Kant. Nonetheless, like many other contemporary German philosophers, he writes about "the Enlightenment" in ways
that are anachronistic, selective and omissive. Significantly, he does not
discuss the major Italian figures or the work of Franco Venturi. Developments in Poland, Russia and Scandinavia are also ignored, as is the entire
Luso-Hispanic world, including Latin America. Many German philosophers, to be fair, write about the Enlightenment as though Cassirer's *Philosophy of the Enlightenment* were an uncompromised contemporary text,
or as if Newton, Locke, Voltaire and Kant belonged to a single club. But in
Habermas's case there are substantive implications. For if it can be shown

10. *Ibid.*, p. 82.
11. *Ibid.*, p. 16.
12. *Ibid.*, pp. 51–52.
13. See, for example, R. Porter et al., *The Enlightenment in National Context*, Cambridge,
1981.

that mystical tendencies and religion were centrally involved in much of what used to be labelled "the Enlightenment" – and Newton is only the most obvious example – then there are implications for Habermas's views about the historical relations between rationalism, arational views, and social emancipation. And if it can further be shown that the very notion of a single "Enlightenment" sets up a literary figure that represses and misrepresents what were in fact multiple and conflicting social processes, then Habermas's terms of analysis are in jeopardy.

## 5. What "Dialectic of Enlightenment"?

Habermas also relates thinkers whom he discusses to an alleged "dialectic" or contradictory trajectory of Enlightenment, a term taken from Horkheimer's and Adorno's *Dialectic of Enlightenment* (1947). Habermas is too sharp to be taken in by Horkheimer's and Adorno's pessimism, and thoroughly criticizes the theses advanced by them in *Dialectic of Enlightenment*.[14] Nonetheless, the notion of a "dialectic of Enlightenment" survives, even though it is problematic, together with a controversial emphasis on philosophical ideas, as if they were central to modernity, rather than, say, science, technology or capitalism. The exact terms of reference are unclear, and there are ambiguities between reference to "the Enlightenment" as an alleged movement in European cultural history, and "enlightenment" as an alleged process, achievement, or goal. Often these senses become conflated so that it is a process, achievement, or goal that is meant, but these are construed in ways that depend crucially on positive facts associated with "the Enlightenment" as an historical development or "the Enlightenment" is referred to in ways that derive from the postulate of a process, achievement, or goal, rather than from detailed recent studies of school reform in Austria or administrative reform in Naples. Insofar as such ambiguity arises, the notion becomes hard to tie down. Just as there are reasons to doubt that it is acceptable to posit that there was a single Enlightenment, so there are also reasons to challenge the notion that a single Enlightenment led to, allowed or "inherently contained" a single "dialectic," let alone the notion that this single dialectic was a dialectic "of Enlightenment."

Moreover, Habermas uses "the dialectic of Enlightenment" in an anachronistic way. He refers, for example, to Hegel as wanting to develop "the dialectic of Enlightenment" out of the difference between reason and understanding,[15] while Nietzsche is said to "leap out of the dialectic of

14. *Ibid.*, chapter V.
15. *Ibid.*, p. 133. See P. U. Hohendahl, "The Dialectic of Enlightenment Revisited: Habermas's Critique of the Frankfurt School," *New German Critique* 35, Summer/Spring 1985, pp. 3–26.

Enlightenment" and to bid farewell to the "dialectic of Enlightenment,"[16] which seems to imply that this dialectic can be taken or left. In Habermas's defense it may be urged that the term "dialectic of Enlightenment" is much more natural in German than in English, and that everyone knows broadly what is meant. But the fact that a particular language or cultural tradition encourages certain ways of speaking does not answer the substantive point – which is that multiple trends and multiple logics may be involved, and that talk of "Enlightenment" and "dialectic" misrepresents this situation in ways that have important implications for social theory.

## 6. What "Critique of Reason"?

Habermas's argument revolves around the notion of a critique of reason: a *Vernunftkritik*. The term is a strong one, yet Habermas nowhere clarifies what he understands by it.[17] Nor does he show that any thinker he discusses consciously advanced such a critique. Instead, he implies that because a thinker advanced certain views tending to subvert a particular normative conception of reason, they can be taken to have advanced a *Vernunftkritik*. If, however, it is alleged that the work of a particular thinker tends towards a *Vernunftkritik*, then the exact *Vernunftkritik* has to be spelled out clearly, along with the alleged tendentious motion, so that the evidence for both can be evaluated fairly. Just as it is self-evident that an investigation of the conditions of the possibility of reason should not be confused with criticism of reason, so it should be self-evident that the notion of *Vernunftkritik* cannot properly be used to conflate claims about the conditions of the possibility of particular constructions of historically and socially specific forms of reason with attacks on reason itself. The term *Vernunftkritik*, in short, must not be used to presuppose the notions of a single reason, and of quasi-transcendental norms as to its deployment, that are at issue.

## 7. What Is "A Totalizing Critique of Reason"?

Habermas's argument depends even more crucially on the notion of a totalizing critique of reason. According to Habermas such a critique is to be found in Nietzsche, and reappears in those influenced by him in this respect. Habermas claims that from Nietzsche on a totalizing critique of reason has appeared that leads to unacceptable paradoxes and levellings. This critique is self-referential, and surreptitiously relies on normative

---

16. *Ibid.*, pp. 86–87.

17. Habermas's usage, here, is less problematic for German readers familiar with such terms, although the lack of analytical sharpness remains. See H. Schnädelbach, "Dialektik als Vernunftkritik," in L. von Friedeburg and J. Habermas (eds.), *Adorno Konferenz*, Frankfurt a. M., 1983.

intuitions derived from the rational potential inherent in everyday practice.[18] Once again there is a methodological problem about what Habermas wants to claim here. For what is "a totalizing critique of reason"? And how could one possibly know where and when, if at all, it became *totalized*?

At times Habermas appears to mean that such a critique is unrestricted in its application and in that sense "total." At other times he appears to mean that such a critique is "self-encompassing" or "self-enclosed." In the end the term may just be shorthand for the charge that certain thinkers advance claims that involve them in performative self-contradiction.

Here there are many different issues overcompressed by striking phrases. One is whether specific thinkers assert the claims alleged. Allowing for local overstatement, it often appears that they do not advance such claims as basic theses by which their work should be judged. If so, then the inflatus of Habermas's language seems heteronomic. But even if they did advance such claims, what would follow? Even if such claims were self-referential, Habermas would need to do more than observe the fact. Likewise, even if such claims involved self-contradiction, a stronger burden, it could not be simply assumed that this constituted a fault, since such self-contradiction might, in principle, be coherently handled by relevant paraconsistent logics. Finally, the stress on "pragmatic" also offers only apparent elucidation, since if the charge is about the ethics of dialogue, the substantive views could be unaffected. That is, Habermas needs to show that the claims are open to objection – not that those who advance them are open to criticism as discussion partners, for the latter might be true even though the views concerned could be coherently reformulated. Pragmatic self-contradiction, in short, is not substantive refutation and does not really help to show that any alleged critique of reason is "total" or "totalized."

### 8. What is "The Radical Critique of Reason"?

Habermas also refers to the radical critique of reason, which he associates with both Nietzsche and with recent German writing about "reason and its Other." Once again this writing is reified as the new *Vernunftkritik*, even though the writers concerned might well object to such a regimentative construal of their work.

Habermas claims that the radical critique of reason purports to criticize reason from a standpoint outside of it: that of the Other excluded from it. The notion of an "Other of reason" promotes the illusory idea of an autonomous "reason," which operates on the social scene, including some matters and excluding others. Instead, reason needs to be understood as

18. *The Philosophical Discourse of Modernity*, pp. 336–41.

internal to social practices involving solidarity. According to Habermas, the radical critique of reason, however, remains tied to the presuppositions of the philosophy of the subject – from which it may purport to free itself – and thus generates an "Other of reason" as the mirror image of its construction of reason as power.[19] Habermas's view of "the Other of reason" follows from this:

> Since such totalizing critique of reason has given up all hope of a dialectic of enlightenment, what falls under this totalizing critique is so comprehensive that the other of reason, the counterforce of *Being* or of *sovereignty*, can no longer be conceived of only as repressed and split-off moments of reason itself. Consequently, like Nietzsche, Heidegger and Bataille must reach beyond the origins of Western history back to archaic times in order to rediscover the traces of the Dionysian, whether in the thought of the pre-Socratics or in the state of excitement surrounding sacred rites of sacrifice. It is here that they have to identify those buried, rationalized-away experiences that are to fill the abstract terms "Being" and "sovereignty" with life. Both are just names to start with. They have to be introduced as concepts contrasting with reason in such a way that they remain resistant to any attempts at rational incorporation. "Being" is defined as that which has *withdrawn* itself from the totality of beings that can be grasped and known as something in the objective world; "sovereignty" as that which has been excluded from the world of the useful and calculable. These primordial forces appear in images of a plenitude that is to be bestowed but is now withheld, missing – of a wealth that awaits expending. Whereas reason is characterized by calculating manipulation and valorization, its counterpart can only be portrayed negatively, as what is simply unmanipulable and not valorizable – as a medium into which the subject can plunge if it gives itself up and transcends itself *as* subject.[20]

The radical critique of reason, in other words, leads to an abstract negation of the subject as the principle of modernity. Here it is unclear how far Habermas alleges that a structural logic leads to such position-taking, and how far this is simply what, as a matter of fact, happened.

## IV

Habermas's treatments of individual thinkers in *The Philosophical Discourse of Modernity* also leave a good deal to be desired. In many cases these treatments are anachronistic and misleading to a degree that seems in conflict with Habermas's own aspirations to intellectual propriety. Habermas combines criticism of intellectual tendencies with references to the politics of thinkers he wishes to discredit, using the latter to prejudice the interpre-

19. *Ibid.*, p. 309.
20. *Ibid.*, pp. 102–3.

tation as well as the evaluation of the former. As a result, he regiments the work of individual thinkers to fit into his architectonics, and falls into historical slippage. Like Lukàcs, Habermas has a keen eye for "irrationalism" and an uncomplicated, if often shrewd, sense of its likely outcome. Moreover, like Lukàcs, Habermas allows tendency critique to prevail over the need to take account of the heterogeneous and complex legacies of major thinkers, which seldom correlate exactly with readings of their alleged sociopolitical tendencies. Some methodological problems posed by Habermas's handling of the work of individual thinkers can be illustrated by reference to the cases of Nietzsche, Heidegger, Derrida and Foucault.

### Nietzsche

Habermas's treatment of Nietzsche is brilliant, but anachronistic. To this extent it facilitates a sociologistic reading of Nietzsche that is not informed by exact exegetical or philosophical technicalities. It is now standard practice to reinterpret Nietzsche in light of current debates, despite the violence this does to an historically rigorous approach to his texts. Allowing for the fact that Nietzsche interpretation will always be controversial because of the uncertainties of Nietzsche's corpus and his own habit of making paradoxical or one-sided statements of his views on particular matters, any principled interpretation of Nietzsche's work has to reckon with his classicism, his systematic interest in the sciences, and his engagement with a wide range of technical metaphysical issues. Obviously different scholars will integrate such consideration into their interpretations in different ways. Nonetheless, it is unacceptable to read Nietzsche nontechnically, as if he advanced the simplicities of Nietzscheanism. It is also unacceptable to read a later problematic into Nietzsche's work. Habermas does not entirely avoid either pitfall.

Locating Nietzsche in his context of an alleged "philosophical discourse of modernity," Habermas writes:

> With Nietzsche's entrance into the discourse of modernity, the argument shifts, from the ground up. To begin with, reason was conceived as a reconciling self-knowledge, then as a liberating appropriation, and finally as a compensatory remembrance, so that it could emerge as the equivalent for the unifying power of religion and overcome the diremptions of modernity by means of its own driving forces. Three times this attempt to tailor the concept of reason to the program of an intrinsic dialectic of enlightenment miscarried. In the context of this constellation, Nietzsche has no choice but to submit subject-centered reason yet again to an immanent critique – or to give up the program entirely. Nietzsche opts for the second alternative: he renounces a renewed revision of the concept of reason and *bids farewell* to the dialectic of enlightenment.[21]

21. *Ibid.*, pp. 85–86.

But this reads Habermas's context into Nietzsche, and does not explicate Nietzsche's context, let alone preserve Nietzsche's technical terminology. Habermas also forces different passages from Nietzsche into the following pattern:

> In particular, the historicist deformation of modern consciousness, in which it is flooded with arbitrary contents and emptied of everything essential, makes him doubt that modernity could still fashion its criteria out of itself – "for from ourselves we moderns have nothing at all." Indeed Nietzsche turns the thought-figure of the dialectic of enlightenment upon the historicist enlightenment as well, but this time with the goal of exploding modernity's husk of reason as such.
>
> Nietzsche uses the ladder of historical reason in order to cast it away at the end and to gain a foothold in myth as the other of reason: "for the origin of historical education – and its inner, quite radical contradiction with the spirit of a 'new age,' a 'modern consciousness' – this origin must itself in turn be historically understood, history must itself dissolve the problem of history, knowledge must turn its sting against itself – this threefold must is the imperative of the new spirit of the 'new age' if it really does contain something new, mighty, original and a promise of life." Nietzsche is thinking here of his *Birth of Tragedy*, an investigation, carried out with historical-philological means, that led him beyond the Alexandrian world and beyond the Roman-Christian world back to the beginnings, back to the "ancient Greek world of the great, the natural and human." On this path, the antiquarian-thinking "latecomers" of modernity are to be transformed into "firstlings" of a postmodern age – a program that Heidegger will take up again in *Being and Time*. For Nietzsche, the starting situation is clear. On the one hand, historical enlightenment only strengthens the now palpable diremptions in the achievements of modernity; reason as manifested in the form of a religion of culture no longer develops any synthetic forces that could renew the unifying power of traditional religion. On the other hand, the path of a restoration is barred to modernity. The religious-metaphysical world views of ancient civilizations are themselves already a product of enlightenment; they are too rational, therefore, to be able to provide opposition to the radicalized enlightenment of modernity.[22]

Nietzsche, however, may not refer to myth as "the Other of reason," and Habermas's construal reads Habermas's own version of Hegel into Nietzsche at the expense of Nietzsche's own positions. Certainly Nietzsche would not recognize his own positions in summations such as the following:

> Nietzsche owes his concept of modernity, developed in terms of his theory of power, to an unmasking critique of reason that sets itself outside the horizon of reason. This critique has a certain suggestiveness because it appeals, at least implicitly, to criteria borrowed from the basic experiences of aesthetic modernity. Nietzsche enthrones taste, "the Yes and the No of the palate," as the organ of a knowledge beyond true and false, beyond good and evil. But he cannot legiti-

22. *Ibid.*, p. 96.

mate the criteria of aesthetic judgment that he holds on to because he transposes aesthetic experience into the archaic, because he does not recognize as a moment of reason the critical capacity for assessing value that was sharpened through dealing with modern art – a moment that is still at least procedurally connected with objectifying knowledge and moral insight in the processes of providing argumentative grounds. The aesthetic domain, as the gateway to the Dionysian, is hypostatized instead into the other of reason. The disclosures of power theory get caught up in the dilemma of a self-enclosed critique of reason that has become total.[23]

Habermas, however, uses the synthetic overviews his approach offers to generate even more generality. Thus when summing up Nietzsche's relation to modernity, he writes,

> With Nietzsche, the criticism of modernity dispenses for the first time with its retention of an emancipatory content. Subject-centered reason is confronted with reason's absolute other. And as a counterauthority to reason, Nietzsche appeals to experiences that are displaced back into the archaic realm – experiences of self-disclosure of a decentered subjectivity, liberated from all constraints of cognition and purposive activity, all imperatives of utility and morality. A "break-up of the principle of individuation" becomes the escape route from modernity. Of course, if it is going to amount to more than a citation of Schopenhauer, this can only gain credibility through the most advanced art of modernity. Nietzsche can blind himself to his contradiction because he splits off the rational moment that comes to expression in the inner logic of avant-garde art from any connection with theoretical and practical reason and shoves it into the realm of metaphysically transfigured irrationality.[24]

Once again this conflates different aspects of Nietzsche's thought, and provides unifications that are missing in Nietzsche's texts. For Nietzsche does not claim to offer a critique of reason in the relevant sense, nor does he claim that his exposure of the pretensions of philosophy to access a neutral reason are "outside the horizon of reason." Here the technical distinction between what Nietzsche *claims* and what he *implies* is very important. Nor is it clear that a self-enclosed critique of reason can be attributed to him, or that it makes precise sense to refer to his alleged critique of reason as having become "total." Similarly, Habermas introduces a notion of "rationalization" that is not Nietzschean, again blurring Nietzsche's views with his own:

> Like all who leap out of the dialectic of enlightenment, Nietzsche undertakes a conspicuous leveling. Modernity loses its singular status; it constitutes only a last epoch in the far-reaching history of a rationalization initiated by the dissolution of archaic life and the collapse of myth.[25]

23. *Ibid.*
24. *Ibid.*, p. 94.
25. *Ibid.*, p. 87.

Apart from excessively regimenting the sense of Nietzsche, Habermas's way of reading Nietzsche also leads to a quasi-determinist account of future philosophical possibilities. After Nietzsche, Habermas implies, a totalizing critique of reason had to take the form either of a philosophical critique of metaphysics and scientific objectivism (Heidegger, Derrida) or a genealogy of enlightenment that unmasks the will to power behind all values (Bataille, Foucault):

> Nietzsche's critique of modernity has been continued along both paths. The skeptical scholar who wants to unmask the pervasion of the will to power, the revolt of reactionary forces, and the emergence of a subject-centered reason by using anthropological, psychological, and historical methods has successors in Bataille, Lacan, and Foucault; the initiate-critic of metaphysics who pretends to a unique kind of knowledge and pursues the rise of the philosophy of the subject back to its pre-Socratic beginnings has successors in Heidegger and Derrida.[26]

Habermas's attempts to link Heidegger, Derrida and Foucault with Nietzsche's alleged critique of reason, however, confuse Heidegger's position with two radically different French projects, positing a unity at the structural level that is basically misleading. Thus he alleges that:

> Heidegger and Derrida want to advance Nietzsche's program of a critique of reason by way of a destruction of metaphysics; Foucault wants to do so by way of a destruction of historiography.[27]

But this formulation is technically improper, since it uses Heidegger's term "destruction" but not in Heidegger's sense. It then gives the impression that Derrida stands in an epigonal relation to Nietzsche. This misconstrues Derrida's approach to "metaphysics," which Derrida holds cannot be transcended. Foucault's approach to historiography is also seriously misrepresented, as if Foucault intended a destruction of historiography in general, rather than a critique of specific over-idealist and over-teleological variants of it.

Predictably, Habermas is much better on Bataille, a thinker who is safely dead. The fact that Bataille does not advance technical philosophical theses also means that his work is less distorted by Habermas's broad summaries, while the fact that his views, unlike Derrida's, are not a live option, leads Habermas to produce a more nuanced reading. Nonetheless, once again Habermas ties Bataille to his own reading of Nietzsche rather than to Bataille's reading of Nietzsche. Indeed, Habermas reads both Bataille and Heidegger as advancing totalizing critiques of reason, and as therefore falling into traps that had already claimed Nietzsche:

> The two moments – that of reason and that of its other – stand not in opposition pointing to a dialectical *Aufhebung* [sublation], but in a relationship of ten-

26. *Ibid.*, p. 97.
27. *Ibid.*, p. 284.

sion characterized by mutual repugnance and exclusion. Their relationship is not constituted by the dynamics of repression that could be reversed by countervailing processes of self-reflection or of enlightened practice. Instead, reason is delivered over to the dynamics of withdrawal and of retreat, of expulsion and proscription, with such impotence that narrow-minded subjectivity can never, by its own powers of anamnesis and of analysis, reach what escapes it or holds itself at a remove from it. Self-reflection is sealed off from the other of reason. There reigns a play of forces of a metahistorical or cosmic sort, which calls for an effort of a *different* observance altogether. In Heidegger, the paradoxical effort of a reason transcending itself takes on the chiliastic form of an urgent meditation conjuring up the dispensation of Being, whereas, with his heterological sociology of the sacred, Bataille promises himself enlightenment about, but ultimately no influence over, the transcendent play of forces.[28]

## *Heidegger*

Habermas has both political and intellectual reservations about Heidegger, and the former compound the latter. Habermas, quite properly, makes much of Heidegger's disgraceful involvement with the Nazis, and, less judiciously perhaps, cites Farías's exposé with evident sympathy.[29] He also attempts to insinuate a substantive connection between Heidegger's later philosophical views and his politics. Indeed he implies that Heidegger's involvement with the Nazis was structurally crucial for his philosophical development:

> I suspect that Heidegger could find his way to the temporalized *Ursprungs-philosophie* of the later period only by way of his temporary identification with the National Socialist movement – to whose inner truth and greatness he still attested in 1935. [30]

A comparison here with Philippe Lacoue-Labarthe's *Heidegger, Art and Politics: The Fiction of the Political*[31] is methodologically revealing. Lacoue-Labarthe is able, as Habermas is not, both to present Heidegger's position fairly, and also to diagnose a pathology associated with it that goes to the construction of "the political" in modern German culture.[32] On the other hand, he cannot recognize the structural points at which Heidegger's philosophical development made him susceptible to option taking that is not related to discursive rational argumentation. Here it is Habermas who grasps the link between philosophical technicalities and subsequent catastrophe. Habermas, however, oversimplifies the relevant mediations and

---

28. *Ibid.*, pp. 102–3.
29. See Victor Farías, *Heidegger and Nazism*, trans. by P. Burrell and G. R. Ricci, Philadelphia, 1989.
30. *The Philosophical Discourse of Modernity*, p. 155.
31. P. Lacoue-Labarthe, *Heidegger, Art and Politics*, trans. C. Turner, Oxford, 1990.
32. *Ibid.*

underestimates the extent to which Heidegger's late philosophy could go with many different political enthusiasms, with varying ethical and social consequences. Perhaps because of his general tendency to sublimate rather than to articulate theological choices, Habermas fails to explore why it was Heidegger the reader of Nietzsche who opted for Nazi spiritual revolution rather than the theologically minded German intellectuals who were manifestly attracted by the late Heidegger's philosophical views.

In contrast, Habermas provides a capable exposition of some of the main doctrines of *Being and Time*, but then fails to engage in detail with the rest of Heidegger's enormous corpus. Instead, like Adorno, to whose work he is probably indebted, he seems unable to follow what the late Heidegger sought to convey by terms such as *Ereignis.* Instead, he caricatures Heidegger as a pseudo-seer who returned to the discredited Romantic call for a new mythology and dubs his late thought a temporalized philosophy of origins. Here Habermas misses the philosophical point and force of the late Heidegger's ideas, including their subversive potential, to which scholars such as David Kolb and John Caputo have rightly drawn attention.[33] One could share, as I do, Habermas's distaste for both the methodology and the substantive claims of the late Heidegger without denying that this part of his work demands exegetically rigorous and philosophically precise interrogation. Habermas, however, provides a vulgarized interpretation of Heidegger's strategies, as if Heidegger was a Nietzschean irrationalist who attempted to undermine Western rationalism by a critique of "metaphysics" in a vulgar rather than in a highly technical sense of "metaphysics." Similarly, the parallel with Bataille leads Habermas to suggest that both writers develop "their theory" by way of a narrative reconstruction of the history of Western reason, and that Heidegger interprets reason as self-consciousness, claims that seem colored by Habermas's reading of Bataille.[34]

### Derrida

Habermas on Derrida is magisterial, but off-target in crucial respects. Habermas reads Derrida as an inverted foundationalist positing an arche-writing that is a subject-less generator of structures. Once again his discussion is decontextualized, insensitive to the nuances of Derrida's French (Habermas approaches Derrida via North American literary receptions),

33. See D. Kolb, *The Critique of Pure Modernity: Hegel, Heidegger and After,* Chicago, 1986, and J. Caputo, *Radical Hermeneutics: Repetition, Deconstruction, and the Hermeneutic Project,* Bloomington, 1987. See the more subtle and balanced discussion, "Work and Weltanschauung: The Heidegger Controversy from a German Perspective," especially the footnotes, in J. Habermas, *The New Conservatism: Cultural Criticism and the Historians' Debate,* trans. by S. W. Nicholsen, Oxford, 1989, chapter VI.

34. *The Philosophical Discourse of Modernity,* p. 103.

and omissive of problems of changing developments from book to book.[35]

Habermas has no difficulty in identifying the implausibility of Derrida's early claims about "writing," his attempt to assert the priority of "writing" over speech, and his notion of an "arche-writing" or system of signifiers from which both writing and speech derive. He also goes to the heart of the matter when he notes that Derrida is still committed to a philosophy of the subject rather than to a genuinely social ontology. What is missing in Habermas's treatment is an appreciation of what Derrida is trying to achieve. When it comes to Derrida's engagement with Western metaphysics, Habermas's discussion is flat-footed, as if Derrida wrote a medieval ontology manqué, without irony or wit. Once again, he uses coloring material to prejudice both the exposition and the evaluation of Derrida's oeuvre; in this case alleged links between Derrida and Jewish mysticism.[36] And once again the relevance of such Jewish mysticism is not the issue, as Kevin Hart's superb discussion of Derrida's work in the context of negative theology shows; the issue is Habermas's prejudicial handling of this theme.[37]

Habermas approaches Derrida in the context of the need to reject any levelling of philosophy and literature, and the need to oppose attempts to assert the authority of rhetoric over logic.[38] Here Habermas is concerned to reverse the spread of nonsense emanating from some of Derrida's followers, especially in the United States. Unfortunately, Habermas seems to attribute the vulgarizations of the Derrideans to Derrida himself. Whereas Habermas gives a very careful analysis of Derrida's early work on Husserl, he fails to understand Derrida's later work, and misses the point of Derrida's literary style and suspensive irony. He does not recognize that Derrida does not want philosophy to become literary criticism and himself admits that his own work is "not properly philosophical." He also fails to appreciate that Derrida rejects attempts to reduce logic to rhetoric, and that he is arguing for irreducible contamination, not for the displacement of logic. Four quotations from Derrida give a sense of the vast gap between the straw man Habermas constructs and the French thinker who insists that the problem of the categories is not a problem of language (*pace* Benveniste):[39]

35. For a different but related interrogation of Habermas's reading of Derrida, see C. Norris, "Deconstruction, Postmodernism and Philosophy: Habermas on Derrida" in *What's Wrong with Postmodernism? Critical Theory and the Ends of Philosophy*, London, 1990.

36. *The Philosophical Discourse of Modernity*, p. 182.

37. See K. Hart, *The Trespass of the Sign: Deconstruction, Theology and Philosophy*, Cambridge, 1989.

38. *The Philosophical Discourse of Modernity*, pp. 161–210.

39. For a useful comparison, see R. Boyne's recent study, *Foucault and Derrida: The Other Side of Reason*, London, 1990. Although he is more sensitive than Habermas to the ambiguities of Derrida's French, Boyne sees Derrida as "opposing reason" (p.90).

It is true that "deconstruction" has focused on philosophical texts. And I am of course a "philosopher" in the institutional sense that I assume the responsibilities of a teacher of philosophy in an official philosophical institution – *l'Ecole Normale Supérieure*. But I am not sure that the "site" of my work, reading philosophical texts and posing philosophical questions, is itself properly philosophical. Indeed, I have attempted more and more systematically to find a non-site, or a nonphilosophical site, from which to question philosophy. But the search for a nonphilosophical site does not bespeak an anti-philosophical attitude.[40]

In a certain sense it is true to say that "deconstruction" is still in metaphysics. But we must remember that if we are indeed inside metaphysics, we are not inside it as we might be inside a box or a milieu. We are still in metaphysics in the special sense that we are in a determinate language. Consequently, the idea that we might be able to get outside of metaphysics has always struck me as naive.[41]

The difference between our modes of thought does not mean that I or other "modern" thinkers have gone beyond Plato, in the sense of having succeeded in exhausting all that is contained in his texts. Here I return to what I was describing as the "future" of a Heideggerian text. I believe that all of the great philosophical texts – of Plato, Parmenides, Hegel or Heidegger, for example – are still before us.[42]

It is as impossible to say what philosophy is not as it is to say what it is. In all the other disciplines you mention, there is philosophy. To say to oneself that one is going to study something that is not philosophy is to deceive oneself. It is not difficult to show that in political economy, for example, there is a philosophical discourse in operation. And the same applies to mathematics and the other sciences.[43]

Of course, Habermas makes an outstanding contribution by problematizing Derrida's ability to establish theoreticity for his major claims. Leaving aside the vexed question of Habermas's accusation that Derrida (like Nietzsche, etc.) falls into performative self-contradiction, Habermas is probably right to signal that Derrida's radicalism tends to cultural displacement rather than theoretical problem solving. Indeed, Derrida's subsequent shifts and resorts to ever more refined subtleties provide some support for this.

## Foucault

Habermas's reading of Foucault is also extremely shrewd at the level of tendency critique, but, at least in part, misdirected.

40. R. Kearney, *Dialogues with Contemporary Continental Thinkers*, Manchester, 1984. Interview with Derrida, Paris, 1981, p.108.
41. *Ibid.*, p. 111.
42. *Ibid.*, p. 113.
43. *Ibid.*, p. 114.

Habermas is disturbed by Foucault's refusal to legitimate his social criticism by resort to reasons, by his positivist suspensions of meaning and value, and by his attempts to avoid normative conceptions of reason. He rightly observes that Foucault in revisionary methodological vein tends to overlook the degree to which interpretation is unavoidable and always involves participation in a horizon of socially shared meaning.[44] This reservation, however, in no way justifies Habermas's over-reading of Foucault as a Nietzschean irrationalist, not only because Foucault's debts to other thinkers (Maurice Blanchot, Canguilhem) qualify his borrowings from Nietzsche and the use to which he puts them, but because it is not methodologically justifiable to conclude from the fact that a thinker refuses to assert certain positives that he asserts the negatives of the same positions.

The coercive effects of Habermas's regimentative readings of Foucault's work can be clearly seen in the following passage:

> Schelling and the Romantic philosophy of nature had earlier conceived of madness as the other of reason brought about by excommunication, but of course within a perspective of reconciliation alien to Foucault. To the extent that the bond of communication between the madman (or the criminal) and the rationally constituted context of public life is severed, both parts suffer a deformation – those who are now thrown back upon the compulsive normality of a reason that is merely subjective are no less disfigured than those expelled from normality. Madness and evil negate normality by endangering it in two ways – as what disrupts normality and puts it in question; but also as something that evades normality by withdrawing from it. The insane and the criminal can develop this power of active negation only as inverted reason, which is to say, thanks to those moments split off from communicative reason.
>
> Foucault, along with Bataille and Nietzsche, renounces this figure of thought from Idealism, which is supposed to grasp a dialectic inherent in reason itself. For him, rational forms of discourse are always rooted in strata that limit monological reason. These mute foundations of meaning at the basis of Occidental rationality are themselves meaningless; they have to be exhumed like the nonlinguistic monuments of prehistory if reason is to come to light in interchange with and in opposition to its other. In this sense, the archaeologist is the model of a historian of science investigating the history of reason, having learned from Nietzsche that reason develops its structure only by way of the exclusion of heterogeneous elements and only by way of a monadic centering within itself. There was no reason before monological reason. And so madness does not appear to be the result of a process of splitting off in the course of which communicative reason first became rigidified into subject-centered reason. The formative process of madness is simultaneously that of a reason which emerges in none other than the Occidental form of self-relating subjectivity. This "reason" proper to German Idealism, which was meant to be more primordial than that

embodied within European culture, appears here as just that fiction by which the Occident makes itself known in its specialness, and with which it assumes a universality that is chimerical, at the same time that it both hides and pursues its claim to global dominance.[45]

There is also a problem with the way Habermas reads German systematicity into Foucault's French moralist counter-history. Habermas makes the disastrous mistake of reading Foucault as a systematic thinker. Habermas assumes, for example, that Foucault has *a theory* of power and then argues against Foucault that this theory is self-referential.[46] But he does not show that Foucault intends to advance a *theory* of power. Similarly, according to Habermas, Foucault raises power to the status of a basic transcendental-historical concept, but this, arguably, is precisely what power in Foucault is not.[47] More fundamentally, Habermas misses the spirit and tone of Foucault's texts. He ignores the obvious jokes. For example: the smiling counterpoint of a title such as *Folie et déraison: Histoire de la folie à l'âge classique*. He then points out, quite correctly, the consequences that follow from a prosaic and humorless reading, whereas an exegesis based on an appreciation of Foucault's irony would have led Habermas to grasp both the local objects of many of Foucault's passages (and hence his loyalty to modernity and the Enlightenment) and also his French moralist intentions.

In the same way Habermas fails to appreciate that Foucault's work is not open to the type of objection he raises unless Foucault presents his claims as theory, and not as culturally creative counter-history. When Habermas charges Foucault with performative self-contradiction and alleges that he cannot account for his own position, he is correct vis-à-vis one phase of Foucault's work, the phase in which he played the para-theorist, in self-satirical mode, a point to which again Habermas is less than sensitive. Habermas, in short, gets the genres wrong where Foucault is concerned, and misses the antitotalizing rather than antirational, let alone "irrational" implications of the intellectual challenges Foucault offers, challenges often not necessarily incompatible with his own emancipatory intentions.

## V

Habermas today might accept the thrust of many or some of these scruples, pointing out, quite correctly, that it is unfair to make too much out of "lectures," and noting that it is not difficult to criticize interpretations advanced some years ago in the light of evidence not entirely, or not easily,

45. *Ibid.*, p. 412, footnote 3.
46. *Ibid.*, p. 254.
47. *Ibid.*, p. 359.

available at that time. Certainly it is the case that the lecture format makes the argument of the volume less accessible than it might be, especially since key ideas are presented under topics, rather than in logical order, and are sometimes buried in very rich text. It is also only fair to emphasize that the tendency to read other thinkers in terms of one's own problematics is far from uncommon among philosophers, that Jaspers and Heidegger read both Kant and Nietzsche in just this way, and that much the same can be said for many works on Hegel written by philosophers rather than professional Hegel scholars. It is also only proper to note that historical and exegetical slippage is commonplace in works by Anglo-Saxon and French philosophers. The need for a more articulated ethics of reading where philosophical texts are concerned is endemic, as feminist scholars have insisted for some time. Nonetheless, the doubt remains that the tendency (1) to deploy inflationary and prejudicial terminology; and (2) to read evidence in ways that converge with one's own theoretical commitments, tendencies I have identified in *The Philosophical Discourse of Modernity*, are not entirely absent from Habermas's social theorizing more generally.

## VI

Habermas's outstanding contribution to contemporary social theory lies in his advocacy of a differentiated concept of rationality and in his refusal to endorse various attempts to transcend "reason." He has gained a worldwide audience precisely because, unlike the work of Lukács or Adorno, his claims depend neither on adopting an allegedly correct political standpoint, nor on deriving mysterious insights from Western high art objects. Moreover, in contrast to other thinkers in the Critical Theory tradition, Habermas has again and again shown himself prepared to reformulate his views in the light of relevant objections. In place of political dogma or paraphilosophical uplift, Habermas offers theories that are open to revision when and as relevant criticisms or improvements are suggested. Here Habermas's example has been followed by some of the best post-war German philosophers and social theorists, including Albrecht Wellmer and Axel Honneth.

Habermas's work also draws on many different disciplines. In the process it calls into question the exact status of philosophy and its relation to sociology. The danger, however, is that methodological controls developed in one particular discipline may be lost in a transdisciplinary fusion. Insofar as Habermas's work involves argumentational claims, historical claims, and sociological claims (among others), there is a problem about the methodological controls that discipline his discursive practices. For whereas Habermas has a magisterial command of argumentational claims, it is fair to comment that his sociological claims are more derivative and parasitic on the work of others, and that his historical claims are dramatic and rhetorical rather than analytically rigorous or empirically precise. Of course, it can be said that Habermas is not an intellectual historian but a social and political thinker, and that his interpretations of other thinkers' works are instrumental to his arguments. It is the arguments that matter, even if they turn out not to apply to the thinkers Habermas discusses in quite the way Habermas suggests. But the problem is that Habermas at times constructs the terms of debate in ways that involve inflationary non-analytical terminology and rhetorical rather than critical historical claims. To this extent, it is possible to challenge him to reform his own discursive practices in order to better advance his own critical intentions.

To the degree that Habermas works with inflationary and unclear socio-historical terms, this goes to his theoretical aspirations. This can be seen from statements such as that

> Even in modern societies, a diffuse common consciousness takes shape from the polyphonous and obscure projections of the totality.[48]

or that:

> . . . even modern, largely decentered societies maintain in their everyday communicative action a virtual center of self-understanding, from which even functionally specified systems of action remain within intuitive reach, as long as they do not outgrow the horizon of the lifeworld. This center is, of course, a projection, but it is an effective one. The polycentric projections of the totality – which anticipate, outdo, and incorporate one another – generate competing centers.[49]

Another issue that goes to Habermas's social theorizing generally is the use he makes of idealizations and typologies. Such idealizations and typologies give his work apparent range, but, as in the case of Weber, they open up the danger that patterns found in contingent historical facts are turned into structural principles that explain those facts as if actual history manifested an ahistorical structural logic. This danger is increased in Habermas's case because his idealizing and typologizing is ethnocentric to Western European or even German experience. It also tends to build in a very committed secularist reading of Western sociocultural development that is insensitive to the persistence of religion and to the resilience of antimundane views of the world, especially in non-Western cultures.

A final issue is the effects that Habermas's homologizing tendencies have on his treatment of specific issues. Habermas's approach tends to interrelate issues about the Enlightenment, rationality and modernity in

48. *Ibid.*, p. 359.
49. *Ibid.*

ways that make it difficult to clarify what is contingent in each case, and also the degree to which any one implies the others. Hence, one challenge to Habermas is to consider whether there are not dimensions of human experience that cannot usefully be reduced to "moments of reason." Another is to consider whether modernization and rationality may not need to be theorized separately if the complexity of their undoubted connections is to be adequately explored. Put simply, there are reasons for the difficulties that Habermas has with the type of issues raised by debates about "reason and its Other." Habermas cannot easily accommodate heterological, prediscursive, corporealist, or antimundane considerations, and his difficulties are related to the way in which he opts for a secularized doctrine of the approach (*Logoslehre*) to the particularities and disorders of human social history. There is a certain ethnocentrism in his tendency to construct theoretical issues in terms of the vocabularies of Kant, Hegel, Marx and Weber, and there is a modern chauvinism in his tendency to repeat obviously interested accounts of key concepts such as modernity proposed by German philosophers. Given that the moves which Habermas makes toward intellectually coherent and analytically rigorous social theory are to be applauded, a certain heteronomy and bias, not least at the level of terminology, remains. To this extent, it may be misleading to contrast Habermas's work with that of thinkers who opt for "the Other of reason." For the deployment of "reason" for purposes that go beyond the requirements of strict theoreticity is an issue that arises within Habermas's work itself.

# –8–

# Reconceiving Truth and Reason

## RICHARD CAMPBELL

One of the basic ingredients in the Enlightenment ideal of reason was the assumption that by its exercise we can attain truth and thereby discern what is conducive to the good life. The unabashed optimism of this ideal was itself fashioned in response to the breakdown of the synthesis of Christianity and Aristotelianism, which had been the great philosophical achievement of the high Middle Ages. Reliance on revelation was no longer necessary for learning the truth; the rigorous exercise of human reason could yield knowledge of all reality.

This ideal has now come under intense questioning through widespread disillusion with the capacity of our intellectual faculties to deliver unvarnished truth. As a result, the role of reason has in our time been reduced to the purely instrumental task of calculating the cost-benefits of various possible means to attain preferred ends, the ultimate selection of which is strictly irrational. It is this narrowing down of the scope of reason that has enabled the economists in our time to capture the concept of rationality to such an extent that public discourse concerning rational courses of action is now largely carried on in terms derived from the economic vocabulary. It is ironic that public rhetoric couched in these terms should invoke the resonances of the Enlightenment ideal at the same time as its essential rationale has been whittled away.

If we are to think our way through these issues, we need to investigate how truth itself has been conceived; a radical critique of reason involves a radical examination of the concept of truth. This concept had become problematic long before Kant penned his first *Critique*. Yet although this problem is arguably the constituting issue of the discipline of Philosophy, the philosophers who have most clearly understood its fundamental character have been those writing in the German tradition. One of the most interesting attempts in recent times to grapple with it is to be found in the work of Jürgen Habermas. He has been attempting to develop a "consen-

sus theory" of truth within a refashioned concept of "communicative rationality" in order to salvage something of that Enlightenment ideal. But I
believe that we can only understand his project once it is placed against the
background of the severing of the essential linkage between truth and reason implicit in that ideal. Accordingly, this paper will begin with a sketch
of the crisis in the concept of truth generated by the breakdown of the
medieval Christian-Aristotelian synthesis. I will then outline the responses
of Kant, Hegel, Kierkegaard and Heidegger, by way of introducing the
more detailed discussion of Habermas's recent attempts to reconceive these
two concepts.

## The Breakdown of Medieval Synthesis

The standard medieval definition of truth, coined by Isaac Israeli and
adopted by Avicenna, Thomas Aquinas and many others, was *adaequatio
intellectus et rei*. The crucial question was how this "conformity" of intellect and reality is possible. In brief, the answer, developed most influential-
ly by Aquinas from Aristotelian sources, took it that the very same form
that is individuated in some particular piece of matter can also inform the
intellect of a particular knower. Since the form of an entity, and not its
matter, is what determines its nature or essence, this double occurrence of
the form ensures that the nature or essence of the entity is knowable.

Underlying this epistemology, and giving it plausibility, was the Christian doctrine that everything in the world was created by the Divine Word
and so had an intelligible character. Consequently, there was built into the
creation a *convenientia*, a fitting, of the intellect of a knower to how things
are, which made truth (in this sense) possible. Likewise, the doctrine of
creation also reinforced what I call the "objectual" conception of truth,
which derived from Plato. For him, although statements (*logoi*) are certainly said to be true, fundamentally truth is ontological in status – it means
the unhiddenness of the Real – whereas falsity has its locus not in reality
but in discourse. This conception had entered the theological tradition via
Augustine's Christianized neo-Platonism, which had identified truth with
God (which, of course, makes no sense if truth is fundamentally a feature
of statements). So, applying Israeli's definition to this "ontological truth,"
things themselves could be said to be true to the extent that they con-
formed to the idea of them in the Divine intellect, in accordance with
which they were created. In this way at the hands of the medievals the doctrine of creation provided a twofold support for this definition of truth.
Nevertheless, despite that, it was this same doctrine that eventually undermined the Aristotelian metaphysics invoked by that epistemology and as a
result generated a radical problem about truth.

To understand how this happened we need to look at the model of scientific explanation developed by the medievals out of Aristotle. As I reconstruct that model, to explain some natural phenomenon required a five-step process. The first step is to identify all the particular agents at work in the situation. Next, the "violent" behavior of each entity – i.e., the behavior that results from the imposition of the action of other agents upon its own – can be resolved into the natural behavior of each agent. Thirdly, the natural behavior of any agent is the necessary expression of its nature or essence. Fourthly, the nature of any entity is determined entirely by its form (not its particular matter). Finally, forms can be articulated in definitions, which therefore provide the basic premises for an explanation. In the metaphysics underlying this model, there are only two possible sources of contingency: a) the occurrence of some form in this particular piece of matter, rather than in some other; and b) the conjunction of those particular agents that happened to be at work in the situation. The former plays no part in explaining any phenomenon, and, given the latter, the rest is strictly necessary and so yields strictly deductive accounts of why the phenomenon occurred. That was its attraction as a model of explanation.

But for theologians insistent upon the free and omnipotent sovereignty of God, that was much too much necessity. As they thought through the implications of Christian doctrine, they came to insist that creation involved more than God's choosing to instantiate some selection out of an infinite array of eternal forms, each with its own intrinsically necessary nature. Rather, God could do anything that did not involve a contradiction – and even about this there were debates. Furthermore, there were problems about the status of the Divine ideas, despite some ingenious suggestions of Aquinas. How could they be many and distinct, when Christian theology could admit no real distinctions within God other than the special case of the three Persons of the Trinity? Centuries of complex and technical discussions concerning these issues led, by the seventeenth century, to the abandonment of Aristotelian metaphysics. In particular, this medieval explanatory chain broke apart with what I call the "fracture of the forms." This decisive break is marked by Locke's distinction between the "real essence" of a thing, which in the traditional manner was taken to be its inner constitution from which its natural behavior flows, and the "nominal essence" of a thing, which is what the word naming it means. But in the crucial case of substances, Locke argued that we simply do not know whether these two match.

This fracture had far-reaching consequences, not least for truth. For it set up a dichotomy between thinking, concepts and words, on the one side, and reality, things, or objects, on the other. Unless that gulf could be overcome, the very possibility of truth, i.e., some unity between these two sides, remained deeply problematic. For while the Latin definition of Israeli dropped out of usage, philosophers like Hume still took truth to consist in "the conformity of our ideas of objects to their real existence,"[1] and Kant took truth to consist in the "agreement of knowledge with its object."[2]

## Bridging the Gulf

The British empiricists responded to this crisis about truth by rejecting innate ideas; the very fact that we have ideas shows that we have some intimations of reality. But this approach soon led to Humean skepticism. It was in continental Europe that philosophers took up the notion of an intuitive apprehension of truth within reason itself. But before long, that approach too had to confront Humean skepticism. How to work out constructive proposals that engaged with that problematic became the constitutive task of German philosophy from the late eighteenth century onwards. In this undertaking, the easy optimism of the Enlightenment ideal became more chastened and the issue of the "Other" of reason emerged either as that which had to be consigned to a region beyond the scope of reason, or as that which had to be overcome and assimilated by reason.

Kant's solution was to safeguard truth about objects by giving up on the question of whether things, in themselves, are the same as the objects of our knowledge. He argued that these objects are constituted out of the "manifold of sensation" by the structuring processes of our understanding, as we order that data within a spatio-temporal matrix and conceptualize it in terms of basic categories. But since the forms of space and time, and the categories, are necessary for us, they provide the framework for universal and necessary knowledge of objects.

It was not long before this Kantian solution was attacked, most notably by Hegel. He argued that Kant had committed himself to a study of what appears to be, to phenomena, and such a study can never arrive at what is. At best, he argued, what Kant offered was only a psychological description of the processes of knowing, that could not meet the demand of thought, which will be satisfied with nothing less than showing the necessity of its facts, of demonstrating the existence of its objects, as well as their nature and qualities. Furthermore, by denying the competence of reason to determine anything either with respect to things in themselves, or to the three comprehensive ideas (soul, world and God), Kant had failed to overcome

1. D. Hume, *A Treatise of Human Nature*, ed. L.A. Selby-Bigge, 2nd ed., rev. by P. H. Nidditch, Oxford, 1978, book 2, part 3, 10, p. 448.
2. Kant, *Critique of Pure Reason*, A58/B83, A191/B236, A642/B670.

the pervasive dichotomies that had been opened up by the collapse of the Christian-Aristotelian synthesis. The only effective way to overcome those dichotomies was to demonstrate the intelligibility of what there is and the reality of what is intelligible. Hegel's strategy for doing so involved nothing less than a fundamental rethinking of the concept of truth by means of the integration of history itself into the resulting philosophical system. To those present-day philosophers who unthinkingly follow the tradition (usually attributed to Aristotle but never fully affirmed until Locke), of taking judgments, statements, propositions or sentences as the locus of truth, this Hegelian project seems either nonsensical or confused from the outset. Yet Hegel was consciously and explicitly working against that tradition and was deliberately trying to reinstate that "objectual" conception of truth that is to be found in Plato and classical Christian theology.

So long as truth is conceived as something simply notional, the most it could mean is some correspondence between notion and reality. But insofar as that way of conceiving truth presupposes that thought, language and judgment are distinct from reality, things that can at best only mirror reality, it fails to take seriously that a statement or a thought is itself part of reality. But once that is understood, the problem of truth becomes that of achieving some harmony between those parts of reality that are sayings, judgings, thinkings, and those that are complex, changing things.

It is to Hegel's credit that he saw how the question should properly be posed. His own answer was that such a harmony will only be achieved when every item has found its proper place in the Whole; the "Other" of reason would thereby be overcome. That is why he says, in the context of his discussion of truth, that God alone is the thorough harmony of concept and reality; the existence of finite things does not measure up to their concepts. The invocation of God here is no aberration; on the first page of his *Encyclopaedia of the Philosophical Sciences* he says that the objects of philosophy are upon the whole the same as those of religion: "In both the object is Truth, in that supreme sense in which God and God only is the Truth."[3]

Nevertheless, Hegel was acutely aware, in the light of Kant's *Critique of Pure Reason*, that the very possibility of rational discourse about "the whole" had become deeply problematic. Consequently, simply to proclaim the reinstatement of such a conception of truth would be an act of dogmatism. Hegel saw quite clearly that not only must Kant's restrictions on the legitimate deployment of theoretical reason be overcome, but the shift in standpoint from which reason is deployed – the shift brought about by Kant's "Copernican revolution" – had to be taken fully into account. His guiding idea was that the True is itself engaged in historical development of a quite

3. *The Encyclopaedia of the Philosophical Sciences*, trans. W. Wallace, London, 1892, p. 3.

special kind. Only through development can the True arrive at a comprehension of itself, and become what it essentially is. Hence he writes,

> The True is the whole. But the whole is nothing other than the essence consummating itself through its development. Of the Absolute it must be said that it is essentially a result, that only in the end is it what it in truth is; and that precisely in this consists its nature, *viz.*, to be actual, subject, the spontaneous becoming of itself.[4]

That is, his strategy for finding a way beyond the Kantian restrictions is to reinstate the conception of truth of Christianized neo-Platonism through conceiving of the True as a result brought about by the self-becoming of the Absolute, i.e., the whole.

## Truth as Personal Appropriation

While in this way Hegel attempted to revive the Augustinian identification of truth with God, the harmony of concept and reality, the critical question is: can truth in this sense be attained by human thinking? And the answer must be: only if the Hegelian ambition of actually demonstrating the eventual *Aufhebung* (sublation) of the opposition between thought and reality succeeds. Most famously, Kierkegaard denied that such an outcome is humanly achievable. Kierkegaard does not deny the validity of the System; he simply maintains that, while Reality itself is a system – for God – it cannot be a system for any human individual. His sticking point is that man is necessarily located within the domain of finite existence, and therefore our proper concerns must equally lie there. As Kierkegaard sees it, it is "ludicrous" or "comical" for finite thinkers to attempt to transcend the realm of their own existence. To do so would involve identifying oneself with a universal and impersonal Spirit and forgetting that one is in actual fact human.[5]

It is not surprising that Kierkegaard, in ridiculing this Hegelian project, should develop a radically different conception of truth, summarized (perhaps mischievously) in the slogan: truth is subjectivity. While this infamous slogan is designed to sound shocking, it emerges out of a rigorous adherence to the standard definition of truth – formulated as the conformity of thought and being – that had been adopted by Hume and Kant. Kierkegaard's own account in terms of subjectivity is not an alternative to that, not a replacement for that; rather, it states how truth as traditionally defined has to be thought of, if it is to be humanly attainable.

Concerning this definition, Kierkegaard remarks that if "being" is

4. Hegel, *Phenomenology of Spirit*, trans. A. V. Miller, Oxford, 1977, p. 20.
5. S. Kierkegaard, *Concluding Unscientific Postscript*, trans. D .F. Swenson and W. Lowrie, Princeton, 1944, p. 109.

understood as empirical being, truth is at once transformed into an ideal toward which one strives but cannot ever fully attain. That is because both the knowing subject and the empirical object are in a process of becoming; since neither is a finished product, an identity of the two cannot be claimed. Kierkegaard's argument here is a remarkably insightful anticipation of the position arrived at laboriously by two generations of contemporary philosophers of science who nowadays speak of a "convergence" on the truth of our "best theories."[6] In fact, as Popper was honest enough to acknowledge, there is no guarantee that the process of falsifying empirical theories will ensure that those theories that survive falsification are converging on the truth; his own substitution of "verisimilitude" has been tried and found wanting. Kierkegaard's insight is sharper: as the conformity of thought and being, truth could be attained by objective reflection only when the process of becoming had stopped, but this would mean that empirical being had ceased to be what it fundamentally is.

Since objective reflection fails to provide a way to the truth for an existing individual, Kierkegaard then proceeds to turn attention inward to the subject. To appreciate this, let us reflect first of all on the fact that any doing is performed within the general process of becoming, which characterizes all empirical being.[7] Now, what is special about human becoming is that the process is self-directed; we decide what we shall do. Yet, when I think of something that I propose to do but have not yet done, the content of this thought, no matter how exactly specified it may be, is no more than a possibility. Similarly, if I think about something someone else has done, and so think of something real, I "lift this given reality out of the real and set it into the possible."[8] Thought thus ranges in the medium of possibilities. Translating such a conceived reality, i.e., a possibility, into reality cannot be effected by thought alone; it requires the exertion of the will, moved by interest, to realize possibilities. It is only here, in the moment when I myself deliberately actualize some possibility of which I have been thinking, that thought and being actually conform. Thus, truth, as traditionally defined, is attained only insofar as it is brought about through decisive action.

This has the radical consequence of severing the standard Enlightenment linkage between truth and reason, with the former taken as the proper object of the latter. For it has turned out that truth, as standardly defined, is humanly attainable, not by the exercise of pure reason, but by decisive action. Truth itself has thereby been shifted into the "Other" of reason.

Kierkegaard accepts another consequence of this account – that truth

6. See, for example, H. Putnam, *Mind, Language and Reality*, Cambridge, 1975, p. 290.
7. The approach taken here follows that of M. C. Taylor, *Kierkegaard's Authorship*, Princeton, 1975, p. 42ff.
8. *Concluding Unscientific Postscript*, p. 285.

can occur only momentarily. Once the action has been performed, the moment of truth is past. But not all decisions to act are equally significant. Those that concern Kierkegaard are the ones that have an "essential relationship to existence." Many items of knowledge are not of ultimate significance to me, and the question of truth with regard to them is ultimately a matter of indifference. Any item of knowledge that is not related, in the reflection of inwardness, to the question "how shall I be?" is accidental knowledge. "Only ethical and ethico-religious knowledge has an essential relationship to the existence of the knower."[9] That is why he focuses on "essential truth," that is, the truth that is essentially related to my own existence. Those decisions that resolve such questions – questions that objective reflection cannot determine – are just the ones that engage our passions: "In passion the existing subject is rendered infinite in the eternity of the imaginative representation, and yet he is at the same time most definitely himself."[10]

Kierkegaard locates truth in this tension of subjective inwardness. We can now appreciate his famous definition of truth: "An objective uncertainty held fast in an appropriation-process of the most passionate inwardness is the truth, the highest truth attainable for an existing individual."[11]

The invocation of subjectivity here has nothing to do with the capricious desires or private interests of an individual, nor does it mean that we can call truth whatever we like. It means rather that because an existing individual is always in a state of becoming, his life is a constant, passionate striving to realize in his concrete actions those ethical and ethico-religious ideals that he conceives, for these are the ones that touch upon his very existence. An existing individual can only do that for himself, and has to appropriate, in his own actions, the ideals he conceives in the face of the fact that the ultimate questions have no incontestable answers demonstrably beyond the questioning of reason, wherein thought could rest satisfied. Thus, the meaning of the slogan "truth is subjectivity" is that truth, in Kierkegaard's own words, "consists in nothing else than the self-activity of personal appropriation."[12] In this way, by working through the implications of the orthodox definition of truth for existing individuals, Kierkegaard succeeds in transforming the conception of truth.

## Truth as Revelatory Event

Kierkegaard's notion of existential truth was developed in the face of the failure of the Hegelian ambition. A truth that is lived transcends theoreti-

9. *Ibid.*, p. 177.
10. *Ibid.*, p. 176.
11. *Ibid.*, p. 182.
12. *Ibid.*, p. 217.

cal discourse in the same way as existence transcends thought. Can such discourse then never be said to be true? The answer to that disturbing question depends once more on the conception of truth. We have seen that the Kierkegaardian notion emerges from a rigorous application of the formula: the conformity of thought and being. If the conformity sought has to be taken as total, that is, if truth is attained only when the whole sphere of thought has been rendered identical with the totality of being – which is Hegel's conception of it – then Kierkegaard's persuasive answer is No. But might not our statements direct us toward those existing things that our statements purport to be about? And can we not verify, at least sometimes, that in this orientation towards some entity, it shows itself to be just as it was presented in the statement as being? Can we not then, in a more piecemeal fashion, justly claim that at least some of our statements are true?

It is along just such lines that Martin Heidegger began his life-long meditation upon "the phenomenon of truth." That phrase signals his search for an understanding that would reach deeper than the truth of statements to something more "primordial," to that which grants the "inner possibility" of true statements. His concern is not epistemological; still less is he interested in presenting some theory about how statements are true. Rather, he takes the different tack of addressing directly the conception of truth.

Heidegger begins to subvert the "traditional" assumption that assertion is the proper locus of truth by presenting assertion as a way of being toward the entities we encounter in the world. He argues that in making true assertions of the simple subject-predicate form, we are orienting ourselves, and our audience, toward the entity in question in such a way that this orientation "uncovers," or "discloses," that entity as it is. And when such an assertion is confirmed, what is to be confirmed is that the original orientation has in fact succeeded in uncovering the entity. It has succeeded in showing the entity just as it in fact is.

That is possible only if one has so oriented oneself toward the entity that it can be seen. It has, so to speak, to be brought out of hiding. Heidegger therefore characterizes the being true of assertions as meaning that the entities one is talking about have, in speaking, to be taken out of their concealment; one must let them be seen as something unconcealed (*alethes*); literally, one dis-covers them.[13] That dis-covering is what a speaker does for a hearer. Someone who knows what he or she is talking about "lights up" those entities so that the audience can come to know them too.

In this way, Heidegger argues that the possibility of truth (in the sense

13. M. Heidegger, *Being and Time*, trans. J. Macquarrie and E. Robinson, Oxford, 1973, pp. 56–57.

of the correctness of assertions) is grounded in what makes possible this disclosure of how things are. In *Being and Time* he infers from his analysis that, since being-true as being-uncovering is a way of being that we manifest, what is primarily "true" – that is, uncovering – is our way of being, which he calls *Dasein*. Entities within the world are true in a second sense, of being uncovered.[14]

But what makes this very uncovering possible is still more basic, more "primordial." The uncoveredness of entities that results from this uncovering is grounded in the world's disclosedness. But disclosedness, he takes himself to have shown, is that basic character of Dasein (*Da-sein:* being there) according to which it is its "there." I take that to mean that the basic character of that way of being which we manifest is to be identified with all that is involved with our being here, not just in the sense of being at some particular place, but being here in a worldly environment and projecting ourselves into it, with the finitude, limitations and possibilities such a way of being opens for us. Existing in such a way, we find our own way of being disclosed to us as being-in-the-world; the disclosedness of the world is coordinate with the disclosedness of our own way of being. "Disclosedness," he says, "pertains equiprimordially to the world, to Being-in, and to the Self."[15]

From this analysis, it follows that insofar as Dasein is essentially its disclosedness, to this extent it is essentially "true." This is the third and most basic sense of truth toward which Heidegger's account has been moving. The coordinate openness of the world to this way of being, and of this way of being to itself, is constituted, on Heidegger's account, by state-of-mind, understanding and discourse; that is, these three are how disclosure takes place. And since disclosure belongs in this fashion to the very constitution of our way of being, only with *Dasein*'s disclosedness is the most primordial phenomenon of truth attained.

Heidegger sums up this basic thesis with the theological-sounding slogan: *Dasein* is "in the truth" – a slogan balanced with its counterpart: its state of being is such that it is in "untruth." This latter is also stated as an ontological thesis. To be closed off and covered up is intrinsic to the factual occurrence of our being; that is, we just do happen to be in particular contexts, and our several destinies are inseparably bound up with the route we negotiate through all the other entities we encounter. Our way of being is acted out – as a matter of fact – within whatever are our particular contexts. These entities are always encountered "looking as if . . . ." We can, to some extent, penetrate their semblances and discover more of what they are – and in the process come to a deeper understanding of our own being

14. *Ibid.*, p. 263.
15. *Ibid.*

too – but neither how they nor how we are ourselves is transparent. Hence Heidegger's remark that entities have to be "snatched out of their hidden-ness"; truth (uncoveredness) must be wrested from them, by a kind of robbery. (For that reason, he suggests, it is no accident that the Greeks expressed the essence of truth by a privative expression, *a-letheia*.) Although Heidegger does not show much awareness of scientific practice, the point he is making here is well illustrated by the way an experimental scientist has to manipulate entities in order to get them to reveal what their natures are.

Accordingly, Heidegger presents the possibility of speaking (or writing) the truth as requiring a struggle to appropriate what has been uncovered, to defend it against semblance and disguise and to assure ourselves of its uncoveredness again and again. Even when an event of disclosure has occurred, repeated utterance of the same sentence that expressed that disclosure will not necessarily ensure that the original insight will be conveyed to successive audiences. It takes effort and repeated acts of insight to renew that initial disclosure. In his later writings, Heidegger tried to think his way ever deeper into this basic phenomenon of unconcealment – even to the point of giving away his early identification of it with truth. But despite these obscure and implausible efforts, his earlier analysis remains his lasting achievement.

## Habermas's Synthesis of Marx and Pragmatism

The different conceptions of truth developed by Kant, Hegel, Kierkegaard and Heidegger mark different responses to the pervasive dichotomy between thought and reality opened up by the breakdown of the medieval synthesis. If Hegel's answer of displaying the eventual convergence of the two in the Absolute is not accepted, the problem of truth and its relation to reason clearly remains to fuel contemporary debates. Is anything worth salvaging from the Enlightenment heritage?

One line, which runs from Kierkegaard through Heidegger to contemporary French philosophers like Derrida and Foucault, has proceeded in a neo-Nietzschean vein of denying any transcendent realities or values; all values, including "regimes of truth," are constituted through discourse and ultimately reflect struggles for power. For a spirit that will have nothing to do with universal schemes, foundational structures, or global historiography, even Heidegger is regarded as "too metaphysical." It is fruitless to search discourses for realities beyond discourse; there are just decentered networks of interactions between contending opponents.

The most interesting voice in contemporary German philosophy to engage with these issues is that of Jürgen Habermas. Habermas has come to accept, as do Derrida and Foucault, that the Enlightenment project assumed a subject-centered notion of reason, but denies that the rejection of subjectivity entails the abandonment of rationality. From his early attempt in *Knowledge and Human Interests* to sketch how critical social theory could be grounded in the forgotten experience of self-reflection to his lectures on *The Philosophical Discourse of Modernity*, Habermas has been developing a concept of reason located in linguistically generated intersubjectivity.

One of the objectives of Habermas's program is to restore the essential linkage between truth and reason; if reason can be relocated in intersubjectivity, and if truth can be reconceived as constituted through social action, truth can once again be understood as the proper object of reason. Truth, thus understood, will transcend individual subjectivity without needing to invoke some discourse-transcendent reality. The point of this strategy becomes clear only once it is seen as a response to the breakdown of that linkage between truth and reason, which is why I have devoted the first part of this paper to retracing the dialectic that has generated their severing. Let us now turn to examine in more detail his successive attempts to articulate a "consensus theory" of truth.

The systematic idea guiding *Knowledge and Human Interests* is one suggested by some undeveloped remarks of Kant, which were taken further by Fichte: that reason itself can only motivate rational inquiry, that is, be practical, if there are interests that determine the forms of rationality themselves. In Habermas's development of it, this idea is expanded into a comprehensive philosophical anthropology in which three basic modes of human existence are posited – work, interaction, and power – each of which grounds a "cognitive interest" (technical, practical, and emancipatory) aiming at self-preservation, at communication and intersubjectivity, and at freedom and responsibility respectively. In this scheme, each of these three cognitive interests generates a domain of knowledge: the empirico-analytic sciences, the historical-hermeneutic disciplines, and self-reflective critical theories respectively.

In this work, Habermas argues that the three basic domains of knowledge are not given *a priori* as Kantian forms of pure rationality, unsullied by empirical circumstances. Rather, they have themselves been constituted historically under determinate empirical conditions as expressions of the self-formative processes of the human species. He sees Marx as the first to articulate this central idea, although Marx tried to develop it purely in terms of the instrumental and social relations generated by labor, and so failed to realize the full significance of his own insight. Habermas calls these structures of rationality "quasi-transcendental," a term for which he has been much criticized because of its alleged ambiguity. But by that term

Reconceiving Truth and Reason

Habermas is deliberately signalling how his thinking is breaking out of the Kantian architectonic; the familiar distinctions between what is empirical and what is *a priori* fail to take account of how "transcendental" frameworks for the appearance of possible objects of study have themselves come to be formed under contingent circumstances.

If the forms of rationality arise from social structures through which both its labor is organized and mutual understanding is mediated by ordinary language, the truth of statements is likewise a social construct. In a Postscript, written in 1971, Habermas recounts how in his earlier days, under the influence of Dewey, he "could not always resist the temptation to oppose the realist view of knowledge by stressing the instrumentalist idea of truth implicit in pragmatism."[16] But in the book Peirce is the one he turns to for "a view of reality which critically examines meaning on the basis of a consensus-theory of truth."[17] He sees this as far from instrumentalist, since Peirce had separated problems of object-constitution from those of truth.

Habermas there argues that for Peirce reality is a "transcendental" concept. It is only under the conditions of the process of inquiry as a whole that reality is constituted as the object domain of the sciences.

> If the only propositions that count as true are those about which an uncompelled and permanent consensus can be generated by means of scientific method, then reality means nothing but the sum of those states of fact about which we can obtain final opinions.[18]

While reality is taken here to be independent of what any individual thinks about it, it is no Kantian "thing-in-itself," unknowable "other"; it depends on what that final opinion is, even though that opinion does not depend on how anybody in particular may actually think.

While Habermas argues that Peirce did not adhere consistently to this concept of reality, his principal complaint is that Peirce missed the opportunity, opened up by his own thinking, to take seriously the communication of investigators as a transcendental subject forming itself under empirical conditions. Had Peirce taken that step, Habermas claims, "pragmatism would have been compelled to a self-reflection that overstepped its own boundaries."[19] When investigators attempt to bring about consensus concerning metatheoretical problems, what they are doing is grounded in inter-subjectivity. Of course, when scientists are acting instrumentally they

16. "A Postscript to *Knowledge and Human Interests*," trans. C. Lenhardt, in J. Habermas, *Knowledge and Human Interests*, trans. J. J. Shapiro, Cambridge, 1987, p. 374.
17. *Ibid.*
18. *Ibid.*, p. 95.
19. *Ibid.*, p. 137.

## Richard Campbell

make use of representational signs and technical rules that are conventional. But the rules of empirical-analytic reasoning do not provide the framework for their attempts at reaching a consensus. As Habermas points out,

> It is possible to think in syllogisms but not to conduct a dialogue in them. I can use syllogistic reasoning to yield arguments for a discussion, but I cannot argue syllogistically with an other. . . . The communication of investigators requires the use of language that is not confined to the limits of technical control over objectified natural processes. It arises from the symbolic interaction of societal subjects who reciprocally know and recognize each other as unmistakable individuals.[20]

Reflection on the community of investigators, he contends, is necessary in order to work out thoroughly what is involved in a consensus theory of truth. But to have engaged in that would have burst the pragmatist framework.

Implicit in this analysis is the notion of an ideal speech-situation, where speakers are able to communicate and test each other's claims free from all those social pressures that inhibit and distort full mutual understanding. In *Knowledge and Human Interests* that notion was not at all worked out; in his later writing Habermas has given it increasing attention, so much so that commentators now speak of his "linguistic turn." Responding to critics, Habermas acknowledged in his Postscript that he had not yet sufficiently sorted out what are problems of object constitution and what are problems of validity (*Geltung*). Thomas McCarthy explains that Habermas became concerned with the criticism that the theory of cognitive interests, by tying all forms of knowledge to "deep-seated imperatives" of human life, undercuts the notions of objectivity and truth:

> Anchoring cognitive schemata to action schemata in this way seems to amount to a new form of naturalistic reductionism (in the case of the technical interests) or socio-historical reductionism (in the case of the others). What then becomes of the unconditional character usually associated with claims to truth? How can Habermas claim anything more than an interest-relative truth for his own theories? Doesn't his position involve him in the same type of difficulty that plagued, say, the radical pragmatism of William James?[21]

Furthermore, Habermas came to believe that the epistemological focus of his early work was too individualistic and subjectivistic to yield an adequate conception of consensus, which is structured through dialogue. Accordingly, his later writings are all directed towards working out what he calls a "universal pragmatics" in which the linguistic and logical features of language-use are presented in practical contexts of communicative action.

20. *Ibid.*
21. T. McCarthy, *The Critical Theory of Jürgen Habermas*, Cambridge, 1984, p. 293.

## The Consensus Theory of Truth

Crucial for the consensus theory of truth that Habermas then set about developing is a distinction between discourse and the realm he calls life-praxis, where people act and experience objects in the world. In the latter, action-related experience is acquired and shared. Communication here serves to announce experience; assertions have the role of a piece of information about experience with objects. Experience claims to be objective (by which he means it can be shared intersubjectively) and for that reason there is a possibility of error or deception. In saying this, he acknowledges that one possesses sense certainty concerning one's perceptions; in themselves perceptions cannot be false. So when we deceive ourselves, he says, it must be that there was, not this, but some other perception than we thought; or there was no perception at all even though we thought we had perceived something.[22] But communication in action-contexts does not discuss this possibility of error; its theme is our experience of objects in the world. A statement made in such a context implies a truth claim by presupposing the truth of the stated proposition, but the truth of that claim is not the explicit topic.

What happens, according to Habermas, is that from time to time people engaged in communicative action become aware that the claims they are implicitly making in communicating with one another are in fact problematic; some disagreement occurs which throws them into question. In order to overcome this disruption to interaction, these claims – which can no longer be taken for granted – need to be tested. So communication has, as it were, to be lifted onto another level where precisely the validity of the claims raised in action-contexts can be examined as to their justification. This other level of communication is what he calls discourse.

In discourse, Habermas says, we exchange no information, but rather arguments, which serve to ground or dismiss problematic "validity-claims." In his essay on "Theories of Truth"[23] and in later works like *The Theory of Communicative Action* this expression becomes a central theoretical term. When two or more speakers are engaged in exchanging coordinated speech-acts – i.e., making relevant comments on what each says, like questions and answers, commands and agreements, etc., – they operate in terms of a "background consensus." That consensus persists through their reciprocal recognition of four kinds of claims that all competent speakers implicitly raise with each of their speech-acts. These are:

a) that the utterance is intelligible;

22. "Postscript to *Knowledge and Human Interests*," p. 363.
23. "Wahrheitstheorien," in H. Fahrenbach, (ed.), *Wirklichkeit und Reflexion. Festschrift für W. Schulz*, Pfullingen, 1973, pp. 211–65.

–147–

b) that its propositional content (or the propositions presupposed in it) is true;

c) that it is right or appropriate for the speaker to be making that utterance; and

d) that the speaker is truthful and being honest.

So long as their utterances appear to the participants to be compatible with their experience, they continue to exchange validity claims in a constructive interaction, without explicitly adverting to them. That is, while all four validity claims are raised by every speech-act, they become the topic for discussion only when the verbal interaction is disrupted and the background consensus is shattered.

As his thinking along these lines has developed, Habermas has come to embed this account of the four kinds of validity claim in a much wider analysis of speech-acts. The details of that need not concern us here, although it is important to remark that he recognizes that the claim of intelligibility and the claim to truthfulness are of a rather different order than the other two. The claim to truthfulness, he says, can only be redeemed in action-contexts (i.e., not discursively). Furthermore, intelligibility has to be counted among the conditions of communication, for a hearer can ask "how do you mean?", "how should I understand that?" or "what does that refer to?" and can try discursively to reach agreement with the first speaker about the language they will jointly employ. But the claims to truth and legitimacy or appropriateness, once they are questioned, are genuine claims that have to be redeemed in discourse, and that requires a breaking off from the original communicative interaction.[24]

Having drawn this distinction between two levels of communication – in action-contexts and in discourse – Habermas locates the truth of statements within the latter. Discourse requires the suspension of the need to act and of the pressures of experience, so that the "force" of the argument is the only permissible compulsion and the cooperative search for truth the only permissible motive. In order to conduct discourse, we have to some extent to get outside the contexts of action and experience. As he explains:

> Because of their communicative structure, discourses do not compel their participants to act. Nor do they accommodate processes whereby information can be acquired. They are purged of action and experience. The relation between discourses and information is one where the latter is fed into the former. The output of discourses, on the other hand, consists in recognition or rejection of problematic truth claims.[25]

24. "Wahrheitstheorien," pp. 221–22. Unless otherwise indicated, the author is responsible for the translation of the various quotations.
25. "Postscript to *Knowledge and Human Interests*," p. 363.

Whereas in action-contexts truth claims are uncritically accepted, in discourse they are "rendered virtual" and dealt with hypothetically; we register a "reservation of existence" with respect to objects of experience (things, events, persons, utterances), as well as norms, and look at them under the aspect of possible existence or legitimacy.[26]

In discourse the same statement as occurred in an action-context can be asserted, but now the statement focuses on a state of affairs, an alleged fact, in order to make explicit or question a truth claim. It no longer brings to expression an experience that is objective (or even merely subjective); it now expresses a thought that is true or false. Of course, experience is not irrelevant to questions of truth; it can be cited in relation to an argument. For instance, one can make an experiment, but this experiment withdraws experience from practical life in order to subject it to reasoning, thus in effect transforming experience into data. By asserting a state of affairs, I precisely do not assert an experience (which is objective); I can only draw upon structurally analogous experiences as data in an attempt to legitimate the truth claim embodied in my statement.[27] So for Habermas, a state of affairs (*Sachverhalt*) is the propositional content of an assertion, of which the truth-value is problematic. Facts (*Tatsachen*) are existing states of affairs, but what is meant by that is the truth of propositions. Only states of affairs asserted, for example, by the uttering of statements, can be discussed – not facts. Experiences support the truth claim of assertions, but a truth claim can be redeemed only through argumentation. "A claim based in experience is in no way a grounded claim."[28]

One implication of this distinction between communication in action-contexts and in discourse is that it allows Habermas to state clearly what is wrong with the correspondence theory of truth, which takes truth to consist of the agreement of a statement with a corresponding fact. Following the English philosopher Peter Strawson, Habermas contends that facts have a status different from the things and events, persons and their assertions, that are objects of experience about which we put forward assertions and of which we assert something.[29] I have experience of objects; facts are what I assert. I cannot experience facts and cannot assert objects (or experience with objects). So, if the objects of our experience are something in the world, we may not say in the same manner that facts are "something in the world." But the correspondence theory of truth requires facts to be "something in the world" in just the sense that objects are. That is now seen to be a fatal mistake.

26. "Wahrheitstheorien," p. 214.
27. "Postscript," p. 364.
28. "Wahrheitstheorien," p. 218.
29. *Ibid.*, p. 215.

This objection leads Habermas back to the self-contradiction that Peirce had alleged against the correspondence theory. As Habermas summarizes the point,

> If we can attach no other sense to the term "actuality" (*Wirklichkeit*) than that we connect it with statements about facts, and conceive of the world as the embodiment of all facts, then the relation of correspondence between statements and reality becomes determined anew through statements. The correspondence theory of truth tries in vain to break out of the logico-linguistic sphere, within which alone can the validity-claim of speech-acts be clarified.[30]

Given his account of what facts are, this objection is well taken. If talk of facts has to be assigned to the sphere of discourse and explained in terms of the truth of statements, then it is not possible to explain truth in terms of correspondence between statements and some alleged items in the world called "facts."

All this suggests to Habermas what he calls a consensus theory of truth. Following Strawson, he distinguishes between the speech-act of assertion and the statement thus asserted. Assertions are linguistic episodes that are datable, whereas the statement made is a claim that some state of affairs exists; this is an invariant judgment that has a nonepisodic character. The question that is debated in discourse is whether the validity-claim raised by some assertion is redeemable or not. "We call statements true which we are able to substantiate (*begründen*)."[31] So, like "state of affairs" and "fact," the word "true" belongs to the logico-linguistic sphere; its meaning will become clear once it has been indicated what "redeemable in discourse" means.

Now, while he refers to experimentation as providing data that can be cited in attempts to legitimate a contentious truth-claim, Habermas refuses to take the positivist route of identifying truth as a property of those statements and theories that satisfy certain confirmation tests. The objection to doing so is that such tests do not uniquely determine particular statements and theories that could then be taken as true. At most, experimentation provides data that can be cited in an argument; it is the context of discourse that is paramount. So it is sociologically – by reference to the social circumstances under which assent is justified – that the operational character of truth has to be explicated. Truth may be ascribed only to those statements and theories that are capable of commanding an unforced consensus:

> I may ascribe a predicate to an object if and only if anyone else who could engage in a discussion with me would also ascribe the same predicate to the self-

30. *Ibid.*, p. 216.
31. *Ibid.*, p. 219.

same object. In order to distinguish true from false statements, I refer to the assessment of another – and in fact to the judgement of all others with whom I could ever undertake a discussion (in which I include counterfactually all discussion-partners whom I could find if my life-history were co-extensive with the history of the human world).[32]

Thus he concludes that the condition for the truth of statements is the potential agreement of all others. "Truth means the promise of attaining a rational consensus."

This sounds as if Habermas is defining truth in terms of rational consensus, as Peirce on occasions did. Nevertheless, it would be misleading to understand what is going on here as offering a formal definition of truth (or, indeed, to characterize the link between truth and consensus in the familiar but now contentious terminology of an analytic connection). "True," after all, is already a meaningful word in common use. So this "definition" cannot be just a stipulation; Habermas is trying to explicate what "true" means. For this reason, objections along the lines that he is confusing the meaning of "truth" with the method for arriving at true statements miss the point.[33] Habermas has indeed been widely criticized for confusing "to be true" with "to gain truth," which means something different. But as I read him, Habermas is not claiming that the meaning of "is true" is identical with the meaning of "is able to command a rational consensus." Rather, he is seeking to explain why those statements called true should have the ability to motivate a rational consensus.

Habermas, in fact, is more careful here than his critics. What he is saying is that a statement can be said to be true when the validity claim raised by the speech-act with which we assert that statement is legitimate, i.e., when that claim can be made good. The distinctions here are subtle, but they signify how his concern is not with the semantic meaning of the word "true" but with the pragmatic meaning of an act, the making of a truth claim.

"The truth of a proposition stated in discourses means that everybody can be persuaded by reasons to recognize the truth claim of the statement as being justified."[34] A statement is able to attract a consensus because there are persuasive reasons that can be adduced in its favor. Habermas makes his position quite clear on this point: "Truth is not the fact that a consensus is realized, but rather that at all times and in any place, if we enter into a discourse a consensus can be realized under conditions which identify this as a founded consensus. Truth means 'warranted assertibility.'"[35]

32. *Ibid.*
33. For a discussion of such objections, see T. McCarthy, *The Critical Theory of Jürgen Habermas*, Cambridge, 1978, p. 303.
34. "Postscript," p. 364.
35. "Wahrheitstheorien," pp. 239–40.

So he is not offering a definition of the word "true" (a nominal definition); he is proposing a substantive account of what truth consists of: warranted assertibility. That phrase from Dewey, which has also become prominent in present-day analytic discussions, he has now situated firmly within his overall account.

From this it is also clear that he is not equating truth with the *de facto* achievement of a consensus. Objections that take him to be doing so are thus misconceived. He understands quite well that discursive justification is a normative concept. The question is: under what conditions is an assertion warranted? Thinking about this has led Habermas into successive attempts to characterize what he calls "the ideal speech situation."

### The Ideal Speech Situation

In order to distinguish a founded consensus from one that is merely *de facto*, Habermas presents an account of "the peculiarly unforced force of the better argument" in terms of the "formal properties of discourse." Since he insists that arguments consist not of sentences but of speech-acts, the logic of discourse is not formal in the usual sense of formal logic. The crucial notion is the pragmatic one of cogency (*Triftigkeit*). A cogent or sound argument is one that can survive radical questioning, that is, questioning not only of the data put forward as relevant, but also of the warrant that connects that data to the conclusion (e.g., a general scientific law, a universal moral principle), of the backing for the warrant, which establishes it as plausible, even of the general conceptual scheme within which the claim being defended was originally put forward. Further, if and only if freedom to move between these argumentative levels is guaranteed by the formal properties of the discourse can a consensus be said to be rationally motivated, the result of the "force of the better argument," rather than caused by external constraints or internal barriers that inhibit full communication.

Thus stated, this condition might seem innocuous enough; it accords with much recent discussion of the way scientific theories have in fact been challenged and overthrown in favor of others. But Habermas explores further what is required for the condition to be met. His thesis is that the formal properties of discourse that guarantee the required freedom of movement, the necessary interrogative space, are those realized when the discourse is conducted in an ideal speech situation.

What is "ideal speech"? It is that form of discourse in which there is no other compulsion but the compulsion of argumentation itself; where there is a genuine symmetry among the participants involved, allowing a universal interchangeability of dialogue roles; where no form of domination exists. The power of ideal speech is the power of argumentation itself.[36] Such a situation must fulfil a number of conditions, summed up in the general symmetry requirement that for all participants there is a fair distribution of chances to select and employ speech-acts. Each must be free to put forward any assertion, or to call any into question, with the same chance to express their attitudes, feelings, intentions so that they can all be truthful in their relations to themselves and can make their "inner natures" transparent to each other. Each must have the same chance to command, to oppose, to permit, to forbid, and so on. Privileges in the sense of one-sidedly binding norms must be excluded so that the formal equality of chances to initiate and pursue any line of discussion can in fact be practised.

Only when these conditions are met can an agreement be recognized as rationally motivated, and not open to the charge of being less than rational, the result of open or latent domination. In this way Habermas forges a link between the truth of statements and "the intention of the good and true life," that he had foreshadowed in his inaugural lecture at Frankfurt in 1965. The concept of truth cannot be analyzed independently of freedom and justice. Even to approximate such an ideal speech situation demands an "ideal form of life" – one in which the social and political institutions and practices permit free, symmetrical, responsible, unconstrained discourse.

At this point questions that have been held back during the exposition crowd in. For instance, in what sense is this characterization of speech ideal? Is Habermas proceeding in a Platonic way to describe empirical situations in terms of a pure ideal that is perhaps aspired to but rarely, if ever, realized? It is easy to see why some of his Marxist critics should have accused him of idealism. But that is a misunderstanding. He readily admits that ideal speech is usually (and perhaps even always) counterfactual. But his claim is that it is an unavoidable supposition (*Unterstellung*) of discourse. It is made, and must be made, whenever we enter into discourse with the intention of arriving at rational agreement about truth claims, "on their merits."

Of course, we can never guarantee in advance that the discursive situation is such that only these merits will have force. In retrospect, often we can tell that it was not. But our entering into a discussion on that implicit supposition still makes a real difference. For that reason, in "Theories of Truth" Habermas insists that the ideal speech situation is neither an empirical phenomenon nor simply a construct, but is genuinely anticipated in every discourse. It is operationally effective. So he sees it as more than a regulative idea (in Kant's sense), even though he also acknowledges that no historical reality matches the form of life that could be characterized by reference to ideal

---

36. This summary is given by R. Bernstein, *The Restructuring of Social and Political Theory*, Oxford, 1976, p. 212.

speech. It is the constitutive condition of rational speech. Whether it is a delusion (from which it would follow that rational speech is a delusion) or whether the empirical conditions for its realization can in fact be brought about, cannot be answered *a priori*. Rather, the norms of rational speech contain a practical hypothesis, i.e., this ideal is one we can try to realize by social and political action.[37]

But in that case, how does this theory explain why anyone should try to realize the conditions of rational speech? In his earlier work, Habermas had argued that the forms of rationality must themselves be understood to be constituted by basic human interests. But when that is dropped, the questions return: Under what conditions will agents who have a clear understanding of their historical situation be motivated to overcome distorted communication and strive toward an ideal form of community life? What are the concrete dynamics of this process?

Richard Bernstein, who poses these questions, contemplates a reply that Habermas might give: that to require that a comprehensive theory of communicative competence should answer such questions is to place an illegitimate demand upon it. The aim of Habermas's theory is to provide a rational reconstruction of the formal conditions required for communicative competence. Only when that is clearly understood can we examine the historical forms of social evolution and the real potentialities for future development. But such a reply is not entirely satisfactory. There are different types and levels of action involved in the development of society, and a variety of ways of overcoming the crises that break out; there is no necessity that the resolution of a crisis will take the form of a movement toward an ideal form of community life. The question remains: Do we have reason to believe that the ideal community that Habermas claims is presupposed and anticipated in any form of communication will ever be realized, rather than the more ominous possibilities that confront us? If not, acts of communication will be anticipations of a form of social interaction that always remain utopian.[38]

On the theoretical level, too, there are difficulties with the idea of the ideal speech situation. One of its functions in Habermas's thought is that it enables him to deal with the standard objection to any consensus theory of truth, namely, that it leaves truth relative to a particular culture. Even if in some culture a consensus is achieved, might not the agreed propositions nevertheless be false? The ideal speech situation was invoked by Habermas to rebut this charge, to explain how the understandings of a whole culture could be rationally rejected. But the difficulty is not just that historical

37. "Wahrheitstheorien," pp. 258–59.
38. These questions are posed by R. J. Bernstein, *The Restructuring of Social and Political Theory*, Oxford, 1976, p. 224.

speech situations are in fact ideologically distorted and subject to oppressive constraints, and so not ideal. Mary Hesse has pointed to the deeper problem that there is no theory that uniquely corresponds to the world:

> If one accepts, along with Duhem, Kuhn and Feyerabend, that there is no ideal theoretical framework that would be uniquely "the best" interpretation of nature even in an ideally rational society and even with "complete" empirical evidence, then one is deprived of the notion of a supra-cultural theoretical truth.[39]

She thus defends the rationality of doubt concerning the truth of a consensus achieved in ideal conditions.

Hesse herself suggests that Habermas might interpret the truth of theoretical science, not in terms of a convergence of theories to an ideal single limit in an ideal society, but as a feature of present truth claims:

> Every theory making truth-claims in a particular conceptual framework includes its own "anticipations" of the total nature of the world as far as it is relevant to that theory. The commitment to anticipated consensus is the commitment to abandon falsified positions, and also to abandon conceptual schemes that do not lead to consensus. There is no last theory or theorist in the sense that science stops there, forever frozen in whatever conceptual scheme happens to be then current. But every serious theory and sincere theorist is "the last," in the sense that that is where the accountability in the face of ideal consensus operates for him or her. To enter the scientific community presupposes acceptance of that accountability.[40]

Habermas finds this interpretation of the universality of validity claims "exceptionally attractive."[41] We cannot simultaneously assert a proposition or defend a theory and nevertheless anticipate that its validity claims will be refuted in the future. So the idea of a "final consensus" does not mean that we have to represent to ourselves the limit value of a cumulative progress of knowledge in the form of an "actual sequence of theories;" it determines only the assertoric meaning of assertions, each in its place and at its time.

Accordingly, in his more recent writing Habermas has backed away from presenting his view in terms of ideal speech. He has conceded that at times he was guilty of using short-circuited formulations that ignore the mediations between the ethic of discourse and the practice of life. He no longer thinks it appropriate to speak of a form of life that we anticipate in the concept of an ideal speech situation. We can develop the idea of a soci-

39. M. Hesse, "Science and Objectivity" in J. B. Thompson and D. Held, (eds.), *Habermas – Critical Debates*, London, 1982, p. 108.

40. *Ibid.*, p. 109.

41. J. Habermas, "A Reply to my Critics" in Thompson and Held, *Habermas – Critical Debates*, p. 277.

ety in which all important decision-making processes are linked to institutionalized forms of discursive will-formation. But he now agrees that it is a mistake to think that we have thereby also formulated the ideal of a form of life that has become perfectly rational – there can be no such ideal.[42]

Significantly, in *The Theory of Communicative Action* (1981) the concept of the ideal speech situation does not occur. Communicative rationality cannot now be taken to provide either a utopian critical standard by which to judge concrete forms of life as a whole, or a *telos* toward which human history can be seen to be moving. Habermas agrees with Peter Winch that forms of life represent concrete "language games," historical configurations of customary practices, group memberships, cultural patterns of interpretation, forms of socialization, competencies, attitudes, and so on. "It would be senseless to want to judge such a conglomeration as a whole, the totality of a form of life, under individual aspects of rationality."[43] If we do want to judge whether a form of life is more or less failed, deformed, unhappy, or alienated, we can look if need be to the model of health and sickness; a normal, healthy life is not one that approximates to ideal limit values, but one that exhibits a balance, an equilibrated interplay of the cognitive with the moral and the aesthetic-practical.

## Communicative Rationality and Agreement

Habermas's latest approach is to reconstruct the idea of the ideal speech situation around the notion of communicative rationality. First of all, he distinguishes between action oriented to success and action oriented to reaching understanding. The latter, which is always social, is what he calls communicative action. To support this distinction, he invokes in an elaborated form J. L. Austin's distinction between "illocutionary" and "perlocutionary" speech-acts, that is, the distinction between what I am doing in saying something (e.g., making a promise) and what I am trying to achieve by saying something (e.g., to ward off criticism).[44] Habermas counts as communicative action those linguistically mediated interactions in which all participants pursue illocutionary aims and only illocutionary aims, with their mediating acts of communication.[45] That excludes all strategic use of language, by which one tries to achieve extrinsic ends.

Reaching understanding (*Verständigung*) is now proposed as the inherent *telos* of human speech. Habermas considers it to be a process of reaching agreement (*Einigung*) among speaking and acting subjects. That

---

42. "A Reply to my Critics."
43. *The Theory of Communicative Action*, I, p. 73.
44. J. L. Austin, *How to Do Things with Words*, Oxford, 1962.
45. *The Theory of Communicative Action*, I, p. 295.

requires more than a mood of collective like-mindedness; a communicatively reached agreement is "propositionally differentiated" and has to be accepted or presupposed as valid by the participants. More than a merely *de facto* accord (*Übereinstimmung*), processes of reaching understanding aim at an agreement that meets the conditions of a rationally motivated assent (*Zustimmung*) to the content of an utterance. That is, the speech-act of one person succeeds only if the other accepts the offer in it by taking (however implicitly) a "yes" or "no" position on a validity claim that in principle is open to criticism. Both participants base their decisions on potential grounds or reasons. It is within this model of speech that Habermas now locates his account of the redemption of validity claims through argument.

In developing the notion of communicative rationality in this way, Habermas is seeking to avoid the "idealist" overtones of his earlier formulations. His claim is to have delineated the structure and development of universal features of communication, which in different cultural and historical situations take on different concrete forms of manifestation. The ultimate test he seeks for his account of communicative rationality is its empirical, theoretical and critical fruitfulness for social theory and research.

Is this account of truth compelling? What should give us pause is the fact that, as his thinking has developed, Habermas has simply assumed that truth is exclusively a feature of propositions that occur either as the content of statements or as presuppositions in communicative action. To treat truth in this way is a relatively recent and contentious assumption in the philosophical tradition; the first to narrow truth down to the linguistic domain in this way was Locke. In adopting it, Habermas has taken over the orientation of the American pragmatists, and has left behind the conception of truth hinted at by Marx, which locates it constitutively in the context of action. (In this regard, there is a fascinating parallel between Kierkegaard and Marx, since both, in reaction against Hegel, located truth in the category of action, although in Marx's case that was always sociopolitical action).

Clearly, the crucial move in Habermas's approach is his taking the *telos* of human speech as reaching understanding. Is that evidently so? Of course, language is used with an orientation to reaching understanding. But is that the basic function of language, in terms of which all its other features are to be characterized? Or even of speech? After all, we have already seen how Heidegger explicates communication as "letting someone see with us what we have pointed out" and how, for him, the basic phenomena are the coordinated disclosedness of the world, being-in, and the self. In this vein, truth is to be understood as the disclosure of entities through which an openness unfolds. While communication will aim at mutual understanding, it is grounded in the opening of being.

This Heideggerian approach provides some content to a fundamental objection that can otherwise sound rather vague and empty. We considered above how Habermas tries to steer a course between idealism and relativism. The allegation that is often made against any consensus theory of truth is that an agreement, even one made in ideal conditions, might nevertheless be false. Now, that allegation does not need to be framed in terms of correspondence with the world. It could be framed in terms of there being a conceptual gap between any consensus and the disclosure of being; it could be urged that Habermas needs to supplement his defense of consensus with a Heideggerian conception of truth in order to explain how the reaching of understanding should indeed be considered the attainment of truth.

To be fair, Habermas does acknowledge that "reaching understanding" involves more than an intersubjective recognition of a single validity claim. He points out that in communicative action a speaker selects a comprehensible linguistic expression only in order to come to an understanding with a hearer about something and thereby to make himself understandable.[46] That three-fold characterization of communication does bear some likeness to that of Heidegger. But instead of appropriating the latter, Habermas invokes once again his elaboration of speech-act theory to flesh it out. However, in this account the conception of communication as letting someone share what has been pointed out in its definite character is lost. No room is made for the idea that in effective communication the hearer is "put in touch" with what the speaker is talking about.

What leads Habermas down this wrong path is his overriding concern with a particular form of rationality. He explicates processes of reaching understanding as aiming at an agreement that meets the conditions of rationally motivated assent to the content of an utterance. That is, of course, in keeping with his taking truth as exclusively a feature of statements, as belonging only to the logico-linguistic sphere. On both scores, his analysis of language-in-use betrays the rationalist bias of giving priority to discursive, propositional knowledge (*das Wissen*). It is knowledge of that kind, and not the knowledge of acquaintance (*das Kennen*), that he portrays a speaker as intending the hearer to accept and share. In making his "linguistic turn," for all that he emphasizes communication, Habermas in the end reduces truth in interactions to reaching accord on which propositions warrant assent, and reduces insight to argumentative validity. Accordingly, all that lies outside "the logico-linguistic sphere" remains the "Other" of reason and beyond the scope of truth.

46. *Ibid.*, p. 307.

The root of these difficulties is the adoption here of a form of speech-act theory that takes language use to be a thought-transference procedure, a conception that goes back to Locke. Despite his focus on communicative action, on the use of language in action-contexts, the speech-act model invoked by Habermas assumes that the speaker first of all has a thought, i.e., entertains a proposition, and then selects a comprehensible linguistic expression with the intention of getting the hearer to accept and share that proposition. Truth becomes a property of those claims, raised by the making of statements, which can be justified by discursive argument. This is a very psychologistic approach, one that analyzes language use ultimately in terms of the content of intentional states (beliefs, desires, thoughts, etc.). Paradoxically, it emerges that Habermas's "universal pragmatics" has adopted an analytic model of speech that takes insufficient account of the grounding of meaningful speech in action-contexts.

This criticism in turn calls into question the sharp distinction Habermas draws between communication in action-contexts and discourse. Discourse was described as a form of communication in which both the constraints of action, and validity claims, are rendered "virtual," so that the only motive is a cooperative willingness to come to an understanding, with all facts and norms regarded as hypothetical. But that is problematical. If all validity claims are to be "bracketed," such a notion of discourse would not cover the usual forms of scientific activity. On the other hand, Peirce's fallibilist model suggests a more piecemeal approach. Particular claims can be called into question, and more firmly grounded or rejected, without all being treated as hypothetical. On this model, we are, in Habermas's own words, "always immersed in a sea of interaction" and are able to step out only at one point at a time. Certain specific validity claims can be made the topic for discussion and their discursive justification tested, but that testing will rely on discursively unjustified background assumptions. The move from action to discourse would not require the total shift between communication structures that Habermas appears to be describing.[47]

Along these lines, we can accept much of what Habermas says about how the ascription of truth to statements can be understood in terms of the redemption of validity claims. But while this piecemeal model would still account for the unconditional character of truth claims, and the commitment to final accountability at a given place and time, it does not yield "objectivity" in the sense of a final and absolute consensus. But then no fallibilist position could. If we recognize that we always operate from a vital

47. See T. McCarthy, "A Theory of Communicative Competence," *Philosophy of the Social Sciences*, 3, 1973, pp. 135–56, reprinted in *Critical Sociology*, ed. P. Connerton, Harmondsworth, 1976, pp. 470–97. The points made here, including the private communication from Habermas, are to be found in the latter on pp. 492–94.

stand-point, we are always immersed in a sea of interaction. We can usefully retain the distinction between claims simply accepted and those regarded as discursively grounded, but which claims are classified as warranted will change over time.

For that very reason, it is not enough to characterize truth as warranted assertibility. While a well-tested consensus will warrant (for the time being) the ascription of truth to certain statements, the conceptual gap between attaining a discursive consensus and the disclosure of Being is not thereby bridged. Nor can it be, as long as we remain in the logico-linguistic sphere, which treats all facts and norms as hypothetical. The "bracketing" of validity claims, as discourse requires, necessarily abstracts from that interaction with reality that could yield a disclosure of Being. The latter has thereby been excluded from the sphere of reason and become its "Other."

On the contrary, I would argue, the sense in which it is plausible to say that reaching understanding is the *telos* of human speech implies that one has been put in touch with what has been pointed out, one has encountered how things are, so as to gain insight into the things themselves. But when the reaching of understanding is reduced to the attaining of (rationally motivated) assent to the content of utterances, this encounter with how things are is not actually secured. One has only established what to say. An encounter with how things are requires the kind of openness that is only given in an action-context. So if the reaching of understanding is to be considered the attainment of truth, an adequate conception of truth for our time must take our involvement in action-contexts even more seriously than Habermas admits.

My hunch is that developing this will require us to appropriate much more of Kierkegaard's novel contribution to how we should conceive of truth than has been done hitherto in the contemporary debate. Far from taking a "linguistic turn," it will require a recovery of the original signification of "truth" as faithfulness, primarily located in action. And since action is intrinsically teleological, such a reconceiving of truth will permit once again something that has become puzzling for contemporary philosophers: why truth should be seen as an end, a value normative for both speech and nonlinguistic action.[48]

When truth is reconceived in this way its scope will be wider than that of discursive rationality. But it will not thereby become the "Other" of reason; if reaching understanding is the *telos* of human speech in the sense I have argued, the scope of reason will also be seen to be wider than the purely discursive. This is the only way I see to overcome effectively the nar-

48. This is argued in detail in my *Truth and Historicity*, Oxford, 1992, upon which much of this paper is based.

rowing of reason to the purely instrumental task of calculating the cost-benefits of various possible means for attaining preferred ends, the ultimate selection of which is strictly irrational. A conception of reason that encompasses both *noesis* and *dianoia*, both insight and discursive calculation, might not satisfy the Hegelian ambition, but it could help overcome our own pervasive alienation.

.

# –9–

# Reason and Its Other
# in the Work of K.-O. Apel:
# The Case of Human Action

## DIETER FREUNDLIEB*

Gernot Böhme has argued that in order to go beyond the impasse of a radical critique of reason, we need to recognize much more fully that as human beings we are part of nature, and that all attempts of reason to assimilate what is considered the Other of reason come at a considerable price.[1] Philosophies that distinguish strictly between a *res cogitans* and a *res extensa*, the phenomenal and the noumenal, the factual and the normative, the ontical and the ontological, and the *Geisteswissenschaften* and the *Naturwissenschaften*, seem to be particularly plagued with the problem of how to account, given such a dichotomy, for the fact that human beings partake of both realms. A version of such dualism, together with the anti-naturalist tendencies that follow from it, is prominent in the history of German philosophy from Kant to the present. Nor has it been overcome by the two contemporary German philosophers who are the most well-known defenders of a substantive, though nonmetaphysical, concept of reason: Karl-Otto Apel and Jürgen Habermas. Apel's work on the methodology of the hermeneutical sciences, in particular, is based on an understanding of human beings that is dualist in a Kantian sense, in spite of all the semiotic and pragmatic revisions to which Kant's metaphysical system is subjected in Apel's philosophy. Neither Apel nor Habermas pretend that the natural can be entirely assimilated to reason, and they clearly provide a systematic space for what is natural in human beings. But, in the end, their dualist premises prevent them from finding satisfactory solutions to some of the important problems they address.

* I am grateful to Wayne Hudson for his very helpful criticisms of earlier drafts of this essay.

1. See his contribution to this volume and his book *Das Andere der Vernunft*, co-authored with his brother Hartmut Böhme, Frankfurt, 1985.

In this essay I would like to show how problems arising from the implicit reserve toward what is natural about human beings, and from the anti-naturalism built into the concept of the *Geisteswissenschaften,* manifest themselves in the work of Karl-Otto Apel. In particular, I attempt to demonstrate that Apel's conception of the natural as an Other of reason prevents him from giving a satisfactory account of the explanation of human action. Since Apel has developed his theory of action explanation in confrontation with a number of action theorists in analytic philosophy and the well-known debate between Neo-Wittgensteinians and their causalist opponents, a discussion of some of the issues raised in this debate will be necessary. First, however, we need to make some general comments on Apel's philosophical project as a whole.

# I

Karl-Otto Apel's transcendental-pragmatic philosophy, which in many ways is very similar to Jürgen Habermas's project of a universal pragmatics and which was developed in close contact and cooperation with Habermas, is one of the most sustained and forceful contemporary attempts to define and defend a notion of reason based on universal principles. These principles can allegedly be found when we reconstruct the universal rule system underlying human communication oriented toward reaching agreement in matters of linguistic meaning as well as matters concerning social and ethical norms. Whereas Habermas seems prepared to accept a general fallibilism, even for his own philosophical project, Apel maintains that the reconstructed principles of communication can be and need to be philosophically grounded. Drawing on insights gained from the speech act theories of John L. Austin and John R. Searle, Apel argues that four types of validity claims are made in every speech act we perform:

(1) the claim to speak intelligibly, that is, within the shared rules of a grammatical system;

(2) the claim to speak the truth as far as the propositional content of speech acts is concerned;

(3) the claim that the speech act performed is in conformity with universally acceptable social norms; and

(4) the claim to speak truthfully in the sense of a genuine expression of an inner state.

The first claim means that we can at any time engage in a discussion of what the words and sentences we use mean, but unlike in the case of the other three validity claims, a certain base-level intelligibility must always already be presupposed, since no discussion could even begin if we could not assume that there was a common semantic ground.

The other three validity claims are associated with three different worlds: the external world of facts, the social world of norms and expectations, and the subjective world of internal mental or emotional states that can be truthfully and authentically expressed. While the last claim can only be redeemed through subsequent action and behavior of the speaker consistent with the validity claim, the two remaining claims are considered redeemable in an ideal speech situation, and their redeemability is said to be counterfactually presupposed by anyone who is prepared to engage in an argumentative discourse. This so-called *a priori* of communication, i.e., the fact that one cannot engage in a process of argumentation unless one has already accepted, at least implicitly, certain fundamental ethical norms regarding one's dialogue partners, is one of the main reasons for Apel to insist that even in the natural sciences there is always a complementary hermeneutical process of communication taking place that is aiming at the settlement of the validity claims raised by scientists. Reason, for Apel, is thus largely the willingness to accept what he considers to be an irrefutable philosophical insight into the *a priori* of communication and to act in accordance with the principles derived from this *a priori*. We cannot, on pain of committing a performative self-contradiction, argue against basic ethical norms, because without such norms argumentation would lose all meaning and purpose.

Like Habermas, Apel is perfectly aware of the fact that in real life human beings often, perhaps even predominantly, use arguments for strategic purposes rather than for the purpose of furthering a communal search for factual or normative truth. But he argues that this does not affect the philosophical validity of his program of a *Letztbegründung*, i.e., an ultimate foundation for a "discourse ethics" (*Diskursethik*), since the validity of his program, on the one hand, and its factual acceptance by concrete individuals, on the other, are two entirely separate issues from a logical point of view.

Nonetheless, the fact that individuals still have to *decide* to accept communicative reason raises the question of how a disembodied notion of reason can be reconciled with the fact that as human beings we are part of the order of nature. In other words, how can nature and reason be combined? Is nature necessarily the Other of reason, and if so, what are the consequences? As I suggested above, it is the aim of this essay to point out the difficulties Apel gets into in his attempt to give a coherent account of action explanation, an explanation that accepts the fact that Kant's dualist distinction between the empirical and the noumenal self remains unsatisfactory, and that envisages a way in which causalist and intentionalist explanations can and sometimes need to be combined. An examination of his theory of action explanation will show that Apel's approach remains, ultimately, within a dualist Kantian framework in which what is natural and what is guided by reason require two completely different, though allegedly complementary, accounts.

Both Apel and Habermas assert that there are two entirely different kinds of sciences, associated with two different conceptual frameworks and two knowledge-guiding interests:[2] the natural sciences, which explain natural phenomena on the basis of a concept of natural law and which provide us with technologically useful knowledge, and the critical social sciences, which explain human actions on the basis of concepts such as intention, reasons and motivation, requiring not an objectivating but a performative attitude toward its domain of objects (which are really other subjects). For Apel, the two types of sciences are strictly complementary in the senses that neither can be reduced to the other, and that both are necessary for the survival of the species.

The complementarity of the two types of science manifests itself primarily in two ways. First, all forms of science presuppose the necessity of reaching agreement about the interpretation of signs.[3] Second, the explanation of human actions in the hermeneutical social sciences is necessarily different from the explanation of natural events. As far as the first point is concerned, a communal process of sign interpretation is seen by Apel as necessary and complementary to natural scientific explanation primarily because he believes that perceptual evidence, while indispensable for the justification of scientific hypotheses, is initially prelinguistic and therefore in need of subsequent interpretation in terms of a "mediation" with an already established sign system. This can only be done in a discursive process leading to an intersubjective agreement on validity claims.[4] As far as the second manifestation of the complementarity of the two sciences is concerned, the need to distinguish between them is based on the fact that while natural events can be explained in terms of the natural laws that gov-

2. Habermas has dropped his earlier concept of knowledge-guiding interests but otherwise concurs with Apel on the basic differences between the two types of sciences.

3. Elsewhere I have tried to demonstrate that Apel's use of C. S. Peirce's "pragmatic maxim" in order to show the complementary nature of the interpretation of theoretical terms in the natural sciences is open to serious doubt. See my "Peirce's Pragmatic Maxim and K.-O. Apel's Idea of a Complementary Hermeneutical Science," forthcoming in *Peirce's Doctrine of Signs: Theory, Applications, and Connections* (Proceedings of the *Charles S. Peirce International Sesquicentennial Congress* held at Harvard University, September 1989).

4. Apel relies here on his reading of Peirce's semiotics according to which "Firstness" and "Secondness" are preconceptual. According to Apel, perceptual judgments are theory-independent and noninterpretive. See, for example, his essay "Die Logos-Auszeichnung der menschlichen Sprache. Die philosophische Relevanz der Spechaktheorie" in *Perspektiven auf Sprache*, ed. H.-G. Bosshardt, Berlin and New York, 1986, pp. 45–87.

ern them, the explanation of human action is open to an internal perspective that allows us to understand actions in terms of their underlying intentions and reasons. Apel's complementarity thesis can thus be seen as part of his dualist conception of the world as divided into the natural, which is only accessible to us externally, and the human world of intentions, reasons and norms to which we have an internal access.

Within the context of action explanation, however, there are cases in which this strict complementarity needs to be broken down. Whenever human behavior is not guided by intentions that are transparent to the actor and that can be reconstructed as "good reasons" in a subsequent hermeneutical action explanation, a "quasi-nomological" explanation becomes necessary. But according to Apel, such explanations, although modelled on the natural sciences, do not serve a technological purpose. Instead, they are designed to lead to an enhanced self-understanding of the agent. Psychoanalysis and the critique of ideology are seen, by Apel, as paradigm cases of such nontechnological knowledge of human behavior. Apel suggests that an emancipation from natural forces within ourselves, but beyond our present understanding – or beyond the understanding of a person afflicted with certain psychical disturbances – is a regulative idea that we need to uphold, and that is justified philosophically through his program of a communicative rationality. Thus in Apel's philosophy nature is considered an Other of reason: something that we can never completely overcome as long as we remain human beings made out of flesh and blood, but nonetheless something that needs to be held in check by reason. In fact, he sees human history as having its *telos* in the realization of rational principles as "ideal laws." Action explanation is one of the prime sites where the relation between nature and reason comes to the fore. Let me therefore now turn to a detailed analysis of how this relation is unfolded by Apel.

## II

Apart from a number of essays, Apel has devoted a book-length study to the problem of explaining action, entitled *Die Erklären:Verstehen Kontroverse in transzendental-pragmatischer Sicht* (*Understanding and Explanation. A Transcendental-Pragmatic Perspective*),[5] in which, as the German title indicates, he analyzes the well-known "explanation versus understanding

5. Frankfurt, 1979. English translation: *Understanding and Explanation. A Transcendental-Pragmatic Perspective*, Cambridge, Mass., 1984. Apel has also addressed these issues in his essays "The Erklären-Verstehen Controversy in the Philosophy of the Natural and Human Sciences" in G. Fløistad (ed.), *Contemporary Philosophy: A New Survey*, vol. 2, The Hague, 1982, pp. 19–50, and "Diltheys Unterscheidung von 'Erklären' und 'Verstehen' im Lichte der Problematik der modernen Wissenschaftstheorie" in *Dilthey und die Philosophie der Gegenwart*, ed. W. Orth, Freiburg, 1985, pp. 285–347.

controversy" that was conducted within analytic philosophy from the standpoint of his own philosophy of a transcendental pragmatics. In this book Apel begins with a reconstruction of the early history of this debate, which goes back to Droysen, Dilthey and the Neo-Kantians, but in the main body of the book he concentrates on the debate between intentional-ist Neo-Wittgensteinians and their causalist adversaries, focussing, in partic-ular, on von Wright's well-known book *Explanation and Understanding*.[6]

Apel's interest in von Wright's theory of action explanation is not sur-prising when one examines von Wright's analysis of what he believes to be an intimate connection between the concept of causality and the concept of action in the sense of a free experimental intervention in nature. Accord-ing to von Wright, our understanding of the concept of causality is logical-ly dependent on the concept of experimental intervention in natural processes, a view with which Apel entirely agrees, and which he takes to be a demonstration of a strict complementarity between causal necessity and free human action. If natural necessity were indeed incomprehensible without presupposing our ability to intervene, experimentally, in a natural causal chain, and if it were true that such an intervention cannot itself be regarded as part of another chain of purely natural events, but only as a non-caused free action, then Apel would have already achieved one of his main aims. He would have established an irreducible difference between agent causation in the Kantian sense of a "causality from freedom," and natural causation, thus separating an important aspect of the human world from the natural world. Reason, in the shape of the rationality of experi-mental testing, could not possibly be part of the natural world, because it is considered a transcendental-pragmatic condition of the possibility of our knowledge of nature.[7] At the same time, von Wright's analysis of causality could be assumed to have established the complementarity between the *erklärende* and the *verstehende* sciences. Thus Apel says:

> It seems to me that von Wright has provided a foundation for a theory of con-ceptual complementarity between causal necessity and free action and thus, at the same time, a theory of the conceptual complementarity between causal explanation in the natural sciences and subjective-intentional understanding (*Verstehen*) of teleological actions.[8]

6. G. H. von Wright, *Explanation and Understanding*, Ithaca, New York, 1971. See also C. Landesmann, "The New Dualism in the Philosophy of Mind," *Review of Metaphysics* 19, 1965, pp. 339–49.

7. It should be noted here, however, that Apel's concept of agent causality differs from Kant's notion of a causality from freedom insofar as Apel does not completely accept Kant's metaphysical theory of the two worlds. While in Kant's system the noumenal world cannot have causal effects on the phenomenal world, Apel argues that agent causality, though clearly distinct from natural causality, has the power to affect external causal events. See "Diltheys Unterscheidung" p. 329/30, note 52.

8. Apel, "Diltheys Unterscheidung," p. 318/9. Author's translation.

However, it is by no means certain whether von Wright's account of causality is tenable. Indeed, Apel realizes that von Wright himself is somewhat ambivalent about the nature of the interdependence of the two concepts.[9] It seems, in fact, that the belief in the possibility of a successful intervention in natural processes presupposes the belief in, and thus the concept of, the law-like behavior of objects.

For example, I can only meaningfully try to prevent an undesirable natural event from happening if I believe that unless I interfered in the appropriate way, something would *cause* the dreaded event to happen in accordance with natural necessity. To be sure, no full-blown science would be conceivable without controlled experimentation. But a basic concept of causality could be entirely innate or merely dependent on the perception of natural regularities in order to be developed ontogenetically. It seems, therefore, that an objectivistic notion of causality is not *derived from* the notion of a (free) intervention, but is a *condition for* this concept to make sense. Apel's use of von Wright's notion of the dependence of the intelligibility of causality on the concept of a free action beyond a naturalistic explanation, as well as his arguments from within his own project of a transcendental pragmatics, are therefore insufficient to justify Apel's separation of reason and nature in the explanation of human action.

Although Apel believes that he is entitled to postulate the existence of a Kantian "causality from freedom," i.e., the idea of an act of intervention that is causally effective while not itself determined by natural causes, he agrees with the causalists that actions can, in principle, be described as spatio-temporal events in the world, and that any explanation of an action *qua* event must identify the causes of this event. He does not, for example, accept the so-called "logical-connection-argument" promoted by some of the Neo-Witgensteinians, which says that reasons or intentions cannot be (Humean) causes since in action explanations cause and effect are logically dependent on each other. As the critics of this argument have shown, the *having* of reasons, and the act that is performed for these reasons, are sufficiently independent of each other ontologically to stand in a cause-effect relationship.

Now the simultaneous acceptance of the two ideas – the idea of free actions involving uncaused causes, and the idea that actions are spatio-temporal events subject to causal analysis – puts Apel in a very difficult position. In fact, as I will try to show, Apel is forced to resort to a rather implausible metaphysics in order to solve the problems generated by such dualism.

First of all, let us see why Apel agrees that an explanation of an action

9. Apel, *Understanding and Explanation*, p. 85f.

must identify the intentions underlying this action as causally effective. One of the main reasons seems to be that otherwise we could not hold a person responsible for the results of an action. To identify a certain intention, and to identify a subsequent action as an action that apparently satisfies the intention, is not enough. This becomes clear when we look at the cases known in the literature as the "wayward causal chain." An example of this is the following story, the original version of which seems to have been invented by Chisholm:[10]

> A nephew desires to inherit the fortune of his uncle whom he has never seen. He believes he can only acquire the money if he kills his uncle. The wish to kill his uncle agitates him so much that he picks a fight with an unknown person in a bar and kills him. This person turns out to be his uncle. In this case we have both the desire or the intention to kill the uncle and the actual killing of the uncle. Nonetheless, we do not have the right kind of causal chain. The intention to kill his uncle was not causally operative in the act of killing – or at least not directly and in the right way. The existence of the desire and the associated belief, together with the performance of an action that could be truthfully described as the fulfillment of the desire, are not necessarily immediately connected with each other.

Now if Apel admits that mental states such as intentions play a causal role in actions, and if he also concedes that actions are spatio-temporal events, but insists that agent causality cannot be identified with natural causality, then he must give an account of how these two types of causality go together. Yet we will see in a moment that Apel is unable to offer a plausible analysis of the interaction between these different types of causes. In other words, he does not provide a satisfactory account of the relation between the description and explanation of an action *qua* action and the description and explanation of an action *qua* spatio-temporal event in the natural world.[11]

The notion of a "causation from freedom," i.e., the notion of a cause that is not itself caused by something else, is an anomaly that cannot be reconciled with a scientific world-view. In the light of the history of science it is *prima facie* not plausible to assume that human beings should be the only organisms in the known universe that do not belong to the order of the natural insofar as they are capable of performing acts that are not themselves caused (or, alternatively, purely accidental in an indeterministic

10. R. M. Chisholm, "Freedom and Action," in K. Lehrer (ed.), *Freedom and Determinism*, New York, 1966.

11. It is possible that Apel over-emphasizes the distinction between agent causation and natural causation because, as far as the latter is concerned, he operates with a Humean notion of regularity rather than a realist notion of causal powers or natural necessity. This is in part, perhaps, why he cannot imagine human intentions as simply a special case of natural causes. See for example his paper "Diltheys Unterscheidung," p. 330.

sense).[12] If Apel thinks that we are forced to make this assumption because of a dualism built into our language that distinguishes between mental and natural phenomena or because we have a fundamental interest in understanding the reasons underlying human actions as well as an interest in natural laws, or because of the so-called "meaning-critical" (*sinn-kritische*) arguments based on such dualisms, then it may well be that there is something wrong with our language and with Apel's arguments. Like the argument from category mistakes, the two-languages argument may turn out to be unnecessarily conservative and is likely to block future progress in knowledge, because it assumes that basic linguistic categories must be immune from revision.

To the committed realist, this looks like a remnant of pre-Kantian rational metaphysics in the sense that it is assumed that somehow ordinary language can tell us something about the fundamental characteristics of the universe *prior* to testing our language against this world. Meaningfulness can never be an absolute and final criterion, because it is always relative to current languages and our current concepts and beliefs. It is possible that both will have to be changed in order to deepen our understanding of the world and ourselves, including, for example, our understanding of what intentions are and what kind of causal role they play in human action. Similarly, fundamental cognitive interests may be seen as the basis on which some kind of "meaning"-disclosure or world-disclosure is possible, but it is logically perfectly conceivable that the world is such that our ways of making sense of it need to be transcended.

Like Habermas, Apel seems to deny that with respect to human action he is committed to a dualist ontology. In fact, he agrees with his opponent A. Beckermann[13] that "the object of reference in the interpretation of an event as an action is 'numerically identical' with the object of reference in the natural scientific apprehension of the event."[14] Beckermann argues that if this is the case, then "the causes of the bodily movements corresponding to an action must at the same time be the causes of that action."[15] Apel, however, rejects this conclusion and gives a different account that leads back to a dualist ontology.

According to Apel, actions cannot, as actions, be completely determined by natural causes. But how does the second type of causality, i.e., the causality from freedom that ultimately brings about the action, interact

12. A very detailed critical discussion of a whole range of philosophical attempts to establish a notion of freedom of action can be found in Ulrich Pothast's book *Die Unzulänglichkeit der Freiheitsbeweise*, Frankfurt, 1987.

13. See A. Beckermann, *Gründe und Ursachen*, Kronberg, 1977.

14 Apel, *Understanding and Explanation*, note 18, p. 268.

15. A. Beckermann, "Handeln und Handlungserklärungen," in Beckermann, (ed.), *Analytische Handlungstheorie*, vol. 2, Frankfurt, 1977, p. 32.

with the natural causality present in an action as an event in the world? According to Apel, a causally effective intention causes certain events to happen in the brain (or at least codetermines them) which then, in turn, cause certain bodily movements such as the raising of one's arm (in order to wave goodbye, for example). Because of the fact that the brain process is brought about by a nonnatural cause, i.e., an intention, this initial brain process is not "objectifiable" in the way the rest of our body is. Apel calls this phenomenon the "*Leibapriori*," i.e., a bodily function that must be separated from those aspects of the body (i.e., the *Körper*, not the *Leib*) that are accessible to natural explanation. The intermediary function of the *Leib* is introduced, it seems, in order to avoid what von Wright calls "animism," i.e., the idea that the mental has a direct, nonmediated causal influence on the physical.

But this strategy is hardly convincing, for it merely introduces another ontologically and epistemologically mysterious entity, i.e., the *Leib*, and it still leaves intentions as the ultimate nonnatural origin of all the natural and intermediary causal processes involved in the performance of an action. As Hilary Putnam once said in another context, "just postulating mysterious powers of mind solves nothing."[16] As a result, Apel's account does not make it clear how the peculiar type of causality manifested in intentions can be integrated in the system of natural causality most scientists think of as closed. Apel cannot, without contradicting himself, both admit that the referent of an action description and the referent of a description of the corresponding spatio-temporal event are *identical*, and at the same time use two semantically and ontologically *incompatible* languages to describe the action/event. The idea of the *Leibapriori*, then, is introduced in order to overcome the dichotomy between freely formed intentions and natural causality, in other words, between reason and its Other in human action. But it remains unclear how this mediation is possible since it does not really suspend the initial dualism.

Apel gets entangled in a further contradiction when he argues against Beckermann that, according to transcendental-pragmatic principles, it is *a priori* not meaningful to talk about numerically identical objects of reference independent of a definite horizon set by a language game (i.e., a conceptual framework).[17] What is at stake is precisely whether both language games, the intentionalist and the naturalist language, are valid and applicable to human actions. If it turns out, as it does, that what the two frameworks force us to say about an identical object cannot be reconciled, then the conclusion should be that *at least one* of the two frameworks must be inadequate. A numerically identical referent cannot have properties that

16. H. Putnam, *Reason, Truth and History*, Cambridge, 1981, p. 2.
17. See Apel, *Understanding and Explanation*, p. 268, note 18.

logically exclude each other. In other words, if Apel's transcendental-pragmatic account of human action is valid, then an action cannot, at the same time, be a natural spatio-temporal event.

Apel contends that his transcendental-pragmatic conception can avoid Kant's antinomy of causality and freedom, i.e., the idea that as empirical objects human beings are part of nature and therefore causally determined, but as noumenal beings they are capable of free actions.[18] Apel's construction, based on transcendental-pragmatic principles, is more complicated than Kant's because he has to show how the noumenal and the phenomenal, to use Kant's terms, can be mediated. But since this mediation is not successful, I do not see how it can prevent similar problems from arising.

Human beings, according to Apel, have a double, or even a triple, nature. First, they are part of the natural world of physical things. Second, they have what Apel calls a "quasi-nature," that is, the unconsciously or unintentionally formed and socially and historically determined habits and motives that can be investigated by quasi-nomological social sciences. Third, human beings are capable of free actions based on rationally formed reasons. Because of this latter capacity, the quasi-nomological social sciences can never give us the whole truth about human beings and their actions. In fact, these sciences must be complemented by *critical* social sciences, for these are able, at least in principle, to transform the rationally unintelligible causes of pathological or ideological behavior into intelligible rules and reasons. Rather than hiding their results from the subjects investigated (in order to allow social engineering and avoid self-fulfilling or self-refuting prophecies), the critical social scientists use their results to deepen the self-understanding of the participants in the scientific process, i.e., both the investigators and the investigated.

The trouble with this conception is that it does not really avoid the problem of how the idea of two entirely different types of causality and their interaction can be made intelligible. For the type of free agent causality that Apel postulates must not only be capable of intervening in external causal chains as in the example of scientific experimentation and in internal but natural causal processes going on within the brain of a single individual. It must also, in order to bring about a "cure" of a psychologically or ideologically afflicted person, be able to intervene causally in *another person's* brain processes. On the basis of Apel's model of emancipation from psychological disturbances through a rational insight into the natural mechanisms causing these disturbances, it must be possible to achieve a cure through the causally effective operation of the rationality inherent in the analyst's discourse and his or her dialogue with the patient. The acceptance of the analyst's account, and the cure effected by it, cannot be con-

18. *Ibid.*, p. 131ff.

ceived of as a rational acceptance of reasons *before* the cure has been achieved, because it is precisely the lack of this ability that causes the disturbances in the first place. In other words, the cure must be understood, even on Apel's own account, as brought about through a causal impact on the patient's mind. The fact that this cause would perhaps be seen by Apel as an example of agent causality rather than natural causality makes little difference. It would still be the case that the analyst's actions are technological in much the same sense as other forms of technology. What this shows again, I think, is that the attempt to separate reason and nature in the way assayed by Apel is not viable. Nature is not an Other of reason, but the two are inherently intertwined.

### III

While we have to admit that human action and its explanation is one of the most difficult philosophical (and scientific!) problems, I suggest that the solution to it should be sought in another way. Perhaps the problem can be solved, or at least more fruitfully attempted, within the framework of concepts developed by John Searle in his writings on intentionality.[19] So let me make some brief and very sketchy comments on Searle's account as a possible alternative to Apel's dualism.

Searle's investigations are carried out within a non-reductive, but thoroughly naturalistic conception of the philosophy of mind, thus avoiding the postulation of an agent causality that is ontologically distinct from natural causality. At the same time, he puts forward a critique of the traditional Humean idea of causality as "regularity." According to Searle, causal relations between events or states are perfectly real and mind-independent. On the other hand, there is a special case of what he calls "Intentional causation;" it is part of the content, not the object, of perceptual experience as well as the experience of acting. Although there are certain similarities here between Searle's and von Wright's notion of causality and its relation to the concept of action, Searle's account differs from Wright's in important respects. For Searle, action is not privileged over perception in a sense that would require us to give primacy to interventionist action over perceived causality, and there is only *one* basic concept of causation, with "Intentional causation" as a special case insofar as it is immediately experienceable. He leaves open the question whether there is a universal determinism, as his own account of the explanation of action does not, in his view, commit him to such a view. But it seems that if intentional causes are natural causes, the question of what causes intentions to be formed is certainly mean-

19. J. Searle, *Intentionality*, Oxford, 1983.

ingful, particularly within a naturalistic framework. In fact, in the last chapter of his book *Intentionality* Searle says that "mental states are caused by biological phenomena and in turn cause other biological phenomena."[20] The desire to drink (i.e., thirst) is a case in point. Here the biological causation that leads to the desire to drink, and thus to an intentional action, can today be traced quite successfully in brain research.

What Searle, and anyone opposed to Apel's "complementarity thesis," must show is that the notion of intention and other mentalistic terms do make sense within a naturalistic theory of the mind. The last chapter of Searle's book *Intentionality* is an attempt to demonstrate the compatibility of the two languages. Searle argues that most attempts in contemporary philosophies of mind to reduce mental phenomena to something more basic are complete failures. They do not do justice to the fact that we *do have* desires, wants, beliefs, intentions, pains, etc. Searle suspects that the attempts to reduce these phenomena are motivated by the fear that otherwise we will end up with an incoherent Cartesian dualism. His strategy is to show that the acceptance of a mentalistic vocabulary does not necessarily commit us to either antinaturalism or a mind/body dualism.

We have seen that Apel tries to avoid the full philosophical consequences of an ontological dualism, but he still upholds the idea of two languages that are complementary to each other. So when it comes to explaining human actions, he must show that the two languages can be integrated with each other after all. But this leaves him with a questionable concept of agent causation whose relation to natural causation remains unexplained. The statement that human action *qua* action cannot be completely accounted for in terms of natural causation, and the statement that action descriptions and descriptions of actions as spatio-temporal events have identical referents are not compatible. They ultimately leave Apel with an incoherent doctrine. Searle's naturalism promises to avoid this problem by showing that mental terms such as "intention" are high-level descriptions of biological phenomena that have causal powers just like other biological phenomena.

If Searle's admittedly sketchy attempt is tenable in principle, we can see how brain processes might naturally cause certain intentions to be formed that in turn cause bodily movements – and all this within a naturalistic, but nonreductionist, framework. The fact that we experience the formation of an intention as free is in itself no proof that such intentions are caused by prior brain processes, as experiments with posthypnotic suggestion have shown. Nonetheless, it would be premature to say that Searle's and similar projects are without problems. On the other hand, the strategy

20. *Ibid.*, p. 264.

of a nonreductionist naturalism seems to be more fruitful than a program whose questionable status is already visible and unavoidable within the system. Searle's naturalistic account would have the advantage of showing how intentions as reasons are intimately linked with the natural order and can be investigated as such. Reason and nature would no longer confront each other as ontologically distinct and somehow inherently antagonistic.

## IV

Apel's accommodation of some of the arguments of the causalists concerning the possibility, in principle, of treating human actions as spatio-temporal events that can be explained causally does not mean that Apel is prepared to abandon his thesis about the necessity of a complementary conception of different types of sciences. On the contrary, he argues that the dispute between intentionalists and causalists can be dissolved only if one approaches the problem of action explanation from the perspective of the two basic cognitive interests: the interest in the technological control of nature and the interest in reaching communicative agreement between subjects. But this means that Apel still insists on the strict separation between causal explanation, which in the case of human action is considered possible to a certain degree because many human actions are contaminated, as it were, by natural causes – and hermeneutical understanding of reasons as "good" reasons. The latter is considered both sufficient and adequate in the case of the explanation of rational human behavior. Questions about the natural causes of the formation of rationally justifiable intentions and subsequent actions are ruled out as unintelligible by Apel because they contradict the dualist assumptions in his philosophy. The hermeneutical sciences are thus guided by the cognitive interest in the improvement of human communication and mutual understanding and only resort to causal explanations if the actions they wish to understand remain unintelligible.

A paradigmatic example of an almost purely hermeneutical science is the history of the natural sciences because here it is precisely the rationality of scientific progress that the historian of science focuses on. In the case of the history of science, the historian is usually not interested in a causal explanation, but in the good reasons for which certain theories were accepted or rejected. And even in other cases, outside the history of science, an historian may wish to approach the actions of past agents exclusively in terms of the reasons for which they were performed. *All* historiography is thus seen as guided primarily by the cognitive interest in the improvement of human communication – even across generations and cultures. But the history of science, at least insofar as it is "internal" history in Lakatos's sense,[21] is said to be a case of a pure hermeneutic science, because here the hermeneutic idealization, i.e., a prior assumption of rationality, is in fact empirically justified (unlike in the case of ordinary history where we often deal with unintelligible, because irrational, actions). According to Apel, it is also a science that tries to understand the past very much in terms of what we can learn from it about present problems in the philosophy of science. It is thus concerned almost exclusively with the realm of the rational. In the history of science as conceived by Apel, the natural can only appear as an Other of reason.

Now it must be admitted that nonreductive intentional explanations are the only explanations we can at present hope to provide in most disciplines concerned with the explanation, in a wide sense, of individual human actions. And it is, of course, possible, and in certain contexts also justified and reasonable, though not necessary, to assess the reasons for which an action was performed. Apart from answering the question why a certain action was in fact performed, we would then ask the question: Is it rational or otherwise justified to act for these reasons (described as logical entities, not as causes) when a person is in a situation of this kind? Apel, it seems, wishes to combine the two questions – and this is of course possible. Applied to the history of science this means that we look at the intentions underlying particular actions or deliberations, but also ask the question whether the effective reasons were, and potentially still are, good reasons.[22] Apel's point is that we can still *learn* from the classical texts in the sense that they might motivate us to alter our own current standards.[23]

No doubt, we need to concede Apel's argument that the process of reasoning, both in science and in other areas, cannot, of course, be *replaced* by naturalistic explanations. And insofar as the history of science can provide us with possible reasons for decisions in specified situations, I can see no reason why Apel's idea of a hermeneutic history of science should be reject-

21. See I. Lakatos, "History of Science and Its Rational Reconstructions" in *Boston Studies in the Philosophy of Science* VIII, 1972, pp. 91–136. Lakatos's dichotomy of internal versus external history of science is another manifestation of the nature/reason dualism to be found in Apel's work.

22. This conception differs, as far as I can see, from Lakatos's model, according to which it does not really matter whether the reconstructed reasons actually were the operative reasons, because his aim is to reconstruct as *internal* as much as possible of the history of science. But this means, whether Lakatos was aware of this or not, that the standards by which we judge the reasons are always already presupposed as valid; they are derived from Lakatos's own conception of research programs. The more of the actual history of science can be reconstructed in the light of this conception, the more this is taken as a confirmation of Lakatos's philosophy of scientific research programs.

23. See Apel's discussion in his "History of Science and the Problem of Historical Understanding and Explanation," unpublished manuscript, Frankfurt, 1981.

ed. What must be kept in mind, however, is that when we combine the identification of intentions and reasons underlying human action with the normative and methodologically relevant assessment of reasons (as logical entities) in the light of our present knowledge and presently accepted norms and standards, we are still dealing with two logically distinct activities. That such an assessment could lead to a change in our present standards is certainly possible, though perhaps not very likely in the case of the natural sciences. In any event, what we have here is simply a combination of an explanatory historical science and the process of an objective assessment of reasons in the light of currently available norms. I do not see, therefore, why such an activity should be regarded as something quite different from what is possible within a nonpositivist analytic philosophy of science. Apel would, of course, insist that the normative part of such a mixed approach can only be understood within the framework of his transcendental pragmatics. But this is by no means certain.

Similarly, it is possible to explain other human actions in history and at the same time assess the rationality or otherwise of the reasons and intentions that were operative in these acts. But again I do not see why we have to postulate a separate cognitive interest in communication and the rest of the transcendental-pragmatic conditions in order to deal with such cases, for we would again be dealing with a double-barreled activity – an empirically adequate intentional explanation and, in a second step, a normative assessment of the action. The framework of the knowledge-guiding cognitive interests unnecessarily creates a dualist ontology and epistemology of reason and nature in a way that makes it impossible to ask what is natural within reason.

## V

In conclusion, let me return once more to our initial question of the relation between reason and its Other in Apel's project of transcendental hermeneutics. It is obvious from Apel's account of the explanation of human action that he sees human beings as belonging to at least two different orders simultaneously: the order of the natural and the order of the logical, the normative and the rational. Reason has to contend with what is natural in us, and while Apel is under no illusion about which one of these forces, for the most part, is winning the battle in the real world of history, he insists that free action, uncaused by natural necessity, is possible. In Apel's foundationalist philosophy, reason is conceived of as something that must overcome not only unreason or irrationality, but *nature as such* – at least as far as human beings are concerned. Hence his postulation of an agent causality distinct from natural causality, endowed with the power to intervene in nature. And it is only because we are (still) natural creatures that Apel sees a necessity for "quasi-nomological" explanations of human behavior. If we were completely rational, we would be transparent to each other and to ourselves, and only two kinds of sciences would be required: the natural sciences and the empirical hermeneutical sciences. But since there is always an Other of reason to be reckoned with when we investigate human action, we must explain its natural mechanisms in order to reduce its blind power over reason.

There is an Enlightenment belief here in the beneficial counter-power of reason that is admirable in one way, but questionable in another. It is admirable in the sense that it is directed at the removal, in all human life, of all unnecessary coercion; but it is questionable in the sense that it tends to denigrate and negate what will always be there and what need not be sublimated into pure communicative reason for an improvement of the human condition to be possible. Radical critiques of reason, as both Apel and Habermas have shown, cannot be defended argumentatively. But too strong an insistence on the importance of reason can lead to an equally undesirable result, namely, the loss of nature in the sense of an antinaturalism in the human sciences and an attitude toward the natural that conceives of nature as an irreconcilably Other of reason.

As the discussion of Apel's account of action explanation has indicated, the problem of freedom and necessity, or reason and nature, no doubt one of the thorniest and intractable problems in philosophy, has not been finally resolved by Apel.[24] The main reason why Apel did not succeed seems to lie in his unwillingness to leave behind the dualist paradigm that has been influential in German philosophy since the days of Kant. A more promising, more naturalistic avenue, but one that Apel is not prepared to pursue, might be to recognize that for each normatively relevant human decision a causal story can, in principle, be told, at least in hindsight. As Apel rightly argues, this would not mean that we could ever *replace* normative deliberations with causal explanations. But it might well be that causal explanations of human actions, even down to the nitty-gritty of neurophysiology, will give us factual information about ourselves that could be useful not only technologically in a straightforward sense, for example in the medical field, but in future normative discourses. We need to know how rationality, understood in Schnädelbach's sense,[25] as a high-level dispositional attribute, is acquired ontogenetically. In other words, we need to know more about what it is that makes people act rationally, what educational

24 The comprehensive bibliography on the topic of freedom and necessity in human action included in U. Pothast's *Die Unzulänglichkeit der Freiheitsbeweise* lists no fewer than 1,390 items.

25. See H. Schnädelbach's contribution to this volume.

styles promote rationality and what social structures support it. Apel would no doubt agree with these aims, but given his conception of a transcendental-pragmatic philosophy, a naturalistic approach to these problems is ruled out. This is why an allegedly inherent opposition between reason and its Other needs to be overcome.

# –10–

# *Vernunftkritik* as Critique of Scientistic Reason*

## A. T. NUYEN

The critical tradition is alive and well in Germany today, more than two hundred years after the publication of Kant's *Critique of Pure Reason*. Halfway between then and now, it was Wilhelm Dilthey who supplied extra nourishment to the critical spirit by adding to Kant's critiques of reason and judgment what he called "critique of historical reason." The present phase of German critical thought owes a great deal to Kant and Dilthey, even though the focus is somewhat different. There is now a concern that reason has been construed instrumentally, and as a result, restrictively. Furthermore, this kind of reason is generally believed to be all-encompassing, in the sense that anything that falls outside its reach is not an object of knowledge. The current phase of the German critical tradition could be characterized as attempting to draw attention to the "Other" of reason. For my purpose, I take 1936, the year in which Parts I and II of Husserl's great last work, *The Crisis of European Sciences and Transcendental Phenomenology*,[1] were published, as marking the beginning of the current phase. Since then, different writers have given different contents to the claim that reason has its "Other." In this paper I wish to examine the Husserl-Gadamer theme that reason, construed as the method of the natural sciences, does not have the all-encompassing epistemic power that has often been claimed for it. For Husserl and Gadamer, the "Other" of reason is a whole area of human experience that the method of science cannot capture, which can only be captured by some other mode of understanding. More importantly, not only does this mode of understanding have an

---

*A slightly different version of the material in Sections I to III forms part of a paper, "Truth, Method and Objectivity: Husserl and Gadamer on Scientific Method," which appeared in *Philosophy of the Social Sciences* 20 (1990). I wish to thank the editor of that journal for permission to incorporate that material here.
1. Trans. by D. Carr, Evanston, Illinois, 1970.

epistemic legitimacy, it is in a sense epistemically prior to science itself. It will be clear that, for Husserl and Gadamer, the "Other" of reason is not irrationality, and as such their views deserve a better reception within the "analytical" tradition, where there has been a suspicion of any talk of the "other" of reason. Indeed, I shall end the paper by arguing that there are many strands of analytical philosophy that can be woven into a fabric matching that of German thought.

## I

The nature of the scientific method, the method of the natural sciences, can be gauged from the property most often associated with it, namely, objectivity. "Objectivity" is commonly taken to refer to the claim that science is "value-free." Roughly, the claim amounts to this: Nature itself is neither good nor evil; it follows that an understanding of nature and the applications made possible by such understanding are neither good nor evil. Understood in this way, the claim is somewhat misleading. Since the most obvious contrast of "objectivity" is "subjectivity," the claim is misleading in that it suggests that all values are necessarily "subjective," that there is no such thing as an "objective value." More significantly, the value-free claim thus understood is not an important element of the objectivity of the scientific method. Indeed, one may argue that it is a claim not relevant to a concern about method, because it is about science itself rather than about its method. For my purpose at least, I take it that the objectivity of the scientific method has to do with the relationship between the scientist and the object of scientific enquiry.

The first thing to notice about this relationship is that it is one of detachment. The nature of the scientist, what makes someone a scientist, is independent of the nature of the object – what makes it the object that it is. It matters not to the object whether or not it is investigated scientifically, or who does the investigating. It matters not to the scientist whether this or that object is studied, and in what way (although as a scientist he or she has to study something scientifically). In Hans-Georg Gadamer's terminology, one may say that the relationship between the scientist and the object is not a "hermeneutical" one, as it is between, say, a work of art and the person who tries to understand it. The latter is described by Gadamer as follows: "(The) work of art is not an object that stands over against a subject for itself. Instead the work of art has its true being in the fact that it becomes an experience changing the person experiencing it."[2] I shall return to this point later. To be sure, some scientists do get "personally involved,"

2. *Truth and Method*, trans. W. Glen-Doepel, New York, 1975, p. 92.

but this is not part-and-parcel of the scientific enterprise, and should ideally be avoided. In any case, how a scientist's life has been changed by what he or she is investigating is not supposed to go into the scientific report. By contrast, how one is affected by a work of art is the whole idea of understanding it. To put the point somewhat differently, science is not concerned with the meaning that an object has for the person who is investigating it, nor indeed with the meaning of that investigation for the investigator, not just as a matter of value but also as a matter of fact. The objectivity of the scientific method also lies in the fact that the individuality, or particularity, of the object is not at all relevant. Indeed, science transcends particularity and rises to the general. The ultimate goal is the formulation of a general law. With this in mind, the scientist has to eliminate the non-standard, the peculiar, the contextual, i.e., everything that gives this object an identity, making it stand out from the anonymity of the series of similar objects. If the object has to be accounted for at all, the scientist will give an explanation of it, i.e., accounting for it by subsuming it under the generality of a law or a hypothesis. The scientist's task is not to understand the object in its particularity, i.e., what makes it this object. Once a law has been established, the consideration of an individual case merely adds yet another confirmation, and contributes nothing to the law as such. The law, on the other hand, does not show how it comes to be that the object is just as it is.

What is involved in the scientific method? A casual observation will reveal that there is a high level of mathematical abstraction. The certainty of the mathematical proof, or deductive reasoning generally, was recognized by the Greeks, whose contributions still serve as the foundation of mathematical knowledge. However, it was Descartes who elevated this type of reasoning to its unique epistemological position. It is not a coincidence, then, that the natural sciences are held in high regard while they embrace mathematics in their method. Nevertheless, science could not achieve the success that it has by being purely deductive. Inductive reasoning and experimentation form the other half of the scientific method. Francis Bacon gave a detailed exposition of this aspect of the method, but it was J. S. Mill who gave it a logical legitimacy.

The spectacular success of the natural sciences has led to an idolization of their method. For many, scientific reasoning is the highest form of human reasoning, the pinnacle of rationality itself. Many hold the view that it is the method to be applied in the pursuit of all kinds of knowledge. Mill himself has advocated the use of induction, as formalized by him, in all areas of scientific work, including the so-called human sciences. Mill's *Logic* was translated into German; it was widely read and had a major impact on nineteenth-century German thinking. His advocacy of the use of scientific induction in the human sciences was quite well received. Indeed, Gadamer opens his *Truth and Method* with the claim that, due to Mill's influence, the "logical self-reflection which accompanied the development of the human sciences in the nineteenth century is wholly dominated by the model of the natural sciences."[3] The question is: Has this influence been beneficial to the pursuit of truth and knowledge generally? For Husserl and Gadamer, the answer is "No" if the reason of science based on the scientific method characterized here, or what I call "scientistic reason," is seen as having a totalizing, or all-encompassing, power. For them, scientistic reason itself has an "Other" that it is inherently incapable of capturing. Yet, without understanding its "Other," scientistic reason lacks a fundamental rationalization. For Husserl in particular, the result is a crisis in science.

## II

Husserl admits that one cannot speak of a crisis if one has in mind only the technical accomplishments of the sciences. There is a "primary sense" in which the sciences are "unimpeachable within the legitimacy of their methodic accomplishments."[4] However, if we have in mind the understanding of human existence, then science has indeed led us astray, and to the extent that science is part of that existence, it has led itself astray. We could speak of a crisis in this sense. This is why in Husserl's work, the word "crisis" often appears in quotes. In what way have we been led astray, into a "crisis"? As we saw above, Gadamer observes that the human sciences in the nineteenth century were dominated by the model of the natural sciences. Husserl, in fact, had made the same observation, saying that the total world-view of human existence in the second half of the nineteenth century allows itself to be exclusively "determined by the positive sciences and . . . blinded by the 'prosperity' they produced," and that means an "indifferent turning-away from the questions which are decisive for a genuine humanity."[5] According to Husserl, the "crisis" began with Galileo's mathematization of nature, and developed as a result of "the surreptitious substitution of the mathematically substructed world of idealities for the only real world, the one that is actually given through perception, that is ever experienced and experienceable – our everyday life-world."[6] What is the effect of this substitution? It is nothing less than a turning-away from the "actually experienced and experienceable world in which practically

3. *Ibid.*, p. 5.
4. Husserl, *Crisis*, p. 5.
5. *Ibid.*, p. 6.
6. *Ibid.*, pp. 48–49.

our whole life takes place."[7] Yet, human existence is existence in this life-world. There is truth in science, but there is also truth in our everyday experiences. It is true that the sun will rise tomorrow, no less than it is true in the scientific sense that it will not. As Gadamer was to put it later, the sun always rises even for the person who knows that it is the earth that revolves around the sun.[8] For Husserl, the "crisis" is the result of the failure to realize that one truth is more "primordial" than the other, and serves as the ground for it. To turn away from the more primordial, the ground, is to undercut oneself. If turning away from the life-world is the problem, returning to it is the obvious solution. Indeed, this is what Husserl attempts to do in Part III of the *Crisis*. I shall consider later some basic features of Husserl's proposal for a proper understanding of human existence. For now, it is worth pointing out that Husserl has warned us that it is not easy to break loose from the influence of scientistic reason. Any concern with the "extrascientific" life-world would be regarded as lacking in objectivity and thus having no value. "If the intuitive world of our life is merely subjective, then all truths of pre- and extrascientific life which have to do with its factual being are deprived of value."[9] Reflections on the life-world, coming particularly from "a nonmathematical, nonscientific circle of scholars," are likely to be "rejected as 'metaphysical'."[10] This is the result of the idolization I mentioned earlier of the scientific method. In fact, since it was the Greeks who laid the foundations for mathematical knowledge, as I have pointed out, it is no wonder that Husserl blames the idolization of the scientific method on the Greeks, who "saw fit to recast the idea of 'knowledge' and 'truth' in natural existence and to ascribe to the newly formed idea of 'objective truth' a higher dignity, that of a norm for all knowledge."[11]

For Husserl, then, there are kinds of knowledge and truth that cannot be revealed by the scientific method. Husserl also goes further, claiming (following Heidegger as we shall see) that the validity or legitimacy of the sciences must be grounded in the knowledge and truth revealed by our reflections on human existence. Husserl's argument for this claim will be considered later. Given this claim, nonscientific reflections on human existence are indispensable. Husserl's approach to such reflections is, of course, phenomenology, while Gadamer's is hermeneutics.

I shall not go into the phenomenology of Husserl or the hermeneutics of Gadamer. Instead, I shall try to show why, for these writers, the objectivi-

---

7. *Ibid.*, pp. 50–51
8. Gadamer, *Truth and Method*, p. 407.
9. Husserl, *Crisis*, p. 54.
10. *Ibid.*, p. 57.
11. *Ibid.*, p. 121.

ty of the scientific method makes it inappropriate for a large class of human concerns.

## III

Among these human concerns is, paradoxically, the concern to understand science itself. Doing science is one of the things we do, and pretty well at that. Can the scientific method help us understand this human activity? As I pointed out above, the objectivity of the scientific method is such that the relationship between the scientist and the scientific task is one of detachment. Science is not concerned with the meaning of the scientific enterprise. Further, for science to understand itself, it has to posit itself as an object of enquiry. To understand science is to understand its origin, its possibility and its continued significance for human existence. That is, to understand it as a particular human phenomenon. Yet, the objectivity of the scientific method requires that science transcend the particularity of the object, and subsume it under some general law. As such, science is not capable of understanding itself. Its very method does not allow it to do this. Metascience is not science, just as metaphysics is not physics. Can we do without this understanding? Husserl is quite adamant that we cannot. It is an understanding of the ground of science itself, and the absence of it contributes to the "crisis" of science. Yet, Husserl points out, science itself cannot provide this understanding. Any attempt by science to understand itself will "lead to a regressus in infinitum."[12]

The "crisis" can be overcome, for science and for human understanding generally, only if we return to the experienced and experienceable lifeworld. Thus, "the proper return to the naïveté of life – but in a reflection which rises above this naïveté – is the only possible way to overcome the philosophical naïveté which lies in the [supposedly] 'scientific' character of traditional objectivistic philosophy."[13] Following Heidegger, Husserl argues that the validity of science itself derives from the validity of the surrounding world of life, which is taken by us all for granted. Thus, argues Heidegger, the "ontological inquiry" into human existence is "more primordial, as over against the ontical inquiry of the positive sciences."[14] This ontological inquiry will reveal "the a priori conditions . . . for the possibility of the sciences."[15] For instance, since the "ontology of life . . . determines what must be the case if there can be anything like mere-aliveness,"

12 *Ibid.*, p. 52.
13. *Ibid.*, p. 59.
14. *Being and Time*, trans. J. Macquarrie and E. Robinson, London, 1962, p. 31.
15. *Ibid.*

and since biology presupposes living bodies, "biology as a 'science of life' is founded upon the ontology of *Dasein*, even if not entirely."[16] Being founded upon the ontology of *Dasein*, science derives its validity from that ontology. Yet science itself cannot provide that ontology. This theme is repeated in Husserl's *Crisis*. Since "science in general is . . . an accomplishment of human beings who find themselves in the world . . . of general experience,"[17] it is this world that provides the ground of science's "cognitive accomplishments."[18] "When science poses and answers questions, these are from the start, and hence from then on, questions resting upon the ground of, and addressed to, the elements of this pregiven world in which science and every other life-praxis is engaged."[19] This pregiven world, then, is "the constant ground of validity" for science. Husserl calls this world the "subjective-relative" and claims that it is the source of self-evidence and verification from which our theoretical and logical reasoning draws its validity. Yet, as we have seen, the objectivity of the scientific method prevents it from being applied to the "subjective-relative." Science cannot account for its own foundation. Heidegger's solution is an existential analytic of *Dasein*, while Husserl's is the phenomenology of the life-world. Naturally, these solutions are meant to apply generally to questions concerning human existence, of which science is just one of the elements.

While both Heidegger and Husserl are concerned with "laying bare" what science conceals, which is the ground of science itself, Gadamer is concerned with the general phenomenon of understanding (of which understanding science forms a part). In *Truth and Method*, Gadamer discusses the understanding of things such as historical events, laws, and works of art (literary texts, musical compositions, plays, paintings, sculptures, etc.). Very early in that work, Gadamer draws the following distinction between an object of understanding and a scientific object:

> The individual case does not serve only to corroborate a regularity from which predictions can in turn be made. Its ideal is rather to understand the phenomenon itself in its unique and historical concreteness. However much general experience is involved, the aim is not to confirm and expand these general experiences in order to attain knowledge of a law, e.g., how men, peoples and states evolve, but to understand how this man, this people or this state is what it has become – more generally, how has it happened that it is so.[20]

The point here is that an object of understanding must be understood in its full particularity. The identity of the object does not drop out of the

16. *Ibid.*, p. 75.
17. Husserl, *Crisis*, p. 118.
18. *Ibid.*, p. 116.
19. *Ibid.*, p. 121.
20. Gadamer, *Truth and Method*, p. 6.

understanding. The object is not a means to something else, but must be understood in itself as an end; not something that we pass over hurriedly on our way to a generalization, but something that we dwell on. Gadamer's point can be illustrated by the following example. Consider a case of civil unrest, such as a riot. One can look at such an event in a scientific way and try to explain it, perhaps in causal terms. In doing so, one can call upon observed regularities. Perhaps riots are more likely to occur at a certain time of year (e.g., in the summer when the weather is warm), and after certain triggering events (e.g., police action resulting in a fatal shooting). This kind of explanation can be useful in that similar incidents can be prevented or controlled. But there are truths to be learned and knowledge to be had in understanding this event in its full particularity, by understanding just how it has happened that people's fears, frustration and anger exploded in a riot on this occasion.

Gadamer also makes the point that, unlike the relationship between a scientific object as a particular case and a scientific law, there is a hermeneutical relationship between a particular case of understanding and the more general rule, if there is one. He illustrates this point with respect to law and morality as follows: "The judge does not only apply the law *in concreto*, but contributes through his very judgment to the development of the law. . . . Like law, morality is constantly developed through the fecundity of the individual case."[21] Thus, unlike an object of science, which is always just an example of a general law, an object of understanding is "not exhausted by being a particular example of a general law or concept."[22] Every encounter in an individual case is a unique experience, contributing in a unique way to the whole of a person's life. "Every experience is taken out of the continuity of life and at the same time related to the whole of one's life. . . . Because it is itself within the whole of life, in it too the whole of life is present."[23]

An object of understanding also differs from a scientific object in its relationship to self-understanding. A certain amount of self-understanding is required (Gadamer calls it "prejudices") with which to approach the object, but that understanding itself will be altered by the confrontation with the object. "We learn to understand ourselves in the object."[24] Because of this reciprocal relationship between the self and the object of understanding, the task of understanding is different from the scientific task. In the former, one brings one's life to bear on the object, and lets the object transform one's life. Both the self and the object are affected in the

21. *Ibid.*, p. 37.
22. *Ibid.*
23. *Ibid.*, p. 62.
24. *Ibid.*, p. 86.

act of understanding and as such both are full partners in the understanding process. Thus, for the hermeneutical task, we need to understand first of all ourselves, our past experiences, our tastes and preferences, our prejudices, our history and tradition, and our sense of the community (*sensus communis*). In this respect, Gadamer follows Husserl and Heidegger. For Gadamer too, "life constitutes the real ground of the human sciences."[25] The life-world is a "personal world, and in the natural attitude the validity of this personal world is always assumed."[26] In a sense, then, the object of understanding is constructed out of one's life-world, and that makes it different from an object of science. In the case of history, for instance, "it is senseless to speak of . . . an object in itself towards which its research is directed," unlike in natural sciences, where the object "can be described *idealiter* as what would be known in the perfect knowledge of nature."[27] Clearly, then, the scientific method cannot be the method of understanding. For Gadamer, that method is hermeneutics.

We have seen that, like Husserl and Heidegger, Gadamer has drawn our attention to the limitations of science and the scientific method. However, unlike them, Gadamer does not lay stress on the claim that truth and validity in science are derivative of truth and validity in human experiences, although he does not argue against this. Instead, Gadamer stresses the point that understanding has its own truth and validity. His point is that there is a kind of knowledge that cannot be had by an application of scientific reasoning, but will be revealed by the hermeneutics of the human sciences. Life experiences are a "different source of truth from theoretical reason."[28] They contain ordinary human passions, and "human passions cannot be governed by the universal prescriptions of reason."[29] Of the kinds of truth to be had in experiences, one can mention moral truths, aesthetic truths, even religious truths. The knowledge of these nonscientific truths can have certainty too, but again it will be a kind of certainty different from that associated with scientific truths. "The kind of certainty afforded by a verification that has passed through doubt is different from the immediate living certainty with which all ends and values appear in human consciousness when they make an absolute claim."[30] He concludes that "a logical application of this [scientific] method as the only norm for the truth of the human sciences would amount to their self-annihilation."[31] To illustrate Gadamer, we may say that by talking about light-wave refraction, pig-

25. *Ibid.*, p. 199.
26. *Ibid.*, p. 219.
27. *Ibid.*, p. 253.
28. *Ibid.*, p. 23.
29. *Ibid.*
30. *Ibid.*, pp. 210–11.
31. *Ibid.*, p. 19.

mentation, and color spectrum, science annihilates paintings, sunsets and rainbows;[32] by trying to be scientific, structuralists annihilate prose and poetry; by computer-analyzing the structure of the New Testament, biblical scholars annihilate faith and worship.

I have discussed Husserl's and Gadamer's views that scientistic reason has an "Other" that it is inherently incapable of understanding. Indeed, for Gadamer, science does not understand: it only explains. It is clear from the discussion that the "Other" of reason is not irrationality, nor is any attempt to understand it "irrational." Thus, the not uncommon belief that those "Continental" philosophers who discuss the theme of reason and its "Other" are mounting an attack on rationality itself is mistaken. No doubt, any talk of the "Other" of reason is apt to arouse suspicion. There is also a suspicion, among those more familiar with the "Continental" concern, that the proposed epistemology results in rampant relativism. The time has come to dispel all such suspicions.

## IV

It goes almost without saying that from the methodological point of view, there is nothing irrational about the procedures adopted by Heidegger, Husserl and Gadamer. Indeed, by any standard, these authors display meticulousness and thoroughness that border on the tedious. Throughout *Being and Time*, Heidegger insists on theoretical rigor, although the result is not the kind of mathematical rigor that many have come to expect. In the case of Husserl, one must not forget that he was the author of *Logical Investigations* and other logical and mathematical works. In the *Crisis*, as elsewhere, Husserl often stresses that skepticism and irrationalism have to be rejected. Indeed, he believes that an account of the pregiven life-world must be such that "we can arrive . . . at scientifically defensible assertions" about it, and this "requires special care in preparatory reflections."[33] The reflections and the answers we can come up with must be "based on rational insight."[34] As for Gadamer, his statement of his mission in the Introduction to *Truth and Method*, that he is concerned "with knowledge and truth,"[35] should put anyone at ease. Furthermore, he states later that this

32. One is here reminded of the following lines by Keats:
   Philosophy will clip an Angel's wings
   Conquer all mysteries by rule and line,
   Empty the haunted air, and gnomed mine –
   Unweave a rainbow.
   *Lamia*, II, 229.
   To be fair, what Keats calls "philosophy" here should be replaced by "science" or perhaps "scientific philosophy".
33. Husserl, *Crisis*, p. 122.
34. *Ibid.*, p. 6.
35. Gadamer, *Truth and Method*, p. xi.

concern has to be discharged within "responsible philosophizing."[36] In the Foreword to the second edition, he states that he "did not remotely intend to deny the necessity of methodical work within the human sciences."[37] What follows, of course, could well serve as a model of methodical work.

The question we really need to address is whether the theories themselves lead to irrationalism and relativism. The charge of irrationalism could be directed at any theory that advocates a return to a prescientific life-world, a world of ordinary experiences. To make this charge stick, it will have to be argued that such a world is essentially irrational, that beliefs, desires and actions in it are on the whole irrational, and that to ground truth and knowledge on such a world is to end up in irrationality. In reply, it may be pointed out that the premise of the argument, namely, the claim that the pregiven life-world is essentially irrational, is not true. One can give an argument in terms of evolution to refute this premise. Thus, if rationality has to do with attaining goals or purposes, then how could the human race survive and win the competitive game of nature if human actions are essentially irrational? Critics of the notion of life-world may argue that, at the very least, the emotions and passions of our experiences are not rational and should not be the ground of truth and knowledge. However, the distinction between the "rational side" and the "emotional side" of human life is nothing more than a cliche. Even within the analytical tradition, the distinction is by no means unproblematical, and is rejected in works such as de Sousa's *The Rationality of Emotion*.[38] Again, given the evolutionary story, one wonders how wildly irrational emotions, which tend to be destructive, could ever have become the norm. On the other hand, it is not uncommon that a scientist succeeds in the end by following his or her passions in the first place. In any case, the objection does not apply to Gadamer, who does not argue for grounding knowledge in life experiences, but only for recognizing them as a source of a different kind of knowledge equally worth having.

I turn now to the charge of relativism. The accusation is that the emphasis on subjectivity and in particular Gadamer's concept of understanding will lead to relativism. Concerning the latter, it may be said that understanding is always an understanding for me, that one person's understanding is just as valid as another's. However, this is so only if Gadamer's view implies that there can be no criteria by which to judge among rival understandings. This is what Gadamer explicitly denies. To say that one "way of understanding . . . is . . . no less legitimate than another," that there is "no criterion of an appropriate reaction" is for Gadamer "an untenable

---

36. *Ibid.*, p. xv.
37. *Ibid.*, p. xviii.
38. R. de Sousa, *The Rationality of Emotion*, Cambridge, 1987.

hermeneutic nihilism."[39] Gadamer can reject relativism on the grounds
that his notion of understanding is such that one's understanding is conditioned by tradition, history, the *sensus communis*, and particularly language. These are shared elements, common to all of us. Together, in some
dynamic way, they yield the criteria we need to prevent rampant relativism.

Concerning subjectivity, it cannot be denied that the German critique
puts an emphasis on the subjective. Indeed, the reason that the scientific
method is thought inappropriate is precisely that it is "objective" in the
way I have explained, and as such it cannot deal with the subjectivity of
human understanding. But, goes the objection, doesn't this emphasis lead
to subjectivism, which in turn leads to relativism? For Kant, and certainly
for Gadamer, the answer is "No." In the *Critique of Judgement*,[40] Kant
argues that the aesthetic judgment is necessarily subjective, but the ground
of this judgment, "namely the final harmony of an object . . . with the
mutual relation of the faculties of cognition," is universal.[41] Because of this
universal ground, the judgment, though subjective, can lay "claim, like
every other empirical judgment, to be valid for every one."[42] The charge of
relativism makes the mistake of not distinguishing between the kind of
subjectivity associated with matters of personal taste such as tastes in food
and wine, and the subjectivity associated with Kant's aesthetic judgments,
or Gadamer's understanding. In the case of the former, it is true that there
is no disputing taste: *de gustibus non disputandum*. In the case of the latter,
however, there are universal conditions, which are also *a priori* for Kant,
underlying our judgments such that they can "rightly lay(s) claim to the
agreement of every one." According to Kant, such judgments have "a claim
to subjective universality."[43] What is universal cannot be relative.

I have tried to show that a rejection, or dismissal, of the German critique
of scientistic reason on the basis that its results are against the ideal of rationality, and its methodology is contrary to the standard of "responsible philosophizing," cannot be justified. It is not irrational to try to understand
the "Other" of reason, even if this "Other" consists of irrationality. Husserl
himself would say that his claim that science cannot understand itself is
itself a scientific claim. The theme of reason and its "Other," at least the
way it has been treated by Husserl and Gadamer, is clearly legitimate, as
well as highly significant. Indeed, one may go as far as to say that, at its
core, the theme transcends philosophical traditions. This can be shown by

39. Gadamer, *Truth and Method*, p. 85.
40. Kant, *Critique of Judgement*, trans. J. C. Meredith, Oxford, 1952.
41. *Ibid.*, p. 32.
42. *Ibid.*, p. 31.
43. *Ibid.*, p. 51.

a cursory examination of certain themes more familiar to "analytical" philosophers.

Within the analytical tradition, any talk of deriving truth and knowledge from everyday experiences will be instantly recognized as empiricist. It is not surprising, then, that if we are to find within this tradition views similar to those discussed here, it is in the empiricist writings. Naturally, it will have to be the "old-fashioned" empiricism of Berkeley and Hume, before it was taken over in this century by the positivists, who turned empiricism against all kinds of "metaphysics." Hume in particular would have agreed with many of the claims made by Husserl and Gadamer. Hume's distinction between "demonstrative reasoning" (also "abstract reasoning" or "cogitative reasoning") and "experimental reasoning" (also "reasoning from cause to effect" or "moral reasoning") is an attempt to separate the sphere of knowledge based on mathematics or deductive reasoning from the knowledge of everyday experiences. The latter is based on regularities observed in our actual experiences. Thus, in a sense, it is based on inductive reasoning, but not the formal kind as formulated by J. S. Mill. Rather, it is of the "prescientific" kind based on custom or habit. Admittedly, Hume attempts to formalize it in the *Treatise*,[44] but formal rules are never meant to replace the authority of custom. For Hume, ordinary life experiences do give us a knowledge that we can rely on with confidence. Indeed, for practical purposes, custom is a more reliable guide than sophisticated reasoning. Hume would have found the idea of a life-world as the source of truth and knowledge most congenial. Hume separates what we know in this respect from what we know from "demonstrative reasoning" (both are distinguished from "probable" judgements). Thus in the *Enquiry Concerning the Human Understanding*, he says that "arguments" can be divided into "*demonstrations, proofs*, and *probabilities*."[45] Demonstrative reasoning has its own kind of certainty, but so does reasoning based on custom or habit. Judgments based on the "proofs" provided by custom or habit are "entirely free from doubt and uncertainty."[46] For by "proofs" Hume means "such arguments from experience as leave no room for doubt or opposition."[47] Life is capable of providing us with such proofs. As Hume says in the *Enquiry*, "the first and most trivial event in life will put to flight all . . . doubts and scruples."[48] Compare this with Gadamer's

---

44. Section XV, Part III, Book I, "Rules By Which to Judge of Causes and Effects." All quotations are from the Selby-Bigge eds., rev. by P. Nidditch, of the *Treatise*, Oxford, 1978, and the *Enquiry*, Oxford, 1975.
45. Hume, *Enquiry*, p. 56.
46. Hume, *Treatise*, p. 124.
47. Hume, *Enquiry*, p. 56.
48. *Ibid.*, p. 160.

statement cited earlier: ". . . in the natural attitude the validity of this personal world is always assumed."[49]

Hume can be said to have drawn limits around reasoning based on deduction and scientific induction. Beyond these limits is another world, the world of human experiences, where custom is king, with its own truth and validity. In this world, human actions are governed by passions. Indeed, when there is a conflict between scientific reasoning and what one feels like, the latter is always victorious. Arguably the most famous line from the *Treatise* is "Reason is and ought only to be the slave of the passions."[50] Compare this with Gadamer's statement cited earlier: ". . . human passions cannot be governed by the universal prescriptions of reason."[51] Interestingly, Hume has been accused of irrationalism and skepticism, just the sort of accusation that has been leveled at the views discussed previously. Again, the basis of the criticism is the belief that Hume cares little for reason. Barry Stroud, for instance, claims that "in Hume's hands the denigration of the role of reason and the corresponding elevation of feeling and sentiment is generalized into a total theory of man."[52] The charge of relativism is also not far behind this. With regard to this, one can defend Hume along more or less the same lines as discussed above. Indeed, Hume could be said to have in mind just the evolutionary line when he talks about the uniformity of nature and how it endows us all with the same natural tendencies. In discussing the artificiality of justice, Hume also talks about the role of community education in much the same way as Gadamer talks about the *sensus communis*. Since this sense of community is what we are all subjected to, or share in, Hume's subjectivism can also claim to be a subjective universality that tends to check relativism. As for the charge of irrationalism, I have argued elsewhere that Hume by no means can be said to be "denigrating reason."[53]

Turning to contemporary writings, the works of Peter Winch show that he shares most of Husserl's and Gadamer's concerns. Like them, Winch stresses the roles of linguistic as well as life contexts in understanding human actions, particularly the actions of those from a different culture. He argues that there is a reciprocal relationship between a person's understanding and the background context. In a passage containing ideas that could have come from Gadamer, he writes,

49. See footnote 26.
50. Hume, *Treatise*, p. 415.
51. See footnote 29.
52. B. Stroud, *Hume*, London, 1978, p. 10.
53. See my "David Hume on Reason, Passions and Morals," *Hume Studies* 10 (1984), pp. 26–45, and "The Role of Reason in Hume's Theory of Belief," *Hume Studies* 14 (1988), pp. 372–89.

A child is born within, and grows up into the life of, a particular human society. He learns to speak and to engage in various kinds of activity in relation to other people. . . . Along with this development there comes a growth in his understanding of what constitute problems and difficulties for them. . . . This growth in his understanding of other people through his dealings with them is at the same time a growth in his understanding of himself, which is in its turn a development of the kind of person he is.[54]

What follows from this passage is as clear a statement as one can get about the hermeneutical relationship between the agent and his or her life situations: The way a person develops in these dimensions will be influenced by the kinds of people, the kinds of situation and the kinds of problems he finds himself confronted with in the course of his life. But of course it is also true that his growth will depend on what he himself brings to the situations he faces.

The intimate, reciprocal relationship described here implies that an act of understanding is always an understanding of something in its particularity. In a recent collection of essays, Winch quotes the German writer, Grete Henry-Hermann, approvingly: "If someone is indignant about a lie, then it's about the particular lie that he heard or that was told to him. He is not indignant about the class of all possible lies."[55] What is generally true, about lies in this case, has an effect on us, but we do not make use of that generality in our understanding as we would use a scientific law, or a logical premise. Suppose, Winch says, one forms the belief that a man will suffer as a result of receiving some bad news. Such a belief represents our understanding of this man, and it is not arrived at "scientifically" or "logically" as a conclusion of some syllogism such as "'All men suffer at such news. This is a man hearing such news. Therefore. . . '."[56] Science deals in generality and is inapplicable here. Thus, "as an account of how I came to fear that this man would suffer, the syllogism is a completely mythological construction."[57] He goes on: "Yes, the life I have lived with other human beings is responsible for my reaction, but not by way of any general theoretical beliefs it has led me to hold." Life produces generalities, but none of them "could play the same role as that in the major premise of a syllogism or, for that matter, as that in a theory about what kind of thing a person essentially is."[58] Clearly, then, there is a separation between "scientific theorizing" and "understanding." At one point, Winch claims that the nature of human actions, or deeds, is such that they can be "described" by being

54. P. Winch, *Ethics and Action*, London, 1972, p. 84.
55. *Trying to Make Sense*, Oxford, 1987, p. 74.
56. Winch, *Ethics and Action*, pp. 151–52.
57. *Ibid.*, p. 152.
58. *Ibid.*

put in a specific context. This makes "deeds" different from scientific "objects": "One important difference is that deeds, unlike 'objects' can be described; another is that emphasis on the deed opens the door to an understanding of how new concepts can be created and to a way of grasping concepts and ways of thinking very different from our own."[59] The suggestion here seems to be that there can be only one context for "objects," namely the scientific context, and only one understanding, the scientific kind. More importantly, science cannot displace other kinds of understanding. For instance, science may "squeeze out the practices and judgments in which talk of oracles and witches finds its expressions," but "this is not to say that the 'belief in oracles and witches' has been refuted – perhaps by showing that the world does not contain such things."[60] One is here reminded of Gadamer's view that science has not refuted the belief that the sun will rise tomorrow. And since there is a context in which it is wrong to say that the sun rises, Winch points out that none of this "is to say that belief in oracles and witches (or in God) cannot be criticized – there are more kinds of criticism than one."[61]

Not surprisingly, Winch has been accused of relativism. However, Winch's defense does not seem to go as far as the defense one can mount on behalf of Husserl and Gadamer. One gets the impression that Winch accepts a kind of relativism but tries to minimize its negative impact by arguing that it is all right for the disputants to hold opposing positions provided that each can support his or her own position and each tries to understand how the other could hold the opposite position. "One way in which a man exercises his reason in such disputes is precisely in understanding the . . . positions of others opposed to his own, along with the difficulties in them, but equally in allowing them to highlight the difficulties in his own position."[62] At one point, Winch talks about "ethical neutrality" and seems to suggest that he would prefer this label to "ethical relativism."[63]

Moving toward the heart of analytical philosophy, we find that there are themes within the philosophy of action that could be construed as being supportive of some of Husserl's and Gadamer's crucial claims. In this respect, one could mention, for instance, G. E. M. Anscombe's view on intentionality. Indeed, the notion of intentionality discussed by Anscombe is precisely Brentano's, a notion that was later to play a key role in

59. *Ibid.*, p. 53.
60. *Ibid.*, p. 207.
61. *Ibid.*
62. *Ibid.*, p. 199.
63. *Ibid.*, p. 191.

Husserl's phenomenology.[64] Intentionality is tied up in the idea of human action, in that an action can be described in terms of the intention the agent has in performing that action, which in turn involves what the agent believes. If this is what an action is essentially, then the world of human actions, the life-world, is an intentional world. That makes it fundamentally different from the natural world, in which events occur without intentionality. From this it seems only a small step from the claim that the method of the natural sciences is inappropriate to a study of human actions.

Some of the more recent works in the theory of action[65] account for human actions in terms of belief and desire. While both states are intentional in Brentano's sense, desire differs from belief in that it is further removed from natural "reality." Indeed, Anscombe herself has characterized this difference in terms of "direction of fit": to believe is to believe something to be true, hence we assess the belief in terms of the extent to which it "fits" the world; to desire, on the other hand, is to desire that the world be in a particular state, and the satisfaction of the desire is the extent to which the world "fits" the desire. If desire has a major role to play in human action then clearly for the scientific method to be appropriate, it will have to be able to account adequately for desires. This requirement becomes more urgent if it is believed that while both belief and desire are involved in an action, it is desire that ultimately motivates one to act. To hold such a view is to complete the circle back to Hume. For it is, as Michael Smith has pointed out, just the Humean theory of motivation.[66]

The conclusion for any analytical philosopher is that if Hume is right, we had better try to account satisfactorily for human desires, or passions. It does not look as if it is possible to do so without paying attention to the social, personal and hermeneutical contexts in which desires come about. It does not look as if we can understand a person's passions without understanding his or her life-world. But this is just what Husserl and Gadamer are saying. Hume himself has experienced the frustration of trying to understand certain life experiences in purely "philosophical" (for which we can read "scientific") terms. For instance, he expresses in the Appendix to the *Treatise* his frustration at being unable to come to terms with his philosophical view about the self. And in the conclusion of Book I, he admits

---

64. "The Intentionality of Sensation," in R. J. Butler (ed.), *Analytical Philosophy*, Oxford, 1965, 2nd ed., p. 13. D. Davidson, "Action, Reasons, and Causes," *Journal of Philosophy* 60 (1963), pp. 685–700.

65. E.g., D. Davidson, "Action, Reasons, and Causes," *Journal of Philosophy* 60 (1963), pp. 685–700.

66. M. Smith, "The Humean Theory of Motivation," *Mind* 96 (1986), pp. 36–61.

that there is a side of him that "determin'd" him to "live, and talk, and act like other people in the common affairs of life," and to regard the philosophical views as "so cold, and strain'd, and ridiculous."[67] One can almost hear the word "*Lebenswelt*" in the phrase "the common affairs of life." Is it not the case that Hume is here talking about the "Other" of his philosophical reason? The theme of reason and its "Other" is more widespread than we may think.

67. Hume, *Treatise*, p. 269.

# –11–

# Reason, Identity and the Body: Reading Adorno with Irigaray

## MICHELLE WALKER

> Disenchantment of the concept is the antidote of philosophy
>
> ADORNO, *Negative Dialectics*

The discourse of reason within Western philosophy sustains an illusion of the primacy of the concept. This logic of identity attempts to smooth over the contradictions and antagonisms of thought and experience. Reason, relying on the priority of the concept, is elevated to a governing operation that attempts to reduce everything to an unambiguous self-identity. The Other of reason refuses to identify with the rational concept, and thus exceeds the logic of identity that attempts to contain it.

The debates on modernity in German culture are characterized by an interrogation of reason as a category of identity that excludes and represses its Other. While for some, nature represents the significant Other of reason, for others it is the body, the passions, or the literary that transgresses the bounds of rational thought. The psychoanalytic intervention into these debates is dominated today by a French rereading and contextualizing of the German texts. It employs the language of the unconscious to explore what is repressed by the dominating imposition of rational thought.

In *Totem and Taboo* Freud argues that the rational process entails a propensity toward unity, connection and intelligibility. Earlier he had forged the links between thought and the dream-work in *The Interpretation of Dreams*, when he wrote of secondary revision as a function similar to the philosophical or interpretative enterprise. By filling in "the gaps in the dream-structure with shreds and patches,"[1] secondary revision behaves much like the philosopher who is unable to acknowledge the gaps in rea-

---

1. S. Freud, "The Dream-Work," in *The Interpretation of Dreams*, trans. J. Strachey, New York, 1965, p. 528; *Standard Edition*, London, 1958, vol. 5, p. 490.

son. Reason, like the dream, becomes a totalized structure. The process of secondary revision is a dissimulating function that characterizes not only the dream work, but also the intelligibility of reason in Western thought.

Rational thought involves the tendency to "grasp the whole universe as a single unity from a single point of view."[2] Unity and totality become synonymous with the interpretative enterprise. For Freud this totalizing gesture remains bound to the emerging unity of the narcissistic ego; the singular view and unity reflecting the apparent unity of this ego. As Samuel Weber explains:

> The pursuit of meaning; the activity of construction, synthesis, unification; the incapacity to admit anything irreducibly alien, to leave any residue unexplained – all this indicates the struggle of the ego to establish and to maintain an identity that is all the more precarious and vulnerable to the extent that it depends on what it must exclude.[3]

The French elaboration of Freud's work continues these themes, stressing the illusory nature of (self) identity. For Jacques Lacan the construction of unity represents an illusory mastery on the part of the ego. As a result of the ego's formation during the mirror stage (Lacan's secondary revision of Freud's narcissistic ego?) the emerging subject will henceforth seek an imaginary wholeness, a unity, in an attempt to master his environment.[4] This unity, this desire to comprehend, is precisely what motivates the act of interpretation, the desire to connect. Julia Kristeva reminds us that interpretative mastery, the desire to give meaning, "is rooted in the speaking subject's need to reassure himself of his image and his identity" and is thus "the apogee of the obsessive quest for A Meaning," a single and ultimate Meaning.[5]

The desire to interpret and to unify is central to the construction of reason within Western metaphysics. Reason enacts the mastery of thought by reducing it to discrete conceptual unities. The concept is therefore an attempt to unify and totalize meaning. It is an attempt to repress that which escapes reason. Disenchanting the concept thus becomes a means of deconstructing the illusory mastery of reason.

The German critique of reason and identity is represented in the work of Theodor W. Adorno. He argues that the concept needs to be severed from the dominating logic of identity, opening it to that which lies beyond

2. *Totem and Taboo,* Standard Edition, vol. 13, p. 77.

3. S. Weber, "A Problem of Narcissism," in *The Legend of Freud,* Minneapolis, 1982, pp. 13–14.

4. J. Lacan, "The mirror stage as formative of the function of the I as revealed in psychoanalytic experience," in *Ecrits,* trans. A. Sheridan, New York, 1977.

5. J. Kristeva, "Psychoanalysis and the Polis," trans. M. Waller, in W. J. T. Michell (ed.), *The Politics of Interpretation,* Chicago, 1983, p. 84.

reason. While Adorno claims that "necessity compels philosophy to operate with concepts," he contends that "this necessity must not be turned into the virtue of their priority."[6] Changing the direction of conceptuality, turning it toward nonidentity is the basis of Adorno's project of negative dialectics.

Similar concerns preoccupy the French philosopher and psychoanalyst Luce Irigaray. Her critique of identity, however, is motivated by the need to dispel specifically masculine constructions of language, meaning and thought. Rational thought, she argues, is a predominantly masculine enterprise that aims to repress that which refuses its logic. For Irigaray the feminine represents the repressed Other of reason. Because of this it cannot be expressed in rational terms: "to claim that the feminine can be expressed in the form of a concept is to allow oneself to be caught up again in a system of 'masculine' representations." Obviously, disputing "femininity" as a concept cannot be merely a matter of elaborating another concept, "unless a woman is renouncing her sex and wants to speak like men."[7]

For Irigaray the identitarian nature of rational thought is an expression of the metaphysical separation of mind and body. The denial of the body and the violence she argues this denial implies, is a condition of phallocentric discourse – a discourse ensuring the mind's own identity precisely by rejecting all that is not mind. For phallocentrism, privileging as it does unity and distance, identity becomes the dominant logic. This logic entails the cultural distancing of man from his body. According to Irigaray, "Historically, they have chosen sex and language against or in spite of the body. The depositories of the body are women. That is, men can find the body in women . . . but women cannot find this in men."[8]

The phallocentric nature of rational thought is a focus for Irigaray's critique of conceptuality. Through the authority of the concept, thought is reduced to an economy of the same. It is this economy that Irigaray labels masculine. Thus sameness, oneness "is always also a project of diversion, deflection, reduction of the other in the Same . . . its power to eradicate the difference between the sexes in systems that are self-representative of a 'masculine subject.'"[9] Woman is constructed as a lack or negative within Western discourse. Within this logic "female sexuality cannot articulate itself, unless precisely as an undertone."[10] What does not reduce to one, to the masculine, is repressed as a violation.

6. T. W. Adorno, *Negative Dialectics*, trans. E. B. Ashton, London, 1973, p. 12.

7. L. Irigaray, *This Sex Which is Not One*, trans. C. Porter, Ithaca, New York, 1985, pp. 122–23.

8. L. Irigaray, "Women's Exile," *Ideology & Consciousness* 1, Spring 1977, p. 76. This suggests the need for men to theorize their bodies, something usually associated with female theoretical endeavors.

9. Irigaray, *This Sex Which is Not One*, p. 74.

10. Irigaray, "Women's Exile," p. 64.

While Adorno adopts a similarly critical posture toward the unity of thought, it would be misleading to represent his project as the same as Irigaray's.[11] Instead, I propose a reading of Adorno with Irigaray in order to foreground the centrality of the body in his critique. By emphasizing Irigaray's insistence on the masculine body as the locus of identity, I suggest that, in Adorno's account of domination and objectification, it is the displaced relation between mind and body that in fact prefigures the relations of domination inherent in both conceptuality and intentionality.

This (unorthodox) heterosexual coupling of Irigaray with Adorno, while vaguely troubling, represents an appropriation of his text; an unframing[12] that emphasizes the role of the body within his critique of reason. Irigaray's account of the masculine nature of identity implies that Adorno's critique cannot be understood without taking into consideration his discussion of man's denigrated body. While this may appear to some to be a marginal element of Adorno's work, I argue that it informs the entirety of Adorno's critical process. This argument entails a reading of the German exploration of the limits of reason and the concept, in Adorno's text, with the radical inflection of the body from Irigaray's French (psychoanalytic) context.

## Negative Dialectics as Process

The following discussion provides an outline of Adorno's fragmentary process. It is an attempt to situate his claims in a manner that ironically risks reproducing what Adorno was most suspicious of; that is, the extrication of "the content of ideas from the form of their presentation."[13]

11. For a discussion of Adorno's critique of specular rationalism see K. Salleh, "Contribution to the Critique of Political Epistemology," *Thesis Eleven* 8, 1984, p. 25; n. 5 p. 41. While Salleh's discussion entails an overview of the "Frankfurt School," Adorno's work is usefully distanced from such *identification*. The influences of Hans Cornelius, Siegfried Kracauer and, most importantly, Walter Benjamin upon Adorno's criticism of the Hegelian tendencies toward totality (*Vernunft*) and reconciliation, distance his thought significantly from that of his colleagues, such as Herbert Marcuse, whose work on art, for example, retains a belief in the revelation of an original plenitude. For an extensive discussion see M. Jay, "Theodor W. Adorno and the Collapse of the Lukácsian Concept of Totality," in *Marxism and Totality: The Adventures of a Concept from Lukács to Habermas*, Berkeley, 1984. For a critical appraisal of Jay's position, see J. Gumley, "Adventures of the Concept of Totality: Thoughts on Martin Jay's *Marxism and Totality*," *Thesis Eleven* 15, 1986, pp. 111–21.

12. For a discussion of the politics of framing/unframing, see J. Frow, "Limits: The Politics of Reading," in *Marxism and Literary History*, Oxford, 1986.

13. M. Jay, *Adorno*, London, 1984, p.12. Gillian Rose, in *The Melancholy Science*, London, 1978, makes a similar point. She writes, "It is impossible to understand Adorno's ideas without understanding the ways in which he presents them, that is, his style, and without understanding the reasons for his preoccupation with style. . . . Adorno's work is the most abstruse, and . . . still the most misunderstood. This is partly a result of its deliberately paradoxical, polemical and fractured nature, which has made it eminently quotable but egregiously misconstruable." (pp. 11, ix.).

Nonetheless it seems necessary to run this risk in order to convey the process of his negative dialectics.

While Adorno's writing is often located within the general field of Marxist humanism, or more specifically, left-Hegelianism, this depiction does little to elucidate the distinctive quality of his thought.[14] Far from (re)presenting humanistic concerns and priorities, Adorno's thought is critical of the anthropomorphic tendencies inherent within much Western discourse. His refusal of the Cartesian subject and its implicit mind-body bifurcation denies the validity of the logical separation of the domains of human intentionality and natural determinism within Western reason. Adorno rejects historicism and philosophical anthropology, but nonetheless seeks to find a way out of the paradox of adopting an "anti-humanist" stance by "undermining humanism on its own grounds."[15] While his critique of anthropomorphism is most evident in his discussion of idealism, it is also a central concern in his approach to dialectical materialism.[16] He argues that the positive anthropology of much Marxist discourse "implied an acceptance of man's centrality, which in turn denigrated the natural world."[17]

Adorno's critical posture toward humanism is symptomatic of his indebtedness to Friedrich Nietzsche. Nietzsche's grasp of the self-abrogation of Enlightenment contributed significantly to Adorno's formulation of the dialectics at play. Adorno's criticism of Hegel's "hypostasis of mind" and "homage to the speculative concept" can be understood in light of Nietzsche. For Adorno, Nietzsche's "liberating act, a true turning point of Western thought and merely usurped by others later, was to put such mysteries into words."[18]

Adorno's work is heavily influenced by Nietzsche's idiosyncratic writing. For both the question of the text's content is indistinguishable from its style of presentation. Preferring the uncompleted essayistic form to deduction and mathematical analysis, each develops what Peter Pütz calls a "paratactic form of representation. . . . The sections need not be read in the

14. For a critical discussion of the characterization of Adorno as humanist, see M. Jay, "The Frankfurt School's Critique of Marxist Humanism," *Social Research* 39, 1972, p. 287.

15. Rose, *The Melancholy Science*, pp. 138–39. For a similar rejection of a simplistic "anti-humanist" label see J. Whitebook, "Saving the Subject: Modernity and the Problem of the Autonomous Individual," *Telos* 50, 1981–82, pp. 79–80.

16. Jay, "The Frankfurt School's Critique of Marxist Humanism," p. 293.

17. M. Jay, *The Dialectical Imagination: A History of the Frankfurt School and the Institute of Social Research: 1923–1950*, Boston, 1973, p. 266. Here Jay refers to both Adorno and Horkheimer. Indeed he notes (fn. 45, pp. 348–49) that "Alfred Schmidt has tried to distinguish between Adorno as a 'real humanist' and other conventional humanists." However, Adorno "dislike[d] . . . the positive connotations of any static definition of human nature . . . [and] fear[ed] that anthropocentricity would mean the concomitant denigration of nature."

18. Adorno, *Negative Dialectics*, p. 23.

sequence in which they have been printed. . . . The thoughts often circle around central statements in the form of *aperçus* and aphorisms."[19] The Nietzschean influence is readily observed in Adorno's "On the Nature and Form of the Essay," where he argues that thought "thinks in breaks because reality is brittle and finds [itself] through the breaks, not by smoothing things over."[20]

Throughout his work Adorno argues against the logical unity and cohesion of rational thought, favoring an approach characterized by fragmentation and disintegration – once again a decidedly Nietzschean motif. In developing Nietzsche's critique of identity philosophy, Adorno attacks "identity thinking" as a dominating imposition of the concept. He argues against the fundamental identity of thought and being, rejecting what he sees as the Hegelian inclination toward synthesis and identity:

> The task of dialectical cognition is not, as its adversaries like to charge, to construe contradictions from above and to progress by resolving them – although Hegel's logic, now and then, proceeds in this fashion. Instead, it is up to dialectical cognition to pursue the inadequacy of thought and thing, to experience it in the thing . . . dialectics aims at what is different. It is as philosophy's self-criticism that the dialectical motion stays philosophical.[21]

Adorno attempts to turn conceptuality toward nonidentity. He attacks the Hegelian domination of identity over nonidentity, universality over particularity, and subject over object. However, he avoids absolutizing this methodology. Negative dialectics remains a process, not an end point. Adorno refuses the Hegelian synthesis, which stresses the overcoming of contradiction within a higher-order unity. He displaces the Hegelian dialectic and emphasizes the consistency of nonidentity, bringing us back to Nietzsche and his belief that "nothing happens in reality that would strictly correspond to logic."[22]

Adorno introduces multiplicity, heterogeneity, and difference within the rigidity of the philosophic calculus by employing a variety of playful styles. The use of ironic inversion, irony as the use of words to convey the opposite of their usual or recognizable meaning, is a strategy employed widely in his aphoristic text *Minima Moralia*. This constitutes part of Adorno's immanent critique of the difference between ideology and reality. Adorno's use of Hegelian terminology relies upon this Nietzschean

19. P. Pütz, "Nietzsche and Critical Theory," *Telos* 50, Winter 1981–82, p. 111.

20. Adorno, "On the Nature and Form of the Essay," cited in J. Lindsay, *The Crisis in Marxism*, Wiltshire, 1981, p. 67. And further: ". . . one cannot construct a continuous argument with the usual stages, but one must assemble the whole from a series of partial complexes . . . whose constellation, not [logical] sequence produces the idea."

21. Adorno, *Negative Dialectics*, p. 153.

22. In Pütz, "Nietzsche and Critical Theory," p. 110.

strategy of textual inversion. Other strategies involve the use of chiasmus – half argument, half trope, the positing of antinomies, and the formation of constellations.[23] Adorno's method of criticism involves a process of dialectics without the identity of synthesis. His signifying practice discloses the "tensions between opposed levels of meaning hidden" within a concept or term.[24]

In order to expose the double character of concepts, Adorno employs a process whereby, dialectically, concepts are used against each other to demythologize reality. Susan Buck-Morss suggests that "to understand this procedure is to grasp the essential mechanism" of Adorno's negative dialectics. The fragmentary nature of Adorno's concepts, their deliberate ambiguity, creates a barrier against easy assimilation: "It was precisely his intent to frustrate the categorizing, defining mentality which by the twentieth century had itself become 'second nature'."[25]

## Negative Dialectics and Deconstruction?

Given that Nietzsche's influence has also had a profound effect upon the work of Jacques Derrida, it is not surprising to discern a striking similarity between the projects of deconstruction and negative dialectics. Nietzsche serves as a meeting point between French and German critiques of reason. Derrida's appropriation of Nietzsche's texts rehearses an active translation of German concerns into a peculiarly French context. Various writers have commented on the Nietzschean motifs that inform both Adorno and Derrida's work. For Martin Jay, Adorno represents the proto-deconstructionist, his work and critical method demonstrating an acute anticipation of later deconstruction.[26] According to Michael Ryan, the two tendencies share strong affinities, although he quite rightly argues that to identify them as the same project "would be to betray the spirit of each."[27] Nonetheless he goes on to develop a "critical articulation" of Adorno and

23. In her chapter "The Search For Style," G. Rose, in *The Melancholy Science*, outlines very clearly the difficult strategies employed within Adorno's texts.

24. A. Salleh, "On the Dialectics of Signifying Practice," *Thesis Eleven*, 5/6, 1982, p. 79. I am indebted to Salleh's insightful analysis of Adorno's work.

25. S. Buck-Morss, *The Origin of Negative Dialectics: Theodor W. Adorno, Walter Benjamin, and the Frankfurt Institute*, Sussex, 1977, pp. 58–59.

26. Jay, *Adorno*, pp. 22, 108, 112. Jay also notes the "striking parallels" between Foucault's "analysis of the disciplinary, carceral society of modernity and Adorno's *administered world.*" Indeed, a similar parallel is also drawn by S. Aronowitz, *The Crisis in Historical Materialism: Class, Politics and Culture in Marxist Theory*, New York, 1981, pp. 26–27. Here Aronowitz points to Adorno's anticipation of many of the concerns of French poststructuralist theory, concerns linked to a conception of modernity as discontinuous and fragmentary.

27. M. Ryan, *Marxism and Deconstruction: A Critical Articulation*, Baltimore, 1982, p. 73.

Derrida, pointing to both their similarities and incongruities. For Ryan negative dialectics and deconstruction involve "immanent critiques of philosophies of identity and transcendence." For example, Derrida uses the language of metaphysics in his erasure, while Adorno uses the concept to explode the concept.[28] In both instances the aim in deconstructing the dualisms of identity and nonidentity, subject and object, mind and body, is not merely to reverse the hierarchy but, more importantly, to displace it.

Adorno's negative dialectics involves an immanent critique that would seem to prefigure Derrida's deconstructive practice. Both are preoccupied with the demolition of hierarchical oppositions within rational thought.[29] Adorno argues that it is insufficient merely to reverse existing hierarchies; they must be abolished: "It is not the purpose of critical thought to place the object on the orphaned royal throne once occupied by the subject. On that throne the object would be nothing but an idol. The purpose of critical thought is to abolish the hierarchy."[30]

While Derrida's deconstructive practice does involve reversal, he considers this one phase of the larger process of dismantling relations. His deconstructive process involves an eventual disruption, not just its reversal. He speaks of the double gesture of deconstruction, which first involves the overturning or reversal of hierarchy:

> On the one hand, we must traverse a phase of overturning. To do justice to this necessity is to recognize that in a classical philosophical opposition we are not dealing with a violent hierarchy. One of the two terms governs the other (axiologically, logically, etc.), or has the upper hand. To deconstruct the opposition, first of all, is to overturn the hierarchy at a given moment. To overlook this phase of overturning is to forget the conflictual and subordinating structure of opposition.[31]

While deconstruction differs from negative dialectics in certain tactical and strategical ways, it is arguable that Adorno's methodology informs Derrida's practice. In this context the affinities between negative dialectics and deconstruction are clear. As Terry Eagleton notes,

---

28. *Ibid.*, pp. 73–74.

29. For a critical discussion of the similarities and differences between negative dialectics and deconstruction in this respect, see P. Dews, *Logics of Disintegration: Post-Structuralist Thought and the Claims of Critical Theory*, London, 1987, pp. 38–44.

30. Adorno, *Negative Dialectics*, p. 181.

31. J. Derrida, "Positions: Interviews with Jean-Louis Houdebine and Guy Scarpetta" in *Positions*, trans. A. Bass, Chicago, 1981, p. 41. Derrida adds, "When I say that this phase is necessary, the word *phase* is perhaps not the most rigorous one. It is not a question of a chronological phase, a given moment, or a page that one day simply will be turned, in order to go on to other things. The necessity of this phase is structural; it is the necessity of an interminable analysis: the hierarchy of dual oppositions always reestablishes itself" (pp. 41–42).

Long before the current fashion Adorno was insisting on the power of those heterogeneous fragments that slip through the conceptual net, rejecting all philosophy of identity . . . and denying the intentionality of signification. Indeed there is hardly a theme in contemporary deconstruction that is not richly elaborated in his work.[32]

Negative dialectics stresses the gaps and ruptures in identity philosophy, the ruses of reason. In so doing it turns the dominating impulse of conceptuality against itself by using the same term in contradictory or multiple senses.[33] This constitutes, to use Adorno's words, a "logic of disintegration . . . a disintegration of the prepared and objectified form of the concept." He argues that thought "need not be content with its own legality . . . we can think against our thought, and if it were possible to define dialectics, this would be a definition worth suggesting."[34] Definition, of course, is exactly what Adorno must avoid. Negative Dialectics is, then, "a protest lodged by our thinking against the archaicisms of its conceptuality . . . [and] amounts to thinking so that the thought form will no longer turn its objects into immutable ones, into objects that remain the same."[35]

## Fragmenting the Concept: Natural History

Adorno's formulation of "Natural History" provides an example of his fragmentary and disruptive process. He attempts to expose the preconceptions of history and nature by using each against the other. He rejects the formal abstractions of historicism and naturalism, denying the logical hierarchy that is in each case presupposed. The falsely resurrected metaphysics of historicity, he claims, "glosses over the painful antithesis of nature and history," requiring the "identity of the non-identical, removing by suppo-

32. T. Eagleton, *Walter Benjamin or Towards a Revolutionary Criticism*, London, 1981, p. 141. While Adorno's writing is suggestive of contemporary deconstruction in its attacks upon an epistemological tradition that privileges the subject in the process of cognition, Michael Cahn argues that his "position can never be *equated* with the deconstructive attempts to privilege the signifier over the signified, unless one intends to cancel out the epistemological relationship altogether." M. Cahn, "Subversive Mimesis: Theodor W. Adorno and the Modern Impasse of Critique," in M. Spariosu (ed.), *Mimesis in Contemporary Theory, Vol. I: The Literary and Philosophical Debate*, Philadelphia, 1984, fn. 27, p. 60.

33. "Dialectics," for example, is used by Adorno to refer to both his negative dialectics and Hegelian dialectics, forcing the reader to grapple with the ambiguity.

34. Adorno, *Negative Dialectics*, pp. 145, 141. Or as Fredric Jameson, in *Marxism and Form: Twentieth Century Dialectical Theories of Literature*, Princeton, 1971, pp. 45, 56, contends: ". . . dialectical thinking is a thought to the second power, a thought about thinking itself . . . [Negative dialectics results] in a thoroughgoing critique of forms, in a painstaking and well-nigh permanent destruction of every possible hypostasis of the various moments of thinking itself." It is important to note that Adorno's method of doubling concepts, while in keeping with the spirit of his negative dialectics, provides the production of a positive textual strategy designed to unbalance and displace the logic of unity structuring the text.

35. *Negative Dialectics*, pp. 153–54.

sition of the concept . . . whatever would resist the concept."[36] Equally untenable is the naturalist ideology "that society is subject to laws . . . immutably given by nature."[37] For Adorno, then, history and nature are not identical. This does not suggest, however, that he himself constructs them as hierarchically-ordered dualities. Accordingly, it is up to thought to see all nature as history and all history as nature, while remembering that "The moment in which nature and history become commensurable with each other is the moment of passing."[38]

In his rejection of the customary antithesis of history and nature, Adorno reiterates his challenge to rational thought. Just as the concept attempts to dominate that which it designates, so too does human intentionality (perceived as history) attempt to dominate the other of nature. Indeed Adorno argues that the logic of identity within Western metaphysics is the sublimated expression of the desire to actively subordinate nature. He contends that the Cartesian mind-body dualism later comes to imply the separation of human intentionality and natural determinism. For Adorno it is necessary to deconstruct this antithesis. His formulation of natural history rejects the primacy of either individual intentionality or invariant natural laws. Against Hegel's conception of history as totality, Adorno argues that it forms "no structural whole," that it is instead "discontinuous, unfolding within a multiplicity of divisions," guaranteeing no "identity of reason and reality;" its force being the spaces between reason and reality.[39] Accordingly, Adorno rejects the typical characterization of history as progress, and it is this theme that pervades his critique of the Enlightenment doctrines of mastery and control.

With the Enlightenment stress upon the emancipation of reason from nature, rational control or mastery over nature became synonymous with historical progress, thus enshrining an instrumental rationality of domination. With the identification of progress and freedom, an attitude of domi-

36. Adorno, *Negative Dialectics*, p. 359. See also Adorno, "The Idea of Natural History," *Telos* 60 (1984), pp. 111–25.

37. *Negative Dialectics*, p. 355.

38. *Ibid.*, p. 359. Adorno's great debt to Walter Benjamin becomes obvious when he quotes his *Origins of German Tragedy*: "When history, in tragedy, makes its entrance on the stage, it does so as writing. The countenance of nature is inscribed 'History' in pictographs of passing." For an excellent discussion of the influence of Walter Benjamin on Adorno's thought see S. Buck-Morss, *The Origin of Negative Dialectics*. See also E. Lunn, *Marxism and Modernism: A Historical Study of Lukács, Brecht, Benjamin and Adorno*, Berkeley, 1982, Part Three.

39. Buck-Morss, *The Origin of Negative Dialectics*, p. 47. As Buck-Morss points out, "Adorno had no concept of history in the sense of an ontological, positive definition of history's philosophical meaning" (p. 49). And further: "He used history, in connection with nature as its dialectical opposite, as a critical cognitive concept, a theoretical tool to demythify socio-historical phenomena and rob them of their power over consciousness and action" (p. 57).

nation toward nature became inevitable. Thus the Enlightenment focus upon the mind polarized human intentionality against nature. In *Dialectic of Enlightenment*, written with Max Horkheimer, Adorno contends that "[t]he program of the Enlightenment was the disenchantment of the world; the dissolution of myths and the substitution of knowledge for fancy . . . the human mind . . . [was] to hold sway over a disenchanted nature."[40]

As a result of the Enlightenment, formal logic became the unifying science, providing the "Enlightenment thinkers with the calculability of the world." Number became the "canon of Enlightenment."[41] Adorno and Horkheimer note that "to the Enlightenment, that which does not reduce to numbers, and ultimately to the one, becomes illusion; modern positivism writes it off as literature."[42] Within this process, thinking objectifies itself and becomes an instrument. It denies its critical, negative quality. "Factuality wins the day; cognition is restricted to its repetition; and thought becomes mere tautology."[43] Reason or intellect separates itself from sensuous experience only to subjugate it, leaving both thought and experience impoverished.

Far from representing freedom, the rejection of nature by its subjugation to reason implies the triumph of domination. Human freedom becomes nothing other than the dominating impulse to overcome the otherness of nature, simply by making it into an extension of ourselves.[44] For Adorno, this principle,

> . . . which antagonistically rends human society, is the same principle which . . . causes the difference between the concept and its subject matter . . . whatever does not bow to its unity will not appear as something different from and indifferent to the principle, but as a violation of logic.[45]

The conceptual imperialism of this dominating impulse is thus evidenced in the conquest of nature by reason.

For many this antagonism is perceived as resulting primarily from a separation of "man" and "nature," the fundamental principle of Enlightenment or bourgeois society being the domination of nature.[46] Adorno argues that this antagonism cannot be understood outside of the fundamental violence of the Cartesian separation of mind from body. For

40. T. W. Adorno and M. Horkheimer, *Dialectic of Enlightenment*, trans. J. Cumming, London, 1979, pp. 3–4.

41. *Ibid.*, p. 7.

42. *Ibid.* And further: "Unity is the slogan from Parmenides to Russell," p. 8.

43. *Ibid.*, p. 27.

44. I. Balbus, *Marxism and Domination: A Neo-Hegelian, Feminist, Psychoanalytic Theory of Sexual, Political and Technological Liberation*, Princeton, 1982, p. 18.

45. Adorno, *Negative Dialectics*, p. 48.

46. This has become a popular theme in contemporary criticism of Marxist philosophy. See, for example, Aronowitz, *The Crisis in Historical Materialism*.

Adorno, "the compulsive urge to cruelty and destruction springs from the organic displacement of the relationship between the mind and body."[47] Indeed, in his call for the writing of the history of the body, the "subterranean history of Europe," Adorno anticipates Foucault. Both are critical of an instrumental rationality that inflicts violence and discipline upon the "prerational sphere" of the body.[48] Adorno writes,

> Europe has two histories: a well-known, written history and an underground history. The latter consists in the fate of human instincts and passions which are displaced and distorted by civilisation. The relationship with the human body is maimed from the outset.[49]

Adorno comments upon society's ambivalence toward the body, suggesting that, while often scorned and rejected as inferior, the body is at one and the same time "desired as something forbidden, objectified, and alienated." Physicality becomes "an object of attraction and repulsion." Further,

> Culture defines the body as a thing which can be possessed; in culture a distinction is made between the body and the spirit, the concept of power and command, as the object, the dead thing, the "corpus." In man's denigration of his own body nature takes its revenge for the fact that man had reduced nature to an object for domination, a raw material.[50]

The foregoing passages reveal the primacy of the body in Adorno's critique of domination. Here, rational thought is perceived as that which subjugates and silences the body, the instincts, and the passions. The violent separation of the body from the superior realm of the mind establishes the hierarchy that prefigures all other relations of power and domination.

### Exposing the Phallus

The same. . . . Same. . . . Always the same.[51]

Luce Irigaray attempts to deconstruct identity as the privileged form of representation within Western metaphysics. In so doing her aim is to

47. Adorno and Horkheimer, *Dialectic of Enlightenment*, p. 233.
48. For a discussion of Adorno and Foucault see A. Honneth, "Foucault and Adorno: Two Forms of the Critique of Modernity," *Thesis Eleven* 15, 1986, pp. 48–58. Honneth points out not only the similarities in their critiques but, perhaps more importantly, the differences in their approaches to the question of subjectivity. See also Jay, *Adorno*, p. 88.
49. Adorno and Horkheimer, *Dialectic of Enlightenment*, p. 231.
50. *Ibid.*, pp. 232–33. And further: "Those who extolled the body above all else, the gymnasts and scouts, always had the closest affinity with killing. They use the body and its parts as though they were already separated from it. Jewish tradition contains a disinclination to measure men with a foot-rule because the corpse is measured in this way for the coffin. This is what the manipulators of the body enjoy. They measure others, without realizing it, with the gaze of a coffin maker" (p. 235).
51. Irigaray, "When Our Lips Speak Together," in Irigaray, *This Sex Which Is Not One*, p. 205.

expose the phallocentric logic inherent within its construction. Like Adorno, she is critical of the dominating impulse behind the rational will to identify. Similarly, she attempts to displace the violence of abstracting body from mind. However, unlike Adorno, she conveys an acute awareness of the sexual specificity of this process, revealing the manner in which critics of identity have themselves ignored the masculine bias of their own logic. While acknowledging the embodied reality of their existence, such critics have largely overlooked the significance of their own sexual positioning. This is evidenced, she claims, in the masculine appropriation of any theory of the subject.[52]

Phallocentric logic, assuming as it does the universal nature of the masculine standard, seeks to identify objective reality with the perceptions of a disavowed masculine subject. It is this very logic that Irigaray attempts to reveal. The use of terminology such as "exposure" and "revelation" entails a certain irony in any discussion of Irigaray's work. She is critical of the specular nature of the masculine economy, valuing as it does "property, production, order, form, unity, visibility . . . and erection."[53] For Irigaray the hierarchically dominating tendencies of identity, sameness and visibility are the preconditions for representation within Western reason. These tendencies are precisely what must be challenged, disrupted and displaced. Given that philosophy establishes itself as the "discourse on discourse," it is within philosophy that such disruption should initially occur: "Whence the necessity of 'reopening' the figures of philosophical discourse – idea, substance, subject, transcendental subjectivity, absolute knowledge. . . ."[54]

Rejecting the absolute sovereignty of the (masculine) subject, thereby displacing the authority of the concept, facilitates a critique of the phallocentric logic of philosophical discourse, a critique that does not remain enclosed "within the same type of utterance as the one that guarantees discursive coherence." Irigaray does not propose a (re)production of philosophy with woman as subject or object, but rather a process "of jamming the

52. L. Irigaray, *Speculum of the Other Woman*, trans. G. C. Gill, Ithaca, 1985, p. 133.

53. Irigaray, "Così Fan Tutti," in Irigaray, *This Sex Which Is Not One*, p. 86. For Salleh, specular culture is based on the notion of "unity, presence, identity, the tangible positive," while the "female morphologic suggests a principle of non-identity, an absolute defiance of the classic, patristic Aristotelian rules of Identity. . . ." Salleh, "Contribution to the Critique of Political Epistemology," p. 33. For Hegel, speculative thought (*Spekulation*) concerns itself with reconstituting unity; a structured totality. According to Gasché, "This idea of totality, whereby absolute reflection *measures itself up* to the idea proper of philosophy – that is, its claim to completeness – has constituted philosophy since its inception in Greece." R. Gasché, *The Tain of the Mirror: Derrida and the Philosophy of Reflection*, Cambridge, 1986, p. 55. Emphasis added, M.W.

54. Irigaray, "The Power of Discourse and the Subordination of the Feminine," in Irigaray, *This Sex Which Is Not One*, p. 74.

theoretical machinery itself, of suspending its pretension to the production of a truth and of a meaning that are excessively univocal."[55]

Irigaray's exploration of an ethics of sexual passion involves an intimate reading of masculine philosophical texts. Much of her work involves a dialogue with the modern tradition of German philosophy, and as such might be read as part of the ongoing French deconstruction of the German text. Nietzsche and Heidegger (standing in for a certain Germanic tradition) feature in the series of texts Irigaray devotes to elemental philosophy. In *Amante Marine* Irigaray explores a fluid philosophy that would counter the excessively rigid metaphors of Nietzsche's texts, while in *L'Oubli de l'air* she attempts to aerate Heidegger's work, to inspire his texts with a breathless and excessive logic.[56]

In an earlier text, *Speculum of the Other Woman*, Irigaray investigates how woman has been silenced within Western philosophy. Her discussion of Freud and Plato disrupts the construction of philosophy that has encoded the feminine as the repressed Other of reason. She argues that female sexuality cannot articulate itself within this dominant Aristotelian logic, and urges us to speak outside this discourse, to speak otherwise. The exploratory prose of "When Our Lips Speak Together" follows upon her deconstruction of Western metaphysics in both *Speculum* and the explanatory essays of *This Sex Which Is Not One*. Here she abandons an adherence to formal linguistic and logical structures in her attempt to formulate "an ideological space in which to speak female."[57] However, establishing this discursive space does not entail, for Irigaray, a mere reversal of phallocentric logic. This would amount to succumbing yet again to the dominating impulse of unity and the singular truth it implies.[58] For Irigaray, "a feminine language would undo the unique meaning, the proper meaning of words, of nouns which still regulates all discourse. In order for there to be a proper meaning, there must indeed be a unity somewhere."[59]

Irigaray confronts the phallic unity and form of Western discourse, which weaves a complex web of language, privilege and sexual positioning. The masculine, assuming as it does the privileged status identity (unity or

55. *Ibid.*, p. 78.
56. *Amante Marine: de Friedrich Nietzsche*, Paris, 1980. *L'Oubli de l'air: Chez Martin Heidegger*, Paris, 1983. For a discussion of Irigaray's elemental texts see E. Grosz, *Sexual Subversions: Three French Feminists*, Sydney, 1989, pp. 168–72.
57. See C. Burke, "Introduction to Luce Irigaray's 'When Our Lips Speak Together'," *Signs* 6(1) 1980, p. 67.
58. See E. Grosz, "Irigaray and Sexual Difference," *Australian Feminist Studies* 2, 1986, p. 76.
59. Irigaray, "Women's Exile," p. 65. And further: "Hers are contradictory words, somewhat mad from the standpoint of reason. . . . For if 'she' says something, it is not, it is already no longer, identical with what she means." Irigaray, *This Sex Which Is Not One*, p. 29.

oneness in Irigaray's terminology), allows no logic other than its own. Thus the feminine is repressed, censured, and permitted no space within which its own self-affection or expression might be voiced. Accordingly,

> all Western discourse presents a certain isomorphism with the masculine sex: the privilege of unity, form of the self, of the visible, of the specularizable, of the erection (which is the becoming in a form). Now this morphologic does not correspond to the female sex: there is not "a" female sex. The "no sex" that has been assigned to the woman can mean that she does not have "a sex," and that her sex is not visible, or identifiable, or representable in a definite form . . . what the female sex enjoys is not having its own form.[60]

Irigaray thus invokes the morphology of the body to convey the intimate relation between discourse and sexuality. Not for Irigaray a brute and unbending anatomy, but rather a rich and metaphorical description of the complexities involved in the active inscription of the body with meaning and significance.[61]

In her confrontation with the privileged unity/identity of masculine discourse Irigaray employs a deconstructive style, displacing the oppositional structures inherent within masculine discourse. She presents the authority of the subject over the object, the self over the other, the *cogito* over the body, as examples of the masculine logic of exclusion, a logic in which the world becomes divided into simple oppositional binarisms. Thus her immanent method aims "to utilize already existing systems of meaning or signification, to exceed or overflow the oppositional structures or hierarchizing procedures of phallocentric texts."[62]

This approach situates Irigaray's work within the Derridean practice of deconstruction. However, her relation to Derrida is hardly straightforward. Her use of Derrida remains tactical, rather than reverent, allowing a

60. Irigaray, "Women's Exile," p. 64.

61. It is worth noting at this stage that Irigaray's morpho-logical description has been variously interpreted. *First* by those claiming that she invokes the static, essential body – Monique Plaza being perhaps most characteristic of this position – and *second* by those who argue that her account actually denies the specificity of the female body – for example, Alison Caddick. See M. Plaza, "'Phallomorphic Power' and the Psychology of 'Woman'," *Ideology and Consciousness* 4, 1978, pp. 5–36, and A. Caddick, "Feminism and the Body," *Arena* 74, 1986, pp. 60–88; also K. Reiger, "The Embodiment of Resistance: Reproductive Struggles and Feminism," *Arena* 79, 1987, p. 96. For an alternative reading, see E. Grosz, "Philosophy, Subjectivity and the Body: Kristeva and Irigaray," in C. Pateman and E. Grosz (eds.), *Feminist Challenges: Social and Political Theory*, Sydney, 1986, p. 136. Indeed, for Jane Gallop the seductive pleasure and political efficacy of Irigaray's *poétique du corps* lies precisely within the *tension* between her combination of obvious modernist poetics with an inevitable referential gesture: "For if Irigaray is not just writing a non-phallomorphic text (a rather common modernist practice) but actually constructing a non-phallomorphic sexuality, then the gesture of a troubled but nonetheless insistent referentiality is essential." J. Gallop, "Quand Nos Lèvres S'Ecrivent: Irigaray's Body Politic," *Romanic Review* 74, 1983, p. 83.

62. Grosz, "Irigaray and Sexual Difference," p. 74.

critical appraisal of Derrida's own project.[63] Or, as Burke would have it, his "presence" is experienced "intertextually" within Irigaray's writing![64]

Irigaray employs the Derridean suspicion of master concepts and the authority they presume. Deconstruction allows her to play with concepts while at the same time questioning this very process of deconstruction: "The referential status of language is put into question and, furthermore, each deconstruction can, in turn, be deconstructed."[65]

For Irigaray the language of the "feminine" – of women – would differ dramatically from that of the morpho-logic of masculine discourse. Rejecting the Aristotelian logic and linearity of "subject-verb-object," and the unified subject this implies, she seeks to "overthrow syntax by suspending its eternally teleological order."[66] Castrated of words within the "one logos," the voice(s) of women have been effectively silenced by the dominant systems of representation. It is a matter, then, of turning "everything upside down, inside out, back to front," in an effort to reinscribe "those crises that her 'body' suffers in her impotence to say what disturbs her." By insisting upon the "blanks in discourse which recall the places of her exclusion," the fabricated coherence and cohesion of reason may be ruptured.[67]

Irigaray's evocation of a contiguous relation between body and language – one that touches upon rather than identifies – facilitates a fluidity in writing. In so doing she inscribes a "corporeal economy of fluids, a multiple economy not organized around the primacy of the One, be it sexual (the phallus), logical (the self-identical), linguistic (the law of the copula), or political (the law of the father)."[68] This inscription of the body through language (writing the body) explores woman's sexuality as multiple, as differences rather than absence. Woman finds her pleasure, she writes,

> almost everywhere. Even if we refrain from invoking the hystericization of her entire body, the geography of her pleasure is far more diversified, more multiple in its difference, more complex, more subtle, than is commonly imagined – in an imaginary rather too narrowly focused on sameness.[69]

In her evocative text "When Our Lips Speak Together," Irigaray

63. Pateman and Grosz (eds.), *Feminist Challenges: Social and Political Theory*, p. 133.

64. C. Burke, "Irigaray Through the Looking Glass," *Feminist Studies* 7, 1981, p. 290. Burke refers to the "presences" of both Derrida and Lacan.

65. *Ibid.*, p. 295 (see n. 36, p. 305).

66. Irigaray, *Speculum of the Other Woman*, "Any Theory of the 'Subject' Has Always Been Appropriated by the 'Masculine'," p. 142.

67. *Ibid.* And further: "Reinscribe them hither and thither *as divergencies*, otherwise and elsewhere than they are expected, in *ellipses* and *eclipses* that deconstruct the logical grid of the reader-writer, drive him out of his mind, trouble his vision to the point of incurable diplopia at least."

68. B. Freeman, "Irigaray at the Symposium: Speaking Otherwise," *Oxford Literary Review* 8, 1986, p. 173.

69. Irigaray, "This Sex Which Is Not One," in Irigaray, *This Sex Which Is Not One*, p. 28.

employs a plurality of voices (evidenced in her elision of "tu/je"), embodying a fluid rather than a fixed or unified subjectivity. Stressing the need to speak otherwise, to break out of the closure of logical discourse, her text warns against the violence of speaking the same: "If we keep on speaking sameness, if we speak to each other as men have been doing for centuries, as we have been taught to speak, we'll miss each other, fail ourselves."[70] And, further: "If we don't invent a language, if we don't find our body's language, it will have too few gestures to accompany our story."[71]

Irigaray calls for a contiguous relation to language that would involve a pleasure in touch rather than sight and identification. Her own textual practice involves an autoeroticism that displaces the masculine economy of desire which relegates woman to passivity.[72] Hers is a process denouncing the dominating logic of reason that separates self from other, while simultaneously dividing all reality into hierarchically ordered binarisms.

## Reason as the Text of Sexual Privilege

The interventions of Irigaray and Adorno, within the debates of reason and identity, relate in complex ways to the fracturing and fragmenting processes of the postmodern gesture. Their immanent critiques of the identitarian impulse of Western reason involve a rejection and deconstruction of traditional humanist formulations of unified subjectivity. This denial of the masterful, knowing subject does not imply, as it does for many, a total elimination of the subject.[73] More importantly, it is a rejection of simplistic identifications of subjectivity with consciousness.

In the Nietzschean approach to the fragmentation and disruption of language and thought Irigaray and Adorno display an acute awareness of the negativity of reason. Irigaray's discursive space in which to "write the body" goes beyond this negativity, and there are also elements of such reclaiming in Adorno's texts.[74]

70. Irigaray, "When Our Lips Speak Together," in *This Sex Which Is Not One*, p. 205.
71. *Ibid.*, p. 214.
72. See A. Dallery, "Sexual Embodiment: Beauvoir and French Feminism (*écriture féminine*)," *Women's Studies International Forum* 8, 1985, p. 200.
73. See Salleh, "On the Dialectics of Signifying Practice," p. 74. See also Jay, *Adorno*. Jay writes of Adorno "While his 'predominance of the object' did mean a refusal to acquiesce in the *reductio ad hominem* of anthropocentric epistemologies, it never went so far as to countenance the total liquidation of the subject. . . . It is this . . . that set Adorno apart from structuralist Marxists like Louis Althusser . . ." (p.71).
74. In his discussion of Adorno and Derrida, Michael Ryan argues that Derrida's project goes further in that he not only criticizes the metaphysics of identity, but that he "forges word-concepts . . . whose undecidability pushes against the logocentric closure of metaphysics." In short, Derrida provides "a method for unbalancing the metaphysical system of equivalences," presumably not found in Adorno's work. Arguably, Adorno's text provides the very undecidability that Ryan refers to. His method of doubling concepts is one example of this.

The convergence of Irigaray and Adorno is characterized by their common denial of any claim to authority for their respective practices. In refusing to hypostasize the process of negative dialectics, Adorno is only too aware of the danger involved in defining exactly what this might involve. "Dialectics is the consistent sense of nonidentity. It does not begin by taking a standpoint."[75] For Irigaray it is not an issue of speaking for women – of creating a single truth, a single struggle or a single understanding. Both Irigaray and Adorno reject the implicit violence of creating universalizing theories and practices.

What distinguishes Irigaray's approach is her radical insertion of sexual difference within a discourse that denies this very difference. She goes beyond[76] Adorno when she posits the morphological correspondence between dominant forms of sexuality and the privileged unity of phallocentric discourse. In so doing she calls into question the relation of theorists – such as Adorno – to this discourse. Might we then position Adorno – albeit with some reservations – as one of "Those mildly estranged members of the subjugating groups with doubts about the legitimacy of their own objective privilege and power"?[77]

Irigaray's work forces us to confront the effects of our sexual positioning. She reminds us that the debates of modernity that revolve around the construction of reason are carried out within a context of masculine privilege. While it is imperative that we question the status of a reason that installs itself by repressing what it cannot tolerate, it is equally essential that we question how and why this process repeatedly encodes the limits of reason as the feminine.

75. Adorno, *Negative Dialectics*, p. 5. And further: "No theory today escapes the marketplace. Each one is offered as a possibility among competing opinions; all are put up for choice; all are swallowed. There are no blinders for thought to don against this, and the self-righteous conviction that my own theory is spared that fate will surely deteriorate into self-advertising" (p. 4).

76. The thought of *going beyond* or *overcoming* is vaguely unsettling in its allusion to a hierarchical principle of authority. As Mihai Spariosu suggests, it might better be a question of turning away, of "digressing" without "transgressing." M. Spariosu, "Mimesis and Contemporary French Theory," in Spariosu (ed.), *Mimesis in Contemporary Theory*, p. 79.

77. S. Harding, "The Instability of the Analytical Categories of Feminist Theory," *Signs* 11, 1986, pp. 656–57.

# Social Theory Without "Reason": Luhmann and the Challenge of Systems Theory

## AN INTERVIEW WITH NIKLAS LUHMANN

Niklas Luhmann, Professor of Sociology at the University of Bielefeld, is one of the most important contemporary German thinkers. Nonetheless, he stands apart from other well-known German social thinkers such as Jürgen Habermas or Albrecht Wellmer. The tone and style are quite different, just as his reception of recent French thought is strikingly different from theirs. On the other hand, Luhmann also differs sharply from the Böhme brothers, despite the fact that he covers some of the same theories from his own inimitable standpoint.

Like other contributors to this volume, Luhmann is radical in terms of older paradigms of reason, consciousness and the subject. Luhmann challenges the claims of Critical Theory by alleging that neither "reason" nor "domination" play *any* role in the explanation of social behavior. He alleges that Critical Theory relies on the ethically committed talk used by individuals, when such talk is not appropriate for the purposes of scientific theory formation. Luhmann, however, is not an enemy of "reason." He distinguishes "reason" from "rationality" and opts for the latter. He also emphasizes the need to historicize European rationality. Further, Luhmann criticizes traditional European discussions of reason, which overemphasized half of a distinction (reason – not-reason) in a one-sided way, and failed to grasp the unity of the distinction: what is the same on both sides. In this sense, he accepts the force of some of the considerations brought by philosophers such as Gernot Böhme against Habermas. His own solution, however, differs radically from theirs. It is to go beyond old European thought altogether – not to revive the complaints and the remedies of German Romanticism. Like some recent French thinkers, Luhmann emphasizes that the contemporary society has no center, no authority or legitimacy, and no power or principle that guides it. But this means something very different for Luhmann than for the French because Luhmann theorizes an antitheodic and antinomic systems-theoretical approach to social evolution.

According to Luhmann, sociology still lacks adequate theory, and a more abstract theory is what is needed. This contrasts strikingly with the views advanced by other contributors to this volume such as Frank and Böhme. Luhmann stands apart among contemporary German thinkers in his unrelenting scientific ambitions and in his positive relation to Darwinian evolutionary theory. He combines a systems-theoretical approach with insights from Husserl's phenomenology and a mathematical theory of complexity-generating distinctions derived from the British mathematician Spencer Brown. Luhmann moves away from an action theory approach to an advanced systems theory that incorporates insights into the production of meaning (*Sinn*). Like his teacher Talcott Parsons, he rejects methodological individualism and speaks uncompromisingly of "the society" or "the modern society." According to his theory, only one "society" now exists. What this means is not entirely obvious, however, because "society" has a technical sense in Luhmann's work, as the interview below makes evident.

Luhmann revises Parson's functional structuralism in a way that emphasizes meaning, diversity and communication. Like Parsons, he takes the problem of order to be central to sociology, but then attempts to account for it in pluralist terms that do not require order to have any single ground or foundation. Again, like Parsons, Luhmann emphasizes the link between systems and the control of action, but Luhmann departs from Parsons by allowing different sub-systems to construct action differently. He offers a new solution to the problem of order, and a new approach to the explanation of societal change by positing autopoietic (i.e., self-shaping) social systems.

Like much contemporary French thought, Luhmann's systems theory tends to embrace aleatory developments and antitheodic possibilities at the expense of the social moralism so evident in the work of Jürgen Habermas. Nonetheless, Luhmann is only antirationalist in the sense of antitheodic. He is a theorist of asymmetric patterns who again and again tries to decouple conventional associations. His critics charge that his work is conservative and incapable of providing critical perspectives on developments. They allege that it simply serves the instrumental demands of the administrative state, and is incapable of taking account of individual human beings.[1] Luhmann, however, denies that his theory liquidates the individ-

---

1. See Habermas's insightful discussion, "Excursus on Luhmann's Appropriation of the Philosophy of the Subject through Systems Theory" in J. Habermas, *The Philosophical Discourse of Modernity. Twelve Lectures*, trans. F. Lawrence, Cambridge, 1987, pp. 368–85.

ual. To the contrary, he claims that his theory makes possible a more extensive treatment of the individual precisely because, in his view, the individual is not in society. Critics also charge that Luhmann reduces power to communication: that his abstractions have their own neoconservative politico-ethical bias. Here they may have a point, but Luhmann's bias is less aesthetico-moral than administrative. If the exact hermeneutical status of Luhmann's claims is often not clear, despite his early commitment in *Sociological Enlightenment* (1971) to a transcendental-interpretative approach, his theory has considerable practical application to the critical study of organizations, a fact that his more philosophically-trained critics often forget.

Similarly, as the interview[2] below confirms, Luhmann's theory is only antihumanist in a technical sense, and can handle an extraordinary range of subject matter, including psychological systems and the development of single individuals. A more serious complaint is that Luhmann's systems theory is too elastic and inclusive: that it can be wrapped around any subject matter because it tends to tautology and metaphorical deployments of what at first sight appear to be determinate technical notions. From this perspective, it is Luhmann's unreformed rationalism that is problematic, and which creates the impression that systems already contain teleological possibilities that are then drawn out from them.

According to Luhmann ontological determinism is false, value judgments are unavoidable and both statistical methods and classical logic are inadequate tools for contemporary sociology. Instead, Luhmann interprets sociological theory as the self-thematization of society. He posits an increasing differentiation of society through social evolution, from segmentation to stratification to functional differentiation. He also stresses the role of communication in the evolution of social systems. Social systems are self-referential systems of meaningful communication. There is an increasing differentiation in the course of social evolution of the binary codes that direct communication. The modern society directs itself according to different codes (true/untrue, right/wrong, transcendent/immanent) in its different functional sub-systems. It is a decentered society, and has no unity apart from such guiding distinctions. Here the parallels between Luhmann's concerns and themes raised in recent French thought and in the German debates about reason and its Other are obvious.

Luhmann implies that an antihumanist sociology is possible which replaces the subject with self-referential systems, and which theorizes consciousness as perception. Thus there are no "social actors" in Luhmann's "society." Luhmann theorizes "society" as a realm of surplus communica-

2. The text below is an edited version of a longer interview and has been approved by Professor Luhmann.

tion, from which some possibilities are selected. He uses information theory to theorize social systems as functional systems that reduce complexity. Luhmann's tactic is to show that an immense range of apparently unrelated social phenomena, including art, logic, and trust, can be explicated in terms of his basic distinctions, e.g., by regard to different types of self-reference. For Luhmann the economy, law, art, and religion are all functional sub-systems in the modern society. Social systems use meaningful communication as their basic operation, and reintroduce the distinction between system and environment with the system.

Despite the mass of technical terms ("operation," "observation," "self-reference," "antinomic substitution," "boundary maintenance," "medium," "form"), Luhmann's sociological systems theory is strangely neoliberal and asocial. The system defines its own boundary, and often appears to have more freedom than the liberal humanist subject. Individuals are dethroned as agents in favor of "codes" and symbolically generalized media, whereas autopoietic systems are self-organizing, closed systems that define their own boundaries, and can form and change their own structures and also produce their own elementary units.

The following twelve theses, which Luhmann presented to a staff seminar at Griffith University in Brisbane in August 1991, summarize some of his main views and are typical of Luhmann's abstract systems-theoretical approach, which is designed to provide a new paradigm for sociology that is not based on "old European thought":

1. For an adequate theory of society we need a new sociological framework based neither on old European thought nor on the sociological classics.

2. Talking about the Enlightenment or modernity will not help.

3. The new theory needs to be nonhumanist. But it also has to account for the individual, as humanist social theory fails to do.

4. A systems-theoretical social theory is required that is more interdisciplinary than the theories of the sociological tradition.

5. Self-referential autopoetic systems are basic to the new theory, not subjects or human actors.

6. Social differentiation (repeating the difference of system and environment within systems) reduces complexity in a way that makes it possible to build up complexity.

7. Modern society consists of functional sub-systems that have positive and negative unintended effects.

8. The modern society has steering media, but these can only be used within sub-systems. There is no center or controlling principle homologizing the sub-systems.

9.  Structural changes intending social reform should be sub-system specific. Nothing else works.
10. Class is not crucial to the evolution of the societal system, but contingency produces accidental evolution of the sub-systems.
11. We should speak of "rationality," not "reason," and ethics should be redesigned to include moral conflicts and moral paradoxes.
12. The modern society describes its future in terms of present risk.

## An Interview with Niklas Luhmann

**Q:**  Professor Luhmann, could you say something about the relationship between your systems-theoretic sociology and the recent German debates about reason and its Other?

**A:**  For me the recent German debates about "reason and its Other" belong to the past. They are more old European thought. Like some of the participants in those debates, I also think that there is a problem about the way "reason" has been theorized in Western thought. A distinction is drawn between reason and nonreason, but there is no discussion of what is the same on both sides of the distinction. There is also a need to recognize the historical specificity of the European notions of reason and rationality.

**Q:**  But your position is also ultrarevisionist. In sociological contexts you want to replace talk about "reason" with talk about "rationality." Why do you take this view?

**A:**  "Reason" always refers to a human capacity, and the capacity that makes reason a distinct phenomenon is always a human capacity. But I think we should look to criteria that can be applied to systems, whether they are social systems or psychic systems. The term "rationality" is better adapted to this task.

**Q:**  So your rejection of reason is compatible with a stronger emphasis on systems rationality. You don't reject the European Enlightenment?

**A:**  The Enlightenment is an historical fact, and it doesn't explain anything to reject historical facts. What I reject is the belief that it will be helpful to apply the principles of the Enlightenment nowadays, especially in the form of a prospect to improve mankind. I don't believe that we can improve mankind.

**Q:**  In effect, you argue from a mixture of structural and historical considerations. But then the interpretation of our contemporary situation becomes important. What do you think about the contemporary discussion of postmodernity?

**A:**  The discussion depends on a distinction between modernity and postmodernity. I do not think it is helpful for anyone attempting to understand our present situation to refer to pieces of knowledge constructed for quite another type of society.

**Q:** But some people use "postmodernity" as a placeholder for a fundamental shift that cannot yet be described.

**A:** On a structural level I do not see any fundamental shift. The change from stratification to functional differentiation began in the middle ages, and we are still living in a functionally differentiated society. The possibilities of such a structure are being worked out, but I do not see any new society about to emerge.

**Q:** But there are many consequences for our horizon formation if one refuses to play the futurologist. Lukács might have accused you of bourgeois irrationalism. How do you theorize the future in your theory?

**A:** I think that increasingly the future is seen as dependent upon decision making. Either present decision making, or past decision making, which we cannot change. The future no longer has a teleological structure, in the sense that there is a goal such as progress or salvation. It is more present as a risk and danger situation. I would theorize the future as probabilities or improbabilities of gains and losses, advantages and disadvantages, depending on decision making.

**Q:** Your approach is in marked contrast to the social Romanticism of many German social philosophers. It is also remote from the hopes of the Enlightenment. Can your theory, however, generate a critical perspective on society, or are you caught in a form of immanentism?

**A:** Whether my theory can generate a critical perspective on a society depends on what you mean by "critical." All theories are critical, in the sense that they make distinctions. If they are good theories, they make more radical and more coherent distinctions than are normally used. It does not make any sense to me to reject a society and to try to live in a different society.

**Q:** But surely you would not opt for an immanentism that encouraged quietism? What about utopia?

**A:** Utopia is a part of the semantics of the society, especially of the late eighteenth century, when utopia had a relation to the future. It is not a very helpful notion in the context of scientific investigation. Of course, it may be helpful for political projects.

**Q:** Although you try to get away from reason, the subject, and consciousness, the term "society" seems to cover too much in your theory. Is "society" not a purely formal concept in your theory?

**A:** It is a very abstract concept, and it is "formal" in a very specific sense. It is not formal in the sense of characterless. Society is formed as a distinction between system and environment, specified by the mode of operation that reproduces the system. Following Spencer Brown, I take the concept of form as a two-sided effect where you can only use one side and the other side is unmarked space. Society is the marked side, but it needs the other side: the environment. In addition, the distinction between system and environment, the distinction that makes a difference, re-enters its own space.

**Q:** So for you there is no "reason and its Other," but there is "Society and its Other"?

**A:** Yes. That puts is very well.

**Q:** If there is an Other, what does this imply for human social life? How, for example, do you theorize religion? As beyond any dualism of rational/irrational?

**A:** In the modern society religion has become a functional sub-system. It is organized as a code by the distinction between transcendence and immanence.

**Q:** But what follows from this in terms of normative issues? Could religion represent an advance in system organization, despite its mythic form?

**A:** Not in general. As soon as functions are institutionalized as systems, religion itself becomes a system. However, the system explains religion, not vice versa.

**Q:** But does religion make distinctions in "the society" that would otherwise not be made?

**A:** Yes, in the sense that the immanence/transcendence distinction is valid only for religion. Perhaps drawing such a distinction serves a function by guaranteeing the meaning of life.

**Q:** To that extent, you might accept a moderate rehabilitation of religion, like some participants in the debates about reason and its Other. Unlike them, however, you have strong natural scientific sympathies. Does your perspective on social evolution reduce the role of reason in social life? In what sense is there a natural evolutionary basis for your theory?

**A:** I think of evolution in quasi-Darwinian terms: as structural change that requires variation, selection and restabilization. The question is whether we can understand human social history in terms of this kind of theory. I think this is possible if we describe what is evolving as a system. I think a match can be made between advanced systems theory and the Darwinian framework. This does not have irrationalist implications, but it implies that moralist talk of "reason" is not enough.

**Q:** Does your theory, however, really allow for human cognition, let alone psyche? Does it not even sociologize psychological changes? Why, for example, do you think that psychic and social systems evolution go together?

**A:** I think in terms of a general model of randomly initiated structural changes, which is basic for both learning and for evolution. I would prefer to understand the structural development of a single individual in terms of "learning," but my theory also integrates a social evolution perspective. In the beginning the social evolution of the society depends on a core evolution of human capacities, but nowadays we have enough human capacities to maintain the communicative network, and communication takes over.

**Q:** Like Norbert Elias, you capture, I think, a crucial connection, whether or not you theorize it successfully. Nonetheless, your work, like that of Elias, does tend to subvert the moralism of traditional social theory. How would you contrast your theory with that of Elias?

**A:** I think that Elias's idea of a trajectory of history is simplistic, and leads to many empirical problems when he tries to understand this trajectory in terms of changes in the self-control of human beings. I also dispute some of his historical contrasts. My evolutionary approach to history would be much more complex.

**Q:** True, but it is often said that your theory is too abstract and general.

**A:** Abstraction is no argument against a theory.

**Q:** But how useful is it to try to relocate "the subject" and "consciousness" in systems theory? Is it really useful to move away from explanations in terms of individuals?

**A:** I think that my theory can explain the evolution of the individual in a new way. The modern systems theory can construct the individual more effectively than traditional sociology by theorizing how individuals build up their own limitations, their own habits, their own memory.

**Q:** But you do concede something to your critics by emphasizing that systems theory has changed. What are the new forms of systems theory that you make use of?

**A:** The new systems theory is a theory about a distinction, not about special objects. In this sense, it is a theory that splits the world into two parts: system and environment. And then you have to select the system reference. Depending on the system reference, you have a different cut. The new systems theory also includes self-reference. The system consults its own state in every state. The system also creates its own elementary units by its own mode of reproduction.

**Q:** But the sense of "world" here is unclear.

**A:** I use "world" in a systematic, not in a popular sense. By "world" I do not mean the scholastic notion of the sum total of all things. I mean the sum total of all distinctions.

**Q:** But although you emphasize the need to break with old European thought, your systems theory is not an ontology, is it? It often seems to involve scholastic refinements.

**A:** The technicalities provide the explanatory power. If you construct a system as consisting of events that are vanishing all the time, and the system is successful in reproducing events, then there is a kind of dynamic stability in terms of the reproduction of elementary units. This is a very different model from a classical static-dynamic model.

**Q:** But although you emphasize the need to break with old European thought, your theory does perhaps resemble a category theory. You produce a set of fundamental distinctions which render certain phenomena intelligible.

**A:** I prefer the term "universal theory." The theory has to cover everything, including itself. The distinction between system and environment is a universal distinction.

**Q:** But is that distinction a concept in the theory? Is the rationality of the theory different from the rationality operational in the world?

**A:** It is a concept in the theory, a device to observe the real world, but a device addressed to real observing systems. The reality is not guaranteed by the outer, but by the real order of observing systems. They construct the world.

**Q:** In effect, you put Husserl's phenomenology into systems theory?

**A:** To some extent. I reinterpret the theory of consciousness in terms of continuous integration of internal references and external references.

**Q:** Again, I hear Husserl. What is phenomenological about your method is that you make the internal interpretation foundational for the character the entities come to have. Is that right?

**A:** The character of entities depends on how they observe themselves, and how they are observed.

**Q:** But that is a characteristically transcendental answer. It raises the question of how far real changes occur in history according to your theory. You seem to understand history like an historian, and it is a very exact understanding. But in your more historical books your systems theory seems to be added on to this more concrete historical understanding.

**A:** I think sociology should be used for historical research, but that traditional sociology is not all that useful because it lacks a sufficiently powerful, that is, a sufficiently abstract, theory. Systems theory provides such a theory. Of course, we need to distinguish between history in the scientific sense, and history in the sense of present history, the importance of which depends upon how you observe your past. I am interested in the possibility of an evolutionary approach to history that explains unintended structural changes. This theory would not postulate a series of phases or epochs. It would be more systematic. I tend to use a Darwinian approach according to which structural changes come about by mass phenomena of small variations and selection. However, contemporary evolutionary theory makes more allowance for jumps and discontinuities. In the same way sociological theory needs to offer explanation in terms of jumps. In my theory, this would mean jumps from segmentary societies to stratification to functional differentiation. At the level of historical research the task is to explain how functional differentiation came about in such a relatively short time.

Q:    You think that systems theory can provide a new agenda for historical research, and that the more it breaks with old European thought the more helpful it will be able to be – in contrast to those participants in the debates about reason and its Other who want to revive neglected parts of old European thought?

A:    Yes.

Q:    But there is a dose of traditional ontology somewhere. Sometimes your theory seems to imply that systems have a natural logic, of which they can eventually become aware.

A:    In my theory the distinctions systems make are historical, not naturalistic, but the type of differentiation gives a frame for possibilities, which then tend to develop out of their situation. The possibilities in a specific historical situation are limited.

Q:    But can a system have a *telos?* And if so, are we not stuck with a doctrine of progress?

A:    There is teleology, but as an effect. The systems test the structural potential of their own autopoiesis. This is not "progress." There is no implication that evolution goes on to better states. Quite the contrary. Thus the modern economy may be incompatible with state planning and so forth. Complexity brings many difficulties with it.

Q:    Your theory seems deceptive at times. Your language goes one way, but the moves you make go another. For example: you often use the language of a strong positive theory, but the content sometimes turns out to be negative rather than positive. You also play up antitheodic consequences of your views, whereas in fact your theory is quite optimistic. Do you really abandon the notion of "progress"?

A:    I take a scientific approach. For me the development of science does not imply that the outcome will be a good society.

Q:    But how do you determine whether it is a good society or not? Surely we are still inside old European thought when it comes to ethics?

A:    For me it is a question of the observer. Value judgments depend on how the observer makes distinctions. They are subjective, but not arbitrary. A decoupling strategy is called for.

Q:    But, despite your disclaimer, do you come close to holding a transcendental cognitive theory that human beings cognize successfully when they learn to make simple distinctions?

A:    I certainly associate cognitive success with making simple distinctions. But not simply "simple," because we need distinctions that build up complexity. For example: "system" and "environment."

Q: On the other hand, you argue that traditional logic is not enough. What sort of new logic is called for?

A: Many valued logic. We need a temporal logic that builds up complexity.

Q: This emphasis on time in sociological theory again takes us beyond old European thought?

A: Yes. It takes us toward more sophisticated theories that we do not yet have.

Q: To put it differently, your radicalism often seems to lie in what you think can be left out. You always emphasize what needs to be excluded from the discussion, what *does not* belong to the process of construction.

A: But you have also to keep in mind what you have excluded. The Other is still there, and may be relevant later.

Q: Finally, a biographical question. Professor Luhmann, why was it you of all the social theorists of your generation who carried systems theory forward as a new paradigm for the social sciences?

A: The answer is autobiographical: a chain of random events. I was a product of the Nazi period and a lost war. After the war I was interested in reconstruction. I studied law and worked as a civil servant, so I learned how to handle legal forms with a view to their strategic consequences. Then I was influenced by functionalist ideas and had an abnormal entry into the sociological profession. My practical experience as an administrator gave me an unusual orientation among sociological theorists. I knew quite at lot about the world of affairs and organizations. Perhaps my crucial decision was to leave administration in 1962, and to go to a new research institute for public administration in Speyer. There I began to write the books. I had no doctorate, and was not in the university. I did not really study sociology. I did my *Habilitation* and my *Promotion* (Ph.D.) in one year. Obviously my year at Harvard, where I met Talcott Parsons, was also decisive. But the most important thing may have been my administrative background, which gives me a very practical approach to theory. I suppose I also have a talent for picking up opportunities.

Q: You are a risk-taker with a strong strategic sense.

A: Yes, but I suppose you could say that I had reasons for taking risks.

Q: Nonetheless, the German reception of your work often gives the impression that you are a conservative social philosopher whose theories promote passive conformity to the instrumental demands of the existing order. Perhaps Niklas Luhmann the practical administrator deserves to be better known. Your work is closer, I think, to jurisprudence than to philosophy. You are not concerned with "philosophical riddles"?

**A:**  That's true. I could never work on Derrida's questions. I use the old philosophical tradition, but I am not in it.

**Q:**  To that extent, you stand out in the contemporary German scene as a thinker who wants to get away from "old European thought," not to revise it?

**A:**  Yes.

*Niklas Luhmann was interviewed by Wayne Hudson at Griffith University, Brisbane, Australia, on the 22nd of August 1991.*

# –13–

# Adorno as a Reader of Heine

## PETER UWE HOHENDAHL

When Theodor W. Adorno presented his lecture on Heinrich Heine in 1956 – the occasion was the 100th anniversary of the poet's death – Heine's status within the German tradition was anything but secure. While East German criticism had begun to include Heine among the canonical authors of German literature, the West German situation was characterized by a curious strategy of resistance that subconsciously continued the fascist repression between 1933 and 1945.[1] Of course, it was quite legitimate now to write about Heine, yet the emphasis of criticism in the new Federal Republic of Germany was on Weimar classicism rather than Heinrich Heine and the Young Germans. Hence Adorno was justified to entitle his lecture, later published in *Texte und Zeichen*, "Die Wunde Heine."[2] Talking about Heine in 1956 meant talking about a Jewish author, about an author who had committed himself to the German language as his medium (even when he resided in Paris after 1830), and finally a writer who, unlike most of his contemporaries, openly criticized the political repression in post-Napoleonic Germany. Adorno was very much aware that he dealt with an author who did not fit the profile of the *German Poet*. Heine was not Eichendorff — notwithstanding the fact that their poems were equally used by major German composers of *Lieder*.

Adorno's defense of Heine must be understood as a response to a situation in which the anomaly of Heine's repression was still treated as normal, a defense that wants to face the problem by lifting the bandages that covered the wound. Yet this attempt to restore the status of Heine in Germany, in a curious way, shares some of the problems it wants to address.

1. For the background, see the comprehensive study by J. Hermand, *Kultur im Wiederaufbau. Die Bundesrepublik 1945–1965*, Munich, 1986.
2. Editors' note: This title was translated as "Heine the Wound" in T. W. Adorno, *Notes to Literature*, ed. R. Tiedemann and trans. S. W. Nicholson, New York, 1991. All translations in parentheses of the quotations from *Noten zur Literatur I* and *II* are based on this edition.

Adorno's essay vindicates some aspects of Heine's *oeuvre*, while others remain in doubt. Among these problematic aspects is Heine's Jewish background, and more specifically, Heine's use of the German language. When it comes to Heine's poetry, Adorno cannot conceal that he has reservations.

How do we account for this resistance? Why is Adorno reluctant to acknowledge the force and the quality of Heine's poetry? After all, Adorno, a Jewish-German author himself, is far removed from the chauvinistic cultural milieu in which Jewish authors were automatically excluded from the realm of German culture. In fact, after his return to Germany in 1949, Adorno considered it one of his major tasks to help the discussion about German anti-Semitism. Adorno was clearly involved in the struggle to unearth and analyze the roots of anti-Semitism. Thus his reservations must not be confused with the indifference of conservative intellectuals or the hostility of unreconstructed nationalists.

Adorno's essay does not deal with crude forms of anti-Semitism, the polemics of Bartels and similar cultural chauvinists; rather, at the very beginning it refers to the criticism of the George circle and that of Karl Kraus. While Adorno is willing to dismiss the resistance of the George circle as motivated by German nationalism, he takes Kraus's negative verdict seriously. According to Kraus, it was Heine's use of the German language that undermined its purity.[3] Heine commercialized the German language of Goethe by introducing the *feuilleton* style into German literature. The corruption of the German language, however, is a threatening notion for Adorno as well – although for different reasons. In his analysis of German fascism, linguistic aspects played an important role. Hence, the Krausean argument directed against Heine and the *feuilleton* touched on Adorno's own experience with the fate of the German language under fascism. For Adorno, the idea of an authentic poetic language remains crucial – particularly after the Holocaust.

Adorno leaves no doubt that he holds Heine's critical prose in high esteem. Adorno praises not only the polemical power of Heine's critical interventions, but also the refinement of his prose. "Diese Prosa erschöpft sich nicht in der Fähigkeit bewußter sprachlicher Pointierung, einer in Deutschland überaus seltenen, von keiner Servilität gehemmten polemischen Kraft" (145) ("This prose is not limited to Heine's capacity for conscious pointed linguistic formulation, a polemical power extremely rare in Germany and in no way inhibited by servility").[4] A decade before young academic critics in West Germany began to discover the importance of this

3. K. Kraus, *Heine und die Folgen*, Munich, 1919.
4. T. W. Adorno, "Die Wunde Heine," in Adorno, *Noten zur Literatur I*, Frankfurt, 1958, pp. 144–52; all page references in the text are to this edition.

prose, Adorno insisted on the Enlightenment tradition in Heine's work and stressed its subversive nature that resisted facile categorization. Adorno's doubts concern Heine's poetry: "Die Wunde jedoch ist Heines Lyrik . . . Heines Gedichte waren prompte Mittler zwischen der Kunst und der sinnverlassenen Alltäglichkeit. Die Erlebnisse, die sie verarbeiteten, wurden ihnen unter der Hand, wie dem Feuilletonisten, zu Rohstoffen, über die sich schreiben läßt" (147) ("The wound, however, is Heine's lyric poetry . . . Heine's poems were ready mediators between art and everyday life bereft of meaning. For them as for the feuilletonist, the experiences they processed secretly became raw materials that one could write about"). Adorno calls Heine's language "präpariert" (147), i.e., ready-made and functional. This critique leaves no doubt about the historical context: Adorno sees Heine's poetry as an example of poetic reification caused by the rise of capitalism in Europe. Heine's poetry has come under the law of the market: "Ware und Tausch bemächtigten sich in Heine des Lauts" (147) ("In Heine commodity and exchange seized control of sound and tone"). It is not the historical situation that Adorno holds against Heine; rather, it is Heine's supposed lack of resistance that Adorno deplores – Heine's seeming willingness to work with the linguistic material of the Romantics. Unlike Baudelaire, Adorno's paradigm for modernism, Heine failed to transform the loss of tradition into "Traum und Bild" ("dream and image"); he reproduced reified language instead of breaking it down.

So far Adorno's criticism uses the arguments already developed in *Dialectic of Enlightenment* (1947) – hence Heine could be called a precursor of the culture industry. Yet Adorno's argument is considerably more complex. Heine, he insists, is both a belated Romantic whose poetry relied on the autonomy of modern art, and an Enlightener who openly foregrounded the commodified character of art and literature. Insofar as Heine's poetry is self-conscious, it imitates and mocks Romantic poetry at the same time – a mode of self-criticism that enraged Heine's German foes, including Karl Kraus. Adorno suggests that the "rage" displaces the reader's feeling of degradation (*Erniedrigung*) caused by social reality to the poem's author.

Here we have reached the center of Adorno's argument. Heine's poetry makes its reader uneasy because it points to the failure of human emancipation, since the process of modernization cannot preserve authentic language – the very language it would need to articulate true emancipation. Heine's lack of authentic poetic language and his proximity to communicative language expose him to anti-Semitic polemic. Heine, the Jewish outsider, who for Adorno stood outside "heimatlicher Geborgenheit in der Sprache" (148) ("a native sense of being at home in a language"), simply makes use of the material he borrowed from the previous generation. The

*Peter Uwe Hohendahl*

result is, in Adorno's words, "das glatte sprachliche Gefüge" (149), a symptom of reification: "Die assimilatorische Sprache ist die von mißlungener Identifikation" (149) ("Assimilatory language is the language of unsuccessful identification"). In Adorno's argument reification, Jewish marginality and anti-Semitic polemic are closely linked. Heine's poetry is singled out by German anti-Semites because it brings into the foreground the power of modernization that they fear but steadfastly deny. Instead of confronting the power of the modern state, they displace their anger onto the marginal group. According to Adorno, the moment of truth in their polemic is the inauthenticity of Heine's language. Yet this lack of authenticity becomes the very reason that Heine's poetry can succeed after all. It prevails by making use of its own deficiency, e.g., by pointing to its own *Bruch* (150) (rupture).

This somewhat surprising argument is more complex than it appears. On one level, Adorno suggests that Heine's text becomes self-conscious and thereby self-critical, yet there is more at stake. What Adorno wants to bring out is a radically changed situation of the reader. The post-World War II reader perceives the poem "Mein Herz, mein Herz ist traurig" in the context of the *Holocaust*.[5]

> Mein Herz, mein Herz ist traurig,
> Doch lustig leuchtet der Mai;
> Ich stehe, gelehnt an der Linde,
> Hoch auf der alten Bastei.
>
> Da drunten fließt der blaue
> Stadtgraben in stiller Ruh;
> Ein Knabe fährt im Kahne,
> Und angelt und pfeift dazu.
>
> Jenseits erheben sich freundlich,
> In winziger, bunter Gestalt,
> Lusthäuser, und Gärten, und Menschen,
> Und Ochsen, und Wiesen, und Wald.
>
> Die Mägde bleichen Wäsche,
> Und springen im Gras herum:
> Das Mühlrad stäubt Diamanten,
> Ich höre sein fernes Gesumm.
>
> Am alten grauen Turme
> Ein Schilderhäuschen steht;
> Ein rotgeröckter Bursche
> Dort auf und nieder geht.

5. H. Heine, *Sämtliche Schriften*, Munich, 1968, vol. 1, ed. Klaus Briegleb, p. 108.

–232–

Er spielt mit seiner Flinte,
Die funkelt im Sonnenrot,
Er präsentiert und schultert —
Ich wollt, er schösse mich tot.

(My heart, my heart is heavy
Though May shines bright on all;
I stand and lean on the linden
High on the bastion wall

Below me the moat is flowing
In the still afternoon;
A boy is rowing a boat and
Fishing and whistling a tune.

Beyond in colored patches
So tiny below one sees
Villas and gardens and people
And oxen and meadows and trees

The girls bleach clothes on the meadow
And merrily go and come;
The mill wheel scatters diamonds –
I hear its distant hum.

On top of the old gray tower
A sentry looks over the town;
A young red-coated lad there
Is marching up and down.

He handles his shining rifle,
It gleams in the sunlight's red;
He shoulders arms, presents arms —
I wish he would shoot me dead.)[6]

Thus its intertextual reference might be Celan's *Todesfuge* rather than
Eichendorff's poetry. The radically new meaning of Heine's poem lies in
its post-Holocaust reception, which was tentatively anticipated in Mahler's
musical setting of this poem. The stigma of reified language becomes the
*signature* of complete alienation that goes far beyond the poem's thematic
concern. Adorno's radical reading cancels *Heimat*, the realm of being at
home, which the poem invokes as the absent space. "Heute, nachdem das
Schicksal, das Heine fühlte, buchstäblich sich erfüllte, ist aber zugleich die
Heimatlosigkeit die aller geworden; alle sind in Wesen und Sprache
beschädigt wie der Ausgestoßene es war" (151f.) ("Now that the destiny

6. Editors' note: The English translation of Heine's poem is taken from *The Complete
Poems of Heine. A Modern English Version*, trans. H. Draper, Boston, 1982, p. 77.

that Heine sensed has been fulfilled literally, however, the homelessness
has also become everyone's homelessness; all human beings have been as
badly injured in their beings and their language as Heine the outcast was")
– a veiled reference to the second World War and the Holocaust.

Grudgingly, as we have seen – so to speak through the backdoor –
Adorno admits Heine to the canon of German literature and assigns him a
place next to Goethe, Eichendorff, Mörike, Nietzsche, and George. His
reservations are grounded in his idea of an authentic poetic language that is
based on Goethe's poetry and that of the Romantics. In his essay "Rede
über Lyrik und Gesellschaft" (1957) ("On Lyric Poetry and Society"),
written almost at the same time as the essay on Heine, Adorno makes it
quite clear that his concept of poetry is confined to modernity and would
not include medieval poems, for instance those of Walther von der Vogel-
weide. Referring to Goethe's "Wanderers Nachtlied," Adorno defines the
completion (success) of a poem as subjectivity that is completely sublated
in its language, i.e., "zum Einstand mit der Sprache selber kommt, dem,
wohin diese von sich aus möchte"[7] ("reaches an accord with language itself,
with the inherent tendency of language"). For Adorno, poetic language is
anything but a vehicle; rather, it is a configuration in which communicative language transcends its pragmatic function in order to articulate the
tension between the subject and the objectified world.

This concept of poetic language Adorno can apply successfully to
Mörike and George, but hardly to Heine, whose texts respond to the trivi-
alization of romantic poetry, the incompatibility of a conventionalized
poetic language and the emergence of a modern society in Germany.
Adorno was by no means blind to this change. In the case of Baudelaire,
for instance, he suggests that the modern poet is a cross between Racine
and a journalist. He argues "In der industriellen Gesellschaft wird die
lyrische Idee der sich wiederherstellenden Unmittelbarkeit, wofern sie
nicht ohnmächtig romantisch Vergangenes beschwört, immer mehr zu
einem jäh Aufblitzenden, in dem das Mögliche die eigene Unmöglichkeit
überfliegt" (97) ("In industrial society the lyric idea of a self-restoring
immediacy becomes – where it does not impotently evoke a romantic past
– more and more something that flashes out abruptly, something in which
what is possible transcends its own impossibility"). Strangely enough,
however, Adorno is unwilling or unable to apply this insight to Heine's
poetry. He fails to grasp Heine's modernity (which is also connected with
his Jewish identity) because he emphasizes the Romantic character of
Heine's poems without much attention to the way in which Heine refunctions this element. Thus the rupture, Heine's self-conscious distance,

---

7. Adorno, "Rede über Lyrik und Gesellschaft," in *Noten zur Literatur I*, p. 85.

becomes nearly invisible. Adorno's resistance to Heine's modernity is particularly remarkable since he argues in another essay[8] that Eichendorff's poetry is post-Romantic. It is closer to Baudelaire than to Novalis or Brentano. Hence we have to ask ourselves: What is the distinctive element in Eichendorff that is supposedly missing in Heine? Adorno suggests that Eichendorff's poetry tends to cancel the subject – "Selbstauslöschung des Subjekts" (127). Eichendorff responds to reified Romanticism in a unique way: through self-cancellation the poetic subject transcends the thematic and linguistic conventions and reaches "Versöhnung mit den Dingen durch die Sprache" (125) ("reconciliation with things through language").

Clearly, Heine's response to the conventional language of Romanticism was very different. Instead of *Selbstpreisgabe* of the subject, Heine reinforces the subject. He openly points to the rupture that, according to Adorno, is the constitutive moment of posttraditional poetry. While Adorno admires Heine's unwillingness to give up his intellectual independence, he seems to be troubled by the unveiled *appearance* of a poetic idiom that is no longer grounded in unquestioned collective language. This is the moment when Heine's Jewish identity becomes important. In Adorno's mind the lack of an authentic language, modernity, and Jewish identity are closely connected and determine Heine's poetry. They bring about a highly problematic configuration that anticipates the catastrophe of the German-Jewish symbiosis.[9]

Obviously, the few remarks Adorno makes about Heine's Jewish background, for example, about his mother and her deficient knowledge of German, tell us little about Adorno's familiarity with Heine's biography or the importance of the Jewish question in the poet's life and work.[10] From his presentation I conclude that he was primarily interested in two aspects – in Heine's social marginality and the relationship between Yiddish and German.[11] The religious question, on the other hand, for instance Heine's decision to convert to Christianity and his later "return" to the Jewish faith – whatever it may have entailed – leaves no trace in Adorno's essay. Since Adorno was not a religious person, the question of Heine's faith is not foregrounded. Heine's complex relationship to the Jewish tradition – his affinity as well as his resistance – comes into view only as an absent space from which Heine moved into the realm of German culture. As much as

8. "Zum Gedächtnis Eichendorffs," in *Noten zur Literatur I.*
9. For the historical context, see S. L. Gilman, *Jewish Self-Hatred, Anti-Semitism and the Hidden Language of the Jews*, Baltimore and London, 1986, pp. 167–87.
10. See L. Rosenthal, *Heinrich Heine als Jude*, Frankfurt, 1973; H. Kircher, *Heinrich Heine und das Judentum*, Bonn, 1973; R. L. Jacobi, *Heinrich Heines jüdisches Erbe*, Bonn, 1978.
11. See the discussion in J. L. Sammons, *Heinrich Heine. A Modern Biography*, Princeton, 1979, pp. 35–42.

Adorno questioned the notion of German culture as an affirmative value, he did not question Jewish emancipation, and with it the breaking down of traditional Jewish culture. In that respect Adorno is very close to Hannah Arendt's thesis that for Heine an unimpaired concept of freedom was the center of his life and work;[12] where they differ is the assessment of Heine's appropriation of the German language. While Arendt celebrates Heine's symbiosis of German, Yiddish, and Hebrew as an enrichment of the German language, Adorno, holding on to a notion of purity taken over from Karl Kraus, rejects the idea of a *mélange*.

What Adorno seems to overlook is the fact that Heine himself was very conscious of the problem of language. Precisely because he was an outsider, socially and legally, he was particularly sensitive about his status within German literature and the possibility of including elements of the Jewish tradition.[13] Not only did Heine realize that Goethean classicism had become unattainable, he also clearly understood the *historical* character of the German language. Heine's understanding of the history of the German language from Luther to Goethe and the Romantics stresses the moment of production, the force that can intervene and change reality. It is clearly not a model predicated on the dichotomy of purity and contamination; rather, it is a model in which the poet and writer is encouraged to draw on various linguistic traditions. In this respect Heine was a conscious and determined anticlassicist. The moment of dissemination and communication is not only essential for Heine's critical prose but also influences his conception of poetry. Irony and parody are used by Heine to subvert the institutionalized aesthetic autonomy. This is particularly true for his late poetry, for instance the "Hebräische Melodien." Heine's attempt to capture the oriental world of the Old Testament and the Middle Ages, his attempt to make it accessible to his German and European readers remains highly ambivalent, integrating and distancing the Jewish tradition – a playful seriousness that always borders on blasphemy. It is not accidental that the *Romanzero* was censured by the Austrian and Prussian governments soon after its publication because of its "unsittlicher Inhalt" (unethical content).[14] The poems deliberately undercut the expectations of a self-enclosed religious world by combining levels of style that were considered incompatible. The seemingly conventional form of these poems is deceptive; its ease is unreliable. Heine's language in "Hebräische Melodien" deliberately subverts notions of poetic purity, for in this context purity

12. H. Arendt, *Die verborgene Tradition*, Frankfurt, 1976, p. 52.
13. See the extensive treatment in S. S. Prawer, *Heine's Jewish Comedy. A Study of his Portraits of Jews and Judaism*, Oxford, 1983.
14. G. Sauder, "Blasphemisch-religiöse Körperwelt. Heinrich Heines 'Hebräische Melodien'," in *Heinrich Heine. Artistik und Engagement*, ed. W. Kuttenkeuler, Tübingen, 1977, p. 140.

would entail a relapse to premodern dogma. Certainly Heine was not simply "in der Sprache," as he, according to Adorno, should have been.

Yet, the notion of a tradition that could serve as *Heimat* is problematic. In his discussions of Goethe and Eichendorff, Adorno was certainly aware of the dialectic of tradition. The very modernity Adorno postulates and holds against Heine's poetry cancels tradition as a premodern category. In fact, Heine's use of the past, of its cultural monuments, reflects his conscious resistance to naive forms of appropriation. But it is also quite clear that Adorno does not appreciate Heine's way of dealing with the cultural tradition. Consequently, he reduces the poet to a second-generation Romantic who is not quite at the critical edge in his use of the poetic language. Unlike Mörike or George, to bring in two examples from Adorno's essay "Lyric Poetry and Society," Heine does not show that tact of avoidance that Adorno demands; rather, he insists on showing his own modernity and that of his readers by invoking and distancing the cultural past through ironic ruptures. Hence the "glatte Fügung" ("smooth linguistic structure") in Heine's poems, which Adorno seems to dislike and reject (as a symptom of Heine's reification), is deceptive; it must not be taken at face value.

It would be too easy, however, to conclude that Adorno simply failed to understand the nature of Heine's poetry, possibly because his own reading was too much influenced by a nineteenth-century reception that saw Heine as the embodiment of German Romantic profundity. The surprising turn at the end of his essay, when Adorno connects Heine's poetry with the Second World War and the Holocaust, points to another level of reception. Here Heine's fate as an outsider and his failure to go beyond the Romantic idiom becomes the touchstone for a general condition of *Heimatlosigkeit*. Now Heine becomes *the* representative modern figure.

The argument, that the fate of the Jew is representative of the fate of mankind, begins to emerge in Adorno's writings as early as 1944 when he and Horkheimer reflected on German fascism and anti-Semitism.[15] In *Dialectic of Enlightenment* the author placed the emphasis of course on the "dialectical link between enlightenment and domination,"[16] which the liberal Jews, relying on the project of assimilation, failed to grasp. Furthermore, *Dialectic of Enlightenment* links modern anti-Semitism to capitalism and defines it as a search for scapegoats. The blame for the inevitable exploitation under capitalism is shifted to the Jews because they are highly

15. On the Frankfurt School, see M. Jay, *The Dialectical Imagination. A History of the Frankfurt School and the Institute of Social Research 1923–1950*, Boston and Toronto, 1973; on Adorno by the same author see *Adorno*, Cambridge, 1984.

16. M. Horkheimer and T. W. Adorno, *Dialectic of Enlightenment*, New York, 1972, p. 163.

visible in the sphere of circulation. When Adorno came back to the problem of German fascism and its anti-Semitism in 1955, the parameter of the public debate had changed. After the discovery of the death camps in 1945, anti-Semitism as well as fascism had become a German question, a problem of German history and German culture that was largely ignored and repressed during the phase of West German reconstruction. His essay "Was bedeutet die Aufarbeitung der Vergangenheit?" (1955)[17] ("What Does it Mean to Come to Terms With the Past?") not only refers to the quasi-official German terms, but also raises the question of why the Holocaust was repressed in postwar Germany. Adorno presents once more both the psychological and the economic arguments that the Frankfurt School had developed during World War II.

Adorno's reeducation program of 1955 invokes the idea of *Aufklärung*, i.e., changing of consciousness through theoretical work, especially sociological and psychoanalytical theory. Adorno stresses at the same time that the failure of reeducation in Germany was not merely or even primarily a matter of insufficient consciousness-raising. He points to the continuation of the objective social conditions that made fascism possible and kept its potential alive: "Daß der Faschismus nachlebt . . . rührt daher, daß die objektiven gesellschaftlichen Voraussetzungen fortbestehen, die den Faschismus zeitigen." ("The reason why fascism is still alive . . . is because the objective social conditions associated with fascism still obtain.")[18] This argument does by no means refer only to the economic system. In fact, the target of Adorno's theory is the culture industry and its ability to neutralize the efforts of the individual in Germany to carry out "die schmerzliche Anstrengung der Erkenntnis" ("the painful effort to reach the truth")[19] because he/she is again under pressure to conform. The real impotence of the individual, Adorno fears, will necessarily undermine the process of critical reflection.

Anti-Semitism, Adorno rightly argues, has little to do with Jews; its mechanisms do not depend on but rather exclude real experience with its victims. At the same time, however, Adorno suggests in his Heine essay that there is a link between Heine's Jewishness and his lack of an authentic language, that there is a real difference after all between a German poet and a Jewish-German writer. Obviously these arguments are not quite compatible. The psychological model of racism as a mechanism in which the victim is replaceable presupposes that there can be no essentially Jewish character. The "Jewish" character, its otherness, is the invention of the racist. Heine's linguistic deficit, his not being quite at home in the German lan-

---

17. T. W. Adorno, *Eingriffe. Neun kritische Modelle*, Frankfurt, 1963, pp. 125–46.
18. *Eingriffe*, p. 139. Editors' translation.
19. *Ibid*. Editors' translation.

guage, on the other hand, appears to be real – a specifically Jewish deficiency that can be recuperated only when it has become a universal human condition, i.e., after the Second World War and the Holocaust.

When Adorno writes about Heine, he becomes caught up in conflicting discourses that he is unable to control. The claim that there is an authentic poetic language that provides the poet with his/her material invites the opposite term and by extension the critical argument that a poet's language can be inauthentic and therefore less valuable. Typically, Adorno uses this construct to stress the need for historical change, since a conventional poetic idiom signals reification and untruth. In the Heine essay, however, the critique of a borrowed language is also concerned with the difference between German and Yiddish. Under these circumstances the meaning of the argument shifts, although not completely. Nowhere does Adorno suggest that Yiddish, Heine's mother tongue, is bad, but he does suggest that someone who comes from that background will find it more difficult, if not impossible, to become fully at home in the German language.

This notion of a "natural" access to German is dubious for two reasons: historically, it is untenable. In the German case, particularly during the eighteenth and early nineteenth century, *Hochdeutsch* was an almost artificial language, a language that was not spoken at home but learned outside.[20] The poet would acquire it only through schooling. This was no less true for Hölderlin and Eichendorff than it was for Heine. They all started out with a regional language that is similar to but not identical with the language of German literature. Since Adorno fails to recognize the historicity of the German literary language, he overestimates Heine's difference. Philosophically, the assumption that there is a "natural" access to an authentic poetic language for native speakers of German relies on the questionable premise that language as pure poetic expression is grounded in the essence of the native speaker who is, then, by definition "at home" in his/her language, while non-native speakers or those who use dialects and regional languages remain outside. There is no space here to discuss Adorno's concept of language in more details; in this context it must suffice to note that Adorno's emphasis on authenticity leads him down a dangerous road. It is not the argument that Heine's language is second-hand and borrowed that I find problematic in principle; it is the link between Heine's way of writing and his Jewish background that leaves me with doubts.

When Adorno addresses the phenomenon of anti-Semitism, he makes it quite clear that he does not believe in Jewish characteristics *per se* – hence there is no Jewish language. In his treatment of Heine he seems to deviate

20. On the history of the literary language, see E. A. Blackall, *The Emergence of German as a Literary Language 1700–1775*, London, 1959.

from this path. The question is: why? It turns out that Adorno is rather ambivalent about the nature of authentic German. His own prose style, involved, complex, and saturated with foreign words (frequently French), was anything but the simple straightforward German that the nationalists, obsessed with the purity of the German language, were recommending. In fact, his prose might have well served as an example for the "Frenchified" German of the typical Jewish intellectual. Adorno was, no doubt, familiar with this discourse and, hence, aware of his own position. His small essay "Wörter aus der Fremde"[21] can be read as an acknowledgement of his own vulnerability – writing un-German/Jewish German. Yet his definition of authentic poetic German is meant to transcend the sophistication of prose – that of Heinrich Heine as well as that of Adorno. But, unlike Heine, Adorno did not attempt to write poetry. Thus he did not directly face Heine's problem of mediating between Yiddish and German, compromised and poetic language. It is interesting to note in this context that Adorno rejects Lukács's claim that the essay is an art form. Instead, he stresses the rhetorical nature of the essay: it is situated between the rigorous argument of philosophy and the pure expression of poetry, a problematic form that can easily collapse under the impact of the culture industry. Hence the modern essay is never too far removed from the *feuilleton* – a mode of journalism that was frequently associated with Jewish intellectuals like Heine. On the other hand, the essay is for Adorno the critical form *par excellence*, precisely because it is "impure" and relies on rhetoric rather than logic.

As we can see, Adorno, when he discusses Heine's language, is more implicated than he seems. The initial distinction between commercialized and authentic poetry, compromised and pure language, finally collapses when Adorno concludes that Heine could succeed only through the open presentation of rupture, "Mißlingen schlägt um ins Gelungene" (150) ("Failure, reversing itself, is transformed into success"). Yet this applies to the essay form as well, since its truth is mediated through its untruth,[22] i.e., through its lack of solidity, its protean character. Thus the ending of the Heine essay points to a dilemma as well as a solution, which includes Adorno the essayist, the refugee, and the survivor of the Holocaust.

21. Adorno, *Noten zur Literatur II*, Frankfurt, 1961, pp. 110–30. Editors' note: This essay was translated as "Words from Abroad" in Adorno, *Notes to Literature*.
22. Adorno, "Der Essay als Form," in *Noten zur Literatur I*, p. 43.

# –14–

# Enlightenment, the Other(s) of Reason, and German Social Democracy (1890–1914)

## ANDREW G. BONNELL

In *Das Andere der Vernunft* (*The Other of Reason*), Hartmut and Gernot Böhme have referred to a "dialectic of appropriation and repression or displacements" (*Verdrängung*) as a characteristic of the process of enlightenment: "a program of emancipation is set into motion simultaneously with a program of repression."[1] For socialist critics of the Imperial German state and society prior to 1914, the project of Enlightenment, including such values as the assertion of the claims of reason against tradition, privilege, and religious dogma, and of natural and civil rights against arbitrary and oppressive government, seemed to offer considerable critical and emancipatory potential. It will be argued below that the belief that the German Social Democratic Party of the period of the Second International was the heir to, and true representative of, the Enlightenment tradition in Germany – which, despite the formal trappings of the *Rechtsstaat*, still fell well short of Enlightenment ideals – was of considerable importance to the self-image and morale of German Social Democrats, even though socialist intellectuals differed considerably over the interpretation of this tradition. To Social Democrats, the Imperial German state seemed to embody the "other" of Enlightenment, with its appeal to premodern forms of political legitimation (dynastic, and to some extent religious) and reactionary constitutional arrangements that were regarded as more backward than the more "rationalized" state structures of the West. In this context, Social Democrats hoped that the Enlightenment tradition of critique, rationalism, and emancipation would be as effective against the Wilhelmine German state as it was thought to have been against the French *ancien régime*

1. H. and G. Böhme, *Das Andere der Vernunft*, Frankfurt, 1983, pp. 14, 17.

before 1789. At the same time, however, German Social Democrats failed to fully appreciate the other side of the "dialectic of Enlightenment" – the limitations of a narrowly-conceived rationalism – and failed to theoretically comprehend a productive and complementary "Other of reason."

The ideology of the SPD in this period was governed by the 1891 Erfurt Program, an explicitly Marxist party program composed by Karl Kautsky with the assistance of Eduard Bernstein, under the influence of Friedrich Engels, who remained in touch with SPD intellectuals and leaders until his death in 1891. The theoretical limitations of the conception of Marxism prevalent in this period have been the subject of considerable academic discussion.[2] Marxism was commonly understood during the period of the Second International – prior to the work of Lukács, Korsch, and Bloch and the rediscovery of Marx's early writings – in the form of "historical materialism," a conception which tended to stress the deterministic, evolutionary and economic aspects of Marxism at the expense of the Hegelian, dialectical, and dynamic aspects. The advantage of such a formulation of Marxism for the socialist labor movement of this period lay in its assurance of a scientific guarantee of ultimate success – a legacy, perhaps, of Enlightenment optimism regarding historical progress. Its drawbacks included a lack of theoretical space for subjective factors that might have made a positive contribution to the formation of a revolutionary consciousness.

For proponents of historical materialist orthodoxy such as Franz Mehring, who did considerable work in applying the "historical materialistic method" to the study of history and literature and to critical commentary on contemporary politics, the claim of the workers' movement to be the heir of the Enlightenment was proven by the Marxist view of history. This claim was held by Mehring to be of profound significance for the historical role of the working class movement. In his *Die Lessing-Legende* (1893), Mehring's critique of existing bourgeois literary history and its representation of Lessing and the Friderician Prussian legend, Mehring followed Engels in proclaiming the proletariat the inheritor of German classical philosophy.[3] Following the reasoning of the Communist Manifesto, Mehring argued that the Enlightenment ideals represented by Lessing had been abandoned by the bourgeoisie and were now the rightful property of the workers (who had constituted part of the same Estate as the bourgeoisie before the rise of industrial capitalism). In Germany the bourgeoisie had surrendered to the old principles of feudal legitimacy, and had

2. See, for example, G. Lichtheim, *Marxism. An Historical and Critical Study*, London, 1980. For the SPD see also H.-J. Steinberg, *Sozialismus und deutsche Sozialdemokratie*, Berlin/Bonn, 1979.

3. F. Mehring, *Die Lessing-Legende* (*Gesammelte Schriften* – hereafter *GS*, Bd. 9, Berlin, 1983), p. 362; F. Engels, *Ludwig Feuerbach und der Ausgang der klassischen deutschen Philosophie*, in K. Marx/F. Engels, *Werke*, Bd. 21, Berlin, 1969, here p. 307.

allowed the revolutionary implications of Lessing's and Kant's work to be forgotten in the pursuit of profit under the protection of the militarist Prussian state.[4] Mehring's study of the literature of the German Enlightenment thus served to support the contention of the Communist Manifesto that the struggle of the working class was a struggle for universal emancipation. (It was a form of argumentation particularly congenial for a former bourgeois radical democrat who had abandoned his earlier class and political affiliations to join the SPD in 1891).[5]

Other Social Democrats, mainly from the revisionist wing of the party, looked to the philosophy of the eighteenth-century Enlightenment – particularly to Kant – not for purposes of historical legitimation, but to provide historical materialism with an ethical base.[6] On the occasion of the centenary of Kant's death, Eduard David declared in the *Reichstag* that the Social Democratic Party alone was able to realize Kant's ethical postulates:

> The central idea of his social ethics was that no-one should use another person as a mere means to an end, because every human personality is a value and end in itself. . . . We wish to see the value and dignity in the self of every human personality made recognizable. That can only happen when an adequate material situation in life is created for everyone, when mass misery and mass deprivation disappear from our culture.[7]

Revisionists such as David, Conrad Schmidt, Ludwig Woltmann, and Eduard Bernstein raised a cry of "Back to Kant," Bernstein arguing in his *Voraussetzungen des Sozialismus* that there was

> need for a Kant . . . to show that the apparent materialism [of the party theoreticians] is in the highest degree an ideology – and therefore most easily misleading, that the contempt for the ideal, the elevation of material factors to omnipotent forces of development, is a self-delusion which was and is exposed as such on every occasion by the deeds of the very men who proclaim it.[8]

The claim of Bernstein and others that historical materialism needed to be supplemented by a recourse to critical idealistic philosophy was sharply rejected by representatives of orthodoxy such as Kautsky, Plekhanov and

4. Mehring, *GS* 9, pp. 357–65.

5. On this development see T. Höhle, *Franz Mehring: Sein Weg zum Marxismus*, Berlin, 1956; G. R. MacDougall, *Franz Mehring: Politics and History in the Making of Radical German Social Democracy, 1869–1903* (Ph.D. diss., Columbia University, 1977), and *idem*, "Franz Mehring and the Problem of Liberal Social Reform in Bismarckian Germany 1884–90," *Central European History* 16, 1983, pp. 225–55.

6. Steinberg, *Sozialismus*, pp. 98–100; see also K. Vorländer, *Kant und der Sozialismus*, Berlin, 1900, and Mehring's reserved response to Vorländer in Mehring, *GS* 13, pp. 183–88.

7. Quoted in Steinberg, *Sozialismus*, p. 101. Unless otherwise indicated, the author is responsible for the translation of the various quotations.

8. *Ibid.*, p. 101f.; E. Bernstein, *Die Voraussetzungen des Sozialismus*, Reinbek bei Hamburg, 1970, p. 217.

Mehring.[9] Plekhanov suspected Neo-Kantianism of being an intellectual weapon of the bourgeoisie and considered its influence among Social Democrats to be symptomatic of opportunistic deviations.[10] Mehring, arguing on the basis of his linear teleological and deterministic view of history, argued that as Kant was the product of a relatively less advanced stage of development of bourgeois society, any "return to Kant" would be a regression from the insights achieved by Marx.[11]

Arguably, SPD intellectuals in this period were unable to formulate a satisfactory philosophical synthesis, either on a "dialectical materialist" or an "ethical socialist" basis.[12] It is questionable, however, how significant such theoretical debates (conducted largely in the relatively low-circulation *Neue Zeit*) were in the crisis facing Social Democracy by 1914 in comparison to factors such as economic conjunctures, changes in the structure of the industrial workforce, the ideological offensive of pro-imperialist groups in German society (combined with outright repression by state organs), the rise of a bureaucratic party and trade union structure, and the growing influence of trade union functionaries in party affairs.[13] This is not the place to pursue these questions in detail. Rather, it is our purpose here to discuss the extent to which the discourse of the organized socialist labor movement[14] emphasized the emancipatory traditions of the Enlightenment. It suffices in the context to note that party intellectuals, whatever their differences and the different uses to which they put Enlightenment literature and philosophy, were alike in regarding the labor movement as the rightful heir to the best, most progressive Enlightenment traditions. (While relatively few rank-and-file SPD members had the leisure or educational qualifications to study theoretical debates about Marx or Kant[15] –

9. Steinberg, *Sozialismus*, pp. 103–105.
10. G. Plekhanov, "Konrad Schmidt gegen Karl Marx und Friedrich Engels," *Die neue Zeit* 17, 1, 1898–99, p. 145. See also the subsequent exchange between Schmidt and Plekhanov: C. Schmidt, "Einige Bemerkungen über Plechanovs Artikel", *ibid.*, pp. 324–34; Plekhanov, "Materialismus oder Kantianismus?", *ibid.*, pp. 589–96, 626–32.
11. Mehring, *GS*, 13, pp. 41f., 54f. Mehring was less one-dimensional and deterministic in his evaluation of art and literature. (See for example *GS* 7 (1980), p. 517). In philosophical questions, however, he was inclined to agree with Engels's statement in the *Anti-Dühring* that Marxism represented "the end of philosophy," and was inclined to dismiss questions of epistemology as "*Hirnwebereien*" (useless speculation).
12. See O. Kallscheuer, "Philosophy and Politics in the SPD," *Telos* 53, 1982, pp. 81–94, whose critique of the SPD ranges from ca. 1900 to beyond the Godesberg Program.
13. For a brief review of the debate on the question of the "deradicalization" of the SPD before the First World War, and the reasons for it, see D. Geary, *European Labour Protest, 1848–1939*, London, 1984, pp. 107–33.
14. It is perhaps worth noting that the following is only intended to apply to the socialist labor movement's cultural milieu, not necessarily that of the working classes as a whole.
15. A point stressed by V. L. Lidtke, *The Alternative Culture*, New York/Oxford, 1985, p. 189; Steinberg, *Sozialismus*, p. 141.

which makes it difficult to analyze specific influences from the Enlightenment tradition with philosophical rigor – it is possible to discern a *general consciousness* in the organized cultural milieu of the SPD that the advance of socialism was an expression of historical progress toward a greater emancipation of humanity as a whole, involving secularization, greater educational opportunities, the triumph of rational forms of knowledge and social organization, and the recognition and realization of human and civil rights).

The equation of the advance of socialism within the realization of universal human emancipation and the unfolding of Reason in human history was a major theme of the most popular socialist book of the period: Bebel's *Die Frau im Sozialismus* (*Women in a Socialist Society*). Socialism would guarantee the free development of the individual personality – in particular, women would have equal rights with men and enjoy complete emancipation: "the 'golden age' of which people have dreamed for thousands of years, and which they have longed for, will come at last. The rule of one class over another will have reached its end for ever, but with it also the rule of man over woman."[16] In achieving this goal, socialists would be realizing the aims of all those who had struggled for equal civil and political rights for women since the French Revolution, in which connection Bebel cites Mme. Roland, Olympe de Gouges, and Claire Lacombe, as well as the Encyclopedists of prerevolutionary France.[17]

Such references to the French Revolution and its emancipatory aims of "liberty, equality, and fraternity" were frequent in socialist discourse of this period. Allegorical representations of the slogans of 1789 made regular appearances at Social Democratic festivals in the form of *tableaux vivants*. In the early 1890s, the socialist poet "C. M. Scävola" composed an "epic-dramatic poem in 12 tableaux vivants" on the French Revolution, which culminated in a representation of "the Republic in the Triumph of Liberty."[18] The melody of the "Marseillaise" was the one that appeared most frequently in Social Democrats' songbooks, serving as the tune for Jakob Audorf's "*Arbeiter-Marseillaise*," the movement's unofficial anthem.[19] The lyrics for such songs "reflected those optimistic notions that forecast the victory of light over darkness, labour over capital, truth over falsehood, and peace and harmony over war and conflict."[20] It is not surprising that the

16. A. Bebel, *Die Frau im Sozialismus*, Berlin/Bonn, 1980, pp. 412, 421–27.

17. *Ibid.*, pp. 271–73.

18. F. Knilli and U. Münchow, *Frühes deutsches Arbeitertheater, 1847–1918*, Munich, 1970, pp. 290–302. See P. von Rüden, *Sozialdemokratisches Arbeitertheater, 1847–1914*, Frankfurt, 1973, p. 155, for an illustration depicting the *tableau vivant* entitled "*Marseillaise*" at the SPD Party Congress at Berlin, 1982. See also Lidtke, *Alternative Culture*, pp. 89f, 153f.

19. See Lidtke, *Alternative Culture*, pp. 122, 126f.

20. *Ibid.*, p. 97.

popular history of the French Revolution by the Social Democratic *Reichstag* deputy Wilhelm Blos was a commonly read item in workers' libraries.[21] For these purposes the historical nature of the French Revolution as a bourgeois revolution that achieved limited aims before its transformation into Bonapartist dictatorship was of less importance than the tradition of revolution against a decaying and repressive *ancien régime* (comparisons could be made with the showy neo-absolutism of Wilhelmine Germany) and the lasting appeal of the ideals of 1789, which included the triumph of Reason against premodern, authoritarian political structures.

One of the forces identified with the *ancien régime* to which Social Democrats were opposed was organized religion – both in its Catholic and Protestant forms. The Catholic Centre Party, which was competing with the SPD for the votes of workers in Catholic areas, and the established Protestant Church were two of the conservative pillars of the Hohenzollern Reich. Socialists such as Bebel saw the conflict with organized religion as a struggle between reason and its Other – between historical progress on the one side and dogma and tradition on the other. For Bebel, religion was a product of, and an ideological prop for, class society, and would gradually disappear along with capitalism.[22] In the 1874 pamphlet *Christentum und Sozialismus*, Bebel had argued that history had shown the Christian church to be "hostile to liberty and culture," and stated, "Christianity and socialism are opposed to each other like fire and water. The so-called good kernel of Christianity . . . is not Christian, but belongs to humanity in general, and what Christianity actually consists of, the whole pile of doctrines and dogmas, is hostile to humanity."[23] Vernon Lidtke has described Bebel as "the German workingman's Voltaire."[24]

After the 1870s, the Social Democrats' militant atheism and aggressive stance towards the churches were modified, partly for tactical reasons, partly because of the Marxian view that religion (like the state) would wither away, but only when its foundations in class society were overcome.[25] The Erfurt Program of 1891 contented itself with declaring religion a private matter for the individual, and demanding the abolition of public expenditure for religious purposes. Churches and religious communities were to be viewed as private organizations that were to run their

21. W. Blos, *Die französische Revolution von 1789 bis 1804*, Berlin, 1923 (first published 1889); Steinberg, *Sozialismus*, p. 139.

22. A. Bebel, *Frau im Sozialismus*, p. 398.

23. Bebel, *Ausgewählte Reden und Schriften*, vol. 1, Berlin, 1983, pp. 294, 298f.

24. V. L. Lidtke, "August Bebel and German Social Democracy's Relation to the Christian Churches," *Journal of the History of Ideas* 27 (1966) p. 253.

25. *Ibid.*, pp. 255–58; S. Miller, *Das Problem der Freiheit im Sozialismus*, Frankfurt, 1970, p. 168f.

affairs independently.[26] Schooling was to be public, compulsory and secular.[27]

Contemporary surveys found a high correlation between secular attitudes towards religion and membership of Social Democratic organizations.[28] The evangelical pastor Martin Rade found that organized workers tended to disbelieve the Biblical account of creation (expressing their opinions in terms influenced by Darwinism) and tended to be critical of church ceremonies and the clergy, even though some of the workers were prepared to concede that Christianity had achieved some positive things historically, or regarded Jesus as a revolutionary figure and a friend of the workers.[29] Organized workers adopted a secularized vocabulary, favoring language borrowed from the natural sciences, which, together with Marxian ideas, fulfilled the need of many for a current *Weltanschauung* in place of traditional religion.[30]

A small minority of workers joined "free-thinking" or "free-religious" communities. These groups encouraged workers to disaffiliate themselves from the established churches, developed nonsectarian life-cycle rituals, defended liberal-humanistic policies in the cultural sphere, and encouraged social reforms in areas from temperance campaigns to the promotion of cremation.[31] While both the "free-thinking" movement and the socialist labor movement believed that popular enlightenment would supersede organized religion, the SPD leadership kept its distance from the (largely bourgeois) free-thinkers, while many of the free-thinkers' leaders had difficulty in embracing the concept of class struggle.[32]

Not surprisingly, the SPD was very active in the field of workers' education. In his well-known 1872 lecture "*Wissen ist Macht*," Wilhelm Liebknecht had discussed the possibilities and limitations of educational work:

> The state and society of today, which we oppose, are enemies of education; as long as they exist, they will prevent knowledge from becoming common property. Whoever wishes that knowledge will be imparted to all in equal measure

26. K. Kautsky, *Das Erfurter Programm*, Introduction by S. Miller, Berlin/Bonn, 1980 (rep. of 1922 edition), p. 256.

27. *Ibid.*

28. V. Lidtke, "Social Class and Secularisation in Imperial Germany. The Working Classes," *Yearbook of the Leo Baeck Institute* 25 (1980) pp. 29–35.

29. *Ibid.*

30. *Ibid.* On the influence of Darwinian scientific thought on German workers, see A. Kelly, *The Descent of Darwin. The Popularization of Darwinism in Germany, 1860–1914*, Chapel Hill, 1981, pp. 123–41, and *idem*, "Darwinism and the Working Class in Wilhelmian Germany," in S. Drescher, D. Sabean, and A. Sharlin, (eds.), *Political Symbolism in Modern Europe*, New Brunswick/London, 1982, pp. 146–67.

31. H. Gorschopp, *Zwischen Bierabend und Bildungsverein*, Berlin, 1985, pp. 67–70.

32. J.-C. Kaiser, *Arbeiterbewegung und organisierte Religionskritik*, Stuttgart, 1981, pp. 115–18, 338–41.

must therefore work for the transformation of the state and society. . . . *The means is political and social agitation* . . . . If we renounce the struggle – the political struggle, we thus renounce *education [Bildung]* and *knowledge*. "Through education to freedom" – that is the wrong slogan, the slogan of false friends. We answer: *through freedom to education!* Only in the free people's state can the people achieve knowledge. Only when the people wins the struggle for political power, will the gates of knowledge be opened to it. *No knowledge without power to the people! Knowledge is power! Power is knowledge!*[33]

Liebknecht's lecture was largely a polemic against liberal and confessional workers' educational associations, which served to deflect workers from independent political activity, but his emphasis on priority for the political struggle remained an authoritative precept, especially for the party's left wing, which stressed the need to actively prepare to take power.[34] However, the great interest that Liebknecht's lecture – frequently reprinted as a pamphlet – aroused, and the wide range of educational activities undertaken by the SPD, show that organized workers wanted both power *and* knowledge. After all, the *"Arbeiter-Marseillaise"* (mentioned above) proclaimed:

"Der Feind, den wir am meisten hassen . . .
Das ist der Unverstand der Massen."[35]
("The enemy we hate the most . . .
Is the masses' lack of understanding.")

These lines testify to an Enlightenment belief in the efficacy of education, and to an emphasis on reason (*Verstand*) as the crucial faculty to which socialists had to appeal.

Broadly speaking, the SPD's concern with educational matters took two forms. One was sustained criticism of the existing school system. In *"Wissen ist Macht,"* Liebknecht had attacked the Prussian *Volksschule*, blaming it, along with military service and the popular press, as responsible for the low educational level of workers:

The school is the most powerful means of liberation and the most powerful means of subjugation – depending on the nature and purpose of the state. In the free people's state the school is a means of liberation, in the unfree state a means of subjugation. . . . The state as it is, that is the class state, makes the school into a means of subjugation.[36]

---

33. W. Liebknecht, *Wissen ist Macht – Macht ist Wissen und andere bildungspolitisch-pädagogische Äusserungen*, ed. H. Brumme, Berlin, 1968, p. 93f. (emphasis in original).

34. See for example Mehring, *GS* 11, pp. 445–49; 10, p. 415; Kautsky, *Erfurter Programm*, p. 169.

35. Quoted in W. Wittwer, "Zur Entstehung und Entwicklung sozialdemokratischer Schulpolitik," *Archiv für Sozialgeschichte* 20 (1980) p. 357.

36. Liebknecht, *Wissen ist Macht*, p. 70.

The *Volksschule*, Liebknecht claimed, stifled independent thought and intellectual curiosity, and aimed principally at producing "fodder for the barracks."[37] In the *Reichstag* (and in state legislatures) the SPD was active in opposing what it perceived to be reactionary legislation concerning education, for example, the extension of the confessional character of the *Volksschule*.[38]

The other form that social democratic education policy took was the sponsorship of workers' education ventures under the auspices of the party and the trade unions. One such venture was the Berlin Workers' Educational School, opened formally by Wilhelm Liebknecht in 1891, with a speech that emphasized again the link between education and the emancipation of the working class.[39] The party's educational work (coordinated by a Central Education Committee from 1906 onwards, to which prominent party intellectuals and leaders belonged) also included extension courses and lectures of various kinds, workers' libraries and cultural organizations such as theater groups.[40]

Writing on the workers' libraries and workers' reading habits has often stressed the limitations of Social Democratic cultural policy – the major works of Marx and Engels were little read, and workers showed a marked preference for sensational fiction and escapist fare such as travel literature.[41] This is not surprising, given what is known about the educational and leisure opportunities available to workers – even the relatively well-off skilled workers who tended to patronize the libraries. What is noteworthy, however, is the steady popularity of books in categories such as the natural sciences and history. Although written at a popular level, such works contributed to the cultivation of the organized workers' outlook on the world. Popular scientific works such as those of Wilhelm Bölsche reflected Darwinistic and rationalist trends of thought.[42] That Otto von Corvin's much-read *Pfaffenspiegel* tended toward the lurid and sensational may be less significant than the extent to which it confirmed anticlerical sentiments. The popularity of utopian novels can be seen as reflecting the desire for a more rationally ordered (and more just) society, just as the popularity of naturalist fiction was at least partly due to its criticisms of existing society (and perhaps also to some extent to its claims to reflect a scientific world-view).

37. *Ibid.*, p. 70f. For the ideological function of the Prussian *Volksschule* see V. Meyer, *Schule der Untertanen: Lehrer und Politik in Preussen, 1848–1900*, Hamburg, 1976; G. C. Field, "Religion in the German Volksschule, 1890–1928", *Yearbook of the Leo Baeck Institute* 25 1980 pp. 41–71.

38. Wittwer, "*Schulpolitik*," pp. 375–77.

39. *Vorwärts*, 25 January 1891 (1.Beilage).

40. On the Central Educational Committee see Groschopp, *Bierabend*, pp. 116–21; Lidtke, *Alternative Culture*, pp. 166–68, 176–79.

41. See Steinberg, *Sozialismus*, pp. 129–42; Lidtke, *Alternative Culture*, pp. 186–88.

42. See the references in note 30.

However limited the reception of Marxism among the rank and file of the SPD was – mediated through pamphlets, speeches, and such unsatisfactory channels as *Vorwärts* editorials – the reading habits of organized workers do testify to a consistent if vaguely articulated worldview as well as to workers' needs for entertainment and diversion.

The self-identification of the SPD with enlightenment and emancipatory principles was also evident in its campaigns for human and civil rights in Wilhelmine Germany. The party had itself suffered from the repressive behavior of the state, having been forced into illegality from 1878 to 1890, and remaining subject to harassment by the police and judicial authorities thereafter. Throughout the 1890s, *Vorwärts* ran a regular column (entitled "Under the New Course") that chronicled the convictions, fines and prison sentences imposed on party members.[43] In 1902, Hans Delbrück wrote, "One of the sources for which the tremendous power of Social Democracy draws its strength . . . is the sense that we in Germany do not live in a system of equality before the law. It is the concept of *'Klassenjustiz'* which awakens a most passionate form of hate."[44] Blatant discrimination against socialists by the courts and such features of the legal system as the arbitrary application of the laws on *lèse-majesté* as a form of political censorship (sometimes resulting in stiff sentences for the editors of SPD newspapers) aroused regular outcries.[45] The SPD program demanded free access to the legal system, popularly elected judges, the right of appeal in criminal cases, compensation for those innocently accused, arrested and convicted, and the abolition of the death penalty.[46] The SPD took a leading part in the opposition to the 1894 *Umsturzvorlage* (Anti-Subversion Bill) and other repressive legislation such as the 1898 *lex Arons* (undermining academic freedom) and the *lex Heinze* (extending censorship).

The SPD also asserted human and civil rights in its opposition to colonialism and to discrimination against women, even if its practice did not always meet the demands of its theory. Although the ranks of the party did harbor some closet (or open) defenders of colonialism,[47] the SPD regularly spoke out on behalf of the rights of colonized peoples, contrasting official claims to be spreading German culture and civilization with the deeds of Carl Peters in East Africa, or General von Trotha in Southwest Africa.[48]

---

43. See also A. Hall, "By Other Means: The Legal Struggle Against the SPD in Wilhelmine Germany, 1890–1900," *Historical Journal,* June 1974, pp. 365–86.

44. Quoted in A. Hall, *Scandal, Sensation and Social Democracy,* Cambridge, 1977, p. 73.

45. *Ibid.*, pp. 72–78; A. Hall, "The Kaiser, the Wilhelmine State and Lèse-Majesté," *German Life and Letters* 27 (1973–74) pp. 101–15.

46. Kautsky, *Erfurter Programm,* p. 257.

47. H.-C. Schröder, *Noske und die Kolonialpolitik,* Berlin/Bonn, 1979; R. Fletcher, *Revisionism and Imperialism,* London, 1984.

48. See for example Mehring, *GS* 14, pp. 134–38; *GS* 15, pp. 175–79.

While there were shortcomings – which have been well documented[49] – in attitudes toward women in the SPD and the Free Trade Unions, the Social Democrats were, at least in principle, staunch advocates of rights for women. The Erfurt Program demanded the abolition of all laws that disadvantaged women in the public or private sphere.[50] Bebel's treatise on the "Woman Question," (*Die Frau im Sozialismus*, mentioned above), was the single most read work of socialist theory in Germany, reaching its fiftieth impression in 1909. Despite the (mainly private) reservations of some figures within the SPD, the SPD's women's organization developed considerable momentum in its campaign for women's suffrage, a campaign that (unlike the suffrage agitation of some mainstream bourgeois feminists) aimed at the removal of *all* discriminatory franchise laws.[51] However, once again, it is possible to discern limits to the SPD's conception of enlightenment. In his discussion of Social Democratic discourse on the "Sexual Question," R. P. Neuman found that "though Social Democratic critics attacked the sexual hypocrisy of the dominant culture, they often reiterated traditional sexual attitudes under the guise of science and self-sacrifice for the class struggles."[52] Attempts to extend the strictly rationalist Marxism of the Second International by integrating it with the subversive implications of psychoanalysis had to await the period after the First World War.

Vernon Lidtke has pointed out the existence of customary forms of communication within the "social-cultural milieu" of organized socialist labor, and the significance of such forms in binding together the various elements of the SPD's constituency. The way in which words such as *"Arbeiter"* (worker) and *"Genosse"* (comrade) were used made them symbols of ideological identification and cohesion rather than mere sociological categories.[53] Similarly, the hostility and repression experienced by the Social Democratic labor movement in its confrontation with the state "intensified its sense of solidarity."[54] To these factors one might add the widely shared assumption of Social Democrats that, in its confrontation with the state and reactionary forces in society, organized labor was the

49. See K. Honeycutt, "Socialism and Feminism in Imperial Germany," *Signs: Journal of Women in Culture and Society* 5 (1979) pp. 30–41; J. H. Quataert, *Reluctant Feminists in German Social Democracy, 1885–1917*, Princeton, 1979.

50. Kautsky, *Erfurter Programm*, p. 256.

51. On the issue of the mainstream bourgeois feminist movement's political conservatism, especially after 1908, see R. J. Evans, "Liberalism and Society: The Feminist Movement and Social Change," in *idem*, (ed.), *Society and Politics in Wilhelmine Germany*, London, 1982, pp. 186–214.

52. R. P. Neuman, "The Sexual Question and Social Democracy in Imperial Germany," *Journal of Social History* 7 (1974) pp. 271–86.

53. Lidtke, *Alternative Culture*, p. 199f.

54. *Ibid.*, p. 201.

bearer of the cause of universal human emancipation, representing reason versus tradition and religious dogma, and human and civil rights versus arbitrary government, and ideas of fraternity versus militarism. The enlightenment elements in Social Democratic thought are perhaps most clearly revealed in such oppositions, which might be theorized as opposition between reason and its Other. These oppositions can be seen to have played an important role in the constitution of the self-image and historical consciousness of the SPD. However, as suggested above, the conception of enlightenment and reason prevalent in the SPD suffered from limitations, which were partly the product of the determinism of Second International Marxism, and partly the consequence of the understandable priority given to immediate political concerns over philosophical reflection. The failure to effectively integrate subjective factors into historical materialism (in the manner of later Left thinkers, such as Bloch's "spirit of utopia" or Lukács's "collective conscious will") limited the SPD's responses to ideological challenges such as that of nationalism in 1914, and contributed to the party's tendency toward a posture of *"attentisme"* as opposed to revolutionary activism. As early as the mid-1890s, some friendly critics of the SPD's cultural policies warned against neglecting the non-rational elements of human experience, a criticism later levelled at the German Communist Party by Ernst Bloch in the 1930s.[55] Nonetheless, enlightenment ideas can be regarded as having a positive value for Social Democratic culture, in enabling Social Democrats to see themselves as being on the side of historical progress and universal human emancipation.

To consider the relationship of German Social Democracy to the Enlightenment tradition after 1914 raises the question of continuity in the history of the SPD as well as the vexed history of debates about reason in German culture and politics in the twentieth century. The split in the socialist labor movement in the wake of the First World War and the Bolshevik Revolution into Social Democrats and Communists, the changes in Social Democrat party programs in the Weimar Republic (at Görlitz in 1921 and Heidelberg in 1925), the suppression of the labor movement by the Nazis, and the division of Germany with the formation of the Socialist Unity Party in the GDR and the transformation of the West German Social Democrats into a fully-fledged *Volkspartei*, jettisoning class-struggle rhetoric at Bad Godesberg in 1959, all combine to problematize attempts at constructing a clear-cut line of continuity in the history of German Social Democracy. Rather, there have been competing versions of Social

55. See W. Hudson, *The Marxist Philosophy of Ernst Bloch*, London, 1982, p. 42f. For an example of earlier criticism, see E. Steiger, *Das arbeitende Volk und die Kunst. Kritische Streifzüge*, Leipzig, 1896, p. 7.

Democratic tradition, as both the SPD in the Federal Republic and the SED in East Germany formulated and laid claim to their own version of the Social Democratic heritage, the ideologists of the SED claiming descent through the revolutionary wing of the German labor movement (from Marx and Engels, Bebel and Wilhelm Liebknecht, through Karl Liebknecht and Rosa Luxemburg, to Thälmann, Ulbricht and Honecker), while SPD historians and the historical work associated with the Friedrich-Ebert-Stiftung in the West gave more weight to reformists such as Bernstein and Ebert, as well as to Lassalle and Bebel. The SPD in the West celebrated its centenary in 1963 (from Lassalle's foundation of the ADAV), while the SED in the East traced its origin back to 1869. In both cases, a strong sense of continuity with party tradition was fostered, supported by some continuity in membership and in leadership, throughout the transformations of the German labor movement.

The debates of the last ten years have demonstrated that "the political use of reason" (to borrow the title of a recent book by Social Democratic leader Björn Engholm) is still an object of lively contention in Germany, in which Social Democrats, and intellectuals more or less loosely aligned with Social Democracy, such as Jürgen Habermas, have played a critical role (in both senses of the term). The *"Historikerstreit"* (historians' dispute about Germany's relationship to the Nazi past) of the mid-1980s saw Social Democratic historians and other intellectuals opposing attempts by right-wing historians – and the Kohl conservative government – to revive feelings of emotional identification with the German nation. Against the threat of a comeback of Teutonic irrationalism, Habermas counterposed the concept of a "postconventional identity" based on "constitutional patriotism," which would draw inspiration from the Federal Republic's democratic institutions and commitment to Western Enlightenment values.[56] After the momentous events of November 1989 that culminated in national unification, revived national sentiment divided the SPD, which was caught between the pressures to identify with the popular aspirations for unification and the need for a rational assessment of its economic and social ramifications. Unification also saw Habermas's notions of postconventional identity come under renewed fire from conservatives, who referred to "constitutional patriotism" as an "anaemic, if well-meaning, professorial fiction," which was superfluous now that the heartland of Germany – Thuringia, Saxony, Saxony-Anhalt, Mecklenburg-Vorpommera-

56. J. Habermas, "Eine Art Schadensabwicklung. Die apologetischen Tendenzen in der deutschen Zeitgeschichtsschreibung," *Die Zeit*, 11 July 1986, repr. in the collection *Historikerstreit*, pub. Piper Verlag, Munich, 1987, pp. 62–76. English translation in *New German Critique* 44 (1988) pp. 25–39.

nia and Brandenburg – was rejoining the Western *Länder*.[57] These political and cultural debates have coincided with a period in which the Western Enlightenment tradition has been subjected to intense criticism in intellectual circles, criticism that has obliged the defenders of that tradition to distinguish between different kinds of rationality – the instrumental rationality of the system of material reproduction under capitalism (a partial, distorted form of rationality), and the emancipatory potential of a concept of reason grounded in communicative action. The more carefully nuanced conception of rationality being worked out by Habermas may provide a way out of the theoretical impasses that have sometimes confronted Social Democratic intellectuals in the past. The resonance of the recent controversies involving the "political use of reason" in Germany, and the enduringly sensitive nature of the historical dimension of these debates, guarantee that these issues will be of continuing concern to German Social Democrats.

57. H.-P. Schwarz, "Das Ende der Identitätsneurose," *Rheinischer Merkur/Christ und Welt*, 7 September 1990. See also K. H. Bohrer, "Why We Are Not A Nation – And Why We Should Become One," in *New German Critique* 52 (1991) pp. 72–83 (originally pub. in the *Frankfurter Allgemeine Zeitung*, 13 January 1990).

# -15-

# Irrationalism, Expressionism, and the Conflict of Generations

## REINHARD ALTER

If influential voices such as that of Joachim Fest, editor of the *Frankfurter Allgemeine Zeitung*, are to be believed, then the socioeconomic "normalization" or "westernization" now underway in the eastern part of a reunified Germany has retroactively invalidated critical perspectives on modernization processes such as those proposed by Jürgen Habermas, Hans and Wolfgang Mommsen, Martin Broszat, Hans-Ulrich Wehler, Jürgen Kocka, and others in the course of the Historians' Debate of the mid-1980s, not to speak of the student protest movement of the late sixties. Beyond their immediate causes, the "upheavals of the past years," according to Fest, "were above all a struggle against the terror of ideas, and the liberation which finally came was a liberation into reality." The figure of Ernst Bloch in particular, whom Fest makes largely responsible for the 1968 student generation's lack of political and historical realism, "towers over the present like an alien, monstrous anachronism."[1]

Such victory celebrations for modern pragmatic rationality over all variants of utopian thought threaten to close all debate not only about the causes of the ideological polarization in Germany since the 1960s, but also about possible sociocultural and generational determinants in the quest for social utopias since the "second industrial revolution" in late nineteenth-century Germany. As far as Ernst Bloch's intellectual generation (the generation of German expressionism) is concerned, it was, even more so than the student generation of 1968, a "fatherless generation" (Alexander Mitscherlich) shaped by tensions between cultural conservatism and economic modernity – tensions that belong to the first casualties of a resur-

---

1. J. Fest, *Der zerstörte Traum. Vom Ende des utopischen Zeitalters* ("The Destruction of a Dream. The End of the Utopian Age"), Berlin, 1991, pp. 78, 81. Unless otherwise indicated, the author is responsible for the translation of the various quotations.

gent instrumental rationality that dissolves all connections between social or cultural criticism and utopian ideas, confuses the diagnostician with the disease, and abrogates the self-critical potential of the very enlightenment tradition it claims as its inheritance.

The German expressionist movement, Alfred Kurella wrote in 1937, was simply the "dreary suds in which . . . the last dregs of three generations of bourgeois thinkers swam helplessly to save that which is beyond all help."[2] And the *Weltanschauung* embraced by expressionist writers, Georg Lukács believed, was "the same . . . subjectivist-idealist one as that of the 'official' philosophy of imperialism."[3] Annihilating verdicts such as those passed on German expressionist literature by Marxist intellectuals in exile begs a number of questions: how was that enlightened, humanist inheritance, which Lukács, Kurella and others required the expressionists to confront critically and develop productively, mediated to this generation? How did it come about, as Kurella rightly indicates – but without differentiating between the Wilhelminian "founding fathers" and the expressionist generation of the 1880s that was coming to maturity in the decade before the First War – that the inheritance of the nineteenth century became "unbearable for the bourgeoisie of the final phase of imperialism"?[4] What stood in the way of the expressionists meeting Lukács's requirement that the good realist seek and find the "mediations which link subjective experience with objective social reality" and that he grasp "lasting characteristics, objective social developments effective over long periods of time"?[5]

Neither does Ernst Bloch's unorthodox Marxist defense of expressionism (that the revolt against rationalization and depersonalization can be driven by "authentic" forms of irrationalism in which utopian impulses are latent)[6] hold all the answers as to how the Wilhelminian cultural inheritance was transmitted to the expressionist generation. Bloch's schematic division of expressionism into "utopian" and merely "regressive" variants passes over important facets of the social-historical framework of Wilhelminian Germany. Most seriously, it neglects those impulses behind the expressionist revolt that gave rise to a decidedly "modern" self-definition –

2. B. Ziegler (= A. Kurella): "Nun ist dies Erbe zuende," in H.-J. Schmitt (ed.), *Die Expressionismusdebatte. Materialien zu einer marxistischen Realismus-konzeption*, Frankfurt am Main, 1973, p. 59. (Unless otherwise acknowledged, all translations are mine).

3. G. Lukács, "'Größe und Verfall' des Expressionismus," in H. G. Rötzer, (ed.), *Begriffsbestimmung des literarischen Expressionismus*, Darmstadt, 1976, p. 34f.

4. A. Kurella, "Nun ist dies Erbe zuende," p. 58.

5. G. Lukács, "Es geht um den Realismus" (1938), in H.-J. Schmitt (ed.), *Die Expressionismus-debatte*, pp. 202, 216.

6. E. Bloch, "Diskussionen über Expressionismus," in *Erbschaft dieser Zeit*, erweiterte Ausgabe, Frankfurt am Main, 1985, pp. 264–75.

as is exemplified most clearly by the case of Gottfried Benn, whose support for the National Socialist regime in 1933 first brought on the debate about expressionism among German intellectuals in exile and moved Kurella (for the wrong reasons, as we shall see) to describe him as the "consequential expressionist."[7]

Benn is the "consequential expressionist" in the same sense that he is the "consequential modernist": namely in his complex – and ideologically ambivalent – sensitivity to tensions between traditional culture and socioeconomic, technological, and scientific modernity. He shares with the modernist temper, in Habermas's sense, the "anarchistic intention of blowing up the continuum of history" and the tendency to replace "historical memory . . . by the heroic affinity of the present with the extremes of history." Such a tendency, as Habermas suggests, can be directed against what might be called "a false normativity in history."[8] Yet, as we shall see, the same revolt against "false normativities" – often in concert with penetrating sociocultural diagnoses – can induce an ideological *salto mortale* whereby a "modern" understanding of self jettisons its own intellectual foundations and redefines itself in terms of its antithesis. This is not to say that the expressionist answer to the "dialectic of enlightenment" is a simple antinomy of "reason" and its "Other." The revolt is not primarily against rationalization and "modernization," but rather against the "official" Wilhelminian culture's implausible endeavors to reconcile modernity with tradition, scientific and technological rationalism with *bürgerlich* social, intellectual, and cultural orthodoxy. In this sense it is an "anti-anti-modernist" revolt.

Furthermore, the "nonsynchronous contradictions" (Bloch) between society and culture in the German *Kaiserreich* – of which the expressionist generation revolt is one of the most palpable symptoms – militate against the recent penchant in Germany, especially since the "Historians' Debate" of the mid 1980s, to reestablish a relationship of concord between the history of the *Bürgertum* in Germany and societal and cultural modernization[9] – or to adduce the expressionist movement as evidence of a progressively liberal and democratic *Kaiserreich* in the years before 1914[10]: a

7. A. Kurella, "Nun ist dies Erbe zuende," p. 59.

8. J. Habermas, "Modernity versus Postmodernity," in *New German Critique* 22 (1981) p. 5.

9. Exemplary for this is T. Nipperdey, *Wie das Bürgertum die Moderne fand* ("How the Middle Classes Found Modernity"), Berlin, 1988.

10. T. Nipperdey, "War die Wilhelminische Gesellschaft eine Untertanen-Gesellschaft?," in Nipperdey, *Nachdenken über die deutsche Geschichte. Essays*, Munich, 1986, p. 178f. This suggests a "silent parliamentarization" before 1918 (M. Rauh, *Föderalismus und Parlamentarismus im Wilhelminischen Reich*, Düsseldorf, 1973) and an evolutionary development of the Wilhelminian system that understates the actual social tensions. Bridges are built to the parliamentary system of the Federal Republic after 1945, which for the most

*Kaiserreich* that affords more agreeable points of identification with present-day Germany than had been possible since Fritz Fischer's work in the 1960s and the subsequent critical social-historical perspectives on pre-1914 Germany uncovered by Hans-Ulrich Wehler, Jürgen Kocka, and others.

# I

Wilhelminian Germany, and in particular the formative years of most expressionist writers around the turn of the century, was one of those periods of rapid transition and reorientation that Karl Mannheim saw as a major determinant in the conflict between generations. "The 'up-to-dateness' of youth," Mannheim observes, "consists in their being closer to the 'present' problems . . . and in the fact that they are dramatically aware of a process of de-stabilization and take sides in it. All this while the older generation cling to the reorientation that had been the drama of *their* youth."[11]

The formative years of the ideal-typical father of the "Wilhelminian generation" (born in the 1850s or early 1860s)[12] were marked by the dramatic economic reversal from a period of middle-class security (which culminated in Germany in the unprecedented boom of 1867–1873 and the euphoria of unification in 1871) to a period of depression in 1873–1879.[13] This reversal left a lasting impression, despite the upswing of 1886–1890

---

part overleap the history of the Third Reich. Cf. V. Berghahn, "Politik und Gesellschaft im Wilhelminischen Deutschland," in *Neue politische Literatur* 24 (1979), pp. 168, 171; H.-U. Wehler, "Kritik und kritische Antikritik," in *Historische Zeitschrift* 225 (1977), pp. 347–84.

11. K. Mannheim, "The Sociological Problem of Generations," in *Essays on the Sociology of Knowledge*, London, 1952, p. 300f. Mannheim's application of this concept represents a considerable advance on Wilhelm Pinder's use of it in his *Kunstgeschichte nach Generationen* ("Art History According to Generations," Leipzig, 1926) to explain, metaphysically and with a strong antisociological bias, the varying spiritual and intellectual time-frames, or "entelechies," that coexist within the same epoch. See H. Jäger, "Generations in History. Reflections on a Controversial Concept," in *History and Theory* 24 (1985), p. 285, and F. Trommler, "Mission ohne Ziel. Über den Kult der Jugend im modernen Deutschland," in T. Koebner, R.-P. Janz, F. Trommler, (eds.), *"Mit uns zieht die neue Zeit." Der Mythos Jugend*, Frankfurt/M., 1985, p. 21ff. The attempt to investigate sociohistorical continuities and discontinuities by way of the conflict between generations will always need to be mindful of Erich Fromm's caution that "the authority which the father has within the family is not a coincidental one which is later 'complemented' by social authorities; rather the authority of the father himself in the final analysis has its basis in the structures of authority of society as a whole. Seen chronologically, the father is the first to mediate social authority to the child; however he is not . . . the model for this social authority, but its representation." E. Fromm, "Sozialpsychologischer Teil," in *Studien über Autorität und Familie. Forschungsberichte aus dem Institut für Sozialforschung*, Paris, 1936, p. 88.

12. M. Doerry, *Übergangsmenschen. Die Mentalität der Wilhelminer und die Krise des Kaiserreichs*, Weinheim/Munich, 1986.

13. H.-U. Wehler, *The German Empire 1871–1918*, Leamington Spa, 1985 (trans. K. Traynor), pp. 32–51.

and the period of sustained prosperity until 1913. Consequently "inherited fear of crisis [the memory of the inflation of 1873–78] and an economically determined sense of power reinforced one another. . . ."[14] In Germany, insecurity of status and social and cultural disorientation were intensified in the mid-1890s by rapid capitalist concentration and rationalization which hastened the transition from a society of *Stände* ("status-groups") to a society of class. The "seemingly successful alloy of elements of the old and the new," Lothar Gall observes, "proved itself to be a deceptive patina. It only covered over the corrosive processes and led to all kinds of self-deception, above all on the part of those to whom it appeared to have lent new strength."[15]

The generation conflict in German expressionist literature indicates several variants of a "process of de-stabilization" (Mannheim) confronting not only the expressionists themselves, but also the generation of the Wilhelminian fathers. In none of these variants is the generation conflict presented as the simple polarity of "irrational" youth in revolt against robust, unproblematical and sovereignly rational fathers.

The fathers' unstable compound of self-confidence and self-deception is most striking where they seek to resolve the tensions between the old and the new by throwing themselves into the front line of capitalist transformation. In Reinhard Johannes Sorge's *Der Bettler* ("The Beggar," 1911) this occurs in the delirious imaginings of the father: his nostalgia for his student corporation days gives way abruptly to futuristic dream-visions of the planet Mars, its wondrous navigation systems, its industry and its battle fleet – all of which serve him as the model for a future Germany to be realized by his son. The tensions between the old and the new are literally suicidal; patricide is an act of deliverance, performed at the behest of the father. On the sociopolitical level, the extremities of finality and optimism that characterize the father are reflected in the satirical panorama of Wilhelminian society in the café scene early in the play, where repressed anxieties are assuaged by nationalistic assertiveness: the gathering of newspaper readers decides to pass over the "negative" items – flood, fire, earthquakes, war – and seizes on the "positive" news: the building of a new German battleship and the birth of a strong, healthy baby boy.

"Modernity" as a refuge from the self is also the driving force in Georg Kaiser's *Die Koralle* ("The Coral," 1917). "Progress," the billionaire/father asserts, "is not: where to – but what from!"[16] The poverty of his working-

14. C.-P. Witt, "Innenpolitik und Imperialismus in der Vorgeschichte des Ersten Weltkrieges," in K. Holl/G. List, (eds.), *Liberalismus und imperialistischer Staat*, Göttingen, 1975, p. 9.
15. L. Gall, *Bismarck. Der weiße Revolutionär*, Frankfurt, 1980, p. 725.
16. G. Kaiser, "Die Koralle," in Kaiser, *Werke* (ed. W. Huder), vol. 1, *Stücke 1895–1917*, Frankfurt/M./Berlin/Vienna, 1971, p. 664.

class youth, his "fear and his weakness," have driven him to amass wealth and power and to seek refuge in the rationalized, depersonalized and exploitative machine-world of modern industrial capitalism. This solution, however, has only heightened his anxiety and intensified his alienation. He seeks to escape the circle by jettisoning his "modern" identity and adopting that of his *Doppelgänger:* his secretary, who has been blessed with an idyllic childhood in the course of which he "saw and heard nothing of the odiousness of the coarse workaday world."[17]

As in Sorge's *Der Bettler*, the contradictory character structure of the father is reflected within the wider social context: the philanthropic open house held weekly at the billionaire's factory points to the social and economic contradictions from which he benefits: the combination in Wilhelminian Germany of systematic, legal suppression of the workers' movement and social legislation designed to mitigate class antagonisms: "Here ruthless exploitation," the billionaire's son observes, "– and there unlimited charity."[18] The integrative and stabilizing force of the welfare state gives way in the sequels to *Die Koralle, Gas I* and *Gas II*, to the "total mobilization" of the workers, who eagerly submit to the moloch of industry and resist all efforts to break the circle of alienation established by the billionaire father in *Die Koralle*. The psychological predispositions of the "authoritarian personality" – above all the simultaneous will to domination and submission – have become an integral part of the *volonté générale*, "fanaticizing" the workers, in *Gas II*, to self-destruction.[19]

The self-destructive logic of Progress as personified in Sorge's and Kaiser's father-figures anticipates the pessimistic critique of Enlightenment outlined by Max Horkheimer and Theodor Adorno in 1944, the sociopsychological facets of which Horkheimer had detailed in 1936 in the introductory chapter of *Studien über Autorität und Familie*, coauthored with Erich Fromm and Herbert Marcuse: "Bourgeois thought," Horkheimer observes,

> begins as the struggle against the authority of tradition, which it opposes with each individual's power of reason as the legitimate source of justice and truth. It ends with the idolization of mere authority for its own sake, which is just as void of specific content as is the concept of reason since justice, happiness, and freedom for humanity have been eliminated as historical watchwords.

The rationale for the father's authority, Horkheimer believes, is that he lays his "moral claim to subjecting [the son] to his power not because he shows himself to be worthy, but rather he shows himself to be worthy

17. *Ibid.*, p. 689.
18. *Ibid.*, p. 685.
19. G. Kaiser, *Gas II*, in *Werke*, vol. 2, p. 66.

because he is the more powerful."[20] This power, in turn – consciously or unconsciously – submits to the political status quo, even where the father is in revolt against it:

> Every middle-class father, even if he fulfills a lowly or humiliating function socially, can play the role of the master in his private life. . . . Thus it is possible that again and again generations arise – and not only from the ranks of the upper-middle classes, but also from among . . . workers or salaried employees – who do not question the structure of the economic or social system, but acknowledge it as natural and eternal, and even permit their dissatisfaction and their rebellion to be employed in the enforcement of the prevailing order.[21]

This lower-class variant of the expressionist diagnosis of the "authoritarian personality" is exemplified in Arnolt Bronnen's drama *Vatermord* ("Patricide," 1920). Herr Fessel, who has barely struggled free of his proletarian origins, vents his impotent and paranoiac political rebellion in tyranny over his son Walter. But he does so in terms that only go to validate the class society that has perpetuated his own subordinate status. He expressly contrasts his paternal mission with that of the state and proudly emphasizes his past Social Democratic candidature in local government elections. Yet he compulsively affirms codes of "obedience" and "duty" that serve to stabilize not only the patriarchal "master-in-the-house" family structure but also the semiabsolutist state – a contradictoriness that is further displayed in the logic of Fessel's "antinationalistic" sentiments: while railing against the "thrashing out of clichés" in war propaganda, he is undisturbed by his younger son playing war games; and he does not believe war is possible, "given our culture."

That the formal, "legal" authority on which the fathers stand betrays their lack of inner conviction about the legitimacy of this authority is also evident where they engage in conservative rearguard actions against the generation of the sons, as for example in Franz Werfel's novella *Nicht der Mörder, der Ermordete ist schuldig* ("'Not the Murderer, the Victim is Guilty," 1920) and Walter Hasenclever's play *Der Sohn* ("The Son," 1913/14). In each case the father is a military officer, embodying for the sons the forces of order represented by state officialdom. He derives a large measure of his paternal authority from his official position;[22] but he is also shown to be hastening the destruction of the very bourgeois identity that he seeks to protect by recourse to the military-bureaucratic ethos – the last

---

20. M. Horkheimer, "Allgemeiner Teil," in *Studien über Autorität und Familie. Forschungsberichte aus dem Institut für Sozialforschung*, pp. 26, 52. Of this logic Kafka's famous letter to his father (1919) is the classic analysis.

21. *Ibid.*, p. 58.

22. P. U. Hohendahl, *Das Bild der bürgerlichen Welt im expressionistischen Drama*, Heidelberg, 1967, p. 81.

bastion against the "modernity" he fears is latent in his son: "what else can I do but give him [the son] a taste of my power!" says the father in Hasen-clever's *Der Sohn* : "Otherwise I am dishonored. . . . It is a duty I owe to myself. . . . I saw active service; I fought with the sword for my honor . . . I must keep my house pure."[23] Similarly, the self-deceptive adherence to a neofeudal code of "duty," "integrity" and "purity" in Werfel's *Nicht der Mörder, der Ermordete ist schuldig* signifies the chasm between Austria's benevolent paternalist social and cultural identity and the training of its young toward an antagonistic world-view (as exemplified by the "enemy images" in Julius Kalender's fairground stall). The news of the vengeance wreaked by Kalender's son upon his father is printed on July 4, 1914, shortly before the outbreak of war, and gives cause for an editorial com-mentary on the responsibility of the young for the social, cultural and political crisis of contemporary Europe. The responsibility for the debase-ment of "liberal" values since the second half of the nineteenth century, in other words, is shifted onto the generation that is to pay the price in 1914–1918: a "liberal man," the commentator declares, is tempted to resort to the "iron broom" to sweep away "the rot and the decay" repre-sented by modernist culture.[24]

This sense of having inherited the accumulated crises of the liberal-bourgeois tradition as personified in the generation of the fathers extends right across the spectrum of expressionist writers. The prevailing culture, as Ludwig Rubiner complains in 1913, "protracts crises."[25] The parents' gen-eration, as the young soldier in Fritz von Unruh's *Ein Geschlecht* ("A Gen-eration," 1915/16) protests, "sneak obtusely and fearfully in their well-worn tracks, blind to all questions that are crying out for answers"; and "for the solution they are evading they look to the children."[26] In Carl Sternheim's *1913* even the unscrupulous capitalist senses that the future is predetermined by the social, economic, and cultural inheritance: "Our generation has taken over the industrial state from you in its finished form," complains Christian Maske's daughter Sofie, "and absolutely rejects all responsibility for what lies at its basis. . . . You have bequeathed to us the main ingredient for all recipes: unscrupulousness. But we cannot see where this is all leading."[27]

23. W. Hasenclever, "Der Sohn," in Hasenclever, *Gedichte, Dramen, Prosa* (ed. K. Pinthus), Cagnes-sur-Mer, 1963, p. 150.

24. F. Werfel, "Nicht der Mörder, der Ermordete ist schuldig," in Werfel, *Gesammelte Werke* (ed. A. D. Klarmann), vol. 1, Stockholm, 1948, p. 270.

25. L. Rubiner, "Der Dichter greift in die Politik" (1912), in Rubiner, *Der Dichter greift in die Politik. Ausgewählte Werke 1908–1919* (ed. Klaus Schuhmann), Leipzig, 1976, p. 260.

26. F. von Unruh, "Ein Geschlecht," in Unruh, *Sämtliche Werke* (ed. H. M. Elster), Berlin, 1973, vol. 3, p. 26f.

27. C. Sternheim, *1913*, in Sternheim, *Dramen I* (ed. W. Emrich), Neuwied, 1963, p. 285.

The fathers' failure to gain assurance from their offspring as to the stability and continuity of the social and political *status quo* prompts them to identify the symptom with the disease. In Hasenclever's *Der Sohn*, for example, the father is a military doctor who defines his paternal role in terms of his official function; and his medical role, too, is subordinated to his bureaucratic function vis-à-vis his son, whom he diagnoses as "a case that belongs in the medical journals." The "official" culture's banishment of the young to the realm of the pathological serves to uphold the illusion of a "healthy" and "innocent" political and cultural *Sonderweg*. The young become the victims of an integratory ideology that, lacking a firm political, social, or economic foothold in the process of capitalist transformation, falls back on a commonality of *bürgerliche Kultur*.[28] It is on behalf of this fragile cultural identity, as the guarantor of social stability and continuity, that the fathers seek acclamation from their sons. When their strategy fails, they project the responsibility for the debacle of their own culture onto the next generation: "The driving force of our culture," Werfel's Karl Duschek writes in his letter of protest to the public prosecutor, ". . . is called rape! And the education we boast of so proudly is nothing but lustful rape, aggravated by self-hatred and the recognition of [the fathers'] own inherent faults – which every father punishes in his son rather than in himself."[29]

Having failed to win acclamation from the generation of the sons, the defenders of the dominant culture not only "protract crises" (Rubiner); they also, in Habermas's terms, "turn . . . attention away from . . . societal processes" and "project the causes, which they do not bring to light, onto the plane of a subversive culture and its advocates."[30] The arbitrary and self-contradictory logic with which the fathers attempt to validate an affirmative, integratory culture indicates a "legitimation crisis" in which "the procurement of legitimation is self-defeating as soon as the mode of procurement is seen through."[31] The most obvious consequence for German expressionism is a painfully felt cultural isolation in the face of a hostile reception.[32] More far-reaching, however, are the ramifications for the expressionists' sense of history, which in turn defines their sense of their own "modernity" – their revolt, that is, against the "confidence-trick perpetrated by the teleological dynamics of development and causation," as

28. L. Gall, "'Ich wünschte ein Bürger zu sein'. Zum Selbstverständnis des deutschen Bürgertums im 19. Jahrhundert," in *Historische Zeitschrift* 245 (1987), p. 619.

29. F. Werfel, *Nicht der Mörder, der Ermordete ist schuldig*, p. 279.

30. J. Habermas, "Modernity versus Postmodernity," p. 8.

31. J. Habermas, *Legitimation Crisis*, trans. T. McCarthy, London, 1973, p. 70.

32. M. Stark, *Für und wider den Expressionismus. Die Entstehung der Intellektuellen-debatte in der deutschen Literaturgeschichte*, Stuttgart, 1982, especially pp. 47–73.

Carl Einstein noted in his review of Gottfried Benn's *Collected Poems* in 1927.[33]

## II

In Benn's early work the expressionist consciousness of the self-contradictory and self-destructive "legitimation" of paternal and state authority is evident in the contradiction between the supreme self-confidence of the figures of authority and the catastrophic historical consequences of their "murderous urge to fix thought upon an end-result."[34] It is the self-validating quality of authority – in Habermas's terms the "turbid fusion" of "claims to power and validity"[35] – that provokes the "irrationalist" counterreaction. In Benn's dramatic sketch *Etappe* (1915), for instance, intellectual authority, bureaucratic function and military rank converge in the person of Prof. Dr. med. Paschen, head of the welfare department in a conquered Belgian province. The "fusion of authority and validity" is evident in Paschen's mindless historical optimism amid the death and destruction of war, and in his self-contradictory vindication of technological and economic modernization in terms of an elitist, essentially antimodern claim to *Bildung* and *Kultur*.[36] The incompatible marriage of the old and the new, as it was later consummated under National Socialism, is taken to its extreme in the babies' dummy invented by the pediatrician Dr. Kotschnüffel, which is the apotheosis of male sexuality, romanticized ancient Germanic heroism, and modern technology: "Here is a model which is especially suited to the spirit of the times, in the shape of an acorn [*Eichel*]: Germanic forests, brimful with primitive elemental force, and highly presentable in terms of material and design."[37]

The social imperialist welfare program Paschen espouses is dismissed by

33. C. Einstein, "Gottfried Benns 'Gesammelte Gedichte'," in P. U. Hohendahl, (ed.), *Benn – Wirkung wider Willen. Dokumente zur Wirkungsgeschichte Benns*, Frankfurt, 1971, p. 124.

34. G. Benn, "Der Garten von Arles" (1920), in G. Schuster, (ed.), *Gottfried Benn. Sämtliche Werke*, Stuttgart, 1987, vol. III (*Prosa 1*), p. 113. All quotations from Benn's prose works, insofar as they have not appeared in English translation, are from this volume or from *Prosa 2* (1989) and will be acknowledged in the text.

35. J. Habermas, "Die Verschlingung von Mythos und Aufklärung: Horkheimer und Adorno," in Habermas, *Der philosophische Diskurs der Moderne*, Frankfurt, 1985, p. 137.

36. See P. Hampe, "Sozioökonomische und psychische Hintergründe der bildungs-bürgerlichen Imperialbegeisterung," in K. Vondung, (ed.), *Das wilhelminische Bildungsbürgertum. Zur Sozialgeschichte seiner Ideen*, Göttingen, 1976, pp. 78, 186. Further to social imperialism, see Wehler, *The German Empire*, pp. 171–76.

37. G. Benn, *Gesammelte Werke in vier Bänden* (ed. D. Wellershoff), Wiesbaden, 1958–1961, vol. 2, Prosa und Szenen, p. 308f. Further quotations from the second and fourth volume of Wellershoff's edition are acknowledged in the text with Roman numeral II or IV.

Benn's persona, Dr. Olf, as "decorative" ethics (II, 317) to vindicate the invasion of Belgium. This "cultural deed of the very highest order" (II, 305) reveals itself, in retrospect, as a proto-fascist combination of social Darwinism, rationalization and total administrative prerogative: "I am to make a speech," Paschen's fellow officer Duke Wildungen insists: "Commonality of goals, which goals? Nationalization of the people's minds, if only the war would bring that about! A committee in attendance at births, extermination of the unfit, a committee of officials to determine which kind of school, and then which profession, a psychological Taylor system – an aim profoundly to be wished!" (II, 314).

In Benn's first dramatic sketch (*Ithaka*, 1914), too, it is the overweening self-confidence of intellectual authority (the medical professor) that provokes the irrationalist counter-sphere: "We have deployed ourselves right across the world: an army, minds that dominate, brains that conquer," proclaims the professor (II, 299). He meets a violent end at the hands of his students; their invocations of Dionysian ecstasies throw overboard all remnants of the mediation they had vainly explored in their demands for legitimation on the part of the professor. In both plays the young protagonists' flight from cultural chauvinism, or pragmatic rationalism, into a vitalist, Dionysian counter-sphere is dismissed by the representatives of authority, as in Hasenclever's *Der Sohn* and Werfel's *Nicht der Mörder, der Ermordete ist schuldig*, as a symptom of illness, degeneracy, or neurasthenia (II, 298, 320).[38]

Benn's early work, then, is anything but a "new justification of that which Thomas Mann called 'power-protected inwardness'," as Alfred Kurella would have it.[39] On the contrary, Benn exposes to view the very functionalization of bourgeois culture toward imperialist aims that Thomas Mann legitimates in his *Betrachtungen eines Unpolitischen* ("Reflections of a Non-Political Man," 1918). Benn's early work does not evade but confronts the contradictions in Wilhelminian Germany between cultural conservatism and modern society, and the arbitrary and despotic logic that sanctions such contradictions. There is no straight line from the alleged "power-protected inwardness" of Benn's early work to the militant metaphors expressive of the bourgeoisie's forward defense against the pro-

---

38. Benn's *Morgue* poems (1912), which explode the myth of a "heile Welt" (intact world order) in prewar Wilhelminian Germany, were received in a similar spirit. "It is not for me as a critic of lyric poetry to write about the perversity of these poems," writes Hans Friedrich in 1912: "I leave this interesting case to the psychiatrists" (in Hohendahl, *Benn – Wirkung wider Willen*, p. 97). It is noteworthy that the expressionists' publishers – e.g., Alfred Richard Meyer (the publisher of Benn's *Morgue und andere Gedichte*), Kurt Wolff, Herwarth Walden, Franz Pfemfert – were of the same generation, or only slightly older, than their authors. See F. Redlich, "German Literary Expressionism and Its Publishers," in *Harvard Library Bulletin* 8/2 (April 1969), pp. 143–68.

39. A. Kurella, "Nun ist dies Erbe zuende," p. 58.

letariat in the essay *Dorische Welt* (1934).[40] The problem of expressionism, as Kurella rightly points out, is the problem of the intellectual inheritance of the nineteenth century in the first third of the twentieth century. But his assessment of expressionism in general and of Benn in particular (that they proffer only the mouldering heritage of the fathers) overlooks the diagnosis of proto-fascist tendencies in Wilhelminian Germany in works such as *Etappe* and, above all, the insight into the false resolution of tensions between traditional culture and social and economic modernity[41] – tensions that the National Socialists later sought to defuse through a spurious coalescence of political guilelessness and combativeness, social concord and economic dynamism.

Yet from the outset Benn undercuts his potentially critical and provocative premises: his attacks on concepts such as nature, progress, development, and humanity, as Hans Kaufmann has pointed out, are directed not only against their misuse in the imperialist present, but also against their actual content.[42] The source of this intellectual short-circuit is to be found in the same provocative impulse that was behind Benn's attack on bogus cultural syntheses – in the "Dionysian" principle. Its driving force is the liberation of the creative imagination from the coercive power of causation, "development" and "history." The "Dionysian" drive for spiritual self-determination replaces causation and notions of linear development with association: "Creative Man!" cries Rönne, the protagonist of Benn's cycle of novellas *Gehirne* ("Brains," 1915/16), "The reshaping of the idea of development away from the mathematical and into the intuitive" (II, 46). The language of Rönne's "Gegenglück" (his "counter-happiness," II, 42) – a formulation that has its source in Nietzsche's definition of art as "die Gegenbewegung" ("counter-movement") – evokes new and surprising combinations in order to resist the dead hand of intellectual, cultural, and social standardization. Furthermore, "concepts," in Nietzsche's sense, represent for Benn the "graveyard of immediacy":

> for the liberated intellect that gigantic conceptual framework and scaffolding . . . is merely a platform and a plaything for his most audacious feats; and when he shatters it, throws it into disorder, ironically pieces it together again, joining together the most alien and separating the kindred elements, he reveals that he

40. *Ibid.*

41. See J. Herf, *Reactionary Modernism. Technology, Culture and Politics in Weimar and the Third Reich*, Cambridge, 1984. The process whereby modern technology was "incorporated . . . into the cultural system of modern German nationalism, without diminishing the latter's romantic and antirational aspects" (p. 2), which Herf observes among a number of the "conservative revolutionaries" in the Weimar Republic, is already evident before and during the First War.

42. H. Kaufmann, "Gottfried Benns *Ithaka*," in Kaufmann, *Krisen und Wandlungen der deutschen Literatur von Wedekind bis Feuchtwanger*, Berlin/Weimar, 1966, p. 191f.

has no need of stopgaps dictated by expediency, and that he is now guided not by concepts but by intuition.[43]

The associative thought structures that Benn rallies against the "tyranny" of causation, development, and history, however, themselves fall back into normative thinking. Associations are mobilized to form antitheses; heterogeneous categories are placed in apposition so as to appear synonymous. The result is an abstract and easily disposable "norm": the milieu of the "engaged" writer is summarily dismissed in Benn's essay *Zur Problematik des Dichterischen* ("On the Problem of Literature," 1930) as "civilization, science, induction, the age of Bacon, the secular epoch of steel, opportunism, liberality . . ." – of everything, that is, "which one can see in summary as Enlightenment" (III, i, 239). It is Benn's self-confessed "summary" treatment of history that enables him to dismiss the "*typical* historical process" (III, i, 238f., my emphasis), and "the imperialistic basis of *all* historical organizations" (III, i, Benn's emphasis). The "norm" appears under the aegis of empiricism, which, through the common denominator of modern civilization, has given rise both to "Marxism" and "Americanism" (*Inquiry among European Writers into the Spirit of America*, 1928, II, i, 194). The "anti-ideological" writer's position is "anticapitalist, anticivilizatory" (III, i, 218). By placing the two concepts in apposition, Benn makes them appear synonymous. Armed with this questionable premise, he can demolish the entire tradition not only of Marxist but of all sociologically or historically oriented self-reflection in the most crudely schematic manner: science automatically gives rise to capitalism; technology inevitably begets war (*Können Dichter die Welt ändern?*, "Can Writers Change the World?", 1930, IV, 214). The "dialectic of enlightenment" – "from system to catastrophe" (III, i, 95) – is a universal and unassailable truth.

The "emancipatory" purpose of the associative technique is to liberate language from the shackles of causation; but the result is a tendency toward stereotypical, even denunciatory antitheses. And in this Benn is exemplary for the ambivalence, noted above, that Habermas has identified in the modernist temper: the refusal, on the one hand, to accept the imposition on history of a "false normativity," and on the other hand the modernist's temptation – anticipated by Nietzsche – to jettison "historical memory" and to "cut the umbilical cord to the universalism of the

---

43. F. Nietzsche, "Über Wahrheit und Lüge im außermoralischen Sinne," in Nietzsche, *Werke. Kritische Gesamtausgabe* (ed. G. Colli/M. Montinari), vol. III, 2 (*Nachgelassene Schriften 1870–1873*), Berlin, 1972, pp. 380–82. On Nietzsche and the early Benn see R. Grimm, "Kritische Ergänzungen zur Benn-Literatur," in R. Grimm, *Strukturen. Essays zur deutschen Literatur*, Göttingen, 1963, p. 298. See also R. Rumold, *Gottfried Benn und der Expressionismus. Provokation des Lesers; absolute Dichtung*, Hanstein, 1982, pp. 108–38.

Enlightenment."[44] The forfeiture of historical perspective and of intellectual differentiation works in the interest of the "autonomous" writer's self-differentiation from his ideological antagonists. In the final analysis he obfuscates all distinctions between participation in political processes and mindless subjugation to them.[45] "To contradict, to say no," Habermas notes in his 1985 critique of Nietzsche, "now means no more than 'wanting to be different' . . . – according to which criterion, then, is criticism to differentiate? It must at least be able to discriminate between a power which deserves to be valued and one which deserves to be devalued."[46]

Like Nietzsche, Benn answers history's disenfranchisement of the creative imagination with an unstable compound of fatalism and heroism: the victim of history is also history's hero. A virtue is made of "necessity" and an enemy of those who would rouse the fatalist to action. Benn's clash with the Marxists Johannes R. Becher and Egon Erwin Kisch in 1929 is a case in point: putting the case for the meaninglessness of history and the inevitability of the social and political *status quo*, Benn underpins his polemics with the self-assertive rhetoric of the "hard and fit man" who has the courage to face nihilism: "It occurs to me," he writes in *Über die Rolle des Schriftstellers in dieser Zeit* ("On the Role of the Writer Today," 1929) "that it might be far more radical and far more in keeping with the powers of a hard and fit man to teach mankind: this is the way you are and you will never be any different, this is how you live, this is how you have lived and this is how you will always live" (III, i, 221). Benn asserts his intellectual and social "status"[47] vis-à-vis Marxist writers by laying claim to Nietzsche's heritage – and to "modern" cultural representativeness – as the destroyer of the self-deceptive, comforting myths of bourgeois culture.

Just as Benn separates reason and creative imagination, so he posits a relationship of mutual exclusiveness between political engagement and artistic integrity. This is the position for which he reclaims Heinrich Mann in March 1931 on the occasion of the latter's sixtieth birthday. In the face of increasing ideological polarization in the latter phase of the Weimar

---

44. J. Habermas, *Legitimation Crisis*, p. 122.

45. See. R. Alter, *Gottfried Benn. The Artist and Politics (1910–1934)*, Berne, 1976, p. 68.

46. J. Habermas, "Die Verschlingung von Mythos und Aufklärung," p. 151.

47. The lack of historical "mediation" is exacerbated by a lack of social mediation. See J. Schröder, *Gottfried Benn. Poesie und Sozialisation*, Stuttgart, 1978. Growing up as the son of a Lutheran pastor in East Elbia, Benn's social milieu encompassed the rural proletariat on the one hand and the children of East Elbian aristocrats on the other. The educated middle-class status of his father hindered Benn from identifying himself with the working-class children, while rigid social barriers stood in the way of his finding full acceptance in aristocratic circles. Consequently he sought refuge in the "asocial" sphere of art, vindicating his sense of personal worth and thus turning his social outsidership to positive account. After 1928 the fear of proletarianization led him to embrace more firmly than ever a compensatory "aristocratic" principle as the basis for his writing.

Republic, he falls back on Mann as expressionism's generational "forerunner"[48] whose trilogy *Die Göttinnen* (to which he had paid tribute in 1913 with his novella *Heinrich Mann. Ein Untergang*)[49] had exemplified for his generation the struggle initiated by Nietzsche: Germany's struggle for an "anti-ideological philosophy . . . an expressive one" (III, i, 318). The precondition for this spiritual renewal is the continuance of Nietzsche's intellectual revolt against the nineteenth century – and against everything for which Benn's antagonists among the Marxists sought to harness Heinrich Mann: against "progress, education, pedagogy, the party-political, but I see [Heinrich Mann] most profoundly illuminated in this Flaubertian-Nietzschean light" (III, i, 321).

Benn's misunderstanding of Mann's adherence to the ideal indivisibility of spirit and power (*Geist* and *Macht*) was only reinforced by Mann himself when in April and again in June of 1931 he privately defended Benn against Werner Hegemann's polemic *Heinrich Mann? Hitler? Gottfried Benn? oder Goethe?* "I do not believe," Mann writes, "that a fascist can write great works of art. In any case, if he could do so, I would have nothing against his fascism."[50] The cross-fertilization between intellectuals and politics that Mann has in view, however, contains an historical (radical-democratic) orientation toward an idealized French history. He had not portrayed Wilhelminian Germany and its subservient middle-classes as the inevitable consequence of liberal-enlightened philosophy, as did many expressionists, but as its debasement; the Wilhelminian Bürger was merely a questionable *deviation* from what is German, not Germanness itself. The *Bürger* represents a "paradoxical" amalgam of tradition and modernity: a dominant type arose who was "neither Bürger nor Junker, but both rolled into one, a being with spurs and a ledger-brain, a walking paradox."[51]

Unlike Mann's middle generation (b. 1871), the expressionists inherited the Empire under the advanced capitalist conditions as they had taken shape by the mid-1890s. They do not delineate the middle-classes' *deviation* from their "true" path – the path to which the generation of the fathers cling. For the sons this path is irrevocably *verschüttet* – buried under

48. "It occurs very frequently," Karl Mannheim observes, "that the nucleus of attitudes particular to a new generation is first evolved and practiced by older people who are isolated in their own generation (forerunners) [Mannheim cites the example of Nietzsche], just as it is often the case that the forerunners in the development of a particular class ideology belong to a quite alien class." Mannheim, "The Problem of Generations," p. 308.

49. The novella celebrates the narrator's salvation from the "pestilence of knowledge" in a journey to Italy, which signifies the abrogation of empirically defined consciousness and a vitalistic rebirth.

50. L. Greve, (ed.), *Gottfried Benn 1886–1956. Eine Ausstellung des Deutschen Literaturarchivs Marbach am Neckar*, 3rd revised ed., Marbach, 1987, p. 135.

51. H. Mann, "Kaiserreich und Republik" (1919), in Mann, *Essays*, Hamburg, 1960, pp. 392, 400.

the rubble of history.[52] The contemporary stage of civilization betokens the dénouement of the entire bourgeois ethos. In Benn's case this disjunction of history and creativeness is taken to its extreme; it leads him to overleap the entire liberal-democratic tradition and to seek, as he proclaims in his notorious radio address *Der neue Staat und die Intellektuellen* ("The New State and the Intellectuals," 24 April 1933), the "breakthrough" of a "new intelligentsia," of an "entirely new compository world-feeling belonging to an historically transformed young generation" (III, ii, 19).

In February 1933 Heinrich Mann (at that time president of the Prussian Writers' Academy, to which Benn had been elected in January 1932) supported the proclamation of a popular front of social democrats and communists against the NSDAP at the elections of 5 March. The importance of this event as a catalyst in Benn's decision to support the Nazi regime cannot be underestimated. Mann's alliance with the communists spelled the betrayal of Nietzsche's heritage and the endorsement of the nineteenth century's despotic sway over the heroic victims of history. Mann had fulfilled Benn's worst fears, voiced in 1932 in his essay *Nach dem Nihilismus* ("After Nihilism"), as to the triumph in Germany of an "old and reactionary" and "backward-looking, backward-acting" materialistic philosophy of history that had begun in the 1860s and that would persist with "all these attacks on the higher man we've had to listen to for the past eighty years . . . the higher, that is to say, the tragically struggling man."[53]

*Der neue Staat und die Intellektuellen,* accordingly, portrays Heinrich Mann and his brother Thomas as the bourgeois Republic's bogus "heroes," who had perfidiously arrogated to themselves the expressionist generation's authentically "modern," revolutionary struggle against the nineteenth century:

> when these intellectual heroes, the Republic's heraldic animals, deigned to descend from their country estates to deliver a lecture, they granted insights into cultivated spiritual abysses and concluded: what is it you want, do calm yourself, we do after all have a democracy; a blessing to us all (III, ii, 19).

The Republic's "representative" culture, in Benn's view, had merely perpetuated, in the name of democracy, the casuistic arguments employed in Wilhelminian Germany's cultural legitimation of social-Darwinist ideolo-

---

52. This image recurs across the whole expressionist spectrum: the demolition of rationalism (or, in the case of Activist writers, the Utopian vision of a new society), involves an historical "clearing" exercise. For Benn the premise for artistic creativeness is the "breaking apart of all connections" (*Epilog und lyrisches Ich* [1921/27, III, i, 132]), while for Rubiner the "free spirit" necessitates the "smashing of all historical constraints" ("Brief an einen Aufrührer," 1913, in *Der Dichter greift in die Politik*, p. 271f.). Both extremes – Benn's fatalism and Rubiner's voluntarism – are driven by a foiled bourgeois heritage and the loss of plausible points of historical reference.

53. V. Sander, (ed.), *Gottfried Benn. Prose, Essays, Poems*, New York, 1987, p. 112.

gy. The contrast Benn makes between the emigrés' "bourgeois nineteenth-century minds" (*Antwort an die literarischen Emigranten*, "Reply to the Literary Emigrés," III, ii, 26) and the young generation of the early 1930s reads like a long-overdue vindication of the expressionist victim/hero against the pusillanimous, unheroic culture of the "Wilhelminian" generation:

> A fine democracy, the young of this generation said to themselves, which gives most people nothing to eat and leaves them in the lurch spiritually as well, a truly heroic patriotism which at the first sign of danger casts about for unobserved border crossings and for properties in Ascona. . . . We have had to listen to all of this long enough, the young generation told itself: freedom of thought: putrefied freedom – anti-heroic ideology! But man strives to be great, that is his greatness; and so the young raised themselves from the cultivated spiritual abysses and the fetishes of a defeatist intelligentsia and pressed forward, in an immensely exhilarating sense of their own generation which the sixty-year-olds could no longer understand, into the vital . . . into the irrational. . . . (III, ii, 19f.)

The "enemy" remains the Wilhelminian generation of the fathers; but in the final analysis the generation conflict functions in lieu of the socioeconomic antagonisms that had reached new levels of intensity since the onset of the economic crisis in 1929. Benn's solidarity with the economically straitened and spiritually impoverished younger generation of the twenties and early thirties does not point to, but rather diverts attention from the historical roots of the crisis in the 1890s.[54]

The impotent expressionist revolt against the seemingly unassailable, self-validating world of the nineteenth-century fathers – whose "standard concepts" Benn saw in 1930 "vehemently ending their historical mission before our eyes" (III, i, 234) – is resolved in a new (but this time welcome) "fusion of authority and validity" (Habermas). The new fascist regime is consistent, authoritative, lasting and, above all, a radical departure from the arbitrariness and self-contradictoriness of the old order:

> The total state, as opposed to the pluralist state of the last epoch . . . presents itself with the claim to complete identity of power and spirit, individuality and collectivity, freedom and necessity, it is monistic, anti-dialectical, lasting and authoritarian (III, ii, 33).

Purged of its president Heinrich Mann and of its other Republican members, and with Gottfried Benn installed as its new vice-president, the reconstituted Writers' Academy represents the rupture with the discredited bourgeois ideology of Wilhelminian Germany and the Weimar Republic, the vanguard of cultural renewal and the reversal of Spengler's prognosis, the "Rise of the West" (III, ii, 190).

54. See F. Trommler, "Mission ohne Ziel. Über den Kult der Jugend im modernen Deutschland," p. 20 (see footnote 11).

When Benn came to the realization that National Socialism was not the "radical" force he had taken it for and that, far from offering the "militant transcendence" (III, ii, 39) of Wilhelminian Germany's cultural legitimation of unfettered materialism and expansionary politics, it had only taken the process several steps further, he emphatically declared his allegiance to his expressionist points of departure. A decisive impetus in his reassertion of a "modern" identity against National Socialism was the experience of *déjà vu* in relation to a fundamental expressionist experience: the shifting of the disorientation, anxiety, and aggression occasioned by economic, social, and cultural modernization processes onto the cultural "modernists" who critically register these processes. In his article *Die neue Dichtung* ("The New Literature," October 1933) the ballad writer Baron Börries von Münchhausen placed Benn's name at the head of an alphabetical list of expressionists whom he denounced collectively as incarnations of "Jewish" corruption. The attack by Münchhausen, who was a newly elected member of the Writers' Academy, contained not only a serious threat to Benn's medical career; it presented him with the very antithesis of National Socialism's hoped-for cultural *tabula rasa* with the spirit of the nineteenth century: "The most important characteristic of today's literature," Münchhausen wrote, "is its strong *sense of morality*, which is doubly apparent when compared with the thoroughly licentious indecency of times past" (i.e., of expressionism), which has "trampled upon everything German . . . with cold-hearted irony, icy rejection. . . ."[55]

Münchhausen's denunciation went to the very heart of Benn's "heroic" perception of himself at the vanguard of a modern German cultural revolution. His outraged reply is couched in terms similar to his reproaches against the privileged, "unheroic" and anachronistic Mann brothers and their pretensions to literary "representativeness" six months previously in *Der neue Staat und die Intellektuellen*: "How can you bring yourself, with your elegant, cultivated and grandseigneurial existence," Benn asks Münchhausen on 15 October 1933,

> to characterize the agonized, shattered, bitter life of my expressionist generation with these insulting remarks? I can understand the desire to keep one's distance from this generation, the desire to fight against it, but let me assure you that this generation bears more marks of pain than you are prepared to notice today, and the shoulders and the minds of this last generation of a doomed world were burdened with enormous existential struggles.[56]

---

55. P. Raabe, (ed.), *Expressionismus. Der Kampf um eine literarische Bewegung*, Munich, 1965, p. 231f., Münchhausen's emphases.
56. R. Alter, (ed.), "Gottfried Benn und Börries von Münchhausen. Ein Briefwechsel aus den Jahren 1933/34," in *Jahrbuch der Deutschen Schillergesellschaft* 25 (1981), p. 157.

Benn's strong sense of solidarity with his literary generation, as the martyrs to the transition from the nineteenth century to the twentieth, also underlies the essays *Bekenntnis zum Expressionismus* ("Confession of Faith in Expressionism," November 1933) and *Lebensweg eines Intellektualisten* ("The Way of an Intellectualist," 1934) and is compounded by the rapidly dawning realization that National Socialism promises anything but the breaking of the circle of rationalism and sterility, progress and decline, culture and conformity – of the consciousness of a "dialectic of enlightenment" that was constitutive for the work of most expressionist writers. The "modern" and "decidedly revolutionary character"[57] that expressionism shares with fascism is

> genuine readiness, genuine experience of a new being, radical and profound, and in expressionism it brought about the only intellectual feat to leave this miserable circle of liberal opportunism, put the purely utilitarian world of science behind it, broke through the world of big business . . . and in the midst of this ghastly chaos of crumbling reality and inversion of values struggled legitimately and with serious means for a new image of man.[58]

Meanwhile the dilemma occasioned by Benn's "revolutionary" and "modern" understanding of National Socialism in the face of the menacing antimodernist tenor of Münchhausen's attack was being resolved in the wider arena of cultural politics. Hitler's speech of 1 November 1933 at the NSDAP's Nuremberg Cultural Congress closely followed Alfred Rosenberg's rabidly antimodernist stance and put to rest hopes that Goebbels's rumored sympathy with expressionism would be reflected in official cultural policy.[59] Rosenberg's harnessing of cultural conservatism to disguise the contradictions and defuse the tensions within social, economic, and cultural modernity was anathema to Benn's expressionist self-definition. Rosenberg's support for National Socialism as an aesthetic answer to a disoriented, fragmented, and polarized culture – "He [the expressionist] was disciplined because he was the most dislocated of them all"[60] – represents a far-reaching misunderstanding of a "new style" as a form of ideological integration with which he had appealed to artists throughout the Weimar Republic. "Art and artists are fragmented," Rosenberg had written in 1925. "This is the – desperate – feeling of thousands today in all camps. They are all in search of a new bond of commitment, a new style, a new

57. "Bekenntnis zum Expressionismus," translated by J. M. Ritchie, in (ed.), *Gottfried Benn. The Unreconstructed Expressionist*, London, 1972, p. 98.
58. *Ibid.*, p. 101f.
59. See H. Brenner, *Die Kunstpolitik des Nationalsozialismus*, Reinbek bei Hamburg, 1963, pp. 63–86.
60. J. M. Ritchie, (ed.), *Gottfried Benn*, p. 104.

ideal of beauty."[61] Ideologically, Rosenberg's concept of spiritual and social integration and renewal – his invitation to leap into "totally new syntheses [which] are suddenly coming to life and capturing all that searches, struggles, and strives"[62] – amounted to social Darwinism thinly veiled by an epigonal German idealism; socially, it gave the illusion of restored middle-class stability and vitality, and psychologically it promised the security of submission under the shelter of an uncomplicated and unified worldview.

Benn's disillusionment with National Socialism, as the autobiographical *Lebensweg eines Intellektualisten* suggests, came of the realization that it represented not the longed-for elimination of rationalization, ideologization, and standardization, but merely a reconstituted version of the contradictions of Wilhelminian Germany – and of an integratory and normative function for art. National Socialism's pseudo-syntheses – elitism and mass appeal, "spiritual" revolution infused with social-Darwinist tenets, self-assertiveness and submissiveness, *völkisch* "unity" wrought by an ideology of implacable struggle – are the legitimation for a refurbished late nineteenth-century ideal of "personality": the "fat ape from the Darwin era who has struggled his way to the top" (III, ii, 184). It is the irrevocable disintegration of this nineteenth-century ideal, as expressed in his own early works through characters such as Rönne in the *Gehirne* novellas, Olf in *Etappe* and Pameelen in the dramas *Der Vermessungsdirigent* (1916) and *Karandasch* (1917), that Benn reaffirms in *Lebensweg eines Intellektualisten*: "Here we really do have the disintegration of an era. In this brain something falls into decay which for four hundred years has been passed off as the 'individual'. . . . Now this heritage is at an end" (III, ii, 171). The fourth section of the essay, entitled *Die neue Jugend* ("The New Youth," III, ii, 192–95), is the barely disguised revocation of Benn's belief in 1933 that the younger generation's sympathy with the National Socialist movement represented the resumption of his own generation's heroic struggle against the nineteenth century's "liberal opportunist" inheritance.

In the face of National Socialism's social-Darwinist ideology and the attendant ideal of *mens sana in corpore sano*, Benn provocatively restates his conviction that the artist is the odd-man-out in his disassociation from the causal processes of development and from the Nazi ideal of art as representing the prototype of healthy normalcy:

61. A. Rosenberg, "Das Künstlerringen der Gegenwart'" ("The Struggle of the Artist Today"), in T. von Trotha, (ed.), *Alfred Rosenberg. Blut und Ehre. Ein Kampf für deutsche Wiedergeburt. Reden und Aufsätze 1919–1933*, 11th ed., Munich, 1936, p. 205.
62. A. Rosenberg, "Der völkische Staatsgedanke" ("The Folkish Idea of the State," 1923), in *Blut und Ehre, ibid.*, p. 118.

There is an enormous number of paralytics amongst the geniuses, the schizo-phrenics bear the greatest names . . . among the 150 geniuses of the West we find fifty homosexuals and sexual deviants, hosts of drug addicts, the unmarried and the childless are the rule, high percentages of the crippled and the degenerate; creativeness, wherever one meets it, is riddled with anomalies, stigmatizations, paroxysms. . . . (III, ii, 183f.)

The Nazi state, moreover, only corroborates nineteenth-century nihilism and does not furnish a contemporary version of Nietzsche's rejoinder to it:

European nihilism: the animalistic idea of development, lacking the complement of an anthropological idea of authority. . . . Suppression of the will to breeding and style. The dominance of low, pragmatic formations of advancement and construction . . . the plausible, the superficial, science as the theoretical interpretation of the world – the situation of Nietzsche. From within this situation my generation started out. (III, ii, 187)

## III

In defending expressionism against Georg Lukács, Ernst Bloch seems reluctant to pursue – either for expressionism in general or for Benn's case in particular – the full import of the ambivalence of the "Nietzschean impulse" he outlines in *Erbschaft dieser Zeit* ("Heritage of Our Times," 1935). On the one hand, he recognizes in Nietzsche an emancipatory drive, directed against the "cold, reified bourgeois" and "the great systematizers of a closed world." However, Bloch cautions, Nietzsche undercuts his iconoclastic "Dionysian" principle by separating the tree of "knowledge" from the tree of "life."[63] It is the first of these impulses that Bloch emphasizes in expressionism when he argues against Lukács's and Kurella's virtual equation of bourgeois "irrationalism," expressionism, and fascism.

Benn, in Bloch's view, is the exception who proves the rule – the rule that the "decay" registered by the expressionists is not "decay for its own sake, but storms through this world so as to make room for images of a more genuine world."[64] Benn is merely the "purveyor of mysticism," the regressive expressionist obsessed with "primeval slime" and "diluvialism."[65] Bloch thus imputes to Benn a completely negative outcome of the "non-synchronous" contradictions between "regressive" and "emancipatory" impulses – contradictions that in Bloch's view contain utopian potentialities in the majority of expressionists. His propensity to polarize expression-

63. E. Bloch, *Erbschaft dieser Zeit*, p. 365.
64. *Ibid.*, p. 260.
65. E. Bloch, "Der Expressionismus, jetzt erblickt," in *Erbschaft dieser Zeit, ibid.*, pp. 256, 260, and passim, pp. 80, 200, 221, 224.

ism into "authentic" (emancipatory) and "inauthentic" (regressive) variants, however, does not allow Bloch to admit the possibility of National Socialist sympathies from a "modern" self-definition; and it blocks access to the main task of the ideological project he had outlined in 1932:

> The task is to extricate from the nonsynchronous contradiction those elements which are capable of antipathy and transformation, namely those elements which are hostile to capitalism and homeless within it, and to reshape them so that they can function in a different framework.[66]

Like Wilhelm Reich, Bloch rightly admonished the communists in the Weimar Republic for failing to appeal to emotional needs of the impoverished middle classes. The communists, he feared, were presenting themselves merely as the obverse of capitalist rationalization and depersonalization: "At a time and in a land where for 'large sections' of the populace capitalism's bad rationalization has also discredited reason, the emotional values inherent in communism are not given sufficient emphasis, the way is not being shown to the genuine and full, the concrete 'ratio'; as liberation from economics, as the means toward a human and total existence."[67] The *sine qua non* for a more effective antifascism, then, is to come to an understanding of how fascism appealed to an "authentic" anticapitalist heritage.

But Bloch does not do for Benn what he would have had the Marxists do for the radicalized middle classes in the Weimar Republic; he falls into the trap he himself had warned against: "The relationship of the 'irratio' to the deficient capitalist 'ratio'," he observes in his introduction to the 1935 edition of *Erbschaft dieser Zeit,* "has been all too abstractly peripheralized, rather than examining each case on its merits and, where possible, applying a concrete application to this relationship."[68] Benn reacted to the Marxists Becher and Kisch in precisely the adverse sense Bloch had warned of. But this response was not merely a regressive, "antediluvian" one; Benn was staking his own claim to an "heroic" and "radical" modernity vis-à-vis "reactionary" nineteenth-century materialism. Bloch's own utopian quest for sources of "authentic" irrationalism within tradition leads him, as Anton Rabinbach has pointed out, to emphasize "the continuity between fascism and the tradition embodied in its ideas" and to "neglect those elements of discontinuity with the past – elements which give fascism its unique power as a form of social organization – so that its actual links to modern capitalism remain obscure."[69] The corollary of this weakness in

---

66. *Ibid.,* p. 123.
67. *Ibid.,* p. 153.
68. *Ibid.,* p. 16.
69. A. Rabinbach, "Unclaimed Heritage: Ernst Bloch's Heritage of our Times and the Theory of Fascism," in *New German Critique* 11 (1977), p. 14.

Bloch's interpretation of fascism is that he overleaps the historical determinants that led many expressionists to lose sight of the "interconnections between economics, society, and ideology" (Lukács). Benn was neither the "consequential" expressionist in Lukács's and Kurella's sense (i.e., that he resolved the tensions between tradition and modernity in the "subjectivist-idealist" spirit of the "official" philosophy of imperialism); but neither was he simply the exception to Bloch's general rule that expressionism contained "anticipatory movements in the superstructure."

National Socialism promised continuity and discontinuity in one, *tabula rasa* with the nineteenth century and yet a "regenerated" *Bürgertum*, an amalgam of stability and dynamism and, for the artist, of intellectual "radicalism" and "representative" status. Benn submitted in 1933 to the new regime's promise to offer an alternative both to capitalism and to socialism. Like significant numbers of the middle classes in the Weimar Republic, he sought a way out of ideological conflict and class antagonism through the "deeconomization" and "depoliticization" of the actual social dilemma.[70] "Anti-ideological" predispositions such as those displayed by Benn enabled National Socialism's rationally planned "pragmatic irrationalism"[71] to harness psychological insecurities and resentments in such a way as to blind individuals to rational perceptions of the economic and social factors that had induced these insecurities. It is in his recourse to an heroically "anti-historical" and "anti-ideological" individualism that nonetheless belies its (bourgeois) social anxieties and aspirations, that Benn shows himself to be highly "representative" in his ambivalent response to Germany's foiled enlightenment heritage.

That fusion of the "victim" and the "hero" that characterized expressionism in general and Benn in particular can be seen at work in Benn's reception in the 1950s; and, in the guise of Benn the "classical modernist," it has resurfaced in the 1980s. The Büchner-Prize laudation of 1951, written by Oscar Jancke and read by Rudolf Pechel, celebrated Benn as "the writer who, sternly true to himself, set out resolutely to pit artistic form against the capricious times and with unrelenting endeavor, erring, suffering, and growing, opened up a new world of expression in verse and prose."[72] In the Benn centenary year (1986) the first volume of Hans-Egon Holthusen's biography presents Benn as the innocent victim of ideological strife who, through his "fierce dislike of leftist *litterateurs*, allowed himself to be driven into his fatal affair with the extreme right."[73] Benn's opposi-

---

70. M. Clemenz, *Gesellschaftliche Ursprünge des Faschismus*, Frankfurt, 1972, p. 220f.
71. T. W. Adorno, *Studien zum autoritären Charakter*, Frankfurt, 1973, p. 366.
72. Hohendahl, *Wirkung wider Willen*, p. 266f.
73. H.-E. Holthusen, *Gottfried Benn. Leben Werk Widerspruch*, Stuttgart, 1986, p. 105.

tion, of course, was not to the Marxists alone, but to the entire (nonconservative) anti-Nazi spectrum – most notably, as we have seen, to Heinrich Mann. The practice, common in Weimar Germany, of subsuming left-liberal opposition under the heading of "communism" continued in the Cold War era, and it was not absent from some of Benn's own postwar work (most notably *Doppelleben*, 1949/50). It is to this tradition that Holthusen reverts in 1986 when, rather than making constructive use of the debates of the 1960s initiated by Hans Magnus Enzensberger's reevaluation of Benn in *Der Spiegel* of 6 June 1962, he resorts to fruitless polemics against "younger scholars who have grown up in the fog of neo-Marxism and the New Enlightenment."[74]

1986 sees Holthusen treading the well-beaten track on which he had embarked in the 1950s: on Benn's one-hundredth birthday the story has changed little since his seventieth in 1956.[75] Intellectual integrity and political or social engagement continue to be mutually exclusive. The historical agnosticism that characterizes Holthusen's variant of "classical modernism" as he sees it personified in Benn can also be found in the tradition of the "neo-conservative farewell to modernity" that Habermas associates with Arnold Gehlen – and with Gottfried Benn himself.[76] Holthusen's "classical modernism" – based as it is on the disjunction of the "creative," artistic self from the personal, biographical self – must, almost by definition, lead the biographer to understate the significance of the social, psychological, and historical factors influencing his subject's ideological and artistic development, and in a manner that affirms his "aristocratic" apoliticism and obscures rather than clarifies the complex relationship between artistic radicalism and social conservatism.

74. *Ibid.*, p. 68.

75. See Holthusen's speech on the occasion of Benn's 70th birthday, in Hohendahl, *Benn – Wirkung wider Willen*, p. 285, and my review of Holthusen's biography in *AUMLA* 70 (1988), pp. 389–91.

76. Habermas has critically remarked on Gehlen's pessimistic prognosis that "the premises of enlightenment are dead, only its consequences live on." The "irresistible acceleration of social processes," Habermas observes, "then appears as the obverse of a culture which has passed over into an exhausted, crystalline state . . . crystalline [in Gehlen's sense] because all possible cultural resources have been developed. . . . Because the 'history of ideas' is closed, Gehlen decides with a sigh of relief that 'we have arrived in the *posthistoire.*' With Gottfried Benn he offers the advice: 'Reckon with the resources you have at hand'." This, Habermas concludes, is "a neoconservative farewell to modernity" (*Der philosophische Diskurs der Moderne*, p. 11f.). For the affinities between Gehlen and Benn, see Gehlen, *Die Seele im technischen Zeitalter*, Hamburg, 1957, p. 25f. If Peter Uwe Hohendahl is correct in his assumption that the later Benn can be classified as "postmodern" (Hohendahl, "Zwischen Moderne und Postmoderne: Gottfried Benns Aktualität," in P. M. Lützeler, (ed.), *Zeitgenossenschaft. Zur deutschsprachigen Literatur im 20. Jahrhundert. Festschrift für Egon Schwarz zum 65. Geburtstag*, Frankfurt, 1987), then Habermas's hypothesis as to an alliance of the "postmodern" with the "premodern" ("Modernity versus Postmodernity," p. 14) can be seen at work in the reception of Benn of the fifties, which worked toward the very "affirmative culture" that Benn himself ostensibly rejected.

Discrepancies between modern economic and social structures on one side and traditional value orientations on the other had resulted, as we have seen in the characters of the authority-figures in expressionism, in insecurity of status and a variety of strategies of evasion in order to maintain at least a semblance of social stability and personal and national identity in a time of rapid transformation. The "legitimation crisis" that manifested itself in their failure to mediate between tradition and modernity was the decisive impulse behind the younger generation's protest. Discredited parental, educational and cultural authorities may well have heightened their sensitivity to fraudulent syntheses, but they also heightened their susceptibility to new – and even more insidious – "authoritative" syntheses.

# Bibliography

Readers interested in the philosophical issues raised by the debates over reason and its Other may find the following works particularly useful:

Adorno, T. W., *Negative Dialektik*, Frankfurt, 1966. Engl. trans. *Negative Dialectics*, London, 1973.
————, *Ästhetische Theorie*, Frankfurt, 1973. Engl. trans. *Aesthetic Theory*, London, 1984.
————, and Horkheimer, M., *Dialektik der Aufklärung*, Amsterdam, 1947. Engl. trans. *Dialectic of Enlightenment*, New York, 1972.
————, et al., *Der Positivismusstreit in der deutschen Soziologie*, Frankfurt, 1969. Engl. trans. *The Positivist Dispute in German Sociology*, London, 1976.
Albert, H., *Traktat über kritische Vernunft*, Tübingen, 1968.
————, *Plädoyer für kritischen Rationalismus*, Munich, 1971.
————, *Transzendentale Träumereien. Karl-Otto Apels Sprachspiele und sein hermeneutischer Gott*, Hamburg, 1975.
————, *Kritische Vernunft und menschliche Praxis*, Stuttgart, 1977.
————, *Traktat über rationale Praxis*, Tübingen, 1978.
————, *Die Wissenschaft und die Fehlbarkeit der Vernunft*, Tübingen, 1982.
Apel, K.-O., *Transformation der Philosophie*, 2 vols., Frankfurt, 1972/73. Engl. trans. *Towards a Transformation of Philosophy*, London, 1980.
————, *Der Denkweg des Charles Sanders Peirce. Eine Einführung in den amerikanischen Pragmatismus*, Frankfurt, 1975. Engl. trans. *Charles Sanders Peirce: From Pragmatism to Pragmaticism*, Boston, 1981.
————, *Die Erklären-Verstehen-Kontroverse in transzendentalpragmatischer Sicht*, Frankfurt, 1979. Engl. trans. *Understanding and Explanation: A Transcendental Pragmatic Perspective*, Boston, 1984.
————, *Diskurs und Verantwortung: Das Problem des Übergangs zur postkonventionellen Moral*, Frankfurt, 1988.
————, et al. (eds.), *Hermeneutik und Ideologiekritik*, Frankfurt, 1971.
Baynes, K., Bohman, J. and McCarthy, T. (eds.), *After Philosophy: End or Transformation?*, Cambridge, Mass., 1986.
Behler, E. and Hörisch, J. (eds.), *Die Aktualität der Frühromantik*, Paderborn, 1987.
Bernstein, R .J., *Beyond Objectivism and Relativism: Science, Hermeneutics, and Praxis*, Philadelphia, 1983.

————, (ed.), *Habermas and Modernity*, Cambridge, Mass., 1985.

Blasche, S. (ed.), *Philosophie und Begründung*, Frankfurt, 1987.

————, (ed.), *Zerstörung des moralischen Selbstbewußtseins: Chance oder Gefährdung?*, Frankfurt, 1988.

————, (ed.), *Heidegger: Innen- und Außenansichten*, Frankfurt, 1989.

Blumenberg, H., *Die Legitimität der Neuzeit*, Frankfurt, 1966. Engl. trans. *The Legitimacy of the Modern Age*, Cambridge, Mass., 1983.

————, *Arbeit am Mythos*, Frankfurt, 1981. Engl. trans. *Work on Myth*, Cambridge, Mass., 1985.

Böhler, D., *Rekonstruktive Pragmatik. Von der Bewußtseinsphilosophie zur Kommunikationsreflexion*, Frankfurt, 1985.

Böhme, G., *Über die Zeitmodi*, Göttingen, 1966.

————, *Zeit und Zahl. Studien zur Zeittheorie bei Platon, Aristoteles, Leibniz und Kant*, Frankfurt, 1974.

————, *Alternativen der Wissenschaft*, Frankfurt, 1981.

————, and Böhme, H., *Das Andere der Vernunft. Zur Entwicklung von Rationalitätsstrukturen am Beispiel Kants*, Frankfurt, 1983.

————, *Anthropologie in pragmatischer Hinsicht*, Frankfurt, 1984.

————, *Philosophieren mit Kant. Zur Rekonstruktion der Kantischen Erkenntnis- und Wissenschaftstheorie*, Frankfurt, 1986.

————, *Der Typ Sokrates*, Frankfurt, 1988.

————, *Für eine ökologische Naturästhetik*, Frankfurt, 1989.

————, et al., (eds.), *Experimentelle Philosophie. Ursprünge autonomer Wissenschafts-entwicklung*, Frankfurt, 1977.

Bohrer, K. H. (ed.), *Mythos und Moderne*, Frankfurt, 1983.

Bonss, W. et al., (eds.), *Die Zukunft der Vernunft. Eine Auseinandersetzung*, Tübingen, 1985.

Bowie, A., *Aesthetics and Subjectivity: From Kant to Nietzsche*, Manchester and New York, 1990.

Boyne, R., *Foucault and Derrida: The Other Side of Reason*, London, 1990.

Brand, A., *The Force of Reason*, Sydney and London, 1989.

Brunkhorst, H., *Theodor W. Adorno. Dialektik der Moderne*, Munich, 1990.

Bubner, R., *Dialektik und Wissenschaft*, Frankfurt, 1973.

————, *Handlung, Sprache und Vernunft. Grundbegriffe praktischer Philosophie*, Frankfurt, 1976.

————, *Modern German Philosophy*, Cambridge, 1981.

————, *Geschichtsprozesse und Handlungsnormen. Untersuchungen zur praktischen Philosophie*, Frankfurt, 1984.

————, *Ästhetische Erfahrung*, Frankfurt, 1989.

————, Cramer, K. and Wiehl, R. (eds.), *Hermeneutik und Dialektik. Festschrift für H. G. Gadamer*, 2 vols., Tübingen, 1970.

Cavell, S., *The Claim to Reason*, Oxford, 1979.

Christensen, D. E. et al., (eds.), *Contemporary German Philosophy*, 4 vols., University Park and London, 1982, 1983, 1984, 1985.

Cramer, K. et al., (eds.), *Theorie der Subjektivität*, Frankfurt, 1987.

# Bibliography

Ebeling, H. (ed.), *Subjektivität und Selbsterhaltung*, Frankfurt, 1976.

Essler, W. K., *Wissenschaftstheorie*, 4 vols., Freiburg, 1970-1979.

Forget, P. (ed.), *Text und Interpretation*, Munich, 1984.

Frank, M., *Das Problem 'Zeit' in der deutschen Romantik*, Munich, 1972.

————, *Das individuelle Allgemeine. Textstrukturierung und -interpretation nach Schleiermacher*, Frankfurt, 1977.

————, *Die unendliche Fahrt. Ein Motiv und sein Text*, Frankfurt, 1979.

————, *Der kommende Gott. Vorlesungen über die Neue Mythologie I*, Frankfurt, 1982.

————, *Was ist Neostrukturalismus?*, Frankfurt, 1983. Engl. trans. *What is Neostructuralism?*, Minneapolis, 1989.

————, *Eine Einführung in Schellings Philosophie*, Frankfurt, 1985.

————, *Die Unhintergehbarkeit von Individualität*, Frankfurt, 1986.

————, *Die Grenzen der Verständigung*, Frankfurt, 1988.

————, *Gott im Exil. Vorlesungen über die neue Mythologie II*, Frankfurt, 1988.

————, *Einführung in die frühromantische Ästhetik*, Frankfurt, 1989.

————, *Kaltes Herz, Unendliche Fahrt, Neue Mythologie*, Frankfurt, 1989.

————, *Das Sagbare und das Unsagbare. Studien zur deutsch-französischen Hermeneutik und Texttheorie*, enlarged ed., Frankfurt, 1990.

————, *Zeitbewußtsein*, Pfullingen, 1990.

————, *Selbstbewußtsein und Selbsterkenntnis*, Stuttgart, 1991.

————, *Der unendliche Mangel an Sein*, revised ed., Munich, 1992.

————, et al. (eds.), *Die Frage nach dem Subjekt*, Frankfurt, 1988.

————, (ed.), *Selbstbewußtseinstheorien von Fichte bis Sartre*, Frankfurt, 1991.

Freundlieb, D., *Zur Wissenschaftstheorie der Literaturwissenschaft. Eine Kritik der transzendentalen Hermeneutik*, Munich, 1978.

Gadamer, H.-G., *Wahrheit und Methode*, Tübingen, 1960. Engl. trans. *Truth and Method*, New York, 1975.

Geraets, T. F. (ed.), *Rationality To-day*, Ottawa, 1979.

Gethmann-Siefert, A., and Pöggeler, O. (eds.), *Heidegger und die praktische Philosophie*, Frankfurt, 1988.

Geuss, R., *The Idea of a Critical Theory*, Cambridge, 1981.

Habermas, J., *Das Absolute und die Geschichte. Von der Zwiespältigkeit in Schellings Denken*, Bonn, 1954.

————, *Kultur und Kritik. Verstreute Aufsätze*, Frankfurt, 1973.

————, *Legitimationsprobleme im Spätkapitalismus*, Frankfurt, 1973. Engl. trans. *Legitimation Crisis*, Boston, 1975.

————, *Theorie des kommunikativen Handelns*, 2 vols., Frankfurt, 1981. Engl. trans. *Theory of Communicative Action*, 2 vols., Boston and Cambridge, 1984.

————, *Moralbewußtsein und kommunikatives Handeln*, Frankfurt, 1983. Engl. trans. *Moral Consciousness and Communicative Action*, Cambridge, Mass., 1989.

————, *Vorstudien und Ergänzungen zur Theorie des kommunikativen Handelns*, Frankfurt, 1984.

————, *Die Neue Unübersichtlichkeit*, Frankfurt, 1985. Engl. trans. *The New Conservatism: Cultural Criticism and the Historians' Debate*, Cambridge, Mass., 1989.

————, *Der philosophische Diskurs der Moderne. Zwölf Vorlesungen*, Frankfurt, 1985. Engl. trans. *The Philosophical Discourse of Modernity: Twelve Lectures*, Cambridge, Mass., 1987.

————, *Nachmetaphysisches Denken. Philosophische Aufsätze*, Frankfurt, 1988. Engl. trans. *The Future of Philosophy. Between Metaphysics and the Critique of Reason*, Oxford, 1990.

———— and Luhmann, N., *Theorie der Gesellschaft oder Sozialtechnologie*, Frankfurt, 1971.

Held, D., *Introduction to Critical Theory*, London, 1980.

Henrich, D., *Fichtes ursprüngliche Einsicht*, Frankfurt, 1967.

————, *Identität und Objektivität*, Heidelberg, 1976.

————, *Fluchtlinien*, Frankfurt, 1982.

————, *Selbstverhältnisse*, Stuttgart, 1982.

————, *Der Gang des Andenkens*, Stuttgart, 1986.

————, *Konzepte*, Frankfurt, 1987.

————, and Horstmann, R.-P. (eds.), *Metaphysik nach Kant*, Stuttgart, 1988.

Hohendahl, P. U., *Das Bild der bürgerlichen Welt im expressionistischen Drama*, Heidelberg, 1967.

————, *Literaturkritik und Öffentlichkeit*, Munich, 1974.

————, *The Institution of Criticism*, Ithaca and London, 1982.

————, *Literarische Kultur im Zeitalter des Liberalismus, 1830-1870*, Munich, 1985.

Honneth, A., *Kritik der Macht. Reflexionsstufen einer kritischen Gesellschaftstheorie*, Frankfurt, 1985. Engl. trans. *The Critique of Power*, Cambridge, Mass., 1991.

————, *Die zerissene Welt des Sozialen. Sozialphilosophische Aufsätze*, Frankfurt, 1990.

————, McCarthy, T., Offe, C. and Wellmer, A. (eds.), *Zwischenbetrachtungen. Im Prozeß der Aufklärung, Festschrift for J. Habermas*, Frankfurt, 1989. Partial Engl. trans. *Philosophical Interventions in the Unfinished Project of Enlightenment*, Cambridge, Mass., 1992.

Horkheimer, M., *Eclipse of Reason*, Oxford, 1947.

————, *Zur Kritik der instrumentellen Vernunft*, Frankfurt, 1967.

————, *Kritische Theorie*, 2nd ed., Frankfurt, 1968. Engl. trans. *Critical Theory: Selected Essays*, New York, 1972.

Hudson, W., *The Marxist Philosophy of Ernst Bloch*, London and New York, 1982.

Hübner, K., *Kritik der wissenschaftlichen Vernunft*, Freiburg, 1978. Engl. trans. *Critique of Scientific Reason*, Chicago, 1983.

————, *Die Wahrheit des Mythos*, Munich, 1985.

Ineichen, H., *Philosophische Hermeneutik*, Freiburg, 1991.

Ingram, D., *Habermas and the Dialectic of Reason*, New Haven, 1987.

Kamper, D. and Wulf, C., *Die Wiederkehr des Körpers*, Frankfurt, 1982.

————, *Das Schwinden der Sinne*, Frankfurt, 1984.

————, *Die sterbende Zeit*, Darmstadt, 1987.

————, and van Reijen, W. (eds.), *Die unvollendete Vernunft. Moderne versus Postmoderne*, Frankfurt, 1987.

# Bibliography

Kelly, M. (ed.), *Hermeneutics and Critical Theory in Ethics and Politics*, Cambridge, Mass., 1990.

Kuhlmann, W., *Reflexive Letztbegründung. Untersuchungen zur Transzendentalpragmatik*, Freiburg, 1985.

———, (ed.), *Moralität und Sittlichkeit. Das Problem Hegels und die Diskursethik*, Frankfurt, 1986.

——— and Böhler, D. (eds.), *Kommunikation und Reflexion. Zur Diskussion der Transzendentalpragmatik*, Frankfurt, 1982.

Lindner, B. and Lüdke, W. M. (eds.), *Materialien zur ästhetischen Theorie Th. W. Adornos. Konstruktion der Moderne*, Frankfurt, 1980.

Lorenzen, P., *Konstruktive Wissenschaftstheorie*, Frankfurt, 1974.

———, *Methodisches Denken*, Frankfurt, 1974.

———, *Politische und technische Vernunft*, Frankfurt, 1984.

Luhmann, N., *Zweckbegriff und Systemrationalität: Über die Funktion von Zwecken in sozialen Systemen*, Tübingen, 1968.

———, *Soziologische Aufklärung*, Opladen, 1971.

———, *Rechtssoziologie*, 2 vols., Reinbek, 1972.

———, *Trust and Power: Two Works*, Microfilm, Ann Arbor, 1979.

———, *Gesellschaftsstruktur und Semantik*, 3 vols., Frankfurt, 1980, 1981, 1989.

———, *Religious Dogmatics and the Evolution of Societies*, Lewiston, 1984.

———, *The Differentiation of Society*, New York, 1984.

———, *Soziale Systeme*, Frankfurt, 1984.

———, *A Sociological Theory of Law*, London, 1985.

———, *Love As Passion: The Codification of Intimacy*, Cambridge, Mass., 1987.

———, *Die Wirtschaft der Gesellschaft*, Frankfurt, 1988.

———, *Ecological Communication*, Chicago, 1989.

———, *Essays in Self-Realization*, New York, 1990.

———, *Political Theory in the Welfare State*, New York, 1990.

———, *Die Wissenschaft der Gesellschaft*, Frankfurt, 1990.

Lukács, G., *The Destruction of Reason*, London, 1980.

Lypp, B., *Ästhetischer Absolutismus und politische Vernunft*, Frankfurt, 1972.

Marquard, O., *Abschied vom Prinzipiellen. Philosophische Studien*, Stuttgart, 1981. Engl. trans. *Farewell to Matters of Principle*, Oxford, 1989.

McCarthy, T., *The Critical Theory of Jürgen Habermas*, Cambridge, Mass., 1978.

———, *Ideals and Illusions: On Reconstruction and Deconstruction in Contemporary Critical Theory*, Cambridge, Mass., 1991.

Menke-Eggers, C., *Die Souveränität der Kunst. Ästhetische Erfahrung nach Adorno und Derrida*, Frankfurt, 1988.

Michelfelder, D. P. and Palmer, R. E. (eds.), *Dialogue and Deconstruction. The Gadamer-Derrida Encounter*, Albany, 1989.

Pöggeler, O. (ed.), *Hermeneutische Philosophie*, Munich, 1972.

Poser, H. (ed.), *Wandel des Vernunftbegriffs*, Freiburg, 1981.

Pothast, U., (ed.), *Freies Handeln und Determinismus*, Frankfurt, 1978.

———, *Die Unzulänglichkeit der Freiheitsbeweise*, Frankfurt, 1987.

Rasmussen, D. *Reading Habermas*, Oxford, 1990.

————, (ed.), *Universalism vs. Communitarianism: Contemporary Debates in Ethics*, Cambridge, Mass., 1990.

Riedel, M., *Studien zu Hegels Rechtsphilosophie*, Frankfurt, 1970.

————, *Zur Rehabilitierung der praktischen Philosophie*, Freiburg, 1972.

————, *Metaphysik und Metapolitik: Studien zu Aristoteles und zur politische Sprache der neuzeitlichen Philosophie*, Frankfurt, 1975.

————, *Verstehen oder Erklären? Zur Theorie und Geschichte der hermeneutischen Wissenschaften*, Stuttgart, 1978.

————, *Für eine zweite Philosophie. Vorträge und Abhandlungen*, Frankfurt, 1988.

————, *Urteilskraft und Vernunft*, Frankfurt, 1989.

————, *Hören auf die Sprache: Die akromatische Dimension der Hermeneutik*, Frankfurt, 1990.

Reinz-Pesce, R.G., *Metaphysik als Metahistorik oder Kritik des unreinen Denkens*, Freiburg, 1987.

Roberts, D., *Art and Enlightenment: Aesthetic Theory after Adorno*, Lincoln and London, 1991.

Schnädelbach, H., *Hegels Theorie der subjektiven Freiheit*, Frankfurt, 1966.

————, *Erfahrung, Begründung und Reflexion. Versuch über den Positivismus*, Frankfurt, 1971.

————, *Geschichtsphilosophie nach Hegel. Die Probleme des Historismus*, Freiburg and Munich, 1974.

————, *Reflexion und Diskurs. Fragen einer Logik der Philosophie*, Frankfurt, 1977.

————, *Philosophie in Deutschland 1831-1933*, Frankfurt, 1983. Engl. trans. *Philosophy in Germany 1831–1933*, Cambridge, 1984.

————, *Vernunft und Geschichte*, Frankfurt, 1987.

————, (ed.), *Rationalität. Philosophische Beiträge*, Frankfurt, 1984.

Schwemmer, O. and Lorenzen, P., *Konstruktive Logik, Ethik und Wissenschaftstheorie*, Mannheim, 1975.

Schweppenhäuser, H., *Tractanda. Beiträge zur kritischen Theorie der Kultur und Gesellschaft*, Frankfurt, 1972.

Seel, M., *Die Kunst der Entzweiung. Zum Begriff der ästhetischen Rationalität*, Frankfurt, 1985.

Sloterdijk, P., *Der Philosoph auf der Bühne. Ein Versuch über Nietzsches dionysischen Materialismus*, Frankfurt, 1986

————, *Kritik der zynischen Vernunft*, 2 vols., Frankfurt, 1983. Engl. trans. *Critique of Cynical Reason*, Minneapolis, 1987.

Spinner, H., *Pluralismus als Erkenntnismodell. Studien zum Popperschen Erkenntnis- und Gesellschaftsmodell*, Frankfurt, 1973.

Stegmüller, W., *Probleme und Resultate der Wissenschaftstheorie und Analytischen Philosophie*, 4 vols., Berlin, Heidelberg, New York, 1973-1974.

Theunissen, M., *Der Andere: Studien zur Sozialontologie der Gegenwart*, Berlin, 1965.

————, *Gesellschaft und Geschichte. Zur Kritik der Kritischen Theorie*, Berlin, 1969.

Thompson, J. B. and Held, D., (eds.), *Habermas. Critical Debates*, London, 1982.

Thyen, A., *Negative Dialektik und Erfahrung. Zur Rationalität des Nichtidentischen bei Adorno*, Frankfurt, 1989.

Tugendhat, E., *Der Wahrheitsbegriff bei Husserl und Heidegger*, Berlin, 1967.

———, *Vorlesungen zur Einführung in die sprachanalytische Philosophie*, Frankfurt, 1976. Engl. trans. *Traditional and Analytical Philosophy: Lectures on the Philosophy of Language*, Cambridge, 1982.

———, *Selbstbewußtsein und Selbstbestimmung. Sprachanalytische Interpretationen*, Frankfurt, 1981. Engl. trans. *Self-Consciousness and Self-Determination*, Cambridge, Mass., 1986.

Wellmer, A., *Methodologie als Erkenntnistheorie*, Frankfurt, 1967.

———, *Kritische Gesellschaftstheorie und Positivismus*, Frankfurt, 1969. Engl. trans. *Critical Theory of Society*, New York, 1974.

———, *Zur Dialektik von Moderne und Postmoderne. Vernunftkritik nach Adorno*, Frankfurt, 1985.

———, *Ethik und Dialog. Elemente des moralischen Urteils bei Kant und in der Diskursethik*, Frankfurt, 1986.

———, *The Persistence of Modernity. Essays on Aesthetics, Ethics and Postmodernism*, Cambridge, 1991.

——— and Honneth, A. (eds.), *Die Frankfurter Schule and die Folgen*, Berlin, 1986.

Welsch, W., *Unsere postmoderne Moderne*, Weinheim, 1987.

———, *Ästhetisches Denken*, Stuttgart, 1990.

White, S., *The Recent Work of Jürgen Habermas*, Cambridge, 1988.

Wimmer, R., *Universalisierung in der Ethik. Analyse, Kritik und Rekonstruktion ethischer Rationalitätsansprüche*, Frankfurt, 1980.

Zuidervaart, L., *Adorno's Aesthetic Theory*, Cambridge, Mass., 1991.

# Notes on Contributors

**Reinhard Alter** is Senior Lecturer in the Department of German at the University of Western Australia. He is the author of studies of Gottfried Benn and Heinrich Mann, and his research focuses upon the relationship between literature and history from Imperial Germany to the end of the Weimar Republic

**Karl-Otto Apel** is Professor Emeritus in the Philosophy Department at the J.-W.-Goethe University, Frankfurt, Germany. He is the leading advocate of a foundationalist approach to philosophy in Germany and the author of a program to effect a transcendental-pragmatic transformation of transcendental philosophy and ethics.

**Gernot Böhme** is Professor of Philosophy at the Darmstadt University of Technology, Germany. He is co-author, with his brother Hartmut Böhme, of *Das Andere der Vernunft* (1983), a manifesto for a major shift in European thought away from the hegemonic exclusions of modern reason.

**Andrew G. Bonnell** is Tutor in the Department of History at the University of Sydney. His research is primarily focused on German Social Democracy and its contemporary implications.

**Richard Campbell** is Dean of the Faculty of Arts and Senior Lecturer in Philosophy at the Australian National University. The author of a distinguished reinterpretation of Anselm's proof of the existence of God (*From Belief to Understanding*, 1976), he has recently completed a major study of changing conceptions of truth from the ancient Greeks to the present (*Truth and Historicity*, 1992).

**Manfred Frank** is Professor of Philosophy at Tübingen University, Germany. A Schelling scholar and the leading contemporary authority on Schleiermacher's hermeneutics, Frank argues that Schleiermacher's hermeneutics can deal with human subjectivity more satisfactorily than recent French philosophy and that many of the key themes of French "post-" or "neo-"structuralism can be found in early German Romanticism.

**Dieter Freundlieb** is Senior Lecturer in Humanities at Griffith University, Australia. His major areas of research are contemporary debates in literary criticism and critical theory. He has published widely on methodological problems in literary theory and on contemporary philosophical hermeneutics, including a monograph on the philosophy of literary studies.

**Peter Uwe Hohendahl** is Professor of German at Cornell University, USA. He is a leading literary and cultural historian and the author of many books exploring institutional history perspectives on literature and criticism.

**Wayne Hudson** is Senior Lecturer in Humanities at Griffith University, Australia. The author of the standard work on Ernst Bloch (*The Marxist Philosophy of Ernst Bloch*, 1981), he is currently completing books on postmodernism and the reform of utopia.

**Niklas Luhmann** is Professor of Sociology at the University of Bielefeld, Germany, and the most important contemporary proponent of a systems-theoretical approach to sociology. The author of some forty books and three hundred articles, Luhmann is arguably the most original German sociological thinker of the last twenty years.

**A. Tuan Nuyen** is Senior Lecturer in Philosophy at the University of Queensland, Australia. An internationally recognized Hume scholar, Nuyen has also published widely on contemporary European philosophy and postmodernism.

**Herbert Schnädelbach** is Professor of Philosophy at Hamburg University, Germany. Originally a disciple of Adorno, Schnädelbach is a leading advocate of philosophical hermeneutics and combines in his many publications systematic insights raised by classical German philosophy with insights gained from more recent perspectives on Anglo-Saxon philosophy.

**Michelle Walker** is Lecturer in Philosophy at the University of Queensland, Australia. Her interests are in feminist philosophy, French philosophy, and German critical theory.

**Albrecht Wellmer** is Professor of Philosophy at the Free University of Berlin, Germany. A follower of Habermas, Wellmer breaks with what he sees as the residues of utopian idealism in Habermas's thought and with his discursive ethics. Unlike Habermas, he responds to the challenges of recent French thought by attempting to rework Adorno's aesthetics and negative dialectics as an alternative to a model of rationality which restricts itself to the identitarian-logical functions of language.

# Sources

Most of the essays included in this volume are original contributions. Earlier versions of the essays by Reinhard Alter, Gernot Böhme, and Andrew G. Bonnell, Wayne Hudson, Peter Uwe Hohendahl, and a. Tuan Nuyen were presented at a conference on *Radikale Vernunftkritik* organized by the editors at Griffith University, Brisbane, in February 1989. A shortened German version of Gernot Böhme's paper was previously published in the journal *Radius*. Karl-Otto Apel's essay was originally appeared in German in *Concordia* 11, 1987. Manfred Frank's essay was published in German in *Die unvollendete Vernunft: Moderne versus Postmoderne*, edited by Dietmar Kamper and Willem van Reijen, Frankfurt: Suhrkamp, 1987, and Herbert Schnädelbach's essay was published in German in *Kommunikation und Reflexion*, edited by Wolfgang Kuhlmann and Dietrich Böhler, Frankfurt: Suhrkamp, 1982. The editors wish to thank the journal *Concordia* and *Suhrkamp Publishers* for their permission to use this material.

# Index

# Index

# Index

Erlangen School, 4
Essler, Wilhelm K., 4
ethics, 11, 29–47 passim, 79, 165, 212, 221, 226, 243
Evans, Richard J., 251 n. 51
existentialism, 3, 79
expressionism, German, 18, 255–79

Farías, Victor, 123, 123 n. 29
fascism, 18, 68, 90, 230, 237–38, 265, 269–76 passim
feminine, 201, 211, 212–16 passim
femininity, 201
Fest, Joachim, 255, 255 n. 1
Feyerabend, Paul, 68, 155
Fichte, Johann Gottlieb, 4, 6–7, 20, 44, 58, 144
Fink, Eugen, 3
Fischer, Fritz, 258
Flaubert, Gustave, 68
Foucault, Michel, 1, 6, 10, 14, 23, 25, 44, 68–69, 76, 90–91, 108, 119, 122, 126–28, 143–44, 210
frame, (*Ge-stell*), 26, 27 n. 11, 32, 38, 39, 40–45, 47
Frank, Manfred, 7–8, 8 n. 9, 11–12, 59 n. 44, 67, 218
Frankfurt School, 4, 70, 78, 92–93, 237–38
Freeman, Barbara, 214 n. 68
Frege, Gottlob, 31, 38
French poststructuralism, 1, 5, 70, 108, 111, 218–19
French Revolution, 245, 246
Freud, Sigmund, 9, 90, 92, 199, 199 n. 1, 200, 212
Freundlieb, Dieter, 15, 48, 66, 85, 94, 163, 166
Frey, Gerhard, 58, 58 n. 42
*Friedrich-Ebert-Stiftung*, 253
Friedrich, Hans, 265 n. 38
Fromm, Erich, 258 n. 11, 260

Gadamer, Hans-Georg, 4–5, 7–8, 10, 15, 23, 34–35, 35 n. 20, 56, 181–98
Galileo, 184
Gall, Lothar, 259
Gallop, Jane, 213 n. 61
Gasché, Rodolphe, 211 n. 53
Geary, Dick, 244 n. 13

Gehlen, Arnold, 278, 278 n. 76
George, Stefan, 73, 234
George Circle, 230
German Communist Party, 252
German idealism, 3, 52, 74, 89, 107–8, 127, 274
German Social Democratic Party, 18, 241–54
Gilman, Sander L., 235 n. 9
global crisis, 24, 37
God, 80, 89, 134–38 passim, 196
Gödel, Kurt, 58
Goebbels, Joseph, 273
Goethe, Johann Wolfgang, 230, 234, 237
Gorschopp, Horst, 247 n. 31
Greve, Ludwig, 269 n. 50
Grimm, Reinhold, 267 n. 43
Grosz, Elizabeth, 212 n. 56, 213 n. 61, 214 n. 63

Habermas, Jürgen, 1–2, 4–5, 7, 8 n. 9, 9, 12–14, 16, 16 n. 13, 19, 25, 36, 36 n. 22, 52 n. 10, 53 n. 13, 60, 60 n. 47, 61, 64, 79–81, 92–93, 95–105, 107–31, 133, 143–60, 163–64, 166, 166 n. 2, 217–18, 218 n. 1, 253, 253 n. 56, 254–55, 257, 263, 263 n. 30 and 31, 264, 267–68, 268 n. 46, 271, 278, 278 n. 76
*The Philosophical Discourse of Modernity*, 107–10 passim, 117 n. 18, 124 n. 34, 125 n. 35, n. 36 and n. 38, 144
Hall, Alex, 250 n. 43
Hamann, Johann Georg, 59 n. 44, 63 n. 55, 88
Hampe, Peter, 264 n. 36
Harding, Sandra, 216 n. 77
Hart, Kevin, 125, 125 n. 37
Hasenclever, Walter, 261, 262, 262 n. 23, 263, 265
Hegel, G. W. F., 4–5, 14, 20, 27 n. 11, 52, 56, 58, 68, 68 n. 3, 71, 85, 91, 102–4, 113–15, 120, 126, 129, 131, 134, 136–38, 138 n. 4, 143, 157, 203, 208
Hegemann, Werner, 269
Heidegger, Martin, 3–4, 6–8, 10–12, 14, 23–27, 27 n. 11, 31–32, 32 n. 14, 33–34, 34 n. 19, 35, 35 n. 20, 38–40, 42–43, 47, 68, 71–72, 108, 113, 118–20, 122–24, 126, 129, 134, 141,

# Index

# Index

# Index

# Index